LAYERED VIOLENCE
The Detroit Rioters of 1943

DOMINIC J. CAPECI, JR.
AND
MARTHA WILKERSON

UNIVERSITY PRESS OF MISS
Jackson

Copyright © 1991 by University Press of Mississippi
Manufactured in the United States of America
Print-on-Demand Edition

The paper in this book meets the guidelines for permanence and durability
of the Committee on Production Guidelines for Book Longevity of the
Council on Library Resources.

Library of Congress Cataloging-in-Publication Data

Capeci, Dominic J.
    Layered violence : the Detroit rioters of 1943 / Dominic J. Capeci, Jr. and
Martha Wilkerson.
        p. cm.
    Includes bibliographical references and index.
    ISBN 0-87805-515-0 (alk. paper)   ISBN: 1604733748
        1. Riots—Michigan—Detroit—History—20th century.   2. Detroit
(Mich.)—Race relations.   I. Wilkerson, Martha Frances, 1944–   .
II. Title.
F574.D49N4326   1991
977.4'34—dc20   91-17486
                                                                    CIP

British Library Cataloging-in-Publication data available

FOR

MATTIE FRANCES HICKS WILKERSON

AND

LE BELLE SORELLE CAPECI,

MARY ELLEN,

CARMELA RITA

E

ANNA MARIE

Contents

MAPS viii

PREFACE xi

ACKNOWLEDGMENTS xv

1. *Riot and Reconstruction* 3

2. *Of Hoodlums and Hillbillies* 32

3. *Faces in the Crowd* 54

4. *And Victims, Too* 87

5. *Causes Célèbres* 122

6. *From Hastings to 12th Street* 144

7. *Broader Perspectives* 174

APPENDIXES 209

NOTES 225

SELECTED BIBLIOGRAPHY 303

INDEX 317

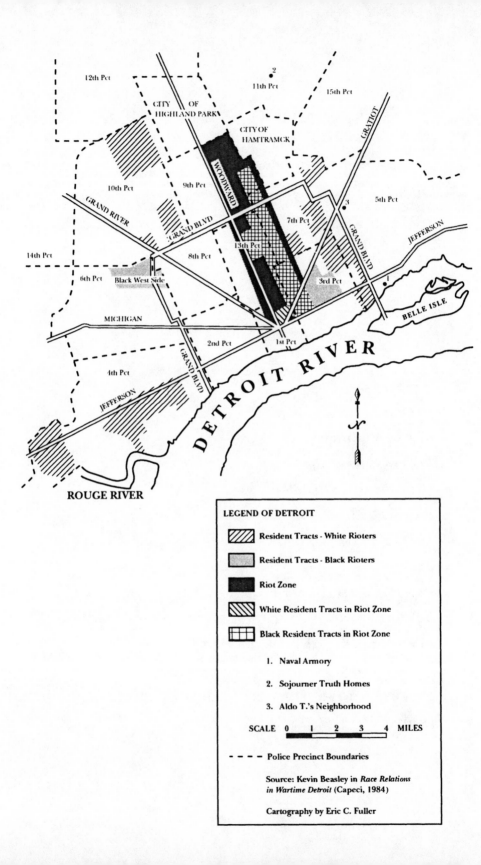

12th Pct

2
11th Pct

15th Pct

CITY OF
HIGHLAND PARK

CITY OF
HAMTRAMCK

GRATIOT

10th Pct

9th Pct

WOODWARD

GRAND RIVER

GRAND BLVD

7th Pct

5th Pct

3

GRAND BLVD

JEFFERSON

14th Pct

8th Pct

13th Pct

6th Pct

Black West Side

3rd Pct

BELLE ISLE

MICHIGAN

1

2nd Pct

1st Pct

DETROIT RIVER

GRAND BLVD

4th Pct

JEFFERSON

ROUGE RIVER

N

LEGEND OF DETROIT

Resident Tracts - White Rioters

Resident Tracts - Black Rioters

Riot Zone

White Resident Tracts in Riot Zone

Black Resident Tracts in Riot Zone

1. Naval Armory

2. Sojourner Truth Homes

3. Aldo T.'s Neighborhood

SCALE 0 1 2 3 4 MILES

- - - - Police Precinct Boundaries

Source: Kevin Beasley in *Race Relations
in Wartime Detroit* (Capeci, 1984)

Cartography by Eric C. Fuller

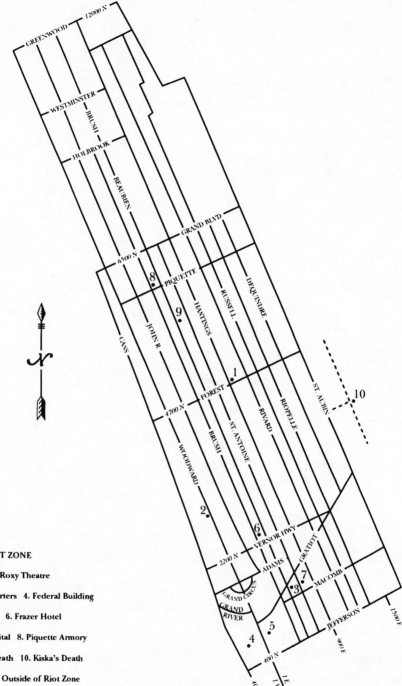

GREENWOOD 12000 N

WESTMINSTER

BRUSH

HOLBROOK

BEAUBIEN

GRAND BLVD

6500 N

8 • PIQUETTE

RUSSELL

DEQUINDRE

9 •

HASTINGS

JOHN R

CASS

1 •

ST. AUBIN

FOREST

4700 N

RIVARD

RIOPELLE

10

ST. ANTOINE

BRUSH

WOODWARD

2 •

6 •

VERNOR HWY

GRATIOT

ADAMS

7 •

2200 N

3 • MACOMB

GRAND CIRCUS

GRAND RIVER

5 •

JEFFERSON

900 E

4 •

400 N

1500 E

400 W

1 W

1 E

LEGEND OF RIOT ZONE

1. Forest Club   2. Roxy Theatre

3. Police Headquarters   4. Federal Building

5. Cadillac Square   6. Frazer Hotel

7. Receiving Hospital   8. Piquette Armory

9. De Horatiis's Death   10. Kiska's Death

- - - - - -   Area Outside of Riot Zone

Cartography by Eric C. Fuller

SCALE   .5   0   .5   1   MILE

Preface

Simply stated, this study contends that the Detroit rioters of 1943 came from diverse backgrounds, exploded for various reasons, and—in rapid succession—piled distinct layers of violence atop one another; their cumulative weight and progressive intensity wrought the most devastating racial upheaval of all previous eras. It challenges the contemporary view of rioters as black "hoodlums" and white "hillbillies," and enables us to understand better the participants of earlier and especially later disturbances. It reveals that the racially proud, politically informed "New Ghetto Man" of the 1960s emerged, as did that entire generation's struggle for racial equality, during World War II.[1] It identifies the additional roles of rioters as protestor, celebrity, hoodlum, unthinking participant, and—much less apparent in previous studies—victim. It verifies the Detroit rioters of 1943 as the transitional figures of racial violence in the twentieth-century: ordinary citizens whose activities represent the last gasp of white fury so prevalent before the Great Depression and the escalating onslaught of blacks first expressed in Harlem of the 1930s.

By focusing on the Detroit rioters of 1943 rather than the upheaval itself, this account approaches racial violence from a perspective overlooked in most previous riot histories.[2] It benefits from those works, in which scholars have noted that violence clustered

xi

around periods of crisis and, in the face of changing demography, shifted from communal bloodshed to commodity disorder—that is, attacks on property.[3] It also adds to their sweeping characterizations of who filled the streets. By presenting more complete portraits of the participants, it contributes to understanding who generated the destruction in Detroit, and—by inference—elsewhere.

Recently available police arrest tickets, court files, and probation records present the first opportunity to establish—within carefully determined parameters—empirical profiles of the Detroit rioters of 1943. Detroit arrestees were among the people in the street and, despite controversy over their being representative of others, they offer an understanding of participants as unique and multidimensional—human beings too often lost in collective interpretations and institutional approaches of civil disorder.[4] Sometimes, for example, the participants articulated their motivations clearly; more often they said nothing, yet acted transparently and in theoretically plausible ways. Few of them were asked why they rioted, but those who did answer this question—in a time of national military crisis, when patriotism was expected—might have spoken more honestly than rioters in a later time of moral imperatives and inflated rhetoric.

Though no documentation exists to compare the Detroit rioters and others who were on the streets as spectators or counterrioters, much evidence indicates that the participants represented the municipal population in many ways. Black rioters were adults, married, educated, employed, long-term city dwellers without criminal records. Their white counterparts were younger, single, slightly more educated workers, longer residents also lacking previous arrests. Certainly, they demonstrate variety among themselves and within their community, as well as positive rather than pathological traits.

For a broader understanding of race riots generally, the Detroit rioters of 1943 disprove some explanations of racial upheaval and furnished support for others. Interacting with their environment, they reveal the "long term factors which build toward violence" and the personal socioeconomic characteristics that affect such behavior; they show that lengthy residence in the city politicized and socialized some blacks toward violence.[5] Thus, they chart shifts in attitudes, images, and perceptions of ghetto inhabitants over time, each generation becoming more physically segregated, racially aware, economically aggressive, politically mobilized, and—when lacking redress—collectively violent. It is hoped that *Layered Violence* will reach beyond the city of Detroit during World War II and stimulate additional inquiries about racial bloodshed in a democratic society.

Acknowledgments

Several individuals helped make our study possible. As often in the past, Profs. Gerald D. Nash of the University of New Mexico and Robert V. Haynes of Western Kentucky University extended continuous support and encouragement. So did Profs. Arvarh E. Strickland of the University of Missouri and William L. Van Deburg of the University of Wisconsin. Profs. William D. Jenkins of Youngstown State University and David J. Hartmann of Southwest Missouri State University provided expert advice on methodology, while Prof. Clifford I. Whipple of Southwest Missouri State University interpreted the psychological data. Their friendship, as well as that of Profs. Federick J. Blue of Youngstown State University, Jack C. Knight, James N. Giglio, and George J. Selement of Southwest Missouri State University, proved invaluable during the trying times.

Archivists were indispensable to our efforts, often going well beyond the call of duty. Joseph F. Oldenburg, assistant director of the Detroit Public Library, first identified the Recorder's Court Files in the Burton Historical Collection and Mary M. Karshner, former curator of manuscripts, made them and untold other collections available. Burton Chief Alice C. Dalligan (retired) and Judy Barmatoski filled innumerable research requests, while Margaret Ward (retired) and Benedict Markowski identified the race and ethnicity of riot participants. Philip P. Mason, director of the

xv

Archives of Labor and Urban Affairs, and his staff—especially Warner Pflug, Pat Bartkowski, Dione Miles (retired), and Mike Smith—offered much good advice and opened several collections. So did Nancy R. Bartlett of the Michigan Historical Collections and LeRoy Barnett and David J. Johnson of the Michigan State Archives.

We also benefited from the staffs of many depositories: the Library of Congress, National Archives, Washington National Records Center, Franklin D. Roosevelt Library, the Municipal Archives of New York City, and the Mullen Library of the Catholic University of America. The United States Justice Department expedited requests for material through the Freedom of Information Act.

Important assistance also came from other law enforcement agencies. Mayor Coleman A. Young and Chief of Police William L. Hart granted us access to Detroit Police Department records. Sgt. Suzanne Fetsco (retired) first located the arrest tickets, while Lieut. Donna Cotton, Sgt. Florence Hall, and especially Insp. Edward J. Zupancic facilitated their use. Inspector Zupancic provided the assistance, insights, and support of an archivist, never too busy to cooperate with our effort. Capt. Alan J. Shaw, Capt. Donald Bennett, and Lieut. Calvin E. Glassford of the Michigan State Police opened pertinent files.

Court officials proved equally helpful. Recorder's Court Administrator George L. Gish and Deputy Court Administrator Julia Penn advanced the misdemeanor calendar and, with the cooperation of Wayne County Adult Probation Services Deputy Director Daniel M. Fontella and Special Services Supervisor George Agnello, the probation files. Their enthusiasm and efficiency, like that of all the police officers, dispelled the myth of reluctant civil servants.

Private citizens—themselves part of Detroit's history—recalled the riot and, in some cases, shared their personal papers with us. Before his death in 1985, Prof. Emer. Donald C. Marsh of Wayne State University inspired this project with candid observations, historical documents, and indomitable spirit. Prof. Emer. Eleanor P. Wolf and Jesse Stewart, retired police officer, also gave interviews, data, and, in the case of Mr. Stewart, permission to consult his personnel file. Aaron and Mendel Shifman answered several queries about commercial activities and race relations in the black east side during the war years, and George C. Edwards granted access to his papers.

In addition, Detroiters and others identified the race and ethnicity of the rioters and proprietors: Phillip Applebaum, Victoria and Judge Elvin L. Davenport (retired), Jerome Kelman, Alvin L. Kushner, Leonard N. Simmons, Louis Wetsman of the Metropolitan Detroit area; Carol Lieberwitz of Springfield, Missouri; Rabbi David J. Zucker of Aurora, Colorado and Rabbi David Wulcher of Huntington, West Virginia.

Several scholars forwarded us copies of their studies of the Detroit rioters, or related work. These included Dr. Elliot Luby of Harper-Grace Hospitals (Detroit), Prof. Sheldon J. Lachman of Wayne State University, Prof. Tyrone Tillery of Wayne State University, Prof. Sidney Fine of the University of Michigan, Prof. Robert M. Fogelson of the Massachusetts Institute of Technology, and Prof. Edward Lurie of the University of Delaware. Their cooperation is much appreciated and their work much quoted, though we alone are responsible for its factual and interpretive presentation in this history.

Financial assistance for our research came from the National Endowment for the Humanities Fellowship for College Teachers (1986) and the Southwest Missouri State University Faculty Research Committee (1986 and 1987), under the auspices of Office of Planning and Policy Director Paul M. Toom. This support, and that of Jeff P. Morrissey, Verna Needem, and Mark A. Oglesby of the Computer Services Department, enhanced our efforts. So did the interlibrary searches by Willa J. Garrett, Carol Lynne Freeman, Frances K. Rottmann, and Byron Stewart of Southwest Missouri State University's Duane G. Meyer Library.

Ed. William T. Bulger granted permission to draw from our article, "The Detroit Rioters of 1943: A Reinterpretation," *Michigan Historical Review* 16 (Spring 1990): 49–72, for material used in various portions of this study. We thank him for that courtesy.

Most importantly, without the sacrifice of our families, we could have neither researched nor written *Layered Violence*. For their understanding, we are most grateful.

Layered Violence: The Detroit Rioters of 1943

ONE

Riot and Reconstruction

June 20, 1943, began as a typical Sunday for most Detroiters, whose numbers had mushroomed during the previous three and one-half years and become increasingly diverse. Defense industries employed multitudes of depression-starved residents and attracted 483,219 migrants, particularly white Southerners and, after 1942, their black counterparts.[1] Detroit now registered a population of over 2 million, and this topsy-turvy industrial and labor expansion caused President Franklin D. Roosevelt's term "The Arsenal of Democracy" to be applied particularly to Detroit. It strained housing, transportation, education, and recreation facilities—and, most ominously, race relations. Competition for substandard rooms, slow-moving streetcars, inadequate schools and parks intensified in the face of congestion, as blacks sought access to previously closed socioeconomic opportunities.

Even before the arrival of most black newcomers—over 35,000—interracial violence occurred in contested neighborhoods, on the Detroit Street Railway (DSR) system, in the public schools, and at Belle Isle—the showcase of city parks. Within the past year, black

3

defense workers fought Polish Detroiters for occupation of the federally funded Sojourner Truth Homes, and they contended with
several white groups, including many long-standing residents, for
skilled positions in union-dominated shops.[2] This charged atmosphere lacked firm, even-handed leadership; instead, mayor, police, managers, and some unionists closed "legitimate channels of
protest" to blacks and promoted hostile racial beliefs.[3] Every real or
imagined affront held the potential for wholesale rampage. "Detroit," commented one reporter, "can either blow up Hitler or it can
blow up the U.S."[4]

To Charles "Little Willie" L.—and, no doubt, to many others
who rose on Sunday morning to clear, sunny skies, summerlike
temperatures, and a day free from monotonous work, the tension
that made Detroit "dynamite" seemed ever-present.[5] Twenty years
old and single, L. lived with his brothers and sisters at 5815 Brush
Street (see Detroit map). His apartment sat in the east side, black
Detroit's oldest, most congested, run-down community, one extending from downtown Adams Street north to Leicester Court,
bounded by Woodward Avenue on the east and St. Aubin Street
on the west.[6] His world, like that of most of the city's 185,000 black
residents, consisted of dilapidated accommodations rendered "almost intolerable" by time and in-migration. Since his arrival from
Brookhaven, Mississippi, five years earlier, Charles L. had witnessed an enormous influx of black newcomers, which had swelled
to 2,100 per month since the previous year and increased the black
population by 24 percent.[7]

Packed into a ghetto three-and-one-half miles square, which
contained several viable institutions, diverse classes, and close-knit
families, Charles L. and his neighbors found employment in the
war-boom economy. He had worked as a laborer in grocery stores
and factories for the past two years, no doubt denied access to well-
paying defense jobs because of low skills, limited education, and
"marked racial feelings." "Little Willie," who stood 5 feet 4 inches,
weighed 140 pounds, and appeared dark-skinned, was considered
"aggressive" and "antisocial"—perhaps the result of his diminutive
size and ghetto experience. He seemed "criminalistic" to the Recorder's Court psychiatrist, although he boasted no arrest record.

He knew discrimination firsthand, however, and had clashed recently with white youths and lawmen.[8]

Seeking escape from the east side's confines, where the temperature broke 90 degrees on Sunday afternoon, Charles L. headed for Belle Isle. Perhaps he brooded along the way, angered by Detroit's inadequate recreation area and agitated by memories of Eastwood Park six days earlier.[9] On Tuesday evening, he was one of fifty black teenagers and zoot suiters accosted by nearly 200 white high school students and servicemen at the privately owned amusement park in East Detroit. He lost the fight, as policemen arrested several whites and ejected all blacks.[10] Charles L. had traveled over seven miles from his home to this amusement park, deep into lily-white territory. Consciously or otherwise, he also did so to protest the restrictive and humiliating conditions placed upon him—upon all black Detroiters. He embodied the "zoot effect," adopting expressive dress—broad shouldered, long-waisted coats, and bloused, pegged pants—behavior, and language that stroked his ego, parried racism, and affronted many of both races, who labeled such antics as abnormal, even gangsterlike, and mocked them in caricatures.[11]

Small wonder that today Charles L. ventured more than three miles to Belle Isle—an island park in the Detroit River connected to the mainland by the Jefferson Avenue bridge—where 100,000 Detroiters converged to escape sultry weather and, ironically, wartime tensions. He arrived in midafternoon, one of many blacks who made up fully 80 percent of the crowd that jammed the isle's 985 acres of ball fields, beaches, and boardwalks, hiking trails and canoe livery, playgrounds and picnic areas.[12] The large proportion of blacks present may have emboldened him, or the growing resentment of many whites, who objected to close racial associations, may have raised his own bitterness.[13] In any event, around 3:30 P.M. he led a milling crowd of blacks in a series of altercations with whites, which officials said "fanned the flame of hatred" and led ultimately to the death of thirty-four persons.[14]

Charles L. shot craps with several youths, both black and white, before a fight broke out over the question of crooked dice. The white cheaters fled the scene, and Charles L. and his friends were unable to catch them. Frustrated, he exhorted seven teenagers to avenge their humiliation in Eastwood Park and "take care of the Hunkies." Quickly he led them in a series of forays, assaulting whites, breaking up their picnics, and consuming their food. In thus evening the score, L. and his marauders reflected the racial tone of other confrontations that began to break out with increasing regularity (blacks and whites scuffling for pony rides or picnic grills). By 9:30 P.M. the exchange of blows and epithets escalated, recording the first hospital casualty—a white teenager assaulted three times within twenty minutes—and Charles L. surfaced again. At the playground, he and his pack attacked fourteen-year-old Gus Niarhos and stole his carfare. Failing to hail a homeward bus or chase down another white target, they headed across the crowded bridge to Detroit. It was now 10:45 P.M. Soon L. brushed against thirty-eight-year-old Joseph B. Joseph, called him a "white motherfucking son of a bitch," and slammed him to the pavement, where other black youths kicked him and suggested hurling him into the river. As the victim struggled to his feet and raced into the path of two white sailors and their dates at the island end of the bridge, L. and his cohorts moved toward Jefferson Avenue.[15]

Pushing and name calling—"black bitch," "white bastard"— turned to mayhem as one of the sailors blew his whistle and rallied some fifty bluejackets stationed at the armory on Jefferson Avenue. Fighting broke out all along the bridge and spilled onto the thoroughfare, where one of Charles L.'s gang unsuccessfully urged blacks to enter the fray, claiming, "a colored woman and her baby had been drowned."[16] By 11:30, however, white numbers had soared and comprised most of the 5,000 persons in the area. Sailors, still smarting from a racial brawl the previous morning, bridge crossers, and nearby residents fought to reclaim the park and reestablish social distance: "We don't want any niggers on Belle Isle." They beat and chased blacks, spreading their vengeance one block either side of Jefferson Avenue and four blocks north on Grand Boulevard. During the next two and a half hours, the crowd dispersed as police officers flooded the intersection and took control without serious loss of life.[17] They handled the disorder, said blacks, by "beating and arresting Negroes while using mere persuasion on whites."[18]

Charles L. was neither among the twenty-eight blacks arrested nor the five injured. He made his way back to the east side and, along with several witnesses frightened by the crazed-looking white toughs, alerted others in the black community.[19] He, or someone else, arrived at the east-side Forest Club at 12:30 A.M. and informed Leo T. of the fighting across-town on Jefferson Avenue (see Riot Zone map).[20]

Thirty-five-year-old T. lived with his wife at 976 Wilkins Street. A resident of Detroit since the age of three, he was familiar with past racial conflicts—the Ossian Sweet incident (1925), the Black Legion terrorism (1930s), and the Sojourner Truth housing disorder (1942).[21] He had brushed with the law as a way of life: thirteen arrests for unarmed robbery, breaking and entering, disturbing the peace, frequenting a gambling place, destruction of property, and, as recently as May 1941, carrying concealed weapons; four convictions, two prison terms, and one probation violation. He had worked as a handy man at the Forest Club, a popular recreation center, since his last police encounter, operating a sound truck, selling dance tickets, and manning the coat room. Literate but crime-prone, he doubtlessly experienced alienation toward white society and especially its gendarmes.[22] His victims, however, had hitherto been fellow blacks.

At the Forest Club that night, Leo T. made his way through the crowd of 700 dancers, climbed atop the bandstand, and stopped the music. Dressed in a dark suit and carrying a briefcase, he identified himself as Sergeant Fuller and announced that a riot was in progress on the island, where whites had thrown "a colored lady and her baby" off the bridge. Everyone "get your guns" and "go out there," he instructed; free transportation awaited outside.[23] Then, having directed his anger against whites, he disappeared, and pandemonium broke out.[24]

Leo T.'s shocking news stampeded Forest Club patrons into the street, but no vehicles idled at the curb for their convenience. Their numbers were unusually large because the night spot, which contained a bowling alley, dance floor, and skating rink, provided one of the few recreational outlets for blacks, and, on June 20, was holding a "big dance" that drew several hundred youths.[25] Galvanized by the rumor of whites killing a black woman and child, which linked a specific violation of sacred mores with general hostile beliefs in white violence, dancers and pedestrians became vengeance-seeking mobs.[26] They filled the intersection of Forest Avenue and Hastings Street, stoning white motorists and trolley passengers while taunting policemen who came to rescue them. One thousand persons of both sexes and various classes struck human targets and overwhelmed lawmen, whose depleted wartime ranks and Belle Isle emergency assignments made answering 500 east-side calls impossible. Unchecked, blacks beat, hit, and stabbed whites who crossed their path, sending one injured person every minute to Receiving Hospital.[27]

Soon rioters roamed throughout "the colored district," flush with victory and, like counterparts of a later generation, "commonality of purpose."[28] South of Canfield on Brush, they knocked unconscious a twenty-seven-year-old white man, who became the first fatality when crushed accidentally by a cab.[29] North of Grand Boulevard on Holbrook, they fought fifty Chevrolet Gear and Axle shift workers, and created disturbances along Oakland Avenue at Owen and Westminster.[30] In this section, a mile above the boulevard, black residents like John T. clashed with police and forced them to detour streetcars.[31] Most in their early twenties, married, and employed as laborers—and well aware of the "hate strikes" that had rocked Detroit for the previous six months, denying promotion of blacks to more skilled, better paying jobs—they might have been pursuing white workers out of revenge.[32]

As police sealed the ghetto and whites avoided it, rioters turned their attention to stores, and, sometime before dawn of June 21, began to loot them. In fact, within one hour of Leo T.'s announcement, they were smashing windows on Hastings Street. Their fury now spread out of control along all the major commercial streets: St. Antoine, Beaubien, Brush, and John R, east to Hastings; Rivard, Russell, Riopelle, and Dequindre, west to St. Aubin. From Adams Street north to Grand Boulevard and ultimately beyond, residents shifted from an interracial or communal upheaval to a riot against property. Hemmed in by physical boundaries, they concentrated on symbols of white domination—lawmen, property, and goods— as white citizens, absentee landlords, and shop owners slept beyond

yond their reach.[33] They confronted officers, injured several, and killed one, but drew deadly, often indiscriminate gunfire, which would ultimately claim seventeen black lives.[34] More often, rioters demolished store fronts and showcases, strewed mannequins and merchandise around the streets in the midst of broken glass, and left large segments of the business district looking as if it "had been bombed from the air with block busters." Looters, in turn, swept through drug and grocery stores, haberdasheries, pawnshops and taverns, confiscating everything from aspirin to liquor. Some stole alone, others in groups; some acted crazy, others deliberate; some targeted any store, but a great majority spared known "colored" establishments or those later identified by hastily painted signs.[35]

At 4:00 A.M., whites began to retaliate along Woodward Avenue, probably having heard of the upheaval from escaping passersby and laborers. Adolescents and young men gathered about the Roxy and Colonial theaters, stoning the cars of blacks that passed along the thoroughfare, which separated black ghetto and white west side, itself characterized by substandard dwellings and transient populations.[36] They also assaulted black patrons exiting from the all-night cinemas and tried to push their way into the black community at Alfred, but were driven back by police officers. In close residential proximity to east siders and competing with them for jobs and status, white assailants, like their predecessors in earlier interracial riots, sought to kick blacks back into their place. And, despite a lull in their activities around 6:30 A.M., they—again like earlier rioters—seemed proud of themselves and threatened further bloodshed.[37]

Before that occurred, Police Commissioner John H. Witherspoon called Mayor Edward J. Jeffries, Jr., other municipal, state, and federal authorities to Detroit Police Department (DPD) Headquarters at 4:00 A.M. For the next two and a half hours, as black and white outbursts raged side-by-side, they discussed the role that police and military units could play in quelling the disturbances. Witherspoon and Jeffries decided against employing other than local policemen and auxiliary officers, however, wrongly believing the riots were subsiding. They knew better by 9:00 A.M., and within the hour, Jeffries called Governor Harry F. Kelly for much-needed manpower. They awaited the arrival of the Michigan State Police, Michigan State Troops (a specially raised wartime home guard), and—as a result of Kelly's eleventh-hour request to the Sixth Service Command in Chicago—soldiers. Meanwhile they endeavored to hold on, unaware of the bureaucratic wrangling over the mobilization of army regulars set in motion by Kelly's entreaty: Presidential aides, military higher-ups, and War Department officials delayed deployment of servicemen for twelve deadly hours, seeking precedence for their action and fearing adverse consequences should something go wrong.[38]

At noon, Mayor Jeffries sped through the east side and met with numerous members of secular and religious organizations at the Lucy Thurman YWCA. He jousted with those brought together by the Citizens Committee, which had organized the previous year's Sojourner Truth housing protest. He drew criticism from delegates of both races about police manhandling blacks but ignoring "Fifth Column" whites, and heard recommendations for mayoral radio pleas, black deputies, and martial forces. Stung by hostile remarks and divided opinion (even over the question of bringing in federal troops), Jeffries insisted that color-blind enforcement would prevail and promised to use whatever force necessary to end bloodshed. He departed abruptly to meet Governor Kelly, tired of the harassment and censure.[39]

While Jeffries and critics fiddled, Rome—in mayoral paraphrase—was burning. Indeed, as they began their well-intended noon parley, hundreds of injuries had already been reported and riot-related deaths numbered eight.[40] White gangs controlled Woodward Avenue, halting traffic to drag blacks from trolleys and automobiles, beat them viciously, sometimes senseless, overturn and incinerate their cars—all pay-back for east-side attacks.[41] They roamed about, with little interference from bluecoats, whose numbers never exceeded 1,000, were divided between two war zones, and generally harbored racial prejudice.[42] Inside the ghetto, where most officers found themselves assigned, blacks continued to break into stores, forage for possessions, and run afoul of patrolmen. Looters represented older, more mature residents, albeit no less resentful than the ruffians led by Charles L.[43]

Rudolph M. certainly would have fought at Belle Isle. A twenty-three-year-old native of Louisiana, who had come to Detroit only thirteen months before the disturbance, he lived with his wife on Edmund Place, two blocks east of Woodward Avenue and midway between Forest Avenue and downtown. He worked in a store stocking shelves for wages far below those paid in the defense industry. Perhaps angered by his environment—slums largely built before 1915, often lacking indoor plumbing, and cruelly dubbed "Paradise Valley"—he turned his anger against absentee owners responsible for his plight.[44] Rather than destroy his own dwelling, however, he selected a more practical target over a half mile from home: Paul's Drug Store at Hastings and Leland. He hurled first a brick and then, moments later, a bottle through the plate-glass window. He was only one of many in the missile-throwing crowd, but he alone drew the attention of police officers, who apprehended him after a short chase. He was found to be carrying a 7-inch butcher knife, a concealed weapon. Though he made no effort to slash his captors, his possession of the blade indicated fear and possibly Southern tradition.[45] Significantly, his presence on the street and repeated attacks on the pharmacy revealed deep alienation and purposeful protest—the combination of ghetto isolation, oppression, numbers, and solidarity with wartime opportunities and anxieties.[46]

Looters carried this racial complaint further. Their early morning plunder seemed symbolically defiant, and soon became wholesale theft by usually law-abiding citizens. Roy S., for instance, watched as several people tossed armfuls of merchandise out of a grocery store at 4717 St. Antoine, half a mile from his home on East Ferry. He and a companion were loading several pounds of pork loins, smoked ham, canned salmon, and cheese—then rare and rationed items—into their car, when police arrested them for larceny. Born in Gregory, Arkansas, but a Detroit resident for the past five years, S. lived with his wife and child and earned good money at Ford Motor Company. Approaching thirty years of age, seeming less disaffected and more established than window smashers like Rudolph M., he nonetheless helped himself to food thrown into the street.[47] Possibly he considered such actions righteous redistribution and redefinition of property—as would some ghetto rioters a generation later. Yet S. never hinted at motivation; he told officers only that he had picked up the goods and indicated which store they came from. That a man like this should engage in behavior normally unlawful—but momentarily acceptable by many in the community—disclosed the drawing power and the grievance of mob activity; that he should collect mostly perishables that would have spoiled if left in the gutters and could have been purchased in the expensive but equitable rationing system, exhibited the ambivalence of moral standards and the anomie among oppressed people.[48] Experiencing mixed emotions and motives in a wholly unregulated and opportunistic setting, Roy S. stole, but he did so for much more than "fun and profit."[49]

Neither Rudolph M. nor Roy S. knew the proprietors of the stores they sacked, despite later contentions by observers that such actions manifested anti-Semitism. Living half a mile away and possessing little if any knowledge of which stores were Jewish-owned, they delivered symbolic attacks on "the white caste." They probably knew that German and, more recently, Russian Jews had occupied the east side before them and still controlled many of its apartments and businesses, yet the antagonisms that fueled the violence were customer-merchant rather than ethnic. They believed themselves exploited by all shopkeepers, not simply the white druggist and the Russian Jewish grocer. Certainly black anti-Semitism—growing out of socioeconomic competition and cultural conflict, which enjoyed a long tradition in the ghetto, and intensified in the face of Nazi propaganda—heightened tensions, but M. and S. reacted as opportunists seizing the moment rather than as ideologues punishing Semites. They struck at accessible, safe targets, emblems of white exploitation and black humility, and they struck as everyday residents, who had neither police records nor apparently political doctrines.[50]

Unconcerned with the motives of M., S., or their white counterparts at this point, Mayor Jeffries sought ways to suppress the outburst, which worsened as high schools released students—ready participants—early. By 3:00 P.M., he agreed to place 250 black counterrioters in the east side, though without firearms or police powers, and he met Kelly (who arrived by plane from the Governor's Conference in Columbus, Ohio). They quickly joined military and state police representatives in the Federal Building on Fort Street, when Gen. William Guthner, emissary of the Sixth Service Command from Chicago, entered the conference. They learned for the first time that the mobilization of army regulars would be given by President Franklin D. Roosevelt only after Kelly declared martial law. Jeffries urged Kelly to comply, but the politically minded Republican governor did not want to appear a failure by requesting aid from the popular Democratic executive. Ultimately the riot situation downtown, where Jeffries and Kelly witnessed 500 whites chase a bleeding black man into the arms of patrolmen and heard reports of 10,000 whites hunting "black meat" in Cadillac Square, caused mayor and governor to address Detroit residents over the radio at 6:00 P.M. Jeffries pleaded for peace, and Kelly finally proclaimed a state of emergency, which authorized the deployment of Michigan State Troops, banned liquor sales, crowd formation, and weapon bearing, and imposed a curfew.[51]

Still, martial law loomed in the future, as slightly fewer than 900 local and state police remained seriously outmanned and mobs ruled important parts of the city.[52] Twenty-one-year-old Erving M., a white man, stood among hundreds of other whites packing the Woodward Avenue-Vernor Highway intersection. Married, employed as a truck driver for the Braun Lumber Company, and earning a good salary despite a ninth-grade education, this Detroit native traveled over five miles from his home on Riopelle Street above McNichols Road to participate in the disturbance.[53] Whatever drew him downtown—curiosity, excitement, idleness, or defense of white supremacy—he appeared willing to fight, possibly even kill blacks. He and two companions walked along the southwest boundary of the east-side ghetto, carrying pieces of concrete. Stopped and searched inside a soda shop by a lone lawman, Erving M. surrendered a gas bomb, which he claimed to have found in the street. A type commonly issued to local and state police, it was probably abandoned during earlier rioting.[54] He was arrested; otherwise, he would probably have been one of hundreds who invaded Paradise Valley at Vernor Highway three and one-half hours later.

That siege, which bluecoats turned back, drew gunfire from frightened blacks in the Frazer Hotel and indicated how desperate the situation had become since Jeffries's radio appeal. White mobsters dominated Woodward Avenue, and black looters picked east-side markets clean, while bluecoats struggled to keep them apart. Indeed between 6:00 P.M. and 9:00 P.M., the death toll surged from sixteen to twenty-six lives, buildings and overturned autos burned beyond control, smoke, tear-gas vapors, small arms fire, epithets, and screams filled the air.[55] More manpower, in Jeffries's opinion, was "needed desperately," especially because the 1,000 Michigan State Troops he requested during this maelstrom would not materialize until dawn.[56] Hence Jeffries prodded Kelly, himself deeply concerned about even greater disorder as daylight turned to darkness, and the governor formally requested federal troops at 9:20 P.M.[57]

Kelly acted none too soon, as rioting spread citywide, ultimately affecting fourteen of fifteen police districts. Concentrated in an enormous rectangle, stretching from downtown Detroit north to the city of Highland Park, running through the heart of the 1st, 13th, and 9th precincts and spilling over east and west into adjacent zones, upheaval also occurred in the black west side and above the Polish city of Hamtramck.[58] Approximately three miles west of Woodward Avenue at Ironwood and Tireman, deep in the black middle-class community to which those who escaped the ghetto had moved, Thomas H. disturbed the peace. Like many living in this stable, upwardly mobile area of homeowners, he was married and employed in a skilled job; unlike most of those milling in the street, he had brushed with the police once before. He might have been displaying anger over reports of DPD brutality in the east side and indifference to white assaults downtown. At thirty-nine years of age, H. and his cohorts were older than most rioters else-where, possibly venting frustration over white society's disregard for their socioeconomic achievements and disdainful rejection of them as mere "niggers."[59]

Not as cohesive as the 30,000 west-side inhabitants, blacks living immediately north of Hamtramck and east of Highland Park (communities which stemmed the east-side ghetto and were themselves surrounded by Detroit) also raised havoc. They threw beer bottles at police officers, expressing perennial and riot-related contempt for these agents of social control, and carried concealed weapons.[60] However, some of those in the Riopelle–Division intersection seemed more victim than participant and hinted at the false assumption of officials (and later investigators) that all arrestees were active rioters. Harding D., for one, left work at the Dodge Main Plant in Hamtramck and had nearly reached home in slum-free north Detroit when he was stopped by patrolmen and arrested for carrying a knife. Almost twenty-four-years-old, single, and residing with a minister since he arrived in Detroit from Winston-Salem one year earlier, Harding D. had found the weapon at work and toted it for self-protection. He had no police record, had attended college for three and one-half years, was draft-classified 4-F (unfit for service), and produced character references from both his roommate and his supervisor. Harding D. appeared genuinely frightened of white toughs and, though found guilty as charged, he was given the choice of probation over prison.[61] His action, in sum, reflected more fear and self-preservation than anger, hostility, and protest. Like untold numbers of others victimized by race war, he had no doubt committed an act of survival and found himself in the wrong place at the wrong time.

Back downtown, Kelly's 9:20 P.M. Mayday for army help brought instant reinforcements and, within two hours, ended the day of bloodshed. Military-police units, which had moved into position several hours earlier, cleared the streets with fixed bayonets and tear gas. The 701st Battalion from Fort Custer dispersed the mobs in Cadillac Square, along Woodward Avenue, and then patrolled the ghetto, combining with the 728th Battalion from River Rouge Park to scatter rioters of both races. In all, eight companies of 1,210 soldiers restored order among several thousand people without firing shots. This demonstrated that impartial, firm policing by adequate numbers of personnel, well-armed and -trained, restrains major violence. Shortly before midnight but long after mobilization, President Roosevelt signed the proclamation authorizing the deployment.[62]

Early Tuesday, June 22, Detroiters awoke in an occupied city. Soldiers, including MPs held in reserve the night before and those of the late-arriving 1st Provisional Battalion, numbered nearly 1,900, bivouacked in armories and public fields, patrolled Woodward Avenue and the ghetto, mounted tanks downtown, and before dawn reopened all DSR lines.[63] Over 2,000 Michigan State Troopers from locations throughout the state also entered the city early in the morning and accompanied army patrols.[64] Neither these reinforcements nor mayoral assurances of public safety and Recorder's Court judges' speedy efforts to try captured rioters, however, restored public confidence completely.[65] Unfounded rumors of black and white combat kept police officers in motion, as did the repeated formation of rock-throwing white gangs five blocks west of Woodward Avenue at Warren and Hamilton. More trouble also continued in the east side below and above Grand Boulevard, though the only riot-related death of Tuesday and the last one of the upheaval—number thirty-four—occurred on Hastings Street at 4:16 A.M.

That killing, which claimed the life of a would-be looter, indicated the difficulty of restoring peace in the shattered ghetto. The looter hid behind a partition, refusing to come out, and told bluecoats to "go to hell" before they let go three blasts from their twelve-gauge shotguns.[66] Black and blue confrontations persisted throughout the day, fortunately with much less dire consequences. Black males, largely laborers from seventeen to fifty years old, congregated along business thoroughfares between John R and Hastings, and north on Oakland Avenue, or they crossed them en route to various destinations. Single youths disturbed the peace and, in the evening, violated the curfew, milling about, throwing brickbats, and picking over already ransacked stores, while married men traveled with knives or, infrequently, firearms. While some of the latter no doubt harbored destructive thoughts as well as weapons, others armed themselves—like Harding D. the previous day—for protection.[67] Such was the case of Harvey G., who sped south on John R at 3:25 P.M. in a car full of companions headed for work. Stopped and searched by police at Medbury and Hastings, the twenty-nine-year-old—a longtime resident of Detroit—admitted that he always carried the small, but illegally sized knife found on him. He was married and employed by the U.S. Rubber Company, "a very substantial fellow" who neither threatened nor harmed anyone despite a previous arrest. He received the token sentence of six months probation and served it without incident.[68] G.'s experience helps explain why so many black males faced charges of carrying concealed weapons after being detained for lesser crimes. It further manifested one of the cultural distinctions between whites and blacks—in this case knife carrying—which set east siders and police at odds and, in several cases, distorted both arrest and felon statistics. Amidst heated outburst, participants and victims became indistinguishable in the eyes of harassed patrolmen—prejudiced and outnumbered, endeavoring both to restore order and to protect themselves.

As June 22 came to a close, so did most of the violence, but not all. That evening on the lower east side, a state policeman shot a twenty-six-year-old defense worker in the back for allegedly shouting "Heil Hitler!" before running into the St. Antoine YMCA. He and fellow officers then charged the Elizabeth Street building and roughed up the "black bastards" and "apes" inside, leaving the critically wounded Y resident lying in his own blood for forty minutes. Their brutality reinforced black hatred for heavy-handed lawmen, but did not escalate into more bloodshed. Officers and fear kept blacks penned in Paradise Valley, while soldiers disarmed and scattered whites east of the ghetto, near Northeastern High School. The arrival of 2,416 members of the Ninth Infantry late Tuesday night and early Wednesday morning, June 23, ended any delusions, black or white, of continuing the disturbance.[69]

Thereafter armed peace slowly gave way to normalcy. Kelly returned to Lansing on June 26 and lifted much of his emergency restrictions two days later, though sizable numbers of soldiers remained in the city well into the next month. Jeffries, in turn, endeavored to explain the riot and—unsuccessfully—restore faith in himself and his police department. As officials and citizens caught their breath in the aftermath of violent public disorder, they realized its staggering enormity. Thirty-four persons were dead: twenty-five blacks and nine whites. Seven hundred and sixty-five injuries had received hospital treatment while hundreds more went unreported. Estimated at $2 million, property damage due to vandalism, looting, and fires—over 100 on June 21 alone— claimed stores, merchandise, and automobiles. One million hours in labor, affecting some defense industries more than others, were lost because of absentee workers, who joined the mobs or stayed home fearing them. It also cost $115,000 per day for federal and state troops to quell the riot. Nor could a price tag be placed on the anguish and heartbreak of those who faced brutality in the streets and jails, learned of a loved one's death, or searched for missing family members. The images of the city and nation also became tarnished.[70] Gleefully, German and Japanese broadcasters spread news of Detroit worldwide, condemning the United States for trying to hide its "abusive social situation" by blaming fifth columnists for the "revolt."[71]

Back home the cost and agony of riot sparked controversy. Several questions arose and centered on those responsible for igniting and quelling disorder: Who and what caused the tragedy? Why did officials wait so long to mobilize federal troops? How come policemen treated whites with "kid gloves" and blacks with deadly firepower.[72] These and similar queries required assessments of those who filled the streets; hence rioters became the focus of conversation—and recrimination.

The numbers and characteristics of those apprehended between June 21 and June 30 affected how the riot was interpreted by many people. Of nearly 2,000 arrestees, young, black males comprised the overwhelming majority, followed by far fewer white males and black and white females. These participants recorded a median age of twenty-five years; surprisingly few of the scores of juveniles seen at the riot were arrested. Regardless of age or gender, blacks filled the ranks of arrestees in greater proportions than their population in metropolitan Detroit.[73] Their spokespersons attributed this gross imbalance to police bias, while bluecoat officials explained it in terms of black aggression.

Throughout the summer and autumn, black and white leaders

debated the question of responsibility. National Association for the Advancement of Colored People (NAACP) representatives labeled DPD handling of the riot as "one of the most disgraceful episodes in American history." Over a period of years, contended national executive secretary Walter F. White, Detroit lawmen had made upheaval possible by permitting "anti-Negro forces" to operate without check. Worse yet, echoed NAACP special counsel Thurgood Marshall, who also journeyed from New York City to gather information firsthand, it was mostly black people whose blood was spilled by police during the hostilities: seventeen dead and nearly 1,000 arrested. The police exerted ultimate force against blacks, thereby cheapening the worth of their lives and inviting unbridled white violence against them. In contrast they employed only persuasion on white rioters, and that, in the opinion of White and Marshall, is what resulted in no white deaths at the hands of patrolmen and far fewer white injuries.[74] Responding to NAACP criticism, Police Commissioner Witherspoon noted that the bloodshed was unavoidable, because blacks started the fight and carried it for many hours. Only blacks, he specified, damaged and looted stores and resisted bluecoats with arms; during the first critical hours of disorder, they injured more whites than vice versa.[75] Witherspoon ignored Marshall's charge that whites assailing black streetcar passengers and incinerating black-owned automobiles also constituted felonies that went uncontested by officers.

Despite this protracted debate over police behavior, which other federal and big city investigators condemned privately, the rioters drew even wider attention.[76] Many officials and observers considered them hoodlums. Jeffries set the tone in his June 21 radio appeal, urging "decent citizens" to comply with the governor's emergency decrees, so authorities could "ferret out the hoodlums and fifth columnists responsible for starting these disturbances."[77] Playing down the reference to subversives, most editors regretted the impact of "hoodlum minorities" on allies and servicemen abroad.[78] Even the Rev. Horace A. White, prominent minister of the Plymouth Congregational Church, sole black member of the Detroit Housing Commission, and supporter of the mayor, laid the greatest blame for disorder on irresponsible "young hoodlums" of both races. As surprisingly, so did the Rev. Gerald L. K. Smith, fundamentalist pastor, America First Committee founder, and recent arrival, who also played up Communist agitation among blacks and deemphasized white southern involvement.[79] Less provocatively, everyday citizens agreed that "teenage boys" who "laugh at law and order" instigated the bloodshed.[80]

More often than not, however, commentators rebuked black rather than white youths. During the bloodletting on June 21, Jeffries claimed that twice as many whites as blacks had been treated for scalp lacerations and broken jaws at Receiving Hospital.[81] He and Witherspoon soon reiterated this interpretation to the Common Council. They identified "white mobs" and "Negro hoodlums"—meaning those teenagers and young adults who engaged in unlawful behavior regularly and repeatedly clashed with bluecoats. Indeed, the police commissioner described white riot behavior as "retaliatory action" (for black-induced violence on Belle Isle and the east side) but referred to perennial antagonisms between blacks and policemen.[82] Black toughs spilled blood first, insisted one white Detroiter, contending that many white rioters were relatives and friends of women who had been insulted on streetcars; black molesters of white women and children, asserted another "taxpayer," cannot be permitted.[83] Besides blatant sexual fears, whites like Sgt. Philip P. Bruno condemned "Negro Hoodlums" for their "militant, abusive, destructive race consciousness," disrespect for law and order, and riotous assault on innocent white people. Petty gangsters over a period of years had built "an unsavory reputation" for all blacks.[84]

White allegations notwithstanding, black leaders revealed the diversity of their community and identified more than thugs among east-side rioters. Editor J. Edward McCall of the *Detroit Tribune* lambasted blacks who disgraced themselves by looting, while John Wood, fellow columnist for the *Michigan Chronicle,* recorded the complaints of those who swelled the streets as anything but criminal. A soldier's mother protested the murder of black servicemen in the South by those they were trained to protect; a family man defended his home from invading white mobs; a qualified woman worker objected to defense employers who "can't hire colored"; a young man criticized police brutality in the ghetto and police leniency on Woodward Avenue, wanting to see "some colored policemen instead of these white so and sos." If these east siders were "hoodlums," concluded Wood, so was everyone else, "no matter what side of the tracks we live on."[85]

The same would not have been said by most black and some white Detroiters about Woodward Avenue and downtown rioters. Army intelligence reported "an unusual amount of traffic" on telephone exchanges in areas of "young white hoodlums," which passed rumors that "niggers" slit the throat of a sailor and raped his girl friend, while prominent residents described whites jammed between Peterboro and Cadillac Square as "mostly hoodlum."[86] And certainly numerous white citizens, locally and nationally, deemed white teenage participants, in the words of Recorder's Court Judge John J. Maher, "typical young American hoodlums."[87] A handful of commentators, such as a later group of Eastern High School students, believed that "base, thrill-seeking" whites were the major cause for violence.[88]

Black or white, younger "Zoot Suiters" and "Jitterbugs" rather than older individuals loomed as the culprits.[89] Those detained in armories before being sent home or transferred to Police Headquarters tended to be "boys in their teens."[90] Few hooligans possessed criminal records, said one commentator, most of them being "just tough youngsters at the dangerous age when vitality greatly outweighs common sense." Consequently, they were egged on by married men on the sidelines.[91] Lacking supervision and adequate recreational outlets, they moved in a war society "with 'fight' written large in it." Some minors enjoyed full employment in the "twenty-four hour work town," but found little time and few places in which to spend their wages. "Nervous tension" resulted, often displaced in "devious opportunities."[92] Four white youths shot an elderly black defense worker simply because they wanted to kill "a nigger." Knife-toting black youngsters and adults terrified the white majority.[93] Armed and surly, so said whites, black jitterbugs fought all along the color line, on streetcars, at Greenfield Restaurant, Eastwood Park, Roxy Theater, and, cataclysmically, Belle Isle.[94]

Several youngsters, probably white zoot suiters, later claimed that they were neither hoodlums nor riot participants but idle, ignored teenagers, yet few Detroiters of either race would have agreed with "One of the People" who accepted their innocence.[95] Instead, most Detroiters envisioned a link between hooligans and riffraff, those individuals marked by limited intelligence and community rejection. In the *News* of June 24, they read of the editor's suspicion that many rioters were 4-F draft registrants and, along with others who committed abnormal acts, should be examined by the Recorder's Court Psychopathic Clinic.[96] *News* readers discovered further that Dr. Lowell S. Selling, head of that unit, agreed and planned to analyze over 1,000 participants. "Hoodlums to Be Given Mind Tests," screamed the front-page story, in which Selling provocatively attributed the "recent emotional explosion" to mostly "feeble-minded" and marginal people. It was not unknown for white boys to be rejected by the armed forces because of "psychopathic failings," but Selling chose to emphasize the alleged problem of mental deficiencies in black youths, who comprised the overwhelming majority of arrestees; Paradise Valley, with its low standard of living, served as a haven for "the mental types who find difficulty in earning a living."[97] Within one day of Selling's announcement, residents learned that Governor Kelly had ordered Dr. C. F. Ramsay, supervisor of the Michigan Bureau of Child Welfare, to determine those "social maladjustments which contributed to the city's worst race riot."[98] Indeed, press coverage of the disorder, which stressed—in photos, tone, and words—abnormality and called for psychiatric evaluations, reinforced the belief that ordinary people did not riot. Representative of the majority's view, if not its politics, the America First Party concluded that upheaval had begun in "the saloons" and "the underworld" by "street brawlers" and "subversive conspirators."[99]

Those who witnessed or read about the rampage also blamed Southern newcomers. When Jeffries stated that an influx of migrant workers contributed to the riot, he sparked the ire of editors like Ralph McGill of the *Atlanta Constitution,* who protested "the cheap and easy habit of blaming any and all racial troubles on the South." Such conflict grew out of civil injustices and economic inequities found in both Detroit and Dixie, lectured McGill, noting also that teenagers, not Southern laborers, had ignited the outburst.[100] Despite McGill's logic, most Detroiters thought like their mayor. Popular *News* columnist W. K. Kelsey ascribed the disorder to scores of Southerners who encountered liberal conditions in the city, where blacks experiencing newfound freedom clashed with whites clinging to "Jim Crow notions."[101] One race appeared "uppity" and the other recalcitrant, both from ignorant and impoverished backgrounds. "The change was too great," added William P. Lovett of the Detroit Citizens League, "the necessity for adjustment too violent."[102] Certainly the mayor and prominent citizens represented their constituents, the majority of whom accused "floaters and drifters," mainly Southerners seeking war work, for the upheaval.[103]

Floaters, like hoodlums, came from both races. Except for Dr. Selling, who described black migrants as highly emotional and overly combative, "ready prey" for antiwhite propaganda, however, most Detroiters focused only on white Southern newcomers. They considered black rioters primarily as hoodlums and white participants as mainly "from the back country." Even Selling described white outsiders as possessing little education and much prejudice, characteristics seen by many others.[104] "Dumber than hell" and harboring hatred for "colored men," the "Hill Billies" struck the first blows on June 21.[105] According to a police reporter who covered the riot, "the lowest element of poor white trash from the South" dominated the early, important stages of bloodshed.[106] They lived in sizable numbers between Canfield on the north and Vernor Highway on the south, immediately west of the black ghetto from Woodward Avenue to Grand River, a deteriorating, highly congested area.[107] Experiencing many of the same abject conditions, cultural alienations, and social humiliations as blacks, they sought security in numbers, which critics dubbed "clannish," and held tight to segregation.[108] "It's about time," wrote Josephine Gomon, who assisted Ford Motor Company workers to find housing, "that someone around here inform the hill-billies, both from the mountains of Kentucky" and the alleys of Detroit, that "we're operating under a democracy."[109]

This last point played to the thinking of longtime city residents in search of scapegoats. "Old" and "Real" Detroiters, proud of their locale's reputation as a refuge for blacks, deplored the riots and blamed it on uneducated, belligerent white Southerners. They castigated newcomers from "backward states," bearing "ignorant prejudices" and undemocratic ideas. "Colored people," declared one resident, "are Americans, too," who were fighting alongside white soldiers on the battlefield of democracy and deserved to live beside them at home.[110] Even "an enlightened Southerner" apologized for "the hill-billies who were largely responsible for the racial trouble."[111]

Some Detroiters, including established Southerners, challenged the majority view, albeit unsuccessfully. "E Pluribus Unum" doubted if those condemning the South had ever been there to witness the absence of "hill-billies" and the presence of harmonious race relations, while "A Reader" contended that the whites arrested for rioting carried no "Southern names."[112] Not content with defending white migrants, "an 'old Southerner'" charged that recently arrived blacks "feeling free" ignited the disturbance, and anonymous bigots from both regions warned that white Americans who "made this country" were not going to give any of it to "the Black Race."[113]

Distinguished Southerners outside the city were irritated by the criticism being heaped on their region. Like McGill, Mayor W. F. Carr of Durham, North Carolina, chided Jeffries for his anti-Dixie remarks.[114] Diplomatically Jeffries replied that he might have been quoted out of context and, if he affronted Carr or others, apologized. Assuming that the South, like all regions, contained individuals with "good, bad and indifferent moral standards," however, he surmised that the "least desirable" came north to exploit "the so-called 'get-rich-quick' formulas" without "contributing anything worthwhile to our community."[115] This position hardly vindicated Southerners, but instead reflected the deep-seated belief, held by most Detroiters and outsiders, that Southern white migrants were troublemakers.

Beyond the view of white rioters as hillbillies, some observers and several Southerners pointed their fingers at ethnics. A former resident of Detroit identified the participants as foreigners, who despised the encroachment of blacks in their neighborhoods, and one eminent liberal Southern Democrat contended that blacks initiated the violence before the whites, mostly from "minority racial groups," could retaliate.[116] More precisely, local high school teachers observed groups of "young Italians" or Mexicans, supposedly identifiable by their "long greasy black hair" and white head bands.[117]

Even so, Detroiters spoke more often of ethnic groups contributing to tensions, which sparked violence, than of their involvement in the bloodshed itself. The Danish owner of Greenfield Restaurant, where blacks protested several times for service, threatened to close the popular Woodward Avenue eatery if forced to serve them in compliance with civil rights law.[118] More often, observers referred to Polish Catholics, who contested blacks for the Sojourner Truth Homes and several neighborhoods east of the ghetto, immediately north and south of Hamtramck—itself an "anti-Negro" enclave.[119] Nevertheless, except for minor skirmishes and a few arrests in Hamtramck, Poles did not stand out in the minds of onlookers as rioters.[120] And some Polish Detroiters, such as W. Kucharski of the *People's Weekly*, considered the "anti-Negro insurrection" a "shameful" episode and a "serious blow" to the war effort.[121]

Because of the latter, many officials and witnesses speculated that subversives lay behind the actions of hoodlums, newcomers, and ethnics, black or white. Certainly that was the belief of "almost every person" attending the Citizens Committee noon meeting of June 21. Hearing black leaders and their white supporters blame the outburst on "fifth columnists," Jeffries broadcast their position and that term citywide at 6:30 P.M.[122] Many Detroiters agreed with him or already suspected treachery. One white resident considered the disorder "a definitely planned maneuver to disrupt production," while a second envisioned it as the result of subversive "mental conditioning" and "physical apparatus."[123] Others noted that the outburst lacked spontaneity and believed that "enemies" manipulated America.[124] "Is it not significant," asked the *Chronicle* editor, who spoke for most blacks on this issue, "that just as our armed forces are about to knock on the doors of Berlin, the unity of our civilian population . . . is being torn asunder?"[125]

Indeed, several citizens of both races believed they had witnessed sabotage during the upheaval. "Please note how the Belle Isle fight spread like wildfire over the city," remarked one Detroiter, who viewed it as "the signal agreed upon by conspirators."[126] The "circulation of fake rumors" troubled many, including Justice Department officials.[127] The story of a black mother and child having been killed duped all rioters, "a Hitler trick" that should have been plainly seen by "a blind man."[128] Other residents reported direction and organization in the rioting. Watching downtown mobs from the vantage point of a third floor office, black social worker Beulah T. Whitby detected "some plan." She saw men in back lots push teenagers onto the street to fight and "certain leaders" repeatedly reorganize dispersed crowds.[129] Lessknown white observers also recorded the presence of leaders and, along Woodward Avenue, well-armed, well-organized columns of defense workers and hoodlums "parading in military fashion," four abreast like "storm troopers."[130] Black victims claimed—and white onlookers suspected—that the "crude dagger-like weapons" and iron clubs used by downtown and Woodward Avenue toughs were forged at Packard Motor Company, Timkin Axle Plant, and other defense industries during the past year.[131] While spectators associated most accounts of subversion with white rioters, only state police suggested the possibility that "un-American activity" had spread false rumors and incited radical groups of both races.[132]

Eyewitness accounts of subversion were heavily reinforced by some black leaders and white reformers, though not simply for the purpose of gaining civil rights improvements as suggested later.[133] Cognizant of recent racial conflicts in neighborhoods, factories, and recreation areas, they pressed the conspiracy theory at the Citizens Committee meeting. Christopher C. Alston, black defense worker and avowed Communist, Harper Poulson, white leftist director of the Greater Detroit Youth Assembly, and President R. J. Thomas of the United Automobile Workers (UAW) held fifth columnists responsible for the riot. Anyone who denied that an organized group lay behind the rioting was "completely wrong," said Thomas.[134] Soon after the gathering of June 21, committee members alerted city dwellers that "the American people were caught off guard by an organized Fifth Column attack on one of our most vulnerable points, that of racial discrimination."[135] Similar charges of a "well-planned, well-organized conspiracy" by Hitler's supporters came from the Civil Rights Federation of Michigan, the Communist Party of Michigan, and the Young Communist League of Michigan.[136] They also came from equally anti-Communist groups, like the local and National Urban League.[137] "All signs," said league officials, pointed to "carefully organized subversive activity in developing racial conflict in war industrial centers."[138] But the league soon abandoned the conspiracy theory.

Given the history of race relations in Detroit, the absence of observations in east-side areas where police barred whites, and the ideology of most leaders commenting on the disorders, the traitors emerged as native fascists. Specifically whites, including former State Senator Stanley Nowak, Metropolitan Detroit Youth Council Executive Secretary Donald M. Thurber, and UAW President Thomas, identified Klansmen as the saboteurs.[139] Shortly after the riot, for example, Thomas informed delegates of the Michigan Congress of Industrial Organization (CIO) convention that he could prove brown shirts led white mobs on Woodward Avenue.[140] Black Detroiters never doubted him, already believing, in the words of *Tribune* editor McCall, that "anti-Negro influences" lay behind the disorder.[141] Melodramatically, *Chronicle* columnist Russ J. Cowans reported a phone call to his office as the riot raged on June 21. "This is the Klan," said an anonymous voice threatening to drive "every nigger out of Detroit."[142]

Leftists, unionists, and blacks took the Klan and other "home-grown Fascists" seriously, though their own motives were suspected by officials.[143] Perennially, Communists and fellow travelers waged ideological war with Klansmen, UAW leaders fought Kluxers for control of their locals, and black Detroiters combated shirt wearers or, in the 1930s, their Black Legionnaire cousins. Most recently in their collective fight for black occupancy of the Sojourner Truth Homes, they defeated more than Polish Catholic homeowners. Indeed federal indictments charged officers of the reactionary National Workers League (NWL) with preventing defense workers from moving into the project. Citizens Committee members believed themselves vindicated and Klansmen, although never indicted, as guilty as NWL fascists for fomenting the housing disorder. Similarly UAW officers, who knew of KKK activities in several locals, blamed them for the hate strikes that shut down several defense plants, including Packard's just before the race riot.[144] And, within one month of the outburst, John Roy Carlson's *Under Cover* exposé of "the Nazi-fascist world" pinpointed how the Klan and NWL stimulated "race troubles in the city" and elsewhere.[145] Hence many, both black and white, imagined everpresent enemies responsible for the blood that stained Beaumont, Mobile, Los Angeles—and now their own Detroit.[146]

Surprisingly, even Gerald L. K. Smith agreed that the Klan was responsible for the "blood uprising," though it shared culpability with the Communist party.[147] If brown shirts encouraged white hoodlums, his leftist foes agitated blacks. In fact, besides the party and its press, fellow travelers included Jack Raskin and the Civil Rights Federation, the Rev. Claude Williams and the People's Institute of Applied Religion, and "fake labor leaders."[148] Smith also struck at the leftists because they held him partly responsible for the upheaval. Raskin, Williams, and local residents referred to Smith as a native fascist demagogue, whose bigotry prepared the ground for Klan sentiments.[149] Similarly, Detroit servicemen of both races placed him alongside Black Legionnaires and Kluxers as "conscious saboteurs," who sparked the disorder so America would lose the war.[150] "The Jews and New Dealers," Smith confided to his soldier son, blamed him for everything "from the weather to Pearl Harbor."[151]

Personal ideology and persecution complex aside, Smith represented a tiny minority seeing more red than brown behind the riot. Military intelligence operatives attributed bloodshed to political mismanagement, economic instability, and "subversive activity among blacks by pro-Communistic and pro-Japanese groups."[152] Similarly State Police troopers told of seeing Communist literature stored in east-side rooms during the upheaval, and a black conductor for the DSR spoke of "a Japanese Movement" behind the violence.[153]

While charges and countercharges—generally along ideological lines and between long-standing nemeses—punctuated the post-riot atmosphere, officials discredited all conspiracy theories. They agreed with black spokesmen and their white allies that "Detroit had long been a storehouse of inflammable material" needing "only a spark to set off the fire," but that did not prove the skulduggery of sinister forces.[154] Despite his broadcast, Jeffries told reporters before and after 6:00 P.M. on June 21 that no evidence existed to suggest the presence of organized, subversive groups instigating trouble.[155] If he spoke in haste about fifth columnists over the radio, perhaps unduly influenced by those present at the Citizens Committee noon meeting, the mayor steadfastly opposed that interpretation thereafter. He was supported by local DPD, State Police, and Federal Bureau of Investigation (FBI) higher-ups, including J. Edgar Hoover.[156] Likewise, military officers, who had originally suspected insidious influences at work, soon concluded otherwise.[157] And later, extensive investigations by state, federal, and army personnel discovered no "enemy agents or sympathizers," Klansmen, or any other subversive group behind the rioting.[158] Rather they found, in Bureau jargon, "spontaneous or internal combustion" in Detroit—and elsewhere.[159]

Some city newsmen and residents, black and white, as well as national civil rights leaders, agreed with their officials. Possibly the Klan or a similar "band of phobics" were in the mobs, reasoned the *News* editor, but rioting was primarily "a spontaneous outbreak of cruelty and hatred."[160] One of no doubt many white readers agreed, noting that no crosses were visible during the disturbance, and Paradise Valley Mayor Chester A. Rentie dismissed enemy agents as the instigators of bloodshed.[161] By July, even National Urban League and NAACP spokesmen shifted from accusing "subversive agents or organizations" of sparking the riot to charging white rioters with following "the Axis line." More than others, however, they stressed the influence of fascist propaganda on race relations, the "traditionally American" nature of the outbreak, and the effort by sinister groups to exploit it.[162] They also contended, like some local unionists and citizens, that the explosion resulted from fundamental interracial strife: "the ever increasing hatred and perpetual abuses . . . heaped upon the Negro Race."[163]

Nonetheless, some blacks and local and national leftists remained unconvinced. The absence of rioters wearing hoods and robes, wrote one black journalist (who might have included the lack of burning crosses), hardly dismissed the evidence of Klan activity in Detroit or its subtlety in riot.[164] More exasperated, the Reverend Mr. Williams wondered if authorities expected subversive rioters to run about with "swastikas on their arms," while *PM* columnist Albert Deutsch of New York challenged FBI findings, for no one was stupid enough to suggest that rioters acted "under direct orders from pro-Axis elements." What, he asked, of the "wealth of evidence" provided the bureau by the Civil Rights Federation, Detroit NAACP, and UAW?[165] Of course, the answer was that agents found it inconclusive and self-serving.[166] Even some of those arrested for rioting claimed no knowledge of "planned action" and reacted individually, impulsively to the disturbance.[167]

Into July black leaders and residents unsuccessfully pressed the conspiracy theory, particularly the Klan's involvement, only to have officials blame them for the riot.[168] Wayne County Prosecuting Attorney William E. Dowling personified this position, jousting with members of the Mayor's Interracial Peace Committee (which Jeffries formed shortly after the upheaval) and previewing the subjective Governor's Fact-Finding Committee appraisal.[169] He had significantly influenced that 8,500-word treatise, *The Factual Report*, which was released on August 11 and almost immediately became known as the Dowling report. Divided into three parts, including thirty-two exhibits of clippings, documents, maps, and photos, it recorded no premeditated plan or "subversive enemy influence" behind the riot, which resulted when black youths incited violence on Belle Isle. It focused on Charles L. the marauder and Leo T. the rumor monger, but relegated "white retaliation" on Woodward Avenue to one paragraph. Unmistakably, it described participants of both races, less the sailors on Belle Isle Bridge, as "youthful," "hoodlums," and "irresponsible." And it held black leaders and newsmen answerable for the "uncontrolled belligerency" of both groups by having exaggerated racial discrimination, exhorted racial militancy, and exemplified "an anti-social and factional outlook." It singled out local NAACP leadership and *Chron-*

icle coverage, which ignited another controversy and ultimately cost Dowling his elected office.[170] Hence, the Dowling report condemned black society, young and old, hooligans, leaders, and journalists without bringing their white counterparts or, more significantly, fifth columnists to task.

The lines were drawn, and the political war lay ahead, but the image of rioters remained one of black ruffians and—less significant in the light of their few arrests and Dowling's report—white newcomers. Hooligans and bums, said news columnist Kelsey, "ignorant Negroes and southern whites," remarked the east-side mayor, evoking images that news photos and, for black participants, official studies would verify.[171] Yet, public beliefs and formal surveys aside, those in the crowd possessed more than criminal faces and few migrant ones. Hoodlums and hillbillies made for easy scapegoats and sensational press, but they hardly reflected the reality of who rioted.

TWO

Of Hoodlums and Hillbillies

In order to identify the rioters more precisely, state authorities and social scientists studied them. They focused on those captured—predominantly black males—and, with one exception, reinforced the official and popular notions of participants as hoodlums, riffraff, and newcomers. However unwittingly, three of their studies undertaken in 1943 and 1944 reflected racial, class and cultural biases; a fourth survey previewed the thinking of a later generation of scholars only to be ignored by virtually everyone. In reality, none of the officials and researchers provided a complete profile of who rioted or what motivated them. Certainly some misfits and migrants filled Hastings Street, but so did protestors and victims: men, women, and teenagers from many backgrounds. Similar diversity existed among those whites who swept Woodward Avenue. Although only black men stood out in the crowd—at least in the minds of lawmen—they, too, wore many faces.[1]

Immediately after the upheaval on June 23, Governor Kelly conferred with state, county, and municipal officials and, soon appointed the Governor's Fact-Finding Committee. He named some of those in attendance—Attorney General Herbert J. Rushton, State Police Commissioner Oscar G. Olander, Wayne County Prosecutor William E. Dowling, and Detroit Police Commissioner John H. Witherspoon—to investigate the riot and those responsible for it. He also ordered committee members to coordinate all the information of those agencies involved in quelling the disorder. What appeared as logical and expedient, however, soon became political.[2]

Under Dowling's leadership, the Governor's Fact-Finding Committee worked quickly and, critics said, subjectively. It held several strategy meetings, collected data from "three federal, one state, one county and one city" agency, and appealed unsuccessfully for information from the public. Within one day, it found no evidence of subversives and quickly persuaded Kelly to oppose a state grand jury probe. Then, for the next seven weeks, the committee undertook its own investigation.[3]

Meanwhile Dowling touched off a major controversy. When representatives of the Mayor's Interracial Peace Committee pressed the county prosecutor to reconsider a grand jury investigation in late July, he said no. He explained that, without evidence of subversion, such an inquiry was unwarranted; he added, however, that if one occurred, it would focus on the local NAACP and certain black newspapers for "stirring up" racial dissension. Besides these irresponsible forces, he blamed "a gang of colored boys and girls" for deliberately inciting and spreading the bloodshed. Black youths, he specified, took the initiative on Belle Isle, circulated rumors, and rampaged in Detroit "several hours before white hoodlums" formed "retaliatory gangs of their own."[4] Despite intense criticism from black leaders and white liberals, who deemed his remarks inflammatory and unfounded, Dowling stood pat and drew backing from the *News* editor and the police commissioner. In fact, Witherspoon revealed additional information, earmarked for the committee's final report: Blacks had provoked over 90 percent of all interracial disorders on streetcars and buses over the previous eight months.[5]

When Dowling released the official findings of the Governor's Committee on August 11, it simply restated his earlier position complete with Witherspoon's reference to DSR statistics as an exhibit.[6] Widely published, the *Factual Report*, coming on top of unsuccessful demands for a grand-jury investigation, intensified the criticism of Dowling, which eventually carried over into his bid for reelection the following year.[7] The report named black instigators—including Charles L., Mattie Mae B., Aaron F., and Leo T.—and blamed black hoodlums for the riot, identifying individual whites only as victims and saying very little about white rioters. Blacks drew first blood on Belle Isle, were responsible for the first stabbing of a middle-aged white man, the first injury of a white policeman, and the first death of an east-side looter (who died from cuts incurred when he broke into a Hastings Street store). The report made no mention of white sailors fighting on the bridge, white rumors circulating along Woodward Avenue, or police maltreatment of blacks on every battlefront. Although condemned, white violence occurred as a reaction to black bloodshed.[8]

The "Factual" or Dowling report also contained statistics on the rioters. Based exclusively on Detroit Police Department (DPD) reports, it recorded 1,893 arrests from June 21 to June 30. Of these, 1,182 were prosecuted (revealing police strategy to disperse crowds by apprehending lawbreakers and spectators alike). Of those arrestees who faced formal charges, 970 were black and 212 were white; only seventy-one were women. Obviously lawmen concentrated on black men and, in varying degrees, ignored white men and women of both races (indicating their own racial bias and deference to gender, as well as female conditioning for nonviolence). Nor was much said about eighty-eight black and forty-eight white youngsters, mostly male and all between ten and seventeen years of age, who were placed in the Juvenile Detention Home, or fifty-eight others who were released. In sum, Dowling's report categorized rioters as "youthful, irresponsible" males, overwhelmingly blacks under thirty-one years of age, who generally disturbed the peace, carried concealed weapons, broke, entered, and looted stores. It lambasted all participants, but singled out blacks. Yet it did little more than itemize their age, race, gender, and crime. Essentially the report offered limited, undigested figures, that disregarded important socioeconomic factors such as education or occupation and any motivation beyond hooliganism.[9]

Long before Dowling released these findings, however, Governor Kelly ordered a second investigation. Realizing that the outburst was "sociological," knowing that the Recorder's Court psychologist planned to examine rioters, and probably sensing the limits of his own committee, he acted for academic and political reasons. Hence on June 25, one day following Dr. Lowell S. Selling's decision to test 1,000 participants and two days after forming the Governor's Committee, he instructed C. F. Ramsay, supervisor of the State Bureau of Child Welfare, to undertake a scientific investigation of the disorder.[10]

Unlike the Governor's Committee, which collected reports from law enforcement and military agencies, Ramsay designed a sixteen question survey and interviewed 340 rioters. He administered the questionnaire to arrestees held at Police Headquarters, Wayne County Jail, and Piquette Armory. With the cooperation of Police Inspector George McClellan of the Special Investigation Squad, he directed a staff of three psychiatrists, four sociologists, and fifty social workers drawn from the Eloise Parole Clinic and the Council of Social Agencies. Ramsay and his researchers conducted all of their face-to-face, twenty-five minute conversations on June 25, questioning individuals previously interviewed by local police, federal agents, and county prosecutors who sought information on possible draft dodgers and subversives.[11]

Following five weeks of tabulation, Ramsay submitted his study to Kelly, who released it to the press on the same date that the Governor's Committee made public its report—August 11.[12] Ramsay might have speculated that Kelly held the findings for nine days so as neither to preempt Dowling's study nor augment the controversy surrounding it. In any case, his own inquiry involved 314 black and twenty-six white males apprehended during the disturbance. That 92.3 percent of these prisoners were black and none female disclosed anew police prejudice; that such a minuscule number were white made analysis of their characteristics even less significant.[13] Consequently, Ramsay found most rioters black, and slightly over half of them thirty years old or older. A sizable majority of blacks, 63 percent, claimed they got into trouble by observing the riot or coming upon it unexpectedly. They reacted to "rumors, hysteria, prejudices and pent-up aggressions," concluded

Ramsay.[14] Yet more than half of those questioned did not know
what brought on the disturbance. Most others attributed its overt
cause to rumors, hoodlums, or subversives, while only a handful
spoke of race discrimination or ghetto conditions as longtime
causes.[15] Interestingly, they disagreed with the interpretations of
both the Governor's Committee and Ramsay.

Ramsay's team also gathered important socioeconomic data ignored by the Governor's Committee. One third of the black participants lived in families that were still intact or had been until their
eighteenth birthdays, and most of the arrestees, 80 percent, grew
up with siblings. More than one third of them remembered their
parents being tolerant toward the "race problem," while only
seven described their mothers and fathers as standing up for
rights. Nearly 40 percent of the black rioters attended high school,
though, strikingly, another 25 percent seemed illiterate to social
workers.[16] While the greatest numbers of prisoners, 73 percent,
had emigrated from the South, a near identical percentage had resided in Detroit for the past five years or longer. Besides stable
childhoods, Ramsay revealed rioters with a stake in society. Over
40 percent were married, a hefty majority of those supporting one
or more children. Almost all participants enjoyed wartime employment, particularly in factories and for competitive wages. In
fact, many of them worked overtime and found few moments for
hobbies or associations. Generally they experienced good health;
only 3 percent showed signs of mental deviation.[17]

In sharp contrast to the hoodlum view presented by Dowling,
Ramsay set forth a very different profile. His participants were
young adult, black males, who had acted spontaneously. Perhaps
unsurprisingly, less than 1 percent admitted to previous arrest. Yet
they represented much more than irresponsible, thrill-seeking or
vengeance-minded youths. Drawn in large numbers from stable,
tolerant homes, living in Detroit for some time, being fairly well
educated, enjoying good health, holding well-paying jobs and, in
many cases, raising families, they seemed representative of upwardly mobile, middle-class black society. Therefore Ramsay believed that blacks reacted to adverse social conditions and racial
prejudice, which aggravated "the problems of life." Perhaps these

factors sparked violence, but because most of them offered no reason for such behavior, Ramsay's view, like that of the Governor's
Committee, represented more conviction than proven fact. And it
became lost in the Dowling controversy.

So did the study of Selling, which was slow getting under way
despite its early conception and ballyhoo by the *News* on June 24.[18]
A month later, his battalion of "sob-sisters"—so-named by military
intelligence operatives—seemed more concerned about "the physical comfort of those incarcerated" than their reasons for rioting.[19]
Originally planning to analyze 1,000 rioters with the assistance of
twenty-three staff members, the director of the Recorder's Court
Psychopathic Clinic encountered several obstacles. He could neither hold arrestees after their arraignment nor release his limited
wartime personnel from everyday assignments, thus dashing plans
for extensive psychiatric investigations of so many individuals.
After much trial and error (including preliminary interviews with
prisoners, conversations with judges, lawyers of defendants, and
leaders of the black community, and consulting Dowling's and
Ramsay's reports), Selling decided upon an examination of convicted riot-related felons, accepting the first 100 referrals from the
Recorder's Court judges. He benefited from information provided
by the Wayne County prosecutor and DPD personnel, but based
his conclusions on physical examinations, psychological tests, personal histories, and professional evaluations—including his own
psychiatric survey of each convict.[20]

Selling publicized his findings in November, long after the upheaval and release of the Dowling and Ramsay reports. He examined chiefly black males under thirty years of age, 27 percent of
them in their early twenties, and provided scant information for
the remaining offenders: five white men and five black women.
Given the age of those surveyed, as well as their intelligence and
psychopathy (detailed below), Selling identified participants between fifteen and twenty-nine-years-old as most responsible for
the disturbance and its so-called hoodlum dimension. Indirectly
he reinforced Dowling's criticism of blacks as the culprits, but also
recognized, as did Ramsay, the impact of a hostile environment on
their behavior.[21]

Also, like Ramsay, Selling uncovered sociological information ignored by Dowling. Providing little statistical information, he highlighted examples of participants of illegitimate and legitimate origins, rejected and loving childhoods, broken and stable homes, whose parents passed on resentment of racial affronts and antagonism against policemen. Again through case studies, he gave the impression that the majority of offenders were single, without children, "well industrialized and well paid." And although Selling made scant reference to the hobbies, physical health, or draft status of the respondents, he revealed that 77 percent of them were born below the Mason-Dixon line (the largest number in Alabama, Georgia, and Mississippi). He also found that only 30 percent of the arrestees had attended high school, but most never graduated. Partly because of their race, Southern backgrounds, limited educations, and prewar poverty, the rioters—despite flush times—experienced insecurity about the future and, Selling hypothesized, acted aggressively.[22]

Instead of establishing socioeconomic characteristics of the rioters, Selling focused on their intelligence and psychiatric composition. He evaluated over 67 percent of all participants as defective: ninety-one and thirty-eight offenders exhibited below average intelligence and some form of feeblemindedness, respectively, while "a large number" of them were also psychopathic. None of the respondents suffered from insanity or psychoneuroses, yet only five appeared psychologically normal. Against these statistics, particularly as they related to the feebleminded, Selling considered many prisoners "abnormally suggestible" and, accordingly, drawn easily into mobs and riot activity. Their offenses involved entering without breaking, larceny in a store, and similar acts related to looting; they wandered into areas already violated by smarter, more fleet-footed rioters only to be caught trying "to get something for nothing." Thirty-four percent of those arrested fell into this category, while nearly 60 percent of the prisoners carried concealed weapons—ironically because they had adopted a knife-toting tradition in the face of inadequate police protection. This antisocial, supposedly Southern phenomenon notwithstanding, Selling pointed out that only five rioters actually attacked other persons. Unlike the shiv carriers, those convicted of assault and battery or felonious assault seemed antagonistic and vicious, incapable of self-control. "As a candle attracts moths," speculated Selling, the riot brought "these persons from their dark places of hiding"; it provided them the opportunity and anonymity to vent personal hostility.[23]

The upheaval, Selling learned, also attracted individuals with previous police contact. Forty-two of the 100 rioters had been arrested before, yet only eight of them had served prison terms for felonies. Those with police records included persons charged but not convicted, individuals arrested for misdemeanor violations, and very few chronic offenders, and thus Selling concluded that recidivism had "little or no place in the riot."[24]

Contradicting Dowling, Selling considered the rioters "by no means hoodlums." Nor did he verify the findings of Ramsay, agreeing only that the participants were young, employed, and affected by abject living conditions. Instead of long-standing, educated, stable family men, somewhat typical of society in general, he profiled long-term and recently arrived, poorly schooled, unattached, Southern in-migrants. Selling judged them rural and semicivilized, living more or less in the last century: "culturally inferior, educationally neglected," and behaviorally primitive. All Southerners (regardless of race or length of Northern residency) required "a great deal of attention in order to bring them in accord with the customs and attitude of the old Detroiter." Although nearly 50 percent of the felons had resided in the city for more than ten years, Selling deemed those of Southern origins "unsatisfactory citizens in time of strain." In sum, he blamed the disturbance on intellectually inferior young adults and uncultured Southerners, rather than average citizens or criminals.[25]

Within the year, Selling's format and, however tangential, interpretation were nearly replicated by staff members of the state prison. On March 9, 1944, sociologist Elmer R. Akers and psychologist Vernon Fox received 105 males convicted of having committed riot-related felonies by the Recorder's Court and sent to the Jackson County facility. They examined extensive prison records for each of the convicts, including police, court, and probation reports, educational, medical, and psychological records, social histories and personal letters. Before the year ended, they published their findings in the *Journal of Criminal Law and Criminology*. [26]

Like Dowling, Akers and Fox identified the prisoners by race and age, the mean for ninety-seven blacks and eight whites being twenty-eight years and two months; like Ramsay and Selling, they categorized the inmates socioeconomically, albeit without the former's thoroughness for family origins, racial attitudes, or military status. While not disclosing complete health reports as did Ramsay, they observed high venereal disease and low drug-addiction rates among the convicts. And, similar to Ramsay and Selling, their subjects were comprised of too few whites for meaningful analysis. [27]

Akers and Fox, nevertheless, reported data resembling that found by Selling. Eighty-nine of the criminals came from below the Mason-Dixon line, mostly from Georgia, Alabama, and Mississippi, representing the greatest proportion of Southerners in any of the riot inquiries. The academic level of all felons was slightly more than fourth grade, even less than that reported by Selling's respondents and partly explains their poor employment records. Almost all of the prisoners were unskilled, and, most striking, twenty-nine of them lacked employment at the time of disorder. Low intelligence quotients and feeblemindedness among eighty-two convicts also might have explained their vocational limits, unemployment rates, and, Selling would have argued, offenses. Slightly more than 50 percent of the inmates entered or looted stores, while 35 percent carried concealed weapons. That many of the latter habitually carried knives reinforced Selling's analysis of Southern heritage; his thesis was further supported by the fact that only a handful of convicts assaulted others and rioted actively. So possibly did the origins, residency, and marriage ceremonies of many felons. Predominantly Southern, living in Detroit ten years or fewer, and involved in common-law relationships, the overwhelming number of prisoners were less than eighty years out of slavery and, therefore, suffering from "cultural lag." Akers and Fox refrained from positing elaborate culture- and race-related theses, yet their findings seemed to substantiate all of Selling's suppositions except one: twenty-three lawbreakers possessed prison records. That statistic appeared to counter Selling's disregard for the role played by recidivists and confirm Dowling's charge of hoodlumism.[28]

All of the studies, then, identified characteristics of the rioters and, less directly, their motives, while also indicating problems of methodology. Dowling listed everyone arrested, but treated them alike, whether they committed crimes during the disturbance or long after federal troops quelled it. None of the other researchers selected their subjects from representative samples. Selling evaluated 100 court referrals, the majority having been arrested throughout the most riotous day, but their small numbers and consecutive order scarcely represented the several hundred persons arrested or convicted on June 21.[29] Even Selling noted that his sample came almost exclusively from Paradise Valley and that a comparable study should be made of those arrested on Woodward Avenue. Ramsay, too, expressed concern over the validity of findings based on 340 subjects, "so few human beings," while Akers and Fox, whose survey included only male rioters serving time at Jackson, acknowledged that a number of participants were still being tried or awaiting trial.[30]

Moreover, the Governor's Committee and the social scientists studied different populations, complicating further comparisons between their conclusions. Dowling examined arrestees released without trial, as well as those tried and found guilty or innocent of felonies and misdemeanors, while Ramsay never disclosed the status or offenses of his rioters. Though Selling and Akers and Fox observed only participants convicted of felonies, their subjects differed significantly; Selling considered primarily those assigned short terms in the Detroit House of Correction, Akers and Fox concentrated exclusively on offenders sentenced to much longer terms in the state prison.[31] Only Dowling and Selling mentioned females in their studies, while all investigators enumerated white males. And Dowling alone identified sizable numbers and percentages of women and whites—but without separating the genders by race and offense.[32]

If Dowling presented mostly one-dimensional police statistics, Selling and Ramsay interviewed the rioters and accepted their self-reporting without corroboration. Perhaps because some of his own "mentally defective" and legally minded respondents were evasive or untruthful in their interviews, Selling endeavored to justify the worth of his study by claiming that Ramsay's subjects "cooperated badly." He contradicted Ramsay's own observation that those interviewed "were eager to discuss their predicament," which a staff member—who marveled at the cooperation of prisoners—later attributed to "the Southern Negro's compliance" with white wishes and the presence of soldiers during interrogation. Whether Selling and Ramsay interviewed cooperative or, of greater consequence, truthful rioters might never be determined, though the question received little attention. Nevertheless, in varying degrees, they, as well as Dowling and Akers and Fox, believed their efforts valid. Ramsay, for instance, presented "some general impressions that may prove valuable" and Selling was certain that his findings would "hold water" for "the Paradise Valley part of the disturbance."[33] Despite serious limitations, investigators centered on different segments of the riot population and provided important insights about them, but nothing about many other participants.

Selling and Akers and Fox also considered their respective studies as the first to present sociopsychological data on rioters, interpretations supposedly enhanced by the utilization of control groups. Selling compared his rioters with groups of murderers, other prisoners, and visitors to the Detroit Physician's Office. He disclosed that there were fewer women and more Southerners among the rioters than among the murderers or visitors, that more than two thirds of the rioters and killers alike exhibited inferior intelligence or feeblemindedness, that the greatest number of murderers, criminals, and especially rioters fell in the twenty-to-twenty-four age group. If Selling's control group reinforced the thesis that intelligence and psychopathy among young adults foster antisocial activity, that of Akers and Fox (a group of 105 state prisoners convicted of felony just before the riot) tended to substantiate greater Southern origins and lower intelligence quotients among rioters than among other convicts.[34] Also discovering that riot participants were significantly older than their counterparts, Akers and Fox considered this unsurprising, because looters and weapons carriers constituted large segments of their study, but few of "the actual rioters"; those responsible for acts of violence and disorderly conduct either escaped because of their youth or were sentenced to the Detroit House of Correction.[35] Neither Selling nor Akers and Fox seemed aware of contemporary criminologists pointing up the need for caution when applying and comparing intelligence tests to criminal populations.[36] These parallels notwithstanding, Akers and Fox avoided Selling's application of psychopathic theory.

Beyond difficulties of methodology, those investigating the rioters exhibited several biases. Dowling, whom blacks endorsed and supported for public office in 1940 and 1942 because of his role in prosecuting Black Legionnaires, promoting black politicians, and employing black assistants, now chose political and class interests over those of east siders.[37] Criticized by some blacks for failing to respond adequately to threats of racial violence that culminated in the Sojourner Truth Homes disorder of 1942, he increasingly questioned assertive black behavior and charges of police misconduct. He, like Jeffries and other public officials who advocated middle-class values, gradualism, and order, became alienated by black juveniles and black leaders. Indeed, three weeks before the riot of 1943, he censured black hoodlums for assaulting victims of both races, blamed their aggression on "rabble-rousing radicals," and warned everyone of a race riot should the activity continue.[38] Despite immediate retorts to his allegations by black "agitators" like Louis E. Martin of the *Chronicle*, who pleaded "guilty" to advocating victory of the democracies abroad, protesting inequality at home, and threatening the status quo everywhere, Dowling repeated his charge in the wake of upheaval. On July 26, he publicized anew his self-fulfilling prophecy and, within two weeks, presented it as official interpretation of the Governor's Committee.[39]

Professionally associated with police officers, politically dependent on white voters, and personally sharing their socioeconomic beliefs, Dowling entered the riot investigation to defend those with whom he shared a stake in the community. He was "a politician," observed the Rev. Horace A. White, who sought to enhance his position with white voters. Worse yet, lamented the black Detroit

Housing Commissioner, his abandonment of east-side constituents and their struggle for racial justice symbolized plans by large, conservative "community forces" to deny blacks progress and disrupt "all kinds" of liberal organizations.[40] In truth, editorialized Martin, Dowling—and his constituents—viewed with alarm black aspirations for equality.[41] Essentially he closed ranks with bluecoats and racists, casting aside his reputation for fairness in order to stem the tide of wartime change.[42] His actions, of course, were generated by the same fears and changing context that impelled white rioters.

Dowling revealed more of his bias than other researchers, none of whom engaged the press regularly or jousted publicly with black Detroiters. Ramsay, for example, projected neither political nor racial overtones in his study, which might have influenced Kelly to bury Dowling's report once it sparked controversy along racial lines. Only as environment and social organization improved, Ramsay informed the governor, could "racial groups hope to realize a reasonable expression of harmony.[43] Politics aside, Selling pressed and Akers and Fox reinforced—albeit very light-handedly—a culture- and class-biased interpretation. Like Dowling, however, Selling publicly anticipated the results of his study long before examining anyone arrested for rioting.[44]

Employing intelligence tests and psychiatric theses, Selling portrayed rioters as dull, feebleminded Southerners, whose culturally backward life-style and economic inferior status invited "prejudice, antagonism, and difficulty in adjustment."[45] His culturally skewed exam and scientifically moot contention (that criminals displayed more psychopathy and feeblemindedness than civilians) held Paradise Valley blacks, themselves victims of racism and poverty, responsible for white society's repression.[46] Linking intelligence, psychopathy, and criminality to Southern black newcomers, Selling reinforced negative racial and regional stereotypes, indicted "some" of the migrants and those government agencies permitting their unsupervised migration. He stereotyped those coming North as principally lower-class dregs, "the well-adjusted competents" having no reason to rove.[47] Like Jeffries, he seemed unaware that black migrants tended to represent a cross section of their society.

Selling also speculated about the social aspects of specific rioters. Of forty-two-year-old Nelson B., a Georgia native who pleaded guilty to carrying a concealed weapon while searching for his daughter on the first day of riot, Selling surmised: "The rural Southern background may have influenced his character." He disregarded Nelson B.'s twenty-four years of residence in Detroit, "good marital adjustment," upright family (including two sons in the armed forces), steady defense employment, clean police record, and normal personality in order to express his own regional and cultural bias. In fact, he knew that Nelson B. had owned the registered .32 caliber Smith and Wesson for thirteen years. Despite all the evidence of fatherly love, social stability, and circumstances, Selling further stated his opinion that Nelson B. hung around with "some delinquent companions."[48] He demonstrated this class bias again by focusing on the social diseases of rioters like Louie H.— twenty-eight years old, well-educated, regularly employed, a five-year resident of Detroit, who came from an "excellent" home environment in rural Tennessee. Selling ignored all these favorable factors to point up Louie H.'s "history of syphilis," while admitting that it had affected neither his mentality nor his riotous behavior.[49]

Nor did he understand the racial and political awareness of blacks, who knew of the independence movement of India, expressed resentment over discrimination in the armed forces and selective service, and experienced tension when Congress defeated bills prohibiting lynching and poll taxes. He recorded as minor and unimportant what another generation of researchers would overstate: violence as protest.[50] Ironically Selling, who called for the upgrading of ghetto conditions, perceived the cultural differences among rioters, and heard their political expressions, failed to recognize his own or the majority's racial and class preconceptions. He challenged the hoodlum thesis and, perhaps inadvertently, laid the basis for the riffraff theory (whereby criminals joined other maladjusted and rejected ghetto dwellers in riot).

Although not as detailed as Selling, all of the inquirers alluded to theories of rioters posited by later scholars. They implied that mostly young people rioted because of their limited socialization, uninhibited personalities, and "animal . . . spirits."[51] Dowling suggested further, as did the subjects of Selling and Akers and Fox, that the rioters were criminals and ruffians, atypical residents repudiated by both races. In addition to identifying riffraff, however, Selling and Akers and Fox described Southern, mainly black newcomers, uncultured outsiders whose rural ways threatened the harmony of Detroit. They sketched what subsequent investigators called the underclass, those poorly educated, underemployed victims of social ills who suffered from inferior intelligence and psychopathic conditions. Dowling and Akers and Fox also observed varying degrees of instability among rioters, whose sociopsychological predispositions resulted in their converging on areas of upheaval.

Only Ramsay, who examined more than the basic statistics of Dowling's report and the convicted felons of Selling and Akers and Fox, presented many employed, married, Northern rioters. In so doing, he provided data that lent itself—as did Selling's matter-of-fact recording of political grievances—to an analysis of black participants as ordinary residents discovering themselves racially and protesting their plights militantly. Moreover, his acts opened the possibility that ghetto conditions socialized black youths toward collective violence.[52] Without postulating any of those theses himself, Ramsay provided information that broke with the other studies and indicated that riffraff, criminals, newcomers, protestors, and others were all viable segments of outburst. Nevertheless he and others failed to realize that several profiles of rioters existed. Ignoring this diversity, they viewed the participants in monolithic terms. They recognized the problems of racism and ghetto conditions, yet, except for Ramsay, blamed black participants for the disorder; they recorded numerous personal shortcomings, everything from irresponsibility to instability. Their conclusions discredited hoodlums and riffraff, while reaffirming the system's legitimacy. Dowling, Selling, and Akers and Fox, then, mirrored and reinforced police actions, official decisions, and public opinion.

Although all of these investigators, including Ramsay, represented the establishment, they possessed additional characteristics that influenced their findings. Dowling (as well as all other members of the Governor's Committee), Selling, and Akers and Fox served law enforcement agencies—the very agencies responsible for capturing, adjudicating, and incarcerating the rioters: natural and unsympathetic adversaries of all offenders. Holding publicly elected, court- and state-appointed positions, they applied their legal training and behavioral disciplines rigidly and conducted their inquiries formally. Professionally, they were used to dealing with hardened criminals, and they responded to the rioters accordingly. No doubt these factors affected their interpretations, as well as the responses that Selling and Akers and Fox evoked from riot-related arrestees—interviewed in isolation by imposing psychiatrists and prison staff members long after the disorder. Conversely, Ramsay supervised a social agency in empathy with the very populations from whose ranks came some of the riot participants. He engaged them as a social worker, probably more informally and sensitively than other officials. He, and his cadre of similarly trained interrogators, spoke with rioters very close to the time of their detention, when emotions ran high, and in crowded holding areas where—despite the scrutiny of lawmen—the presence of their peers tempered fear. In part, then, the backgrounds and positions of each official affected the way he viewed those who rampaged on June 21 and June 22.

While findings of neither Ramsay nor Akers and Fox drew much attention, those of Dowling and Selling stirred emotions, reinforced battle lines, and promoted popular, stereotypical images of rioters. Ramsay's study—which Governor Kelly originally hoped would determine "what kind of folk" rioted and accordingly suggest remedies for better race relations—could not compete with the controversial Dowling report.[53] It attracted the attention of some journalists and officials, and even Dowling inquired about it two weeks after releasing his own conclusions.[54] Nonetheless, once it was published, Kelly backed away from the touchy issue of race and spent much of his time parrying criticism of Dowling and his report. Nor did newsmen, themselves busy choosing sides between Dowling and his critics, pursue Ramsay's results. Even less influential, Akers and Fox published their research in a little read scholarly journal over a year after the disorder and the dispute it generated.

In contrast Dowling's report took center stage and ignited long-standing debate. Its August 11 publication was widespread in Detroit and throughout the state. The *News*, for example, carried front-page headlines and a story on Dowling's findings, printed them in full elsewhere, and endorsed their validity. Describing the report as scientifically thorough, "meticulously detailed," and "authoritative," the editor supported Dowling's every point: "Lawless Negroes" assaulted whites for criminal reasons and as "expressions of resentment against racial discrimination"; their militant leaders and newsmen created an atmosphere for violence, which erupted spontaneously and therefore required no grand jury probe. Anticipating criticism of Dowling for failing to investigate the underlying problems that generated discrimination, the editor noted that the prosecutor's scope was limited to immediate causes.[55]

Jeffries, Kelly, and private citizens also exonerated Dowling. They praised his report and considered it "complete," "factual," and, said the governor, requiring "no further action."[56] Privately, racists applauded Dowling for speaking his convictions, which they deemed segregationist, and threatened further bloodshed should blacks continue to agitate for social equality.[57] Less viscerally, white moderates like William P. Lovett of the Detroit Citizens League admired Dowling's independence and shared his slant on black leaders; and at least one black, perennial gubernatorial correspondent John D. Dixon, blamed racial troubles on them.[58] While debate focused on the question of black protest and leadership, occasional reference—such as that of the *News* editor—reminded everyone that "Negro, not white bullies were typically the aggressors" before and during the outburst.[59]

Most blacks and liberals, as well as several white moderates, however, contested Dowling's findings. Leftists labeled them "biased" and unfair, covering up subversive activity, fabricating black scapegoats, and whitewashing police inefficiency.[60] Dowling's irresponsible statements "might well have come from Martin Dies [the reactionary Congressman from Texas]," said Shelton Tappes of Ford Local 600, or from Nazi propagandist Joseph Goebbels, added Sam Milgram of the International Workers Order.[61] Less sarcastically, liberal *Free Press* writers judged the prosecutor's conclusions "wholly inadequate."[62]

While supporters and critics of Dowling tended to center on his criticism of black leaders and, by inference, black society collectively, the question of black rioters surfaced occasionally. Confidentially, national NAACP Executive Secretary Walter White indicated that blacks were not the aggressors on the night of June 20, while publicly *Tribune* journalists attributed the disproportionately large number of black arrestees to police bias, particularly on Woodward Avenue, where white thugs reigned without check.[63] Given news photos of mob activity on that thoroughfare, asked the Rev. Charles A. Hill of the Citizens Committee, "how could blacks alone be criminals?"[64] They were not, claimed one outstate resident after examining the pictures of several publications. Nelson Williams, Jr., of Northville, Michigan, contended further that neither black nor white youths had caused the upheaval; rather they took "quite a beating, morally and sometimes physically."[65]

Perhaps, but the charges and countercharges provoked by Dowling's summary disclosed more about his own limitations and those of riot commissions generally than about black rioters. Eastside leaders and moderate whites, such as Louis E. Martin and the Rev. T. T. Brumbaugh, pointed to what the report "did not say" regarding the number of black deaths, the violence of police, the presence of slums, and the reality of Jim Crow.[66] Communist Party spokesmen added the Sojourner Truth housing disorder and Packard Company hate strike to their list, while Socialist Judah Drob, among others, resented the blame heaped upon the very victims of discrimination and bloodshed—black Detroiters.[67] "Why do you not say what the major causes are," members of the Metropolitan Youth Council asked the Wayne County prosecutor, "instead of castigating the minor effects?"[68]

Opposing the *News* editor's reply that Dowling's charge prevented an investigation of "underlying social problems," black and white critics offered quite another explanation.[69] In addition to Dowling's preriot judgments, personal and political needs, they sensed other problems. The Governor's Committee lacked a black member, who, argued Walter White, "could supply facts and opinions not otherwise obtainable." It consulted neither the services of any social agency nor the evidence marshaled by NAACP investigators.[70] Instead, the committeemen—all white, mostly under fifty years of age, and bearing law degrees—ignored the basic factors of riot and, said *Tribune* Editor J. Edward McCall, delivered "the kind of report one would expect from a group of peace officers."[71] If they had included a historian or a sociologist, speculated *News* columnist W. K. Kelsey, the tone of their conclusions "might well have been different."[72] Possibly, but dissenters from the National Lawyers Guild and the Civil Rights Federation thought otherwise. Local attorneys observed that two members of the committee—Police Commissioner Witherspoon and State Police Commissioner Olander—headed the very law enforcement agencies under fire for mishandling the disorder. As significantly, fellow committeemen Dowling and State Attorney Rushton were the respective legal counsels of those bureaus. Omitting numerous facts and justifying police activity, the Governor's Committee, accused left-leaning civil rights advocates, defended white rioters and above all, themselves.[73]

It was unsurprising historically that Dowling and his cohorts should have produced "a specialized report" praising bluecoats, castigating blacks, and opposing grand juries.[74] Short on time, limited in scope, and comprised of self-interested elites, who shared concepts of law and order and disdained black protest, they absolved all public servants of responsibility for the outburst or misconduct during it. Under these circumstances they could come to no other conclusions and, as predictably, evinced the prejudices of wartime policy makers.[75] As if to chastise black Detroiters and their white supporters, Dowling released the committee's report as the national convention of police chiefs opened in Detroit.[76]

Thereafter, the Dowling study held center stage. It attracted widespread newspaper and periodical coverage, both locally and nationally, thereby sparking interest among readers of the Detroit *Times, New Republic,* and dozens of similar publications.[77] Long after journalistic attention subsided, copies of the *Factual Report* were sought by numerous individuals and organizations. Over forty days after its release, 17,000 impressions of Dowling's investigation were reproduced by government officials to fill unceasing requests.[78] Addresses by Dowling and controversy involving him and several others, for instance *Harper's Magazine* writer Earl Brown, kept the prosecutor's conclusions alive into the new year.[79] Campaigning for reelection six months later before the Kiwanis Club, Dowling reiterated his view of the riot. He blamed "negro boys" and "dishonorable elements" within black society, and called for the protection of white rights.[80] His resurrection of material from the questionable, year-old report and blatant appeal to segregationists initiated open warfare with black leaders, who considered him more dangerous than ever and worked successfully for his defeat.[81]

While Dowling's report attracted attention and its author moved directly into the circle of white supremacists, that of Selling became available in November of 1943.[82] Surprisingly, Selling's conclusions were well received by black leaders. "At long last," exclaimed McCall, "a scientific and authoritative report" for which east siders were thankful! Specifically, the editor, his *Chronicle* counterpart, and numerous black Detroiters appreciated its "spirit of fairness and earnest endeavor to probe to the root" of violence. They were especially impressed because Selling's report benefited from the input of community spokespersons, including the Reverend Mr. White and Dr. James J. McClendon, president of the local NAACP, and avoided holding only blacks responsible for the disturbance. It stressed abject conditions in Paradise Valley and "anti-Negro prejudice" citywide, while rejecting Dowling's "well worn" hoodlum theory. It suggested several constructive recommendations, including the creation of a municipal department to investigate charges of discrimination and reduce violence-producing tensions.[83] Selling's study, surmised *Tribune* columnist Fred Hart Williams, might have said more about the role of city officials during the upheaval, but given the doctor's municipal position, it represented a "good job" by a reputable professional.[84]

Moderate and liberal white officials echoed these praises. When Arthur E. Gordon, the Recorder's Court presiding judge, presented Jeffries with "A Study of One Hundred Offenders," he considered it "valuable as a scientific observer's factual, objective, and cool analysis of underlying factors not readily discernible by an uninformed public." Hopefully, the mayor and his Interracial Committee would find it of some service.[85] Common councilman

George C. Edwards advised further that his colleagues create the recommended bureau on race relations.[86] While neither Jeffries nor council members reacted quickly to Selling's study or Edward's advocacy of it, black leaders soon expressed hope that the mayoral committee created shortly after the riot would incorporate many of the court psychologist's recommendations.[87]

Selling's findings countered Dowling's conclusions in several important areas, and they did so "scientifically," and that was enough for blacks to trumpet the late arriving study. In their enthusiasm for Selling's report, however, they overlooked its biases. Obviously sniping at Dowling's prejudgments, for example, McCall claimed erroneously that Selling did not build "his conclusions on preconceived personal theories of race relations."[88] In truth, as early as June 25, when Selling announced plans to examine 1,000 rioters, he knew what he would find: inferior intelligence, parents, and homes. "He has found it before in boys from the areas affected," observed one savvy white newsman.[89] Even McCall acknowledged Selling's initial statement, which speculated that ignorance and "substandard mental equipment" underlay the behavior of participants.[90] Nor did black journalists such as Martin question Selling's cultural arrogance and near stereotypical portrait of Southern newcomers, stranded, bewildered, without employment, and carrying knives for protection and as a means of obtaining rights. Until socioeconomic conditions improved in Paradise Valley, it must be considered, according to the Recorder's Court official, "a pilot light which will set fire to any psychologically inflammable mixture."[91]

Besides calling for slum clearance and interracial education, which reinforced perennial crusades of McCall and particularly Martin, Selling also suggested curbing in-migration, which sounded like a plan originally attributed to the United States Attorney General and widely criticized by black leaders as unconstitutional. Martin, for one, labeled Francis Biddle's scheme "incredible," one designed to "enslave segments of the Negro people" and let "Klan-minded whites . . . go their merry way." He recommended that Biddle be rushed to "a mental hospital," if he truly believed that curbing black migration would stem race friction in war centers like Detroit.[92] Yet neither Martin nor McCall (who did not criticize the Attorney General publicly) questioned Selling's challenge to black movement. Themselves concerned over black jitterbugs and Southern migrants, both for reasons of community peace and class bias, they envisioned Selling's report a major retort to Dowling's racist polemic and, as such, embraced it without reservation.

In reality, neither white officials nor white citizens appeared to pay much attention to any study save that of the Governor's Committee. Only it had official sanction, sparked major controversy, and received extensive coverage long after soldiers had quelled the disturbance. Dowling's report probably reinforced the racial beliefs that blacks and whites brought to the point of riot and the mental images they carried away from it: Racists, fretful whites, and exasperated officials agreed with the prosecutor's analysis of aggressive black hoodlums and pushy black leaders; black citizens, newsmen, and spokespersons, as well as their white allies, challenged that interpretation, and observed white prejudice and violence in the face of righteous protest for democratic wartime aims. Most likely citizens of both races—but especially whites—were more impressed with their own or journalistic accounts of the sights and sounds of disorder, with the initial evaluations of responsibility as posited by Dowling and Selling rather than either Ramsay's contradictory findings or Selling's postriot questioning of hooliganism. Their first impressions of bloodletters endured as stereotypes, bolstered by official utterances and research on criminals, newcomers, and riffraff. In the midst of outburst and war, the majority of white Detroiters and their governmental representatives believed experimentation in race relations impractical, embraced racist propaganda against foreign enemies, and relied on force to cow "unruly and criminal elements."[93] That imagery, which surfaced as the riot unfolded, became the prevailing, one-dimensional description of riot participants. Many blacks, including those who contested Dowling's explication of the outbreak, and most whites failed to recognize the faces in the crowd for what they were or answer accurately the query: What manner of men, women, and children rioted?

THREE

Faces in the Crowd

Of course, more than black hooligans and Southern newcomers participated in the Detroit riot of 1943. Despite contemporary studies and public opinion, hoodlums and migrants shared the streets with lawful, longtime Detroiters.[1] Rioters, in fact, included multitudes of ordinary men and women of both races. Their experiences, as well as those of teenagers, identify more completely those arrested for having been in the crowd.

These participants revealed the common and diverse traits of those who rioted. Like their ruffian cohorts described shortly after the disorder, they were mostly black, young, male, employed, well paid, and without previous arrests; like them also, most of those with probation records were without children, came from the South, and had spent five years or more in the city. In contrast, others were white, female, married, and better educated.[2]

Even greater distinctions occurred along racial and gender lines. Black males were the oldest participants, followed by black females and white males. Accordingly, more black men were married than their counterparts; black women tended to be single because of separation from their spouses through estrangement, divorce, or death, while white men remained bachelors largely because of their youthful ages. Economically, too, racial differences unfolded, as black rioters (regardless of their gender) worked at unskilled jobs, whereas among white insurgents, although many also held unskilled jobs, there were many more in semiskilled and skilled occupations. And, in comparison to blacks who destroyed their own neighborhoods, whites traveled far from home to riot.

Beyond these characteristics, which reinforce C. F. Ramsay's portrayal of blacks as stable members of society and challenge those who disregarded footloose white aggressors, the age of participants revealed even more telling behavior patterns. Younger, single rioters of both races committed misdemeanors—largely offenses of misconduct—from midnight to sunrise, while their older, married counterparts engaged in felonies—more serious crimes of violence, weapons, and theft—between noon and the dead of night. Youthful rioters dominated the action on and around Belle Isle, as well as along Woodward Avenue, in comparison to older activists who wreaked havoc all along east-side thoroughfares.[3]

Race and gender disclosed additional features of rioters and patterns of outburst. Blacks committed more felonies than whites, and did so within the ghetto. Men went armed, especially between noon and midnight, which represented both manly behavior and in many cases protection for oneself. Women looted stores during the same time frame, manifesting assertive behavior, but a form culturally accepted for females. Their offenses and places of arrest are similar to those encountered in 1960s riots, when blacks lashed out at white police and white-owned stores. Conversely, roaming white misdemeanants "disturbed the peace"—more accurately, fought with blacks—on Belle Isle or along Paradise Valley borders, a characteristic form of white aggression and black response in earlier communal disorders. Their efforts to penetrate the black community, usually between suppertime and sunrise, often carrying guns, exposed perennial, bloodthirsty motives.[4]

Individually, black male, white male, and black female rioters exhibited even more exact attributes. The largest percentage of black men, slightly more than a quarter, fell between the ages of twenty-eight and thirty-seven, and the median age for all black male participants stood at twenty-seven years. Nearly 63 percent were married, and nearly 75 percent lived in Paradise Valley. Most were literate and employed, and over 85 percent had benefited from the war boom and worked as laborers; 9 percent of the black rioters worked as skilled and semiskilled operatives, suggesting even higher and more stable social standing. Significant also for understanding the spontaneous actions of normally upright residents, most black transgressors were arrested alone and for the first time in their lives. They rioted in their home precincts and within a half mile of their east side addresses.[5]

Information from probation records indicated further social stability for black males. Overwhelmingly born and bred in Alabama, Georgia, and Mississippi, fully half of them had resided in Detroit for nine years or more—the median stay, just short of a decade. Most were married, nearly 40 percent were raising children, and over 50 percent had secured meaningful jobs within the past year; they represented working-class people hopeful of bright futures. Indeed, having endured the Great Depression and blatant racism, they must have sensed the potential for personal and racial advancement: Weekly wages of fifty dollars, median educations of eight years, and several successful protests over housing and employment had surely raised their expectations.[6]

Lester R., twenty-seven years old, married, and father of five children, walked inside a grocery store on Westminster Avenue within a quarter mile of his residence on Delmar at 5:45 P.M. on June 21 and was arrested. Originally from Lexington, Mississippi, he had lived in Detroit for the past three years and presently labored at the Detroit Aluminum and Brass Company. He earned $56 per week despite a sixth-grade education, indicating that war had brought flush times. Possibly because the premises Lester R. entered had already been broken into and he held no stolen produce when arrested, he was placed on probation.[7] Nearly five hours later, in the heart of Paradise Valley, Roy M. also committed a felony. He violated the curfew and carried a concealed weapon. A resident of Detroit for twenty-one years, he had been brought from Virginia at age three and had completed an eighth-grade education. He lived on St. Antoine with his wife and three children, and welded at Chrysler Motor Company for $58 weekly. When apprehended, he stood within a half mile of his apartment and claimed to be returning home after visiting friends. He was found guilty by officials, who considered his knife,—⅝ inch longer than the lawful blade length of 3 inches—as dangerous as the prohibited switchblade. Perhaps he foolishly ignored the curfew and carried cutlery for reasons of work, protection, or custom. In any case, he chose court costs, fines, and two years probation over imprisonment.[8] Neither Lester R. nor Roy M. had ever been arrested before, and both had responsible records (though Roy M.'s probation was extended because he failed to pay all the fees). Acting as individuals rather than in groups set them apart from white rioters and indicated both the defensive and spontaneous nature of much black behavior as the disturbance moved from island to ghetto, and entered the second stage of violence.

While some black laborers and skilled workers undoubtedly knew (as did those interviewed by Selling) the struggles for racial equality nationally and, in the case of India, globally, others were less politically aware. Nearly 40 percent of all black male wrongdoers had faced arrest earlier, and 22 percent had had confrontations with the police two or more times before the outburst. Their recidivism suggested one reason for the deep-seated antagonism that innumerable black participants harbored against bluecoats, and in some instances, it bore out the hoodlum thesis.[9] Over 55 percent of all black male offenses were felonies, with carrying concealed weapons, mostly knives, the most common charge, which fed Selling's theory of Southern cultural deprivation. Nearly 35 percent of the black men were apprehended a mile or more from their homes, providing evidence that some rioters were scarcely pure of heart.[10] As described elsewhere, some recidivists, weapon carriers, and sightseers were victims of circumstance, but others actively went seeking mischief, bloodshed, or adventure.

More often than not repeat offenders were married, employed laborers, Detroit residents, and captured on the first day of riot. Like other participants, however, they shared neither backgrounds nor motivation. James M., thirty years old, without children, and outside the law much of his life, was arrested for the eleventh time when he was caught looting a grocery store on Beaubien Street, while John W., twenty-four years old, unattached, and making $80 weekly, committed his fourth offense: Seeing someone else steal spirits, he lifted several quarts of whiskey from a broken-into market on Hastings Street. Clearly, both James M. and John W. seized the riot as opportunity for self-aggrandizement, but John W.— easily capable of purchasing the $12 worth of liquor that he stole—acted more spontaneously.[11] In contrast, John M., thirty-two years old, father of six children and arrested on three previous occasions, hurled rocks at automobiles passing the corner of St. Antoine and Forest Avenue, no doubt in response to rumors surrounding the Belle Isle fracas. He was apprehended by patrolmen, found to be packing a straight razor, and charged with carrying a concealed weapon. He carried the razor for "a little protection," he said. Still none of these recidivists were Southern newcomers: together they had lived in Detroit for a total of forty years, and John M., his arrest charge notwithstanding, seemed more protestor than rogue. He maintained a "good" probation record, and was inducted into the armed forces five months after the riot.[12]

In sum, usually law-abiding and hard-working men stood side-by-side with lawbreakers. No doubt many of both kinds were politically astute and racially proud. Black laborers and skilled workers, particularly those married, with children and education levels approaching that of whites, knew of—might even have participated in—recent DSR incidents, housing controversies, or hate strikes that sharpened racial animus. Very likely their riot activity arose from the accumulation of blocked socioeconomic opportunities, whch they attributed to white racists. They deemed the Belle Isle rampage and accompanying rumors as final provocation in a series of real and occasionally perceived wrongs. Fearful for their newfound prosperity and status, they struck as much to protect their stake in society as to destroy their enemy, as much out of pride as anger. Black repeat offenders probably clashed with lawmen on familiar ground over perennial grudges. Slightly over 25 percent of all black male participants, however, exhibited calculated or mindless theft as they looted east-side stores, expressly

those on Hastings Street. And a minute number of arrestees attacked white citizens or patrolmen, perhaps displaying a bloodlust
that predated wartime frustrations.[13] In essence, no single profile
or motivation moved black males to action. Protestors and lawbreakers alike took part in several different kinds of riot for equally
diverse reasons.

Ironically, black male rioters sometimes shared characteristics
that affected them dissimilarly. Despite popular and official perceptions that newcomers—those entering the metropolitan area
after 1941 in search of defense employment—swelled the ranks of
mobsters, only 21 percent of the felons had arrived in the city
within the previous twenty-three months. Possibly cultural alienation and social anomie triggered their outburst. For the greater
majority of felons, who had lived as Detroiters for six or more
years, their urbanization most likely promoted stress of another
kind: Long-standing east siders apparently fought for opportunities for advancement, while the younger less-established among
them might have drawn blood because of daily exposure to ghetto
conditions. In other words, recent in-migrants lashed out at the
abnormality of their position, and more rooted residents (depending on age and status) reacted against commonplace racism and
socialization in a Northern, industrial municipality.[14]

Of the black male newcomers, 93 percent hailed from the South
(in somewhat equal proportions from its black belt and upper region). As a rule, they were married laborers in their twenties, educated through the eighth grade, employed in defense work and
had clean records; they usually carried weapons and were apprehended sometime during the first day of riot both within and
well beyond three-fourths mile of their homes.[15] Among them,
Tom M. entered the city with his wife and three children in June
of 1942 and almost immediately found work with Ford Motor
Company and housing in the black west side. He earned $52
weekly, surely more money than could be made by a thirty-two-
year-old black man in Fort Mill, South Carolina, where he came
from. He was one of five passengers in a Ford, heading toward the
Woodward Avenue battle zone shortly before noon on the second
day of bloodshed. The driver, Manley D., attracted police atten-

tion by cutting in front of traffic on West Warren, and M. soon found himself arrested for carrying concealed weapons. He himself carried nothing, but the vehicle contained an illegally large knife, a hunting knife, an iron bar, and three empty soda pop bottles. He and most of his cohorts received one year probation.[16]

In spite of Tom M.'s Southern origins, third-grade education, and weapons conviction, he scarcely portrayed the roughneck stereotype of recent in-migrants embraced by longtime Detroiters of both races. But his presence in the city—and that of others like him—aroused the fears of established blacks, those who had had "a stake in Detroit" before 1935, and who criticized young and Southern blacks for "arousing white antagonism."[17] But Tom M.'s steady job, his residence in the middle-class community, and his release from probation with improvement challenged simple labels and displayed class distinctions among blacks.

Skilled and white collar participants, although not targeted as culprits like Southern laborers, surprisingly shared most of their characteristics. They, too, were married, without police records, and arrested for committing felonies within a half mile of their eastside residences. Clifton T., a twenty-six-year-old presser, wore a suit coat and lugged a "bundle of clothes" from Yockey's Pawn Shop, apparently a selfish act of revolt against the white presence in, and economic dominance of, Paradise Valley.[18] Perhaps equally vindictive and certainly more fearful of whites, twenty-four-year-old William B. carried a gas-ejecting pistol and ice pick on his way home from Lee's Loan Office. He had clerked there intermittently since 1935, while also finishing high school and taking a year of college. A resident of Detroit for eighteen years and separated from his wife and child, he had faced ghetto pressures daily without giving up the struggle for respectability, and had never before reacted to them by breaking the law.[19] Both of these men, though officially counted as rioters, challenged the simplistic rioter stereotypes.

Less concerned about his own safety, seventeen-year-old Frank N. served as one of Charlie L.'s marauders on Belle Isle. He journeyed to the recreation park with twin brother Fred for "sport's sake," congregated with other east-side youths, and munched hot dogs before accosting several white picnickers. City-born and bred, educated through the ninth grade, and employed at Briggs Manufacturing Company, he lived at home with his devoted, hard-working, sometime alcoholic stepfather and equally nervous, shy natural mother. He admired his stepfather, a good provider, but was most attached to his mother. Intellectually below average, physically small, and racially troubled, he felt inferior and behaved immaturely. For these reasons, he followed his brother's lead and, although normally unaggressive at 5 feet 1½ inches and 125 pounds, assailed Gus Niarhos and others. The honorable efforts of his parents notwithstanding, he proved susceptible to racial animosities and resentful peers, as well as his own limitations: all products of a hard-edged, inequitable social structure.[20]

Unsurprisingly, white male rioters were as diverse as their black counterparts. Nearly 65 percent of all white men were younger than twenty-three years old. Their ages extended from seventeen to fifty-four, the median age at twenty years—less extreme than the black range of fourteen to sixty-four and significantly younger than the black midpoint of twenty-seven. Consequently, over 70 percent of the white arrestees were single and over 55 percent worked as laborers, with 4 percent as clericals, 5 percent as semi-skilled, 23 percent as skilled operatives, and the rest service employees or domestics. And, regardless of marital status or occupation, slightly more than 50 percent of all white participants lived relatively close to Belle Isle or on the fringes of Paradise Valley, and 40 percent more traveled over two miles to riot along its boundaries. Fully three quarters of all white offenders left their home precincts, determined to secure the perimeters of Detroit's color line against integrated housing and black upward mobility. Young adults, ordinarily law-abiding, mobilized to avenge past affronts aboard public conveyances, in municipal parks, and at downtown theaters, stores, and eateries.[21]

Probation data reveals that almost all white arrestees were individuals with roots, on the make, and yet insecure. Most—53 percent—identified their home state as Michigan, and only one named the South as his origin; obviously far fewer white Southerners participated in the upheaval than was believed by officials, black leaders, and residents. Surprisingly, white in-migrants,

Southern born or otherwise, stayed pretty clear of the disturbance. Neither Bedford B. nor Leonard O., placed on probation for carrying concealed weapons, qualified as "hillbillies"—those allegedly clannish, dirty, ignorant newcomers from Dixie.[22] One came from a border state, the other from Michigan. Neither possessed police records, and both worked as machinists. They lived with their families, respectively, east of Cass in a neighborhood of white transients and north of Grand Boulevard in a mixed area rapidly becoming an extension of the black ghetto. Separated by nearly twenty years of life (forty-two versus twenty-three) and eight years of education (third grade versus eleventh), they shared little save their whiteness, offenses, and convictions. Both carried weapons, one a butcher knife, the other a nickel-plated revolver, and received sentences of short probation. Occasional drinking problems aside, both met the terms of probation. Having reported regularly, worked steadily, and provided a "suitable home," they were discharged with improvement.[23] Their experiences belied the dominance of Southern or other groups of newcomers among white participants.

Despite Selling or Akers and Fox Southern cultural deprivation theories, over 80 percent of the white felons had resided in the city more than six years. In fact, 50 percent had lived as Detroiters for over seventeen years. Except for being significantly more single than black felons, they registered similar education levels, time of employment, and wages. They competed with blacks for jobs and status, which personalized and sharpened the racial rivalry. Most probably, they recalled the hardships of depression and, facing black competition on every front, feared slipping backward.[24]

Walter J., for instance, traveled over three miles from his home on upper Helen Street to riot across from Belle Isle Bridge at 5:40 A.M. on June 21. He entered the intersection at Jefferson Avenue and Field Street in an Oldsmobile carrying five companions, two knives, and a wrench—one of four vehicles loaded down with from six to "eight and nine fellows in a car." He and others told incredulous lawmen that "they were out taking a ride." Clearly Walter J. and his friends were looking for black targets. J. was nineteen years old, single, schooled through the ninth grade, employed as a laborer, and had spent his entire life in Detroit. He possessed no previous record and was judged innocent of carrying concealed weapons. Thus, he hardly fitted the hoodlum thesis.[25]

White offenders like Walter J. represented various class, ethnic, and religious communities. Fully 10 percent remained unemployed in spite of the war boom, yet fought alongside laborers, semiskilled, and skilled workers, who resented competition from black workers and particularly their upgrading. Eighteen percent of them were Italian Americans and 13 percent Polish Americans, who perennially contested east siders for living space and factory jobs.[26] It was hardly coincidental that rioting Poles followed the footsteps of countrymen, possibly even relatives, who had challenged blacks—Dr. Ossian Sweet in 1925 and defense workers of the Sojourner Truth Homes in 1942—for invading their turf. Remembering these encroachments, some Poles lay siege to the black ghetto. No doubt because of this ethnic dimension, 70 percent of the felons professed Roman Catholicism. Substantial numbers of Protestants joined in the melee as well, though apparently not Jewish Detroiters, who experienced both citywide prejudice of their own and black antagonism over the Jewish-owned shops, particularly in Paradise Valley. Instead of assailing blacks in the riot, Jewish entrepreneurs became the victims of their wrath.[27]

White participants, then, aligned themselves with fellow whites and acted more uniformly and for more similar purpose than did black rioters. Their class, ethnic, and religious differences collapsed in the face of broad-based white supremacy, which momentarily tempered rivalry among themselves.[28] First and second generation immigrants closed ranks with native-born whites to protect their self-interest.[29] Like their white confederates, Italians and Poles fought blacks to secure positions in Detroit's socioeconomic order, but unlike their forebears, they battled less for ethnic integrity and more for white dominance.[30] Hence, white participants of whatever status, nationality, or faith, first and foremost defined themselves racially.

Walter J. and his band indicated how easily white solidarity could overcome ethnic distinctions. The son of Polish immigrants, he traveled with one fellow Pole, two French Canadian and two Ameri-

can youths. He and one of the French teenagers were first generation citizens, yet they associated well with their longer-established
passengers. Moreover, Walter J. lived in Precinct 7, farther from
the riot scene than any of his fellow companions and a mile from
the closest of those in the same police district. Neither he nor those
in Precinct 5 lived within walking distance of one another, which
revealed further the breakdown of neighborhood barriers in the
face of racial conflict. Only two of the six teenagers—Joseph L.
and Arthur O.—resided near the Belle Isle Bridge. Hence Walter
J. came three miles, while Richard T., Paul S., and Clarence J. journeyed two miles or more to riot. Where and how they first met remains unknown, though a common meeting place that bordered
the 5th and 7th precincts, like East Catholic High, might have
served as the nexus.[31] Speculation aside, they acted in unison, uninhibited by their diverse heritages and drawn together by their
race. Indeed, only numbers and age separated ethnics: White
Anglo-Saxons comprised forty-seven arrestees and were younger
than their seventeen Italian and twenty other counterparts from
various backgrounds, but older than twelve Polish youths.[32] However, this particular example showed little age distinction, for Walter J. and his joy riders were all between seventeen and nineteen
years old.

Similar racial unity influenced defense workers of both races.
There was no actual violence within defense plants themselves,
where union leaders controlled shop floors, and the two races
worked side-by-side, but forty-six blacks and five whites engaged
in war production did riot in the streets.[33] Like most black defense
workers arrested during the upheaval, Henry G. was a married laborer (Ford Motor Company, $65 a week), who resided in the city
and possessed no record before he was picked up by police around
suppertime on June 21. He was caught reaching inside a pressing
and cleaning business on Westminster Street, to snatch one coat
and three dresses worth $3.00. That evening he had walked to
meet his wife and, en route, stopped—he claimed—to salvage his
own clothes from the already ransacked store. Perhaps, but he had
no ticket for the merchandise or verification by the proprietor of
his being a customer, and more likely Henry G. saw his chance to

get free clothing for his spouse and four children and took it. He had an eighth-grade education and must have known he was breaking the law, but he was hardly a hoodlum, and had apparently been moved by special circumstances if not conscious protest. He received three year's probation for petty theft and stayed out of trouble thereafter.[34]

So, too, did Leonard O., released after one year probation for carrying a concealed handgun at Woodward Avenue and Vernor Highway early on the morning of June 22. White, married, the father of one child, he had come from Vulcan, Michigan, nine months earlier and, for most of that time, worked for the Ford Motor Company as a machinist. He possessed an eleventh grade education and, at age twenty-three, was somewhat older and better schooled than most white rioters. He never said why he packed the firearm. Acting alone at 7:50 A.M. and within three-quarters of a mile of his home on Brainard Street, he might have been prowling in search of black targets. Or perhaps he carried the weapon for protection. He received the benefit of a doubt from the court and, even after being arrested later for drunkenness, was discharged from probation with improvement. Described as "steadily employed" and maintaining "a suitable home for wife and child," he—like Henry G.—fit none of the stereotypes of rioters as hooligans or Southerners.[35] But both of them, as well as arrested coworkers, represented attitudes of other defense workers who participated in the disorder without getting caught. Most war workers, black and white, either remained at home for security or—as exemplified by Henry G. and Leonard O.—vented their racial feelings against strangers in public areas. Neither urban thugs nor country bumpkins, these rioters acted aggressively at a time and place that promoted racial solidarity and permitted violence, even bloodshed.[36]

Servicemen also closed ranks along racial lines. Over fifty white sailors, stationed at the Naval Armory on East Jefferson Avenue, played a major role in the disturbance on Belle Isle Bridge, though their military status spared them civil punishment (and presumably court-martial).[37] Despite their large numbers and an occasional soldier spotted among the Woodward Avenue crowds, few members of the armed forces were arrested.[38] Donald S., a seven-teen-year-old white sailor in the Merchant Marine, openly carried pieces of concrete on Woodward Avenue just north of Vernor Highway. When he was stopped six or seven blocks from his home at 52 East Willis Street, a concealed blackjack was also found on him. He claimed to be heading for his mother's place of employment to escort her home, and carried the weapons for protection. One of his four companions packed a tear gas bomb, and in consideration of this and their presence in a major riot zone at 6:10 P.M. on June 21, the group seemed anything but innocent. Donald S., a Detroit resident of nine years, was found guilty of carrying concealed weapons despite his alibi and clean record. Because of his maritime affiliation, however, his case was set aside, and he was turned over to his superiors.[39]

Robert B.'s experiences were similar. Black, older, married, somewhat less educated, and much more regularly employed than his white counterpart, B. was a native of Alabama but had been a Detroiter since 1927 and a Chrysler Corporation worker for fourteen years. Now in the Navy, he was on a seven-day furlough when arrested at 7:00 A.M. on the first day of riot. Caught by police among 400 east siders who had broken into stores between Theodore and Farnsworth streets, Robert B. heaped vituperation on his captors. "You rotten son of a bitch!" When he was searched, police found a knife and charged him with carrying a concealed weapon. But he had not brandished the blade, which barely exceeded legal standards anyway, and possessed no previous arrests, so he was given two years probation. Shortly thereafter he returned to active duty—exactly where he had been headed the morning of his arrest—his sentence having been set aside.[40]

Swept up in the disorder as active participants, and doubtless bearing deep-seated racial antagonisms, Donald S. and Robert B. exemplified the experiences of other white and black servicemen, who wore civilian clothes yet escaped capture or were barred from the riot area by Military Police, such as the Fort Custer black troops who unsuccessfully endeavored to seize rifles and a truck in order to assist their families forty miles away.[41] Many black servicemen seemed to be seeking revenge for the much publicized mistreatment of their brethren by white military personnel, police, and civilians in Southern basic-training camps.[42] In short, if circumstances had permitted, many more servicemen would have followed the lead of Belle Isle sailors, Donald S., and Robert B., and tested their combat training on civilians of the opposite race.

Members of both races slated for military induction also participated in the upheaval and, for blacks, in slightly larger percentages. Although arrested for carrying concealed weapons, Detroit native Marquis A. and Southern newcomer James A. represented somewhat different black experiences. Nineteen-year-old Marquis A. was found to have a sheathed hunting knife underneath his shirt when stopped within two blocks of his home at 450 Hendrie Street on the second day of disturbance. A single, eleventh-grade student who attended school in the morning and worked as an Aeronautical Corporation machine operator in the afternoon, he said he had taken the weapon from "a little boy"—ironically to prevent the waif from being arrested. Given his close-to-home location, holstered blade, and unblemished past, Marquis A. was acquitted and shortly inducted into the Army.[43] His story might well have been true, but that of James A. appeared more dubious. He and seven other ghetto youths had piled into a Ford sedan at 2:30 A.M. on June 21 and driven over three miles toward Belle Isle, when police stopped them at Beaufait Street and Jefferson Avenue. Armed with two straight razors, which A. admitted owning, and two knives, they headed for the recreation area "to see what was going on." Clearly they had responded to the rumor of riot and black deaths that circulated in the east side, with little thought that James A. was due to report for military duty in three days. A.'s Georgia background, twelve months in Detroit, and fifth-grade schooling notwithstanding, he hardly seemed criminal. He was single, nearly thirty years old, and steadily employed as a stock handler at Ford-Lincoln, and he had never before run afoul of the law. As for the razors, Marquis A. appeared no different from longtime Detroit workers who also habitually carried blades.[44]

Black and white military personnel, then, entered the disorder in tiny percentages, but in different capacities. Whites were more likely to be trained combatants.[45] Seamen rather than soldiers, they

occupied stations close to Belle Isle and reacted to recent altercations. In contrast, black servicemen were mostly Army draftees—
possibly smarting over their induction into segregated units or perhaps indulging themselves in one final exciting spree. Moreover,
Belle Isle sailors and Fort Custer troops aside, among whites, prospective inductees and men already in uniform appeared in equal
proportions, while black prospective draftees accounted for a somewhat higher percentage than black servicemen—probably a reflec-
tion of their residential patterns. Most significantly, black or white,
servicemen or inductees, the rioters fit no single profile and acted
for several reasons.

All white male rioters, including military members, saw themselves as defenders of the faith, but the actual motives of some
seemed to be vengeful retribution. Numerous combatants trekked
more than two miles, attacked in militialike units, and carried guns
or knives into battle. Nearly 30 percent of the white participants
were arrested on Woodward Avenue, where some of them made
repeated efforts to invade the black ghetto.[46] If blacks and whites
had been within reach of one another rather than separated by
community boundaries and police lines there would have been
carnage.

In addition to their violence and motives, significant differences
separated black and white male rioters. More blacks were older,
married, employed, Southern, and Protestant, while more whites
were younger, single, unemployed, Michigan-born, and Catholic.
Whites tended to be slightly more educated and longer residents
of Detroit, possessing fewer previous arrest records. They also
differed from blacks in riot behavior. Where blacks more often
committed felonies, particularly looting, whites engaged in misdemeanors and, when felons, carried weapons. More blacks were arrested between noon and midnight on Hastings Street and within
a quarter mile of their residents, while more whites were apprehended from 6:00 P.M. to 6:00 A.M., along Woodward Avenue,
and more than two miles from their homes. Black arrests occurred
in the 1st, 3rd, 9th, and 13th police precincts. Essentially, blacks
rioted early and largely inside the ghetto or along its edges, con-
testing whites who recorded more activity later around Paradise

Valley's eastern, southern, and western boundaries. Once youths of both races and white sailors had triggered the outburst on Belle Isle Bridge late Sunday evening and very early Monday morning, blacks took the initiative in the east side. Then whites countered, demonstrably so after 6:00 P.M. on June 21.[47]

Personal characteristics and riot activity also distinguished black female rioters from males of both races. (No data exist for white women, whose participation in the disturbances was completely ignored for the first two days out of the prejudice or chivalry of outnumbered, overtaxed lawmen.) Ranging from seventeen to forty-five years of age, black women tallied a median age of twenty-four and one-half years. Over 65 percent were single, yet almost half of those had been separated, divorced, or widowed. Regardless of marital status, 69 percent of all black females worked outside the home: 43 percent as domestics, cooks, or similar service workers, and 19 percent as common laborers. Their ages, marital statuses, employment rates, occupational categories, and police records identified most of them as predominantly older, mature, working-class, and law-abiding.[48]

Black females rioted in the east side, more often than not within a half mile of their homes, along Hastings Street, and inside the 13th Precinct. During the initial outburst of violence they were less active but between dawn and midnight, on June 21 they turned out. They proved to be much less responsible than black and white males for detonating Detroit's explosion, but they moved quickly to the streets once it began.[49]

Regardless of time, black women committed more felonies (over 57 percent) than misdemeanors. Most of their felonious offenses involved looting, in part indicating the economically and socially marginal position of many ghetto females. Surprisingly in the wartime boom, nearly 30 percent held no jobs, slightly less than 20 percent claimed no occupations, and slightly more than 20 percent possessed previous arrest records. Perhaps they stole in order to provide for themselves and their dependents. Conversely, those working and apprehended for the first time in their lives (slightly more than half of all female offenders) probably stole for other reasons, however self-serving and political. Some entered already smashed stores out of curiosity and, once inside, gathered much-wanted goods, while others may have acted out of resentment possibly expressing righteous contempt for both white society and male dominance. One out of three female looters entered dry goods and shoe shops rather than grocery stores, 43 percent stole clothing and footwear instead of food, all thieves took merchandise worth modest sums (the median value being $15.80)—all of which symbolized elements of status. At some level their theft of mostly white-owned property surely demonstrated racial animosity. And their attacks on black-owned businesses, though few in number, disclosed class conflict among ghetto dwellers. Swept up in an atmosphere of racial defiance and tempted by what had suddenly become open-air markets in a rationed economy, black women looted for reasons of personal need, race, gender, and class. Some of them, like some male counterparts, rationalized their activity as "the socially accepted thing to do."[50]

Goldie W. attempted to steal $20 worth of shoes from Chover Brothers in midafternoon on June 21. A thirty-nine-year-old widow and mother of two married children, she lived marginally with her sister's large family. She traveled around the block from her residence on Holbrook Street to enter the already wrecked store on Oakland Avenue and was standing there with a neighbor, nineteen-year-old Frances D., a single domestic, when patrolmen arrived too late to apprehend a couple of fleet-footed youngsters. Goldie W. received two years probation, while her companion, who was holding nothing when caught, went free. A native of Henderson, Kentucky, Goldie had arrived in Detroit three years earlier with "very low mentality" and a fourth grade education; she had acted inquisitively and probably out of reaction to economic opportunity. Possibly, too, she harbored resentment for not having received government insurance for the accidental death of her husband, a disabled veteran. Other women arrestees, however, like Frances D., showed no signs of supposed Southern backwardness or limited intelligence. They defied Selling's profile, and their clean records scarcely fit the Governor's Committee emphasis on hoodlums.[51]

Indeed, Goldie W.'s life revolved around family. She had married Henry W. in 1917 at the age of thirteen, and lived with him until his death twenty-three years later. She was close to her children, receiving $10 weekly support from her son and, while on probation, visiting Cincinnati several times to see her daughter and grandchildren. After her arrest, Goldie W. established a common-law relationship with an employed man, stayed in close contact with social workers, and remained clear of criminal activity. Small wonder authorities discharged her from probation and suspended her case favorably.

Several other female rioters were married and, in at least two instances, arrested committing crimes in company with their husbands. Mary P. passed $25 worth of whiskey from inside the Columbia Bar to her spouse, Osgood P., who hauled it from 2201 Brush Street to their apartment in the adjacent block. She and her husband looted for personal gain, having made several trips between the beer garden and home before patrolmen caught them in the act at 9:30 P.M. on June 21. Despite two previous arrests and, in Osgood P.'s case, one prison term, neither wife nor husband seemed hardened criminals.[52]

Born in Greensboro, Pennsylvania, in 1906, one of many children, Mary P. had lived a tough life. She was twelve years old when her father, coal miner Henry J., died. After completing the sixth grade one year later, she found domestic work in Youngstown, Ohio. In 1924, her mother, Myrtle J., died, and the following year she entered Detroit with common-law husband William W. and gave birth to a daughter. For the next two decades, Mary P. struggled through economic hardship as a maid and, in really difficult times, a prostitute. Arrested in 1928 and 1931, she "did quite well on probation" and did not appear in court again until the riot. Meanwhile, she experienced lengthy and stable marriages. In fact, she lived with William W. for ten years and Melvin W. for five years, until his death, before legally marrying Osgood P. in 1937. Because Osgood P. had lost a limb and earned little in a barber shop, Mary P. cleaned the home of a northwest Detroiter for $16 per week. She traveled four miles to work and impressed her employer as a "nice person," trustworthy. Thirty-seven years old in 1943 and without responsibility for her daughter (who lived with her father, William W.), Mary P. looked after her handicapped, fifty-year-old husband. Without skills and therefore unable to benefit from the war boom, she stole to help make ends meet.[53]

Perhaps because of Mary P.'s past record and the fact that it was whiskey she stole, she received a sentence of from six months to five years for entering without breaking. Despite recommendations by probationary supervisors that she be spared incarceration, she served four months in the Detroit House of Correction before being paroled. In contrast, Mary P.'s husband was dismissed in spite of his penitentiary stint, probably because he was disabled and had been outside the beer garden when apprehended.

Mary P.'s case reveals clearly the impact of both ghetto life and a period of disorder on basically honest, lower-class residents. Better-off black women did not escape the trauma of upheaval, either, as Louise F.'s experience demonstrated. She and husband, Charles F., both in their early thirties, were racing along Russell Street near Macomb Street, within one-half mile of their residence, when they were stopped at 1:00 A.M. on June 22. She had left a wallet containing $80 and a bank book listing deposits of $3,000 at a relative's home and was hastening to retrieve it, reason enough to fill their Ford with weapons—bricks, pipes, and hammer—and ignore the curfew.[54] Mother of three and a laundress, married to a well-employed defense worker with an excellent record, Louise had never been arrested, and her anxiety over the family's savings during the disturbance was certainly understandable. She was released, but her husband, who had been driving the vehicle, received six months probation for carrying concealed weapons.[55]

If Mary P. was an active rioter—that is, looter—and Louise F. an unwitting participant, both women displayed a diversity of gender and class—and their impact on collective violence—that has long been overlooked by investigators. Mary P. took advantage of the riot; Louise F. sought protection from it.

Other female felons charged with carrying weapons or—the lone case—assault indicated frustrations and racial enmity. Some among the nearly 12 percent who carried weapons did so for protection, but others brandished them offensively. Misdemeanors, for which over 40 percent of all females were arrested, also manifested more than mere delinquency. Many charges of disturbing the peace or disorderly conduct were the result of these women having vented pent-up emotions at white passersby or jousted with white lawmen. Sometimes they seemed unruly troublemakers, at other times protesting residents.[56]

In comparison to black males, black women rioters differed in some important ways. More of them were single, unemployed, or holding low-paying, servile jobs. Although they had few arrest records, their precarious socio-economic status in a materialistic culture and their relative passivity in a male-dominated society led many to steal. Perhaps because of these factors, they entered more clothing stores and traveled shorter distances than black male looters. Unsurprisingly, they stole while their men carried weapons.

Children of both races imitated their elders. Police arrested 194 youths under seventeen years of age between June 21 and June 25. Only 132 of these teenagers entered the Juvenile Detention Home and were identified by name, age, race, address, offense, and arrest precinct. Ninety-seven of them—sixty-four blacks and thirty-three whites, all males ranging in age from ten to sixteen—committed offenses on the first two days of riot. Although no records of their origins exist, all but eight youngsters lived in Detroit; five blacks and one white resided in Hamtramck and Highland Park respectively, while only one white named Monroe, Michigan, as home and another white, no doubt newly arrived, cited Harriman, Tennessee. Within the city, most blacks and meaningful percentages of whites inhabited the east side—predominantly north central and southwest—districts, while a plurality of whites and a good number of blacks occupied respectively far eastern and west-side neighborhoods. Hence both groups contained the sons of lower, working, and middle-class parents, although many more of the latter were white. In almost reverse proportions, white youths traveled beyond their home precincts to riot, and their black counterparts fought on familiar turf. And although the greatest majority of white youngsters bore no readily identifiable ethnic names, nearly 25 percent were Polish, French, and Italian.[57]

Unlike black adult males, black juveniles were younger than

white ones, the youngest being ten years old and the median age being almost fifteen years; like their grown-ups, they engaged in felonies, though in even greater percentages and more as thieves than as armed combatants. Seventy percent broke the law by breaking and entering or looting, carrying concealed weapons, assaulting someone, or destroying property inside the ghetto (usually along Oakland Avenue rather than Hastings Street). Also like adult males of both races and in contrast to white juveniles—who operated steadily over two days—black youngsters overwhelmingly rioted on June 21.[58]

In equally paramount ways, white juveniles differed from and were similar to their elders. Older than black youngsters, they fell between narrower ranges of fourteen and sixteen years, with a median just over fifteen and one-half years. And their arrests, nearly the exact opposite of black teenagers, mirrored those of white adults: 67 percent misdemeanors and 30 percent felonies. White juveniles spread their activity over the 1st and 5th precincts, in and near black neighborhoods. Essentially, black and white youths reversed the age characteristics of their seniors yet retained their categories of riot charges.

Perhaps most significant, juveniles of both races expressed their hostility more openly than grown-ups.[59] Indeed, 16 percent and 21 percent of the black and white youngsters respectively carried weapons, while 11 and 6 percent assaulted someone, and the majority of those arrested for disturbing the peace threw missiles at human targets or passing cars.[60] Their elders armed themselves in greater percentages, but black and white teenagers under sixteen assailed more victims and, once apprehended, verbalized their resentment with less inhibition.

Robert G. seemed typical of those black juveniles most alienated by their surroundings and circumstance. Sixteen years old, unemployed, and living with his parents at 956 East Kirby in the upper east side, he seemed incorrigible. At age thirteen, he committed larceny; at age fourteen, he assaulted and stole again; at age fifteen, he violated probation. Instead of entering reform school, he stayed at home "pending good behavior." Shortly before noon on the first day of riot, he entered a store in the 4700 block of St. Antoine

Street—the crime of entering without breaking. He lied to police officers, claiming to be eighteen years old, waived both pretrial hearing and jury trial, and appeared before Recorder's Court Judge Christopher E. Stein, who found him guilty. Only then did his true age become known, and his conviction was set aside, and his release arranged: parental custody pending further action by juvenile authorities.[61] From one perspective, Robert G. proved Dowling's hoodlum thesis and exemplified Selling's "dangerous character" who, like a moth attracted to light, came out of his dark hiding place to engage in disorder; from another view, he could be a youth striking out at white targets in the ghetto because of deep-seated antagonisms and harsh environmental realities, which generated militant norms among some youngsters.[62] Without additional information, Robert G. remains an enigma, yet he probably wore his delinquency as a badge of courage, and he certainly tested himself by lying about his age and risking a prison term. He—and his peers—carried resentments and manhood into combat, striking and mocking white patrolmen, store owners, and youngsters.

Ironically Robert G. and other juveniles, black or white, failed to attract much bluecoat attention. Concentrating on black adult males, patrolmen pretty much ignored hundreds of youngsters under sixteen years old; in arresting eighty-five black and forty-seven white juvenile males, however, they still exhibited racial bias. Police also overlooked younger girls of both races, just as they ignored adult women. Lawmen held only three black and one white female in juvenile detention—a number so small that it fails to indicate the racial prejudice apparent in the arrest of black adult women, yet displays the gender bias of disregarding females generally. Apparently they concentrated on the handful of girls involved in the Belle Isle fracas that triggered upheaval citywide.[63]

Mattie Mae B., the sixteen-year-old girl who witnessed the beating of Gus Niarhos and exchanged blows with Margaret Hart, for example, was incarcerated as a witness in the case against Charles L. and his marauders. A ninth-grade student never before in trouble, she resided with her parents just north of Hamtramck at 13456 Greeley Street. She scarcely fit the profile for wayward girls, yet she responded in kind and with open hand when called "black bitch" by Hart.[64] Black, proud, and resentful, she unquestionably typified other female minors.

In contrast to youths of either gender, however, seventeen-year-old males were considered as legally liable as their grown-ups. Bluecoats arrested fifteen black and twenty-eight white participants in this age group, whose characteristics and activity provide comparisons for those younger and older than themselves. Black youth roamed the east side and, unlike their elders, had previous arrest records more often than not; white teenagers, instead, possessed no earlier police contacts (as did their elders) when apprehended in the vicinity of Belle Isle or on Woodward Avenue. However, black seventeen-year-olds rioted further north, along Oakland Avenue, and earlier on June 21—67 percent were arrested before suppertime—than did older ghetto participants. They also traveled longer distances from their homes, particularly those venturing from three-fourths of a mile to two miles afield, and committed many more misdemeanors than black elders. In fact, fully 80 percent, or nearly double the percentage of senior blacks, acted disorderly, disturbed the peace, or engaged in some form of misconduct. Although 20 percent of the black seventeen-year-olds looted stores, a proportion half as small as younger and slightly less than that of older felons, they packed no weapons. This was in stark contrast to all other rioters regardless of age, race, and gender, possibly explained by the small number of seventeen-year-olds captured by lawmen. Indeed, among blacks, 16 percent of younger teenage and 29 percent of older males carried concealed weapons, as did 12 percent of adult females.[65]

Ralph C. and Rudolph R. respectively represented black and white seventeen-year-olds. Single, literate, and employed as laborers, both disturbed the peace and received ninety days in the Detroit House of Correction. Ralph C. threw stones on upper Cardoni Street, inside the 9th Precinct at 4:55 P.M. on June 21, while Rudolph R. committed similar mayhem downtown, near City Hall one hour later. Members of large crowds that harassed police and passersby, they drew identical prison terms and early releases for good behavior. Ralph C. had one previous arrest and Rudolph R. none, a common racial pattern among adolescent participants.[66] Still, they appeared more racially agitated than criminally motivated.

Strikingly, white seventeen-year-olds comprised a greater proportion of all white rioters than did their black counterparts, accounting for nearly 30 percent of the whites. White participants were in general younger than blacks and often served as shock troops for their more established but no less threatened parents. Possibly so many white youths were arrested because of some police prejudice; youthful troublemakers had taunted bluecoats earlier at Eastwood Park, projected negative images for the race, and lacked status in their own society. In comparison, black seventeen-year-olds—including three females—made up only 7 percent of all ghetto participants, whose collective older age clearly denoted adult protest for equal opportunities and police disregard for younger blacks of either gender.[67]

White seventeen-year-olds more closely paralleled their older peers than did blacks; like grown-ups they came from afar to riot, 47 percent—almost 6 percent more than senior whites—traveling more than two miles. They committed more misdemeanors than felonies, the latter including only weapons charges; most telling, white youths neither looted nor assaulted. Likewise, they were most active after 6:00 P.M. on the first day of riot; although older whites wound down their activities around midnight, seventeen-year-olds continued agitating until dawn.

White youngsters, whether juveniles or seventeen-year-olds, resembled—probably emulated—rather than differed from adult rioters. Thirty-six percent of those sixteen and under closed ranks with their elders in the 1st Precinct, undoubtedly along Woodward Avenue, while 30 percent roamed with seventeen-year-olds around Belle Isle. They also perpetrated crimes in direct proportion to the older rioters. Caught between adolescence and adulthood, seventeen-year-olds went sometimes one way and sometimes the other. Some, close in age and life-style to many juveniles, joined them on Jefferson Avenue on the night of upheaval and stayed throughout the next day, without the assistance of elder whites. Others, perhaps identifying with adult rioters, battled alongside their models on Woodward Avenue and committed offenses in adult proportions regardless of the combat zone. Overwhelmingly, juveniles and seventeen-year-olds flooded those areas—Belle Isle and downtown Woodward Avenue—where they'd heard race war existed and where they knew blacks and whites intersected. They also exhibited elements of peer influence and the effects of proximity. In short, they did what they saw others doing.[68]

Nowhere was this interaction more painfully exemplified among teenagers than in the celebrated cases of black and white youths accused of having committed cold-blooded murder during the outburst. Black, seventeen-year-old Aaron F. is a case in point.[69]

His family, composed of mother Beatrice, older brother Nelson, Jr., and younger sibling Eugene, had occupied apartment 8 at 5820 Beaubien Street since 1941, and shared it with Henry and Johnel Daniels. This situation resulted from the economic hardship faced by a female-headed family and wartime housing shortage, made worse by race discrimination. Despite difficulties, the F.s were a close-knit upright family, and Aaron F. knew love and stability. His mother, apparently a divorcee who had retained her maiden name and resided in Detroit for many years, stressed education, industry, and religion. Hence he had attended school through the eleventh grade, well beyond the level of most peers, and worked steadily for the Department of Recreation. A regular member of Mt. Zion Baptist Church, he received baptism, served as Sunday School scholar, and, according to the Rev. Robert Wright, was "peaceful and law-abiding."[70]

Aaron F. had never been arrested before the riot. His mother and older brother (who later served overseas in the armed forces), as well as roomers and neighbors provided models of solid, law-abiding citizens. The Daniels, employed and in their thirties, had lived with the family for two years. Hardworking occupants of this and nearby apartment buildings exemplified the community's social cohesion and working-class values.

Like most east-side youth, however, Aaron F. also encountered the disrupting influences of urban society, accentuated by racial competition and war circumstances. Despite accolades from his mother and minister, and undoubtedly without their knowledge, he got into difficulty. He fought some black rivals who had approached him for money and, unsupervised, ran with others who engaged in high jinks.[71] Sometimes he sought recreational opportunities beyond ghetto boundaries and battled whites resisting these incursions. Surely exposed to east-side violence and shady characters, he also witnessed the community's anger over the Sojourner Truth Homes controversy, hate strikes, and similar episodes of interracial antagonisms. Possibly, he even heard his mother, brother, or neighbors complain of such conflict. In essence Aaron F. grew up, as did many ghetto youngsters, both proud and troubled, maneuvering between the respectability of his economically struggling family and the delinquency of his bored, hostile peers. His socialization pitted harmonious, wholesome values of home against militant, violent-prone excitement of the street, which ultimately exploded into riot.

Although not arrested, Aaron F. was among the fifty black youths who clashed with 200 white teenagers, soldiers, and sailors at Eastwood Park on Tuesday evening, June 15. He did not sport a zoot suit, as did many blacks fighting that night several miles from their east-side neighborhood, but he shared their resentment—and probably political awareness—at being denied the recreational facilities granted the very white youths beside whom blacks of draft age would be asked to fight in coming months.[72]

Still mindful of this recent flareup in northeast Detroit, Aaron F. visited Belle Isle five days later. Arriving at noon on June 20, he tired of waiting in the long Sunday line to swim, and, with a seventeen-year-old companion, wandered about in the bright sun and sweltering temperatures. He shot dice at midafternoon in the playground with several teenagers and, after an argument with some of the white gamblers, spoke of the Eastwood Park incident with Charles L. Following the older Charles L., himself a veteran of that encounter, Aaron F. and six others fought whites "like they done us" until dusk. They headed home at 9:30 P.M., crossing the path of white Gus Niarhos near the bridge to Jefferson Avenue. Someone asked the fourteen-year-old Niarhos where he was going, and before he could answer, F. and others beat him to the ground, and Charles L. ripped money from his pockets. On the move again, they chased another white youth before accosting Joseph B. Joseph on the viaduct and inciting riot all across the Detroit River, from isle to mainland. F. battled his way to the street, where he spread rumor—"a colored woman and her baby had been drowned"—

and urged black onlookers back into the fray. He then boarded a bus for the east side, leaving behind a race war, which soon spread to Paradise Valley, its eastern and downtown borders.[73]

Escaping the police dragnet, F. returned safely to his home in the early morning hours and—alleged authorities—committed murder near there at 10:30 A.M. on June 21. One of many teen-agers and young adults gathered on Beaubien Street, he hurled missiles at cars driven by whites who had entered the ghetto un-aware of the riot. He flung concrete at a southbound Chevrolet coupe, smashing its windshields, and watching it swerve around the corner onto Hendrie Street, where it hit a parked car and a pole before coming to a stop in plumes of smoke. The driver, Dr. Joseph De Horatiis, was already unconscious, but Aaron neverthe-less rushed the maroon vehicle and hurled another piece of mor-tar at his head. Coming from a distance of only three feet and landing with enormous force, the blow killed the sixty-four-year-old, Italian-American physician. Identified and convicted several months later of second degree murder, Aaron F. drew the longest sentence of any rioter: seven and a half to twenty-five years in the state penitentiary.[74]

While Aaron F.'s mother was appealing his fate,[75] Aldo T. peered from behind the walls of Ionia State Reformatory and pondered his own dilemma. He was sixteen-years-old when Detroit erupted, a native-born laborer living with his foreign-born parents and nu-merous siblings at 3312 Superior Street.[76] Among many of the 26,277 Italians occupying the area of Russell, Superior, and Gra-tiot, which formed an inverted triangle just west of Paradise Val-ley, he enjoyed strong family and ethnic ties.[77] He possessed, in the opinion of one Roman Catholic priest who knew him and his fam-ily, an exceptionally high intelligence. Yet he never attended high school, because of his own preference and possibly his family's work ethic.[78]

No doubt Aldo T.'s parents, like many of those who comprised the city's more than forty foreign-born nationalities, stressed fru-gality, hard work, and ethnic pride. He knew of their concern for economic security, their belief in social cohesion, and their willing-ness to sacrifice during the war, ever grateful for being citizens and anxious for the future. Perhaps he sensed in them and in their neighbors a willingness to work beside blacks, but deep opposition to living near them. Paradoxically, cultural warmth and first-generation receptivity to newcomers as fellow refugees was offset by ethnocentrism and, especially for Aldo T.'s generation, competition for jobs. T. must have perceived the growing racism among his elders, as well as the anti-Italian, anti-Catholic feelings of other ethnics, who claimed that Italians depreciated neighborhoods, and Catholics might control city schools.[79]

T.'s experience as a second-generation ethnic reinforced the negative racial views of his parents and larger white society. Less survival-minded and more status-conscious than they, he and his peers viewed blacks as inferior competitors to be feared, kept at a distance, and in their place. Ironically, he stereotyped blacks the way many others labeled Italians: aggressive, dangerous, and knife-wielding. Drawing on this prejudice, he embraced—as did earlier second-generation ethnics—racism as part of becoming American.[80]

Aldo T. was also shaped by environment. Intelligence, family cohesion, and community ties aside, he grew up with delinquent friends in a tough neighborhood. "Not too highly trained in the cultural sphere" and emotionally maladjusted in family life, he exhibited—according to court-appointed psychiatrists—resentment and vindictiveness. He seemed preoccupied with himself, indifferent to the rights or interests of other people.[81] Though never convicted of a crime, he crossed paths with patrolmen when he was only twelve years old and he ran with a zoot-suit gang that displayed anti-social and self possessed personalities. Like them, and many black youths, he felt isolated, humiliated, and confined by larger society.[82] Belonging culturally to a minority, he protested against Old World values. Average in size, feeling rejected by everyone, and excited by war circumstances, Aldo T. moved quickly against what he saw as native-born enemies.[83]

Accompanied by Armando M., T. entered his favorite pool room on Superior and Moran streets the afternoon of June 21. He approached Anthony S. and Ralph T. about the riot raging in and about Paradise Valley. Wanting to see the fighting but not be

harmed by it, he located Robert C., borrowed his 1937 Ford Tudor
for transportation, and brought along Armando M.'s .22 caliber
rifle for protection. T. and his band headed west in the black sedan
toward the nearby ghetto that their neighborhood had, for the
past twenty years, rebuffed. "Let's . . . kill us a nigger," said someone, which drew the approval of everyone in the car. Rather than
spark reprisal by shooting into "bunches" of "colored people," the
carload searched for a lone target along Mack Avenue, just above
Gratiot and beyond the east side. Suddenly they spotted Moses
Kiska standing on the corner of Mack and Chene. Ralph T. spun
the vehicle around, slowed it to a crawl, and almost stopped it completely as Aldo T. allegedly fired point-blank at the black man.
After the weapon's muffled report, he accelerated the car east-
ward, back to safe ground.[84] Abandoned at the scene at 6:35 P.M.,
the elder black man died of internal bleeding four hours later at
Receiving Hospital.[85]

Captured in July (Ralph T. surrendered himself in early August), the band received enormous publicity and, ultimately for
three of them, convictions for manslaughter.[86] Singled out as ringleader and "trigger man," Aldo T. faced from five and one-half to
fifteen years in the state penitentiary, while gun owner Armando
M. and driver Ralph T. confronted lighter prison terms.[87] Robert
C., who had stayed behind, and Anthony S. who (might or might
not have) accompanied the death squad as a sixteen-year-old minor were deemed not guilty.[88]

Long before the trial and subsequent appeals by Aldo T., Detroiters read sensational, near boastful newspaper accounts of
Kiska's cold-blooded murder by Armando M. They learned of the
foursome "bumming around" the pool room and deciding to kill
"a nigger," a defense worker whom they did not know and who
had not bothered them. City residents also read that Aldo T. and
Armando M. confessed to the killing, which the Wayne County
prosecutor said they committed with no more compunction than
"normal men would show" for shooting clay pigeons. They read
further that Dowling suspected them of being responsible for the
shooting death of another black man later that evening. Given
these stories, most citizens probably agreed with Detective Lt.

Charles Buckholdt's description of Kiska's slayers as less than human, "utterly vicious and depraved" gang members who acted without provocation.[89] To use the nineteen-year police veteran's single word, they visualized hoodlums.

Much about Aldo T. and his ring reinforced the public belief that young toughs caused and carried on all the rioting. They ranged in age from sixteen to twenty years old, preferred pool hall to schoolroom and unlawful activity to hard work. Aldo T. and Ralph T. experienced earlier contact with authorities, while Robert C. committed a separate riot offense (carrying a concealed weapon) the day after Kiska's death; Armando M. fled Detroit only to be captured a month later as a soldier AWOL. Portrayed as unrepentant and wanton, braggarts unwilling to show their faces to photographers for fear of being identified and consequently assaulted by blacks, they seemed both criminal and cowardly.[90]

Ironically, journalists made little mention of ethnicity or origins.[91] All five suspects had parents born in Italy. Armando M. himself was born in Italy and Ralph T. in Canada.[92] Given their readily identifiable names and existing criminal stereotypes, perhaps newsmen considered comment unnecessary. Most likely, editors also viewed their ethnicity in a city of polyglot nationalities as less significant than their race—and more politically risky to highlight. In race war, skin colors served as the uniforms—the black and white—of urban guerrillas.

"Other people were fighting and killing, and we felt like it, too," Armando M. explained the group's bloodlust—what law-abiding citizens would consider a senseless, criminal motive.[93] His statement reinforced the idea that he and his ilk, especially gunman Aldo T., were mentally defective just as Selling had hypothesized of all rioters immediately after the outbreak. But as diagnosed by three state-appointed psychiatrists, including Selling, none of the five youths exhibited feeblemindedness but instead psychopathic or emotionally abnormal personalities.[94] And, both in popular and legal minds, they appeared old enough to know what they were doing.[95]

Surely Aldo T. and his accomplices also confirmed Dowling's hoodlum thesis, although as white opposites to Charles L. and his band of Belle Isle hooligans. Aldo T.'s and Charles L.'s activities and characters, for instance, were well known to both public and prosecutor before Dowling presented his committee's report to Governor Kelly.[96] In fact, because their celebrated actions dovetailed with the personal prejudices and political needs of Dowling and his committeemen—heads of the law enforcement agencies responsible for quelling and, critics argued, mishandling the disturbance—and because black rioters drew more police attention than any other participants, Aldo T. and especially Charles L. emerged as official prototypes of who rioted and why: young, detached, irresponsible, mostly black male hoodlums.

Their criminal acts notwithstanding, few rioters manifested hoodlum traits. Most participants entered the disorder without previous arrest records, and only 1 percent of blacks and 2 percent of whites attracted police more than once during the melee.[97] Besides Charles L., Aaron F., and Robert C., J. C. G., a white man, broke the law twice. Within forty-five minutes, he committed both misdemeanor and felony at Charlotte Street and Woodward Avenue on June 21. Originally arrested for loitering, he reappeared in the intersection where white gangs were stopping trolleys and automobiles in search of black victims. There at 7:15 P.M., he came across an overturned Ford and removed a tire. Arrested, he pleaded innocent, saying that "some soldier" ordered him to steal the tire. Originally from Tennessee, though an intermittent city resident since 1935, and bearing one previous arrest, he received a prison term for larceny. Nonetheless, he seemed more blue collar than recidivist: twenty-two-years-old, married, father of one child, educated through the eighth grade, and employed as a grinder for Continental Motors.[98]

Even less prone to perpetual lawbreaking, 71 percent of all rioters placed on probation served their sentences "with improvement," while 86 percent of those incarcerated in the Detroit House of Correction were released early for good behavior. And the small percentage who violated their probation, had served previous time in the House, or escaped from that facility shared characteristics—age, marital status, and employment—that did not match the normal image of hooligans.[99]

Two of these probationers, longtime resident William B. and recent arrival James G., had brushed with the law only once. Married, raising families, steadily employed, and educated well above
their peers, they violated probation only after finding better jobs
elsewhere. William B. moved to San Francisco in 1944 and corre-
sponded regularly with his social worker until March of 1945,
when he became "a permanent absconder," while James G. met
the terms of his probation and paid most of his $50 court costs be-
fore leaving for Cleveland after August of 1945. Officially, one was
discharged without improvement and the other sought by authorities, but neither William B. nor James G. represented hardened
toughs.[100] As frightened worker and gambling opportunist caught
up in events, they carried weapons and received stolen goods; as
well-intended breadwinners, they fulfilled their sentences until
new economic horizons placed them beyond probationary authorities. Less upright and more daring, or foolhardy, than east siders
who cleared the streets during the outburst, they depicted com-
munitywide ambivalence toward law and order. They resented
discriminatory treatment yet generally deferred to authority,
aware of the need for neighborhood stability. Their worst fears
and instincts surfaced during the outburst, more often products of
an inequitable social system than of criminal and feeble minds or
flawed characters.

In reality, a variety of individuals rioted for sundry reasons.
Black and white youth, those largely responsible for igniting the
riot on Belle Isle and spreading it to Paradise Valley and beyond,
seemed bent on reprisals for previous affronts throughout the
city's recreational and transportation facilities.[101] Carrying chips on
their shoulders and weapons in their hands, they fought to shore
up or, if black, to tear down the color line in Detroit. White youngsters, themselves children of the depression and witness to their
parents' raised socioeconomic expectations and increased racial
fears, traveled great distances to kick blacks back into their prewar
place.[102] Elder blacks, married and employed, enjoying recently
improved economic status and seeking even greater social stakes,
in turn, struck at police who hemmed them in the ghetto just as
whites generally blocked their opportunities for more jobs, hous-

ing, and human dignity.[103] Eventually black males of various ages and most black females looted predominantly white-owned stores in their community, both to vent anger and to make ends meet. Older whites, kept out of Paradise Valley by police officers, now held the color line along Woodward Avenue. Surely, white and black toughs, as well as their elders, entered the streets for selfish even criminal reasons. Certainly, many white and black rioters responded to the excitement and anxiety of wartime, which ironically, had enhanced their personal prospects while sharpening their intergroup rivalry. In broad sweeping terms, rioters of both races sought to protect and improve their positions in wartime Detroit and, in individual socioeconomic and political terms, protested their relationship toward one another—the difference being that blacks acted out of hope and whites out of fear.

In the process of lashing out at actual or imagined affronts, rioters struck real targets. They seriously harmed, sometimes killed each other, lawmen, and bystanders. They destroyed public and private property, looted ghetto stores, and spread fear citywide. Sometimes they became caught in the maelstrom, victims of circumstance and prejudice. While much was said and written about who wreaked havoc and why they did so, comparatively few words were spent on those—including participants—harmed by the nation's worst World War II domestic upheaval.

FOUR

And Victims, Too

The consequence of disorder staggered all imaginations. Officially, forty-eight hours of rioting left thirty-four dead, 676 injured, and $2 million worth of property destroyed, while costing 1 million hours in war production.[1] Others, according to rumor, died, and many more nursed their own wounds, presumably failing to be recorded by authorities or treated in hospitals. Casualties reduced the ranks of rioters, lawmen, and spectators alike, indiscriminately victimizing all those who stepped into the violence. Whether black or white, civilian or policeman, fighting or bearing witness, their blood spilled as freely in race war at home as in ideological war abroad. And their wrath demolished automobiles driven by unsuspecting blacks along Woodward Avenue and east-side stores owned by white merchants living safely beyond the battle. Ironically, some of those identified as rioters by overwhelmed, often prejudiced policemen and judges were victims. "More often than not," admitted Mayor Jeffries in the midst of disorder, the individual hurt or jailed was "an innocent bystander who got himself mixed up in the melee."[2]

87

More than any aspect of the riot, its wholesale death toll shocked everyone and sparked controversy. Indignant black leaders and white liberals condemned Detroit patrolmen for the lopsided, record number of riot-related black deaths—seventeen of twenty-five—as "willful inefficiency" and "wanton murder."[3] Privately and publicly, national officers of the NAACP, for example, detailed bluecoat prejudice and Nazilike tactics during the disturbance, while local members of the National Lawyers Guild called for investigation of all police killings. Similarly they criticized the disproportion of black arrests, finding it "difficult to square with the known facts."[4] Lawmen's accounts called the slayings and arrests justifiable, supposedly because blacks started the riot, acted more aggressively, carried more weapons, and committed more felonies than their white counterparts.[5] These self-serving versions were dismissed by the critics who marshaled evidence from eyewitnesses attesting to indiscriminate police brutality: blacks denied medical assistance at Belle Isle, beaten outside the Roxy Theater on Woodward Avenue, and shot on the streets of Paradise Valley.[6] They told of patrolmen cooperating with white mobs, shooting into black crowds, and stealing from east-side prisoners, whom they roughed up and called vile names.[7] Although one or two black members of the overwhelmingly white police department also abused east siders, critics, particularly among the NAACP, considered the bluecoat-black confrontations a police riot fostered by racism and past grudges.[8]

Police Commissioner John H. Witherspoon presented another viewpoint, one stressing both black aggression and police courage. Understaffed by 280 officers due to both selective service calls and better-paying defense jobs, his officers worked continuous shifts, stood between the races, and prevented further bloodshed than actually occurred. In the line of duty, they killed only "hoodlums and murderers" and sacrificed themselves. Some donated blood in an effort to save a fallen companion, then returned to their posts; others stayed in the streets despite serious injuries, and one among them died as a result of sniper fire.[9]

On the evening of June 21, Patrolman Lawrence A. Adam paid the ultimate price. He and three other members of the 13th Precinct responded to a radio call of patrolmen needing assistance at Brush Street and Vernor Highway. Arriving on the scene, amid crowds of blacks and whites, they stopped in front of the Frazer Hotel and drew the fire of black tenants, who believed themselves under siege. Leaving the scout car, Adam fell to the ground, downed by buckshot wounds to the right buttock and thigh, while another officer fired and killed the black shooter, Homer E.[10]

Twenty-four-years-old, married, and the father of two children when he joined the force in 1937, Adam represented many patrolmen. Like more than 65 percent of them, he came from the Midwest; like nearly 45 percent of them, he came from a rural or small-town setting; like 22 percent of them, he had worked previously as a craftsman and foreman. Born in Shelby, Ohio, and trained as an auto repairman, Adam shared with fellow white officers—who comprised 99 percent of the department—a stake in the very society threatened by wartime black pride and assertiveness.[11] Yet he broke no police rules and drew no civilian complaints during his six-year career, and he dismissed his shooting as "something a policeman has to expect." He died ten days later of tetanus.[12]

More fortunate than their fallen colleague, seventy-five bluecoats survived riot-related injuries. Of these, forty-five involved assaults, and thirty occurred accidentally (mostly the result of tear gas irritations).[13] Assailed officers usually were struck by missiles, though three were shot. Sgt. Fred Noot, and patrolmen Earnest Hartwick and Russell Reiman converged on Division and Hastings Street shortly before 8:00 A.M. on June 21. They and several fellow officers salvaged the remains of a lower east-side men's store, dispersed a crowd of 250 people, and arrested those like William H. who refused to leave. As policemen were putting the black prisoner into their squad car, he grabbed Hartwick's revolver and shot the patrolman in the leg and the sergeant in the abdomen. Reiman killed William H. almost immediately and was hit himself by ricocheting slugs. All three policemen recovered from their wounds.[14] They and twenty-nine other officers were treated at area hospitals, while nineteen more bluecoats received first aid from police physicians or precinct personnel. Whether victim of attacks or mishaps, nearly 70 percent of all injured policemen required some form of professional medical attention.

However, lawmen spilled more blood than they bled themselves. In contrast to the self-defense deaths of assailants like Homer E. and William H., police killed many others recklessly or, critics said, at random. Patrolman Reiman, for instance, accidentally took the life of Robert D. when exchanging fire with William H.[15] Even less defensible, other bluecoats sprayed black crowds with machine guns and shot spectators who happened to be standing in the wrong place—then offered either no or delayed medical assistance to their victims.[16] They considered everyone in the street rioters, and fired first and asked questions later.[17] Sometimes they shouted warnings or discharged revolvers skyward before killing an east sider, and other times they shot through partitions at threatening voices or disobedient thieves. Seemingly quick-triggered and more apt to protect property than life, they shot fleeing looters in the back and unarmed looters in the chest. Nor did they consider the possibility that some of those fired upon might be hard of hearing or too paralyzed with fear to respond to shouted orders.[18] Frightened and prejudiced, patrolmen often and unhesitatingly employed deadly force. The fact that they did so only against blacks cast a shadow over all departmental shootings, including those involving self-defense, and brought into question official countenance of police shooting. Indeed, of seventeen black deaths at the hands of bluecoats, at least eight seemed unnecessary and one accidental.[19]

Black victims were also killed by both fellow east siders and white marauders. The death of Carrie Hackworth, the only woman of either race killed by rioters, revealed both racial and class divisions among blacks. Twenty-nine-years-old, mother of two sons, and a recent arrival from Birmingham, Alabama, she was riding north on Oakland Avenue with her husband, en route to check on the safety of her sister, when an unknown black youth stepped out from a crowd of rioters and hurled a brick into the passing automobile. Ironically, this "light-skinned negress" died in broad daylight of a crushed skull because one race-conscious east sider mistook her for white.[20] Other "light persons of color," including the Rev. Charles A. Hill, the well-known pastor of Hart-ford Baptist Church and chair of the Citizens Committee for Jobs in War Industries, were attacked out of mistaken racial identity. Most escaped with body bruises, but the Reverend Mr. Hill ended up with head knots "the size of an orange." They pleaded for their lives when possible, but their plight revealed both the black-mulatto schism within the ghetto and the potential for race war between blacks and whites.[21] Carol Crater spoke for many mulatto women when she criticized both elite members of her race, for smugly ignoring the woes of lower-class east siders, and dark-skinned blacks (particularly women), for threatening their brown and yellow sisters.[22] Whether minister or mother, lighter-skinned east siders found themselves the targets of both black and white rioters.

Other blacks also became the indirect targets of fellow east siders. Twenty-four-year-old Annie Jackson, DSR conductorette, witnessed the full rage of a mob above Grand Boulevard, when the Clairmont car she was riding crossed its stone-throwing path. Cut in the left hand and injured in the right eye by flying glass, she became an unintended casualty of blacks smiting white trolley passengers.[23] She nonetheless shared the horror of white victims, perhaps wondering about the irony of holding a job that represented the kind of breakthrough and fair treatment wrought by war circumstances and liberal officials that rioters desired for themselves.[24]

Despite some black-on-black violence, more blacks fell prey to whites. Moses Kiska and Charles S. Grundy collapsed within a quarter mile of one another along the ghetto's eastern border, victims of white assailants. Kiska, a fifty-eight-year-old defense worker, single, whose only relative, his mother, resided in St. Louis, stood at the corner of Mack Avenue and Chene Street at 6:30 P.M. Having worked the day shift at Chrysler Tank Plant and ridden a streetcar beyond his usual transfer point because the rioting frightened him, he waited for the westbound bus to deliver him safely home at 4250 Brush Street. He never made the trip. Instead, a slug was fired into his stomach, and he fell to the pavement. "I am shot?" he asked incredulously, and expired of internal bleeding later that night in Receiving Hospital.[25] Meanwhile, Grundy, a twenty-year-old black youth, about whom very little was

known, died of a gunshot wound in the forehead. When found at
8:45 P.M., lying in the intersection of Dubois and Superior streets,
he lay within a few steps of his doorway and "in the same general
neighborhood" as Kiska. Both east siders, authorities believed,
drew the fire of the same murderers: Aldo T. and company.[26]

Less likely the victims of white rioters than of police and medical
misfeasance, twenty-eight-year-old William McAdoo succumbed
to buckshot wounds of the abdomen. He left work at the Packard
Motor Company to join his wife and two small children for supper
at their apartment in the 900 block of East Willis Avenue. When
nearly home, he walked toward bluecoats dispersing crowds on
Superior Street and, in the middle of tear gas vapors, gun shots,
and stampeding humans, "slumped to the ground." Thereafter,
he lay in Receiving Hospital at least three hours before being
treated and over fifteen hours before being scheduled for opera-
tion. Moved by his worried wife to Diagnostic Hospital, he underwent surgery the afternoon of June 22 and died abruptly, two days
later.[27] Tragically and without identification of his killer, he per-
ished because of indiscriminate police force, overtaxed and insen-
sitive hospital personnel, and possibly wifely love (which sought
private medical help and unwittingly delayed surgery further).

If white rioters killed perhaps as many as six black victims, east
siders—said officials—slew one lawman, one black woman, and
seven white persons.[28] The deaths of Patrolman Adam and Mrs.
Hackworth notwithstanding, Dr. Joseph De Horatiis's killing attracted the most public attention. Born in Agnone, Italy, sixty-four
years earlier, he graduated from the University of Naples and
served as army surgeon before entering the United States in the
early 1900s. He educated himself further at the Detroit College of
Medicine, passed the Michigan medical examinations, and became
a popular physician among lower east side residents and, for the
past fifteen years, Italo-Americans of the Gratiot-McDougall area.
He never married and, since 1930, had lived with the Vincent
Juliano family at 803 Boston Boulevard and devoted himself to his
patients. Predictably on Monday, June 21, another work day, De
Horatiis drove south toward the ghetto, perhaps thinking of his
father, brothers, and sisters in Naples or his patients in Detroit's

Italian colony.[29] He ignored police warnings about trouble in Paradise Valley, noting that a sick person awaited his care, and proceeded through crowds along Beaubien Street.[30] Within minutes, as missiles crashed through the windshield of his maroon coupe, he slumped forward in the vehicle and, veering around Hendrie Street, smashed it into a pole. He probably never knew what hit him when another piece of concrete crushed the left side of his head, damaged his brain, blackened and swelled his eyes shut, and brought blood and spinal fluid to his lips. "Another limp and bloody figure on a stretcher" at Receiving Hospital, he died in a comatose state at 1:30 P.M., three and a half hours after leaving home to fulfill his Hippocratic oath and Roman Catholic faith.[31] He would have forgiven those who murdered him, said lifelong friends, for he lived the command, "love ye one another."[32]

Within hours of the physician's death, other whites died to the north and east of the ghetto. John Holyak fell prey to fifty or so black youths on his way home from work. He and two white female coworkers of the Highland Park Ford plant encountered the gang at Davison Avenue and Greeley Street, well above Paradise Valley, just east of Highland Park and north of Hamtramck. Knocked to the pavement and kicked, the fifty-nine-year-old defense worker sustained a broken arm and threats to his life. "Run home if you don't want to get killed," admonished his tormentors, who also frightened the women but did not harm them. Holyak escaped, hauling a painful broken arm over half a mile to his home at 13471 Anglin Avenue, where he collapsed. Taken to Providence Hospital by his wife Ann, he suffered pulmonary embolism and pneumonia before expiring five days later. Elderly, the father of three sons, including a serviceman held prisoner by the Japanese, Holyak realized the potential for race war anywhere that blacks and whites crossed paths.[33] So did fifty-five-year-old Sally Grabowski, the only white woman killed during the riot. A resident of the mixed community, she was walking along the 5000 block of St. Aubin, on the eastern border of Paradise Valley at 7:45 P.M. on June 21, when a black man entered the street, firing an automatic pistol. She collapsed into a sitting position, a bullet lodged in her head, and died in Chenick Hospital of Hamtramck the following day—the casualty of both tragic happenstance and long-standing black-Polish rivalry.[34]

Interracial violence of whatever origin wounded many more Detroiters than it killed. Officials claimed that whites bore the brunt of injuries, supposed proof that blacks initiated and waged the war. If record numbers of east siders died attacking police and looting stores, they also harmed multitudes of innocent whites, said city officials. Jeffries estimated at noon of the first day of disorder that "twice as many whites" as blacks had been hurt, a statistic reiterated by Police Commissioner Witherspoon one week later.[35] Linking injury to hospital treatment, their contention seemed plausible.

However, Receiving Hospital records told a very different story. Between the outburst's origins Sunday night and its control twenty-four hours later, 222 whites and 211 blacks sought hospital assistance. Thus the racial ratio was almost balanced rather than two-to-one, as claimed by the city. Blacks, who comprised less than 10 percent of the city's population, accounted for nearly 50 percent of the injured. They also made up greater numbers and percentages of those hospitalized for gunshot wounds, stabbings, and beatings, and those who died from their injuries. And more black females than white females received treatment. Blacks lagged behind whites in only one category: emergency treatment and release. In comparison to 185 whites (over 55 percent of the total), they numbered 147 persons. A smaller percentage of black males than white males over age thirty fell into this category, which might have reinforced the official view that younger, black toughs assailed older, white residents.[36]

Nonetheless, whether analyzing statistics for treatment, hospitalization, or death, blacks suffered overwhelmingly and disproportionately. And although Receiving Hospital served the greatest number of riot victims regardless of race, they experienced less access to that public facility than did whites.[37] Nor did their care by private facilities show in the official statistics. Thirty-five east siders, for example, sought treatment at black-owned Parkside Hospital, and smaller numbers found assistance at Harper and Grace hospitals.[38]

Despite evidence of black sufferings, officials played up white injuries as proof of black aggression and, critics believed, defense
for black deaths. Heart–rending stories of injured whites reinforced incomplete and misinterpreted statistics. Earl Bayock became the first person to be hospitalized at 8:30 P.M. on June 20,
following three assaults within twenty minutes' time. After pur-
chasing frankfurters at the Belle Isle pavilion, the white sixteen-
year-old from Vernor Highway, just north of the recreation area,
worked his way back through crowded lines. He drew the anger of
several black youths for bumping them. Refusing to apologize for
what he considered unavoidable and incidental contact, he was
knocked down by the blow of a zoot suiter. He scrambled to his
feet, only to be downed again by another black arm. Momentarily
rescued by patrolmen, he headed for the bus stop, where a third
black male hit him with a bottle. By that time he no doubt felt like a
human punching bag and was finally treated for lacerations by Receiving Hospital physicians.[39]

Within two hours, Gus Niarhos, Joseph B. Joseph, and several
others fell before black assailants as random incidents became full-
scale riot along Belle Isle Bridge. By 1:00 A.M. on June 21, whites
on Hastings Street were finding themselves the target of irate
blacks.[40] Patrolman Stewart Marchant received serious head lacerations when hit by a brick at Forest Avenue, and DSR motorman
John Williams endured consecutive beatings as his trolley twice
crossed the intersection at Hendrie Street. As riot spread outward
from the east-side epicenter, white pedestrians and passengers—
like Henry Huddleston on Grand Boulevard at 4:00 A.M. and
Henry Smolinsky on Alfred Street at 8:00 A.M.—found themselves set upon by "jitterbugs" and crowds. Their experiences—
their cuts and fractures, their white skins and middle ages—made
it plain that full-scale race war was all too possible.[41]

Throughout the remainder of the first full day of disorder,
whites within reach of blacks experienced similar assaults. Some,
George W. Stark for example, entered dangerous territory unexpectedly. Having driven his wife, Anne Campbell, to the Children's
Hospital, within a half mile of the Forest Club, he proceeded south
on St. Antoine Street at 9:00 A.M., headed for work at the Detroit

News. He reduced speed behind a black driver, who slowed "almost to a walk," and suddenly felt one stone strike his right eye, another the base of his skull, and several hands drag his body to the street. The terrified, fifty-year-old columnist recalled being pummeled by a gang before police rescued him and drove him to Harper Hospital.[42]

Other whites injured during the upheaval knowingly ventured into its vortex, drawn there by curiosity or bloodlust. On the evening of June 21, eleven-year-old Raymond M. joined a group of Polish youths who had traveled short distances from their homes just east of the black ghetto to form part of a crowd at Forest Avenue and St. Aubin Street. There they followed black pedestrians and stoned their houses. When a scared, middle-aged black man randomly fired a double-barreled shotgun from inside his home 150 feet away, young M. caught pellets in his buttocks, legs, and right wrist. He received hospital treatment and later pressed charges against his assailant. Whether or not M. intended to harm the gunman, he had appeared at 9:30 P.M. in a neighborhood marked by tension and as part of an assaultive gang. Perhaps for this reason, his attacker left the Recorder's Court a free man.[43] In very different ways an excited eleven-year-old white boy and a frightened forty-nine-year-old black man were victims in Detroit's bloodiest day of turmoil.

Official disregard notwithstanding, wounded blacks also suffered woefully. Gladys House and her date, a man partially crippled by polio, crossed Belle Isle Bridge late Sunday evening and found themselves amid angry whites, who beat them to the ground. Unable to run, the nineteen-year-old female, who lived just below Highland Park, and her escort defended themselves as best they could. They arrived shortly after midnight at Receiving Hospital, where physicians administered first aid for contusions and cuts caused by flying glass.[44] Their brutal ordeal was repeated among other blacks for nearly twenty-four hours, as they encountered white mobs and biased lawmen on Woodward Avenue and elsewhere. Longtime resident Samuel Mitchell, a veteran of World War I, was chased from a streetcar by white thugs, only to be captured by police—and stabbed and hit repeatedly by rioters while in custody. His horrors, doubtless comparable to those he experienced as a doughboy, occurred at 1:00 P.M. on Monday, while those of Henry Griggs happened five and one-half hours later in a virtual combat zone.[45] As 500 whites marched from Woodward Avenue, down Watson and toward John R, where several blacks stood their ground, Griggs watched as patrolmen threw tear gas and opened fire on the "colored people." He fell to the ground, struck by a "machine gun bullet" that hit his lower breast bone, tore through his right kidney, and lodged in his back. Originally carried to Wayne Diagnostic Clinic by another east sider, he received first aid, was transferred to Receiving Hospital, underwent surgery, and—thirty days after his release—stared at a bill for $252.50.[46]

Many blacks suffered both physically and financially as whites brutalized them and destroyed their property. Returning from work at the Ford River Rouge Plant on June 21, John Bell unexpectedly drove into the Woodward Avenue mobs at high noon. He slowed down for a traffic light at the intersection of Elliott Street, suddenly finding himself the target of missile-hurling rioters. As he got out of the car, he felt the blows of a rock, a blunt instrument, and several fists, which opened neck and eye wounds requiring numerous stitches. He broke from the crazed horde, which beat him at every step and downed him twice before giving up the chase at John R Street. Bell escaped into the ghetto, bloodied yet alive, but his abandoned automobile, "burned beyond repair," was left behind like a bombed-out tank lost on a battleground.[47]

Blacks, and doubtless some white car owners passing through the east side early in the outburst, experienced similar ordeals.[48] Pulled from his Ford and beaten unconscious by white marauders on Woodward Avenue, Archie B. Crawford survived to find the vehicle lying on its roof, missing a wheel.[49] Claribel Wright maneuvered through the same gangs that evening, not daring to stop as they ripped off one fender, pushed in another, and dented the roof of her automobile.[50] Whatever the specific details, several car owners, including a handful like the Rev. Henry Powers who talked their way to safety, endured the shock of being terrorized and beaten. And, according to DPD statistics, fewer whites than blacks were injured while their automobiles were incurring damages at the hands of east-side mobs.[51] The loss of cars, in some cases damaged beyond hope of repair or compensation, only intensified the trauma of disorder.[52]

Black and white victims and their loved ones expressed both anguish and, where life prevailed, relief. James L. Moon, black employee at Ditzler Color Company, left for work late Sunday evening aware of the disturbance—"some foolishness which would pass." In early morning, he called home and learned of the riot's gravity and also that his son had gone to class rather than miss final examinations; worried about the boy, he received permission to leave work early. He checked on his mother and nephews first, then on his wife and discovered that their son was trapped in the school by white rioters. He alerted the police and, when told they were too busy to respond, set out with a relative to rescue the boy. Threatened by whites on the school grounds, he and his armed brother-in-law held them at bay until bluecoats came. Ironically, Moon faced arrest, and his son was beaten later by rioters.[53]

Just as Moon represented the trauma of many parents, relatives, and friends of victims, black or white, columnist Stark exemplified their deliverance. "I am grateful that I am alive," exclaimed the white victim who spoke for everyone injured or traumatized.[54]

Store owners too endured hardships. They claimed unprecedented property losses on Jefferson and Woodward avenues and, most indescribably, along east-side thoroughfares as far north as Westminster Street. Ben Levine seemed typical of most Paradise Valley proprietors, having closed his dry-goods store in the 3800 block of Hastings Street at 11:30 P.M. Saturday, only to return three days later and find it in shambles: doors opened, windows smashed, men's clothing and ladies's shoes strewn everywhere. From an inventory of $20,000, he had lost $1,000 worth of merchandise and $250 in cash. He did not know who had ransacked his business, for he lived more than five miles away.[55]

Some of Levine's fellow merchants sustained even greater vandalism and theft. Unsurprisingly 85 percent owned east-side shops, over half of them along Hastings Street, while the remainder did business above Grand Boulevard, mostly on Oakland Avenue. They operated sundry establishments, ranging from pawnshops to pharmacies, but 75 percent of all damage came to dry goods, grocery, and liquor stores in almost equal proportions. Hence retailers of apparel, food, and alcoholic beverages became the target of most rioters and bore the greatest losses.[56]

Store owners resembled one another in several ways. Ninety-eight percent were white, 84 percent male, and, reflecting the community's historical development, 74 percent Jewish, probably of Russian origin. Of the remaining white shopkeepers, Italians comprised the next largest group, although only 6 percent. And, personal characteristics aside, over 65 percent of all merchants lived outside the ghetto, mostly in northeast Detroit (police Precinct 10). Only Jala Robertson, a businesswoman of twenty-five years' experience, resided beyond city limits, on Moss Street in Highland Park. Manager and part owner of a store specializing in ladies wear and located on Alexandrine Street, near the corner of Brush, she reflected the experiences of other female proprietors who made up 16 percent of all retailers. "My store was a complete wreck," she testified; "even the showcases were kicked in."[57]

Robertson's description reinforced that of other shopkeepers, even though their losses varied. Harry Bornoty found his grocery store on St. Antoine Street "upside down," without its windows, appliances, or stock, while Isadora Cohen discovered her dry-goods outlet on Hastings Street "smashed up," less one-third its inventory of men's wear worth over $18,000. And, despite belated measures by some merchants, like Harry Brandt who placed watchmen in his beer garden on Monday, June 21, they "had been blitzed."[58] They claimed individual losses as high as pawn broker Morris Harris's $30,000 and collectively at $2 million.[59] While downtown retailers experienced no such catastrophe and, according to one spokesman, could use the "breathing spell" caused by riot to catch up on inventories, others understood what the upheaval did to "our business!"[60]

Officials, in turn, questioned the amount of losses incurred by east-side merchants. Perhaps because Recorder's Court judges sensed that the City of Detroit might be liable for riot-related de-

struction and theft, they cross-examined retailers about their figures. When, for example, Albert Holbrook testified that rioters ab-
sconded with $20,000 worth of merchandise from his pawnshop
on Oakland Avenue, Judge John J. Maher noted that stock of
$6,000 and loan balances of $8,500 fell rather short of that total.
He concluded, perhaps too sweepingly, that businessmen inflated
their losses.[61] On another occasion, Judge Maher informed Hastings Street store owner Simon Shifman that estimating his loss of
shoes as "a few thousand dollars" meant very little and insisted
that he provide an exact figure.[62] Clearly, he revealed concern that
merchants, themselves victims of disorder, might endeavor to vic-
timize insurers and taxpayers alike.

Possibly some did, but others did not, and none of them received municipal compensation. Like Benjamin Levine, who last
took inventory six months earlier for income-tax purposes, many
merchants did not know the size or worth of their stock.[63] And,
perhaps because others could not fix the exact cost of damage to
their stores, they inflated the worth of their merchandise.[64] Many
retailers recovered "several thousand dollars worth of loot," because bluecoats caught some thieves red-handed, and black neighbors reported others, and this further reduced their losses and
compounded the problem of counting them accurately.[65] Additional complications arose for grocers whose pork loins, cheeses,
and even canned goods—"perishables"—were retrieved by officers and given to Receiving Hospital rather than left to spoil.[66]
Operating small, often family-type, cash-only establishments, many
merchants, regardless of their specific trade, probably estimated
their losses generously or, at the very least, in a way to protect their
livelihoods. Partly for these reasons, their figure of $2 million dif-
fered significantly from that of Detroit Police Department investigators, who cited property damages around $6,000 and mer-
chandise losses slightly over $330,000.[67]

One significant reason for this discrepancy is that police seriously underestimated these losses. Scores of east-side stores, whose
owners, like Isadora Cohen, claimed complete or extensive damage, did not even appear on the official list of buildings where malicious destruction of property occurred. In fact, of 101 addresses,

only one—a poolroom—stood on Hastings Street.[68] Equally startling, merchandise declared stolen by retailers and sometimes cor-
roborated by court evidence and testimony failed to be included in
the departmental report of looted businesses. On Hastings Street,
for instance, Simon Shifman said he lost $3,000 in footwear, and
police caught a looter with $60 worth of shoes, but investigators
placed their worth at $20.[69] Over on Beaubien Street, Baxos Saad
lost groceries he valued at $1,500, a figure agents reduced by one
third, while Rivard Street beer garden proprietor Cecilia Sorgman
identified $60 in stolen equipment and liquor that detectives later
recorded as $2.50.[70] Similar inconsistencies happened to shop-
keepers above Grand Boulevard, where Oakland Avenue pawn-
broker Albert Holbrook estimated purloined stock at $5,950, and
patrolmen recovered jewelry worth $50. Yet his losses appeared in
the final police report as $700.[71]

Apparently merchants suffered because of peculiar and incon-
sistent police methods and incomplete data presented by the department. Only cases involving arrests for malicious destruction of
property, breaking and entering, or entering without breaking became part of the official report, explaining why retailers who
claimed damage and theft found their businesses filed with one or
the other, but rarely both charges.[72] Hence Isadora Cohen's dry-
goods store was not listed among destroyed businesses. Why investigators undervalued items, like Simon Shifman's shoes, even after
court testimony verified their worth, is inexplicable. In some instances when looters, caught inside stores like that of Bernard
Eiseman on Hastings Street, dropped the valuables they were
holding, lawmen considered them empty-handed and reported no
loss to the retailer.[73] On other occasions, when thieves jettisoned
loot if apprehended outside shops—again like that of Cohen's on
Hastings Street—detectives included its price in their tally.[74] Perhaps most puzzling, police noted exact dollar figures for the booty
of a specific, convicted looter, but often estimated much larger
amounts for the theft of unknown perpetrators still at large.[75]
Sometimes they disregarded sums for known thieves and approxi-
mated values for unidentified robbers of the same store, such as
that of Abraham Clover on Oakland Avenue.[76] Clearly officials un-

dervalued the losses of east-side merchants, excluded or ignored damage and theft to additional Paradise Valley stores, and provided no data on destruction done along Woodward Avenue by white rioters.[77] And although most but not all riot-related cases had been adjudicated by the date of police department tabulations in late July, bluecoats presented incomplete figures.[78] Their report notwithstanding, over 300 ghetto stores lost much more than $330,000 in inventory.

Given the merchants' failure to extract compensation from the City of Detroit, their collective losses were never verified. Retailers—as well as some citizens who were injured, lost a loved one or personal property—raised the question of municipal repayment, sometimes within days of the disturbance.[79] Their requests sparked expressions of both support and opposition, some white residents, black editors, and liberal unionists urging assistance of some kind to all victims, and more conservative, even blatantly prejudiced, individuals arguing otherwise.[80]

Private opinion aside, proprietors needed to convince Mayor Jeffries of the city's "liability or authority" for recompense. Quickly they learned that no legal responsibility existed, at least according to corporation counselor judgments.[81] Their claims proved as futile before council members, who followed counselor and, doubtlessly, mayoral advice in determining Detroit's official position.[82] Both individual and test cases, whether presented by Joseph Siade, the Detroit Retail Grocers Association, or the East Side Merchants Association, fell short despite arguments—that the police failed to provide adequate protection during the disorder and that the city bore a "moral duty" to restore riot losses. Best articulated by Samuel J. Lieberman of the east-side organization, business people raised concerns over their ability to pay increasing insurance rates and stay in business without inventory reimbursements. Lacking assistance, some shopkeepers would be forced to close, thereby creating "a negative, far reaching effect on future peace in the city." Hence they sought aid, and legislation to assure compensation should mayhem recur.[83] However, neither east-side association members seeking $500,000 nor Mamie T., who lost her son to police gunfire, swayed authorities. Mayoral appointees sympathized with victims in "a matter over which the City of Detroit had no control," but remained firm about their inability to "rectify this."[84] Unconvinced by such rhetoric, Lieberman's group of sixty-five store owners carried their grievance into the new year and, on the first anniversary of disorder, filed suit in the Wayne County Circuit Court.[85]

East-side merchants appeared to some observers—black and white—as victims of anti-Semitism.[86] Jewish pawnbrokers and liquor salesmen, the Wayne County prosecuting attorney confided privately, systematically fleeced black customers and, through their association, controlled "the leasing of stores to colored people."[87] Their "low down Hebrew tricks," complained another, presumably white critic, forced hundreds of gentile businesses "to the wall."[88] In other words, Jews operating in Paradise Valley provoked vandalism and looting—a black backlash—once riot began, which in turn, said some witnesses, sparked white attacks on black-owned shops.[89] Jewish residents, rumored outsiders as far away as North Carolina and New York, plotted with blacks to "wipe out certain patriotic people" who, instead, urged blacks to attack the stores of Jews.[90]

These allegations by black newsmen, government officials, and knee-jerk anti-Semites emanated from personal motivations and the history of black-Jewish relations in east-side Detroit. Perhaps journalists were seeking sensational stories and authorities cover for "their own failures," while more assuredly bigots searched for simplistic, even preposterous confirmation.[91]

Everyone's knowledge of the past reinforced both motives and prejudgments, for Jews and blacks had shared ghetto experiences since the late nineteenth century. Small numbers of Germans of Reformed Judaism and native black urbanites had settled in Detroit's lower east side, where they were joined by later influxes of Orthodox Russian Jews and Southern black sharecroppers. Despite internal class and cultural differences, by 1920 each group had created largely homogeneous religious and racial communities. These Jewish communities, increasingly Russian in origin, were more urbanized and educated than the black newcomers; they invested in real estate and soon owned apartments and businesses throughout Paradise Valley. Struggling blacks were forced to patronize these, while the landlords moved their own residences beyond Grand Boulevard. Well-heeled blacks also had established homes elsewhere—in the west side and at Eight Mile Road—but it was principally Jews who returned daily to collect rents or sell merchandise along Hastings Street and its confines. This was the situation at the time depression and war sparked a new in-migration of Southerners.

Those contending that the riot revealed both black anti-Semitism and Jewish racism possibly recalled depression experiences, only a few years in the past. Blacks, who had less education and fewer skills than most other Detroiters, had suffered even greater economic hardship than their white neighbors, especially the Jews, who were largely self-employed and recorded smaller jobless rates than the average for all workers. More recently, actions by some greedy Jewish slumlords and shopkeepers had been reported in the press and standard anti-Semitic propaganda had been circulated by black nationalists, Nazi sympathizers, and Klan members. Intergroup cooperation between black and Jewish leaders like the Rev. Charles A. Hill and Samuel J. Lieberman notwithstanding, east-side looting was interpreted by some observers as acts of anti-Semitism, in part provoked by Jewish shylocks and created by recent black-Jewish conflict.[92]

Undoubtedly such clashes did exhibit serious anti-Semitic tensions, and Jewish merchants stood among the victims of riot. Yet it took more than black anti-Semitism and Jewish racism to explain shopkeeper experiences. Consider the representative case of Mendel Shifman who had come to the United States from Russia (via Canada) in 1919 and opened a dry-goods store at 2615 Hastings Street two years later. An Orthodox Jew from a large, close-knit family, he lived in the east side for several years, while it was largely Jewish in composition, and moved his home beyond the ghetto as it developed into a black community. His son Aaron, born in 1924 and involved in the small family business, remembered black patrons becoming increasingly numerous and, after 1930, black proprietors opening area stores (though other Jewish entrepreneurs remained their major competitors). Shifman hired both black and white help, gave credit rarely and only to longtime customers in need, and dealt personally with occasionally drunk or unruly shoppers. Sometimes Aaron Shifman chased a petty thief up and down east-side alleys—"a game"—but Mendel experienced few serious encounters and avoided calling policemen. He served honest, steady customers, who provided him with a good living and, during the upheaval, called him, tried to save his store windows, and escorted his son to safety when he came to inspect the premises. Reopening quickly afterward, he remained on location for another six years.[93]

Other Jewish merchants recorded similar experiences shortly before the disturbance. Surveyed by Wayne State University students under the supervision of sociologist Donald C. Marsh, they dispelled several prevalent notions and, along with white gentile and black respondents, gave pause to merchant-customer conflict on Hastings Street, Oakland Avenue, and Warren Avenue (near the black west side). Of 150 proprietors of all backgrounds, Jews did not monopolize business in any of the districts (which had experienced significant black ownership since the late 1930s). Nor did they open stores on Hastings Street and Oakland Avenue because of beliefs that black shoppers were "easy marks." Rather, Jewish store owners had chosen east-side locations when their co-religionists lived there. Now none of them resided in the Hastings Street area, but neither did 75 percent of the black merchants questioned. And like them, Jewish retailers indicated the same level of satisfaction with black customers. Though few Jews or white gentiles extended credit to their clientele, they did so more often than black tradesmen. Jewish storekeepers, as verified by price surveys, also charged lower prices than their black and white gentile competitors. Neither their rivalry with black shopkeepers nor their hiring of black and white employees led to discord.[94]

Perceptions of Jewish merchants were reinforced by Jews beyond and blacks within the ghetto. In comparison to white gentiles, Jews—of whatever occupation—were far more often willing to reject racist stereotypes and showed far greater tolerance for contacts, personal and impersonal, with blacks. They also reported pleasant relationships with domestics, customers, and neighbors.

Fully 75 percent of 191 respondents also believed themselves obligated to treat blacks—fellow victims of persecution—well. In somewhat smaller percentages, black adults and black youths, respectively comprising 150 and 225 of those surveyed, said they enjoyed pleasant relationships or fair treatment from Jewish employers and landlords, and half of the teenagers admitted that Jews treated them better than did white gentiles.

In addition both the preriot survey, funded by the Jewish Community Council and the Detroit NAACP, and the testimony of Jewish merchants identified most troublemakers as strangers (rather than regular customers). So did a postriot survey, again conducted by Professor Marsh. Proprietors served steady customers, a fact verified by over 40 percent of the black adult respondents and by several instances of black clients who endeavored to protect the stores of Jewish merchants or warned their owners to stay home during the riot.[95] Largely because black patrons were careful to write "Negro" on their windows and to stand guard over their establishments, Jewish shopkeepers believed that it was outsiders—not patrons and neighbors—who damaged and looted east-side stores. They discovered "personal friends" among black clients, as well as those who identified with Jewish insecurity and risked bodily harm.[96] Moreover, when looters were brought into court, owners rarely recognized them as customers. Neither Harry Bornoty nor Bernard Eiseman, for example, knew Roy S. or James S.[97] In the Oakland and Warren avenue districts, Jewish retailers kept their doors open during the upheaval, selling customers "iodine, bandages, and things like that," further exhibiting genuine personal relationships and explaining why they attributed the turmoil to causes other than themselves.[98]

Jewish and white gentile store owners endured almost identical experiences, in fact, which helped them dismiss the interpretation of the riot as anti-Semitic. White gentile proprietors also received the assistance of black customers and neighbors, as attested by court testimony and Professor Marsh's postriot survey. Of 106 retailers interviewed after the outburst, for instance, three fourths of the Jewish and white gentile owners said black patrons attempted to protect their stores and succeeded a quarter of the time. Some of them also served Warren Avenue customers during the riot.[99] White gentile shopkeepers recognized none of the defendants charged with destroying and stealing their property, and like Jewish merchants refused to blame patrons for their losses.[100]

Professor Marsh's surveys verified their beliefs, particularly for Jewish shopkeepers. His preriot study demonstrated that it was socioeconomic conditions that primarily affected black-Jewish conflicts and all customer-merchant relationships, including that of racial ownership. This was particularly prevalent in the Hastings Street area, where black and, even more so, Jewish proprietors experienced conflict with some of their more recent, little-known patrons. Oakland Avenue store owners endured less conflict, and in general it involved youthful street gangs rather than hard-working customers, and Warren Avenue entrepreneurs reported few confrontations of any kind with their largely middle-class clients.[101] Predictably then, merchants in Hastings Street stores incurred the greatest damage during the riot, while those operating on Oakland Avenue lost less and on Warren Avenue almost nothing. Essentially east-side class and riot patterns demonstrated the destabilizing effect of poor environment and changing populations on all social relations. Therefore, Jewish and white gentile shopkeepers who responded to the postriot survey believed themselves the victims of "roving 'stranger' mobs" who invaded and upset neighborhood stability, particularly in Paradise Valley below Grand Boulevard. They interpreted, as did Professor Marsh more eloquently, the destruction and theft of Hastings Street and Oakland Avenue establishments by unknown black mobs as "a symbolic attack on the white caste."[102]

Nevertheless, however much it was an interracial conflict rather than an anti-Semitic riot, the destruction of stores did occur on east-side thoroughfares, not just "in any densely populated area" of Detroit, and did manifest black-Jewish strain.[103] Certainly Marsh recognized and explained the latter in cultural, class, and commercial terms, instead of purely racial or ideological ones, aware that these relationships aggravated the riot but hardly caused it.[104] He noted that Jewish shopkeepers, often foreign born, urbanized, and educated, considered newly arrived customers from Southern

rural backgrounds as unsophisticated and undisciplined, even vio-
lence-prone. Coming from close-knit families and socioreligious
communities, Jews compared blacks to themselves and to their
own way of life and naturally found the latter wanting: weak family ties, aggressive personalities, night-life behavior. Blacks, stereotyped one Hastings Street proprietor, lived to fulfill "their hunger,
thirst, and sexual desire." They, in turn, mocked the European
"language, accent, and gestures" of Jewish merchants and mis-
understood their initial price as final, rather than as the first of
several gambits in "an ancient bargaining ritual." Similarly, domestics considered the demands of Jewish housewives as their
actual expectations. Ever mindful of subordinate caste positions,
which never permitted haggling over prices or tasks in the South,
blacks resented what seemed unreasonable, stereotypical Shylock
behavior.[105]

Lower caste also connoted lower class, for customers experienced less status than proprietors in commercial relationships,
particularly in areas of great poverty and unstable populations.
Jewish store owners and black clientele, admitted Marsh, found it
difficult to develop "positive and constructive relationships" along
Hastings Street, where the struggle for existence proved so harsh
and recent memories of economic depression so bitter. Even in
more socially stable and economically prosperous districts like
Oakland and especially Warren avenues, Professor Marsh found
business settings that assigned Jews a superior status and blacks an
inferior one—and reinforced respective stereotypes of money
grabbing creditors and shiftless debtors. Commercial contacts, in
other words, provided a poor context in which to introduce or
maintain intergroup relations. Blacks sensed their inferior position acutely. Some believed Jewish retailers were powerful enough
to give or withhold the "necessities of life."[106]

Despite what appeared like anti-Semitism, Marsh attributed attacks on Jewish-owned shops—indeed on all white-owned shops—
by black rioters as primarily symptomatic of their socioeconomic
position in a racially defined caste system. Jewish proprietors were
struck more because they represented white dominance than because of their Judaism.[107] Since Jews had settled the east side be-

fore blacks came and still retained control of its commercial ventures, they seemed to ghetto dwellers to be responsible for their plight. Their white presence and proximity became "a logical peg upon which to hang" black resentments.[108] During the riot, they served as convenient, vulnerable targets for angry blacks, who envisioned all white property as a racial "badge" or "symbol" marked for destruction and theft.[109] Many black rioters failed to distinguish between Jew and gentile store owners, referring to all white shopkeepers as "Jews." This reduced a very complicated issue to the simplest of erroneous explanations, a "principle parsimony," as Marsh called it, which ignored the interaction of ethnicity, environment, and economics.[110] Certainly, once riot came, the long history of mixed relations and black-Jewish conflict sharpened east sider aggression. Jewish shopkeepers drew both the wrath of strangers and the protection of customers—contradictory actions expressing the ghetto's diversity and the riot's intricacy.[111]

If community surveys (and court testimony) "exploded" the myth of Jewish traders as Shylocks, they also clarified beliefs about black merchants.[112] Black shopkeepers played an increasingly important role on Hastings Street, Oakland and Warren avenues during the five years before upheaval when many of them opened for business. They enjoyed superior status among east siders, one reason for locating their businesses there while living elsewhere, usually in the black west side or above Grand Boulevard. Oakland Avenue proprietors, few of whom had previous experience, operated the most successful businesses of all and, in the process, belied the stereotype that black entrepreneurs failed for want of commercial training. Operating stores even smaller than Jewish "mama and papa" operations and concentrating on personal services, black shopkeepers charged the highest prices and issued the least credit of all retailers. Nonetheless, they recorded greater satisfaction with both their locations and their customers than did white store owners. They also rated "customer honesty" higher. There was some commercial friction and envy. Even though black shoeshine operators, restaurateurs, and the like did not compete directly with larger, more prosperous haberdashers, grocers, and liquor store proprietors, they resented what they perceived as unfair advantages. Ironically, blacks who operated the same businesses as whites and on relatively equal bases expressed much less conflict. In part commercial and customer relationship displayed racial identification, yet black shopkeepers—like white ones, Jewish or gentile—registered greater problems with transient, lower-class clients in the Hastings Street area than with the more stable customers on Oakland and Warren avenues.[113]

While black shopkeepers were hit nowhere near as hard by the riot as Jewish and white gentile merchants, they did become both victims and beneficiaries of the disorder. Fewer black proprietors incurred the wrath of rioters, who spared outlets bearing window signs saying "colored" or "Negro."[114] Some who found their stores wrecked and looted, might have failed to identify them in time or, like S. C. Gibbon, part owner of the Cut Rate Furniture Store on Hastings Street, failed to convince looters that they were the proprietors.[115] Or possibly, they seemed to class-conscious rioters to deserve their fate, since many looters believed themselves exploited by all entrepreneurs and resented well-to-do black tradesmen. Just as race marked white shopkeepers as victims, socioeconomic standing identified some black ones. However, black retailers generally found themselves in a potentially stronger economic position after the riot, since several Jewish and white gentile retailers moved out of their east side and west side locations because of financial losses or fear of more violence.[116] Existing and new black retailers replaced the departing competition and stood to reap its profits.

Nevertheless, a handful of black merchants suffered greatly and gained little, if at all, from prospects of expansion. J. Cole, for example, was sitting in his shop when a brick smashed through the window, followed by patrolmen who might have hurled it and, for no reason, marched him to the police station. There he was kept standing with his hands raised for two and a half hours, shared one large cell and one broken toilet with 260 other so-called rioters, and slept on the floor before being released.[117]

More directly, Clarence Sharpe found himself drawn into the maelstrom out of fear for his wife's safety. The forty-eight-year-old restaurant operator lived on the corner of Winder and Brush.

Unaware of the disorder, he walked to his Hastings Street café on June 21 and, realizing what was happening, decided to take his first day off in five years. He rested at home with his ailing wife until midafternoon, then returned to his business, which had been neither broken into nor looted, and gathered soup and pork chops for dinner, and returned home. Shortly before 8:00 P.M., he heard warnings that a white mob was approaching. He dashed outside with a .45 caliber pistol, terrified that his wife could not be moved to safety. He joined large numbers of blacks on the corner and stared across the one-block chasm at crowds of bloodthirsty whites. Urged by frightened neighbors to "scare them back," he fired one shot into the air and was apprehended quickly by a police officer. Sharpe pleaded not guilty to carrying a weapon with unlawful intent and later convinced Recorder's Court Judge John J. Maher of his innocence. Possessing a registered gun, facing a hostile mob, having never been arrested before, he seemed a victim of circumstance. His ordeal laid bare the anguish of many blacks, who appeared on police blotters and in the public's mind as rioters but, in reality, committed acts of self-defense.[118]

Sharpe was fortunate. Napoleon M. was not. Forty-three years old, married, and the father of one child, he had arrived from Florida seventeen years earlier with an eighth-grade education. Now he operated a grocery store at the corner of Theodore and St. Aubin streets, along the ghetto's western border, from which he earned a monthly income of $160. Shortly after noon on the first day of riot, he confronted several "white hoodlums" bearing bricks and baseball bats outside his market, and when they refused to disband, he fired an automatic pistol repeatedly. Unintentionally he killed Sally Grabowski, an innocent pedestrian. Napoleon M.'s story of the shooting varied, one version saying that the white youths accosted him inside the store, another stating that they approached him in the street, and still a third claiming that a driver, who appeared armed, struck his car outside the store and that he had shot in self-defense. He also contended that several shots were discharged simultaneously, and it was someone else's bullet that penetrated the woman's skull, but several white witnesses in the mixed neighborhood said that he had entered the thoroughfare firing in the direction of Grabowski. Perhaps because he had been arrested three times before and because of the seriousness of his crime, he was judged guilty of manslaughter and sentenced from two and a half to fifteen years in prison.[119]

Actually Napoleon M. benefited from the compassion of Recorder's Court Judge Joseph A. Gillis, who considered him "an example of citizens who try to take the law into their own hands." Hence he stood trial for manslaughter, not murder, and received a court recommendation for only two and half years incarceration. However irresponsibly, he had endeavored to protect himself, his livelihood, and probably his home, since he lived above his store. He might well have seen in the eyes of white toughs the end of his wartime prosperity—even of life itself. Reacting to an outburst of someone else's making, he had victimized an unoffending Polish shopper and himself.

Calamity also struck many persons wrongly treated as rioters by lawmen and justices. Seven hundred and eleven individuals (nearly 40 percent of all arrests) were discharged without prosecution.[120] Some of these might have engaged in actual riot, but many must have been rounded up by heavy-handed blue coats, purely out of blatant disregard for their civil liberties. Black roomers of My Hotel, located downtown in the lower east side at 410 Clinton Street, endured physical and verbal abuse when patrolmen raided the apartment building at 7:30 P.M. on June 21. Rousted from beds, bullied to the street, lined up, and searched, they were then marched—some in nightshirts and bare feet—to Beaubien Station. Louis Gabbins remained in custody for nearly a week, apparently without being charged, while John Smith stayed in jail for over three days, having been accused of "running a red light" though he neither owned nor had ever driven a car.[121] Their experiences typified those of other boarders, just as that of John Lewis portrayed the tribulations of many others who never faced arrest. Dressed in his Army uniform, he left home early in the day to enjoy a movie and traveled from above Grand Boulevard to Brush and Brewster streets. Grabbed from behind and pummeled to the pavement by one of several officers dispersing east siders, he ultimately made his way to Receiving Hospital. Perhaps Lewis's military dress, which symbolized black status and respectability, infuriated the police, who received little respect in the ghetto. In any event, according to witnesses, they attacked Lewis without cause.[122]

Black females experienced similar trauma, though fewer serious injuries or arrests. Residents of Frazer Hotel on Vernor Highway, for instance, drew the attention of state and local police, who converged on snipers in and near their building around 8:30 P.M. on June 21. Herded to the street, Cora Lee and Miss Brooks, her ninety-four-year-old roommate, stood with hands high near puddles of blood left by the slain bodies of black shooters and listened to vile language, "God damn niggers," as law officers ransacked and stole their belongings. Miss Brooks finally received permission to sit down, but was kept outdoors until close to midnight. In the midst of such scenes, an occasional black streetwalker, looking for action of quite another kind, was arrested like a common rioter.[123]

Many of those arrested—and often convicted of riot-related offenses—were also victims (though incomplete data makes their precise numbers impossible to determine).[124] Other black women entered the streets to protect family members, only to be arrested by policemen, who could hardly distinguish their intent from that of assailants. Sometime after 11:00 P.M. and long past the official curfew, Ella Mae H. left her apartment at 8794 Cardoni Street with a two-foot-long iron bar, which she carried "concealed against her clothing." Forty-eight-years-old, married, and employed as a domestic, she worked her way north, weaving through excited crowds and torn-up neighborhoods, and crossed Holbrook Street in front of a scout car. She attracted the attention of bluecoats, who arrested her without inquiring about her purpose or destination. In truth, Ella Mae H. was on her way to meet her sister arriving by streetcar and carried "part of her stove equipment" for protection. Perhaps because she toted the instrument openly, possessed no previous record, and profited from her sister's corroborating testimony, she was judged innocent. Still she endured incarceration and, eventually, had to post $2,500 bail money. Victimized by the circumstance of riot, she would ordinarily never have dashed to the DSR, violated an emergency decree, or packed a weapon.[125]

Aside from individuals like Ella Mae H., who were trying to protect loved ones during the outburst, several arrestees carried weapons and occasionally used them for self-defense. Police, responding to a truck driver's tip, flagged down Albert H.'s Checker Cab at 7:00 P.M. at Woodward Avenue and Adelaide Street. Thirty-seven years old, white, and married, the cabbie surrendered a revolver, while Robert P., his white passenger, yielded up a .300 Savage rifle. H. claimed to have bought the loaded revolver from Robert P., who had, only moments earlier, assured him of its registration. Both driver and passenger expressed their need for protection, Albert H. concerned about operating in the riot zone, and Robert P. anxious over his mother-in-law living on the east side, just above Grand Boulevard. Albert H. went free when prosecuting attorney and municipal judge dismissed his case, but Robert P. was given one year's probation and paid $100 court costs. Less victimized than Ella Mae H., they also responded emotionally to terrifying events and—perhaps because of their circumstance and race—received relatively lenient judicial treatment.[126]

Occasionally so did blacks like Samuel P., who became the target of crazed whites. Twenty-seven years old and single, he was returning from work at the Parkstone Apartments in Indian Village, north of Detroit, shortly before 8:00 P.M. on June 21 when he suddenly found himself accosted by several rioters at the Harper-Van Dyke DSR stop. Almost two miles from Paradise Valley's eastern border and three miles from his Euclid Street home north of that community, he retreated, firing two shots as thugs chased him in cars and on foot. He ran into police officers who, responding to reports of the shooting, struck him with a gun butt and kicked him several times. He lay in his own blood, needing first aid for a lacerated scalp and bruised ribs, while bluecoats allegedly stole his watch and empathized with bloodthirsty mob members who gathered on the scene wanting to "kill the Black So-and-So." Arrested for carrying a concealed weapon, he sat in jail while local newspapers reported his having been shot in the head, and homicide detectives refused his sister information about his condition or whereabouts.[127]

Samuel P. must have been shocked by his encounter. Born in

Jacksonville, Florida, and raised in Detroit, he worked as a receiving clerk, earned $25 weekly, paid taxes, and belonged to the local NAACP. He enjoyed a close relationship with his sister, Dorothy, who complained bitterly about his injuries. His story was that someone on the streetcar, seeing the mob approach, handed him the unregistered .22 caliber pistol, but this probably swayed magistrates less than his clean record and his mistreatment by patrolmen. P. received only two years' probation, which he served without incident. Whatever the origins of Samuel's weapon, he was surely more victim than assailant.

Some looters were arrested because of sheer bad luck, having shown up in the wrong place at the wrong time. Isaiah J., a twenty-five-year-old, Montgomery, Alabama, native who had arrived in Detroit in 1941 with two sisters and a tenth-grade education, found steady employment and flush wages—$70 weekly—at Ford Motor Company. He married and began a family within one year of arriving, and was living on Theodore Street when the riots started. Around suppertime on June 21, he walked to Louis Thomas's grocery store at 5047 Beaubien Street and entered it through the rear door. Inside he came upon more than half a dozen people, including fifty-three-year-old laborer Dee G., himself a married, employed, nine-year resident of the city. Within seconds of his arrival, Isiah J. heard someone holler "Law!" as a police sergeant entered the store and, while others fled, apprehended him and Dee G. Empty-handed yet caught in the store with its rear door wide open, front window partially smashed, and floor strewed with bacon, ham, and cheese, he received two years' probation for entering without breaking.[128]

Isaiah J. hardly seemed like a deliberate thief or even a spontaneous looter. He had lived in the neighborhood for two years and, according to the proprietor who knew him, his wife, and his mother-in-law as customers, he shopped in Thomas's grocery "practically every day."[129] He knew about the riot, but entered the store through its open back door, as he and everyone living on Theodore Street was accustomed to doing, unaware of the break-in or the owner's absence. Seeing others loot, he did not join in but turned back to the alley just as the policeman entered the store.

He knew none of the others inside, had no police record more serious than traffic violations, and believed himself innocent of any
wrongdoing.

Dee G. also innocently appeared in the wrong place at the wrong
time. He and his second wife came from St. Louis, Missouri, in
1935, leaving behind his ninety-seven-year-old mother, brother,
sister, and the youngest of seven children from a first marriage
that ended with his wife's death. His children ranged from eleven
to twenty-three years of age; all were married except the eleven-
year-old in Missouri, two were serving in the Army, and none was
living at home. He and his present wife of several years had no
children of their own, but cared for four orphans between the
ages of four and eight. Illiterate yet employed for $50 weekly by a
scrap dealer, who vouched for his "good reputation," G. lived on
Theodore Street and patronized Thomas's store. He too entered
the grocery by the rear door during the riot as people—customers, he thought—were coming and going. He intended to "buy
something" but took nothing and stood empty-handed when arrested with Isaiah J. Although he did not know the younger defendant, he was well known by the grocer. He had lived around the
corner for two years and had worked at his trucking job for four.
He was well liked by his employer, who accompanied him to court
and wanted him back at work. For these reasons, the absence of
previous violations, and the similarities with Isaiah J., he also drew
only two years probation.[130]

Despite their differences in age and education, these two defendants shared much in common and no doubt represented other
east-side married men. Both came from Southern and border
states and urban backgrounds, and apparently adjusted easily to
industrial society. They enjoyed stable family relationships, both as
children and adults—in Dee G.'s case, to the point of adopting an
orphan family. They worked hard and were law-abiding, and, predictably, they received favorable probation releases from the courts.
And yet, like untold numbers of others caught up in the disorder,
Isaiah J. and Dee G. went down in official and news reports as hard-
case felons deserving their fates.

Several misdemeanants had similar experiences, and in the official statistics became rioters and hoodlums, riffraff, and Southerners of the public stereotype. Lee J. was one of them. When a squad car halted in front of his Winder Street address at midafternoon during the first day of turmoil, he never expected to be arrested. He was unarmed and at home, one block north of Vernor Highway and within three blocks of Woodward Avenue, where gangs of white youths roamed. A married home owner, forty-four-years old, he was prepared to protect his family and house from "invaders." He had resided in Detroit since 1937 and worked at Briggs Manufacturing Company, abiding by the laws—he claimed never to have been in trouble before, though police reported one previous arrest—and doing whatever possible "for the war effort." Nevertheless, police charged him with disturbing the peace. Considering his background, his unarmed status, and circumstances— not to mention police behavior that day—he seemed guilty only of expressing fear for his family and property. He served eighty days in the Detroit House of Correction and was released early for "good time"—indicating anew an upright rather than a criminal personality.[131]

Howard G. shared a similar fate, although it ended more fortunately. On Monday morning, standing on the corner of Hancock and Beaubien, near the epicenter of the violence and far from home, he looked every bit a hoodlum to bluecoats who arrested him for disturbing the peace. He became, in the words of lawmen, "very violent and abusive," but aggressive behavior seemed wholly out of character to fellow defense workers, who knew G. as "a very mild man." "The very thought of his participation in any overt act," wrote the secretary of Ford Local 600, was "ridiculous." Twenty-eight years old and married, he had merely been watching the police disperse crowds for reportedly stoning motorists when an officer "insisted" that he be arrested. Howard G. fared well before jurors, who believed his testimony over that of policemen and judged him innocent of all accusations.[132]

Howard G.'s ordeal showed that innocent and guilty alike could expect to be swept up in police dragnets—handicapped persons not excepted. Thirty-seven-year-old James G., an employed truck driver, happened upon a patrolman and several state troopers at

1 : 20 A.M. on the second day of the disturbance. Deaf and mute, he could not explain his presence on Hastings Street after the curfew or the 4-inch knife he carried in his pocket. He possessed no record and threatened no one as he was returning from work. Found guilty of carrying a concealed weapon during racial unrest, he was placed on probation for two years and, before completing the sentence, released to join his wife and five children in New York City.[133]

In what his lawyer called "a moment of terror" for all Detroiters, James G. faced special difficulties. A newcomer who had arrived only four months earlier from New York City, he did not know the legal length for carriable blades. He neither heard nor spoke, communicating only by reading and writing, skills taught him in the New York School for the Deaf, and hence, when stopped for violating the curfew, he had no way of indicating that he was returning from work and therefore legally exempt from the curfew. If not for the riot, James G. never would have been stopped, much less searched and arrested.[134]

Less innocently, other hearing-impaired rioters acted aggressively. Elry T., a partially deaf black youth, was cornered by patrolmen in an east-side loan office and killed for verbally threatening them from behind a difficult-to-see hiding place. By contrast three white mutes paid little price for their violence.[135] James N., Edward T., and Virgil G. joined the Woodward Avenue gang that overturned and burned the 1941 Ford sedan of John Jarrett. Responding to the excitement of an interracial fight, they "just entered into it." Charged with malicious destruction of property, they initially pleaded innocent but later admitted their guilt and drew one-year probations. Unquestionably treated leniently because of their disability and possibly their race, they served no prison time and paid no property damages (though the automobile's value exceeded $425).[136]

Although their escapades occurred on the first day of outburst, James N., Edward T., and Virgil G. eluded arrest for four days before someone recognized N. in newspaper photographs, and then he identified his friends.[137] All three lived very near the riot scene at Davenport and Woodward, cheek by jowl with blacks and, except for T. who earned $50 weekly at Ford Motor Company, held lower-paying, nondefense jobs for a laundry and candy company. Two of them had high-school diplomas and the third, Virgil G., had attended classes through the sixth grade; they communicated by sign language and handwriting. Seventeen, twenty, and twenty-eight years of age and single, they came to Detroit in search of employment. Tennessean Virgil G., the youngest, arrived in February 1942, and Michigander Edward T. appeared five months later, neither as established as three-year-resident Coloradan James N., the oldest. How much regional, religious, and cultural baggage they brought with them is uncertain, but Virgil G. and Edward T. were Protestants and James N. a Catholic Greek of the first generation.[138]

Beyond the emotional appeal of bloodlust, then, these three deaf-mute rioters entered the fray for reasons of race and status. Living in the Woodward corridor, they knew of contested housing; working as tool-and-die maker, Edward T. must have been aware of shop conflicts over the issue of upgrading blacks, while as clothes presser and common laborer respectively, James N. and Virgil G. may well have felt the economic-racial rivalry keenly. Handicapped or not, they shared the prejudices and fears of other whites, particularly those in close proximity and direct competition with blacks. Usually law-abiding and never previously arrested, they expressed, in a flash of action on Woodward Avenue, deep-seated anger and anxiety, and they did so as white males rather than as disabled persons, again signaling the disorder's decidedly racial dimension.

Race and class distinctions further victimized riot participants, especially if black, in overt and subtle ways. Early in the riot, Mayor Jeffries condemned as "unpatriotic" all rioters, curiosity seekers, and fun lovers who had sparked the violence or interfered with official efforts to restore order. The shameful events were "not 'fun'—not for anyone but the Nazi and the Jap," he admonished all Detroiters as the race war raged out of control.[139] And while the mayor was envisioning witless saboteurs in search of good times, other public figures also called into question the character and motivation of those who engaged in riot.

Shortly after the upheaval was quelled, Dr. Lowell S. Selling declared publicly that feebleminded black newcomers had fallen prey to "distinctly anti-white" propaganda circulated by a pro-Japanese organization, and white country boys, rejected by selective service for "psychopathic failings," had exercised their race prejudice.[140] He and local journalists pushed his opinion as proved medical diagnosis and stigmatized all rioters. Meanwhile, he completed arrangements for his investigation with the Recorder's Court, whose judges referred 23.5 percent of all accused felons for psychological examinations and, in the very act of doing so, reinforced Selling's thesis.[141]

State and local investigators employed similar middle-class yardsticks. State prison researchers Elmer R. Akers and Vernon Fox, for example, selected "venereal condition" and "drug addiction" as variables for their comparison of riot and nonriot prisoners. Their choice clearly indicated a prejudgment of riot participants, the underlying assumption being that troublemakers consisted largely of lower-class, maladjusted hoodlums. Their confirmation that "a very high proportion of common-law relationships" existed among the rioters reinforced the racial, regional, and cultural perspective of Selling.[142] Similarly, social workers considered such marriages less than satisfactory. Women's Division Supervisor Vemba M. Dunlap of the Detroit Department of Probation, for one, judged Mary P. an individual "with low standards of personal relationship." Dunlap regarded Mary P.'s most recent legally recognized marriage as acceptable, but that was insufficient to offset her earlier attachments. The supervisor seemed incapable of understanding the cultural norms that took such unions for granted or of appreciating the caring and stable relationships that Mary P. had established, living with one man for eleven years before leaving him and joining another common-law husband until his death five years later.[143]

Investigators victimized rioters by impugning, if not ridiculing, their life-styles. They seemed primarily critical of blacks, those farthest removed from their own mores and most numerous among their cases. They focused their studies on alien class traits that blurred distinctions among rioters and made them appear as homogenous misfits. The cases they studied no doubt did include "socially maladjusted" lifetime recidivists and antisocial loners like fifty-year-old Duke B. and thirty-seven-year-old James G., the deaf mute, who might well have possessed low intelligence.[144] But they also included hard-working, loving fathers and honest aunts such as Nelson B. (see Chapter 2) and Edna A., who avoided trouble for thirty-nine years, worked steadily for twenty years, resided in Detroit for fourteen years, and, most recently, paid for the boarding-house care of a six-year-old niece. Neither Nelson B. nor Edna A. carried police records into the disorder, and both were apparently victims of circumstance. Edna A. was curious, "thinking there was no harm in looking around" a Hastings Street store that others had broken into.[145] Researchers also observed teenagers like Frank N., and emphasized all the negatives. Selling, for instance, recorded that Frank N.'s mother separated from his natural father and married his stepfather, who despite a drinking problem supported the family well and was worshipped by the stepson. Instead of stressing these facts, the father's honesty, or the "family circle," he concluded that Frank N., one of those who assailed Gus Niarhos on Belle Isle, suffered from "beginning alcoholism" and "a broken home background."[146]

Most victims, in sum, fell into several categories and represented every constituency imaginable. Regardless of race, gender, or class, physical or other impairments, civilian or military status, they and their families endured the riot experience without relief—and soon were forgotten. In contrast a handful of the most celebrated rioters sought redress for having been mistreated—indeed, they insisted, victimized—by authorities. Their claims carried into the future, keeping alive memories of race war and questions of police ethics.

FIVE

Causes Célèbres

Startlingly—some might have said deservingly—a couple of the most notorious rioters found themselves victims of zealous, angry officials. Aaron F. and Aldo T., the highly publicized killers of innocent, upstanding Detroiters, both claimed they were framed by detectives, prosecutors, and judges for crimes committed by others. They—one young black man, one white—and supporters moved from individual redress to collective crusade, ironically closing ranks behind an interracial, interreligious freedom effort. In the process, their causes célèbres detailed both the retribution and the compassion fostered by hostile outbreak.

Aaron F. faced court examination in December 1943 for the murder of Dr. Joseph De Horatiis, fully six months after it occurred and nearly five months after his arrest for accosting Gus Niarhos. Belatedly identified by neighborhood youths, he allegedly charged the physician's sedan on Hendrie Street and crushed his skull with a piece of concrete. He emerged, testified witnesses, from a nearby, missile-throwing crowd that struck the automobile, forcing it out of control and finally to stop. He hit his prey deliberately and at point-blank range, said those who knew him. Singled out by Cleveland R. and five other teenagers as "the last person" to assail the doctor, Aaron F. was charged with murder, remanded without bail, and held for trial.[1] He soon stood before three psychiatrists, including Dr. Lowell S. Selling, who judged him as having "no mental disorder or ailment which would impair his responsibility."[2]

Given these legal and psychological proceedings, Aaron F. entered the courtroom on March 1, 1944, and, within two weeks, departed for Jackson State Penitentiary to serve from seven to twenty-five years for killing De Horatiis. His trial lasted only three days, and his all-white, female jurors deliberated less than seven hours, very much influenced by some of the same teenagers—Cleveland R., Ross C., and Reginald P.—who fingered him three months earlier. Aaron F. himself collapsed, for example, when sixteen-year-old Reginald P. stated under oath that he had originally tried to protect the defendant by lying to prosecuting attorneys. The Aaron F. family and several neighbors testified that he had been at home on Beaubein Street, watching from a window, when De Horatiis crashed around the corner. But jurors, disbelieving the family's story, found Aaron F. guilty of second degree murder. Recorder's Court Judge Joseph A. Gillis handed down the long sentence without recommending less than the maximum number of years in prison.[3]

Indignant at the verdict, Aaron F.'s mother, Beatrice B., began a long crusade to vindicate him. She employed a private investigator immediately after the trial, instructing him to scout the neighborhood for witnesses to the assault on De Horatiis. Although James Leveye of the Michigan Detective Bureau completed his work in October of 1944, she lacked the funds to pay for a copy of the court testimony, which cost $125, or for a lawyer to examine the new information and the existing record. Hence she worked and saved for nine months before hiring attorney Asher L. Cornelius in February 1944.[4]

Attorney Cornelius, impressed with Beatrice B.'s effort and probably horrified by her findings, quickly and successfully petitioned the court to clear the way for a belated new-trial motion.[5]

He contended that the court had committed several errors, such as calling the jury's attention to the charge of murder rather than to the question of Aaron F.'s guilt. He also challenged the testimony of witnesses for the prosecution and compared it with that of neighbors, six swearing that the defendant was home during the bloodshed and six more describing an older, larger male as De Horatiis's killer. Cornelius's most compelling arguments also lay in the discovery of "important new evidence" that "should effect" the outcome of a new trial.[6]

Having gained the right to file the motion for a new trial in April 1945, Cornelius then spent eight months arguing why the court should act favorably on it. He reiterated earlier concerns about court error, yet in much greater detail impugned the prosecutor's witnesses. Although the slaying of De Horatiis had occurred on June 21, on "a public street," "in plain sight of dozens of people" and, one might have added, in broad daylight, he noted that nobody was arrested or charged with murder "until the following November." Of those who stepped forward, in a court of law, and finally identified Aaron F. as the killer, four were "self-confessed juvenile delinquents" and, in the case of Ross C. and William P. who fleeced the pockets of De Horatiis as he lay dying, "self-confessed thieves."[7] Cornelius also knew that Cleveland R. had fought with F. twice before his arrest and threatened revenge, while Fred M., himself declared feebleminded by the Probate Court and among the rioters, was serving time in reform school. He knew still further that Reginald P., the only teenager without delinquency status, had changed his story, first denying F.'s presence at the scene of De Horatiis's death and then saying F. had struck him with a piece of concrete. Each of these witnesses suffered coercion and "physical violence in connection with this case."[8]

Cornelius enumerated his charges. He noted that, during the examination and trial, police maintained direct control of delinquents Fred M., Ross C., and William P., as well as probationer Cleveland R., and held Reginald P. incommunicado until he agreed to testify against Aaron F. In vulnerable positions, he added, they were bullied, paddled, and threatened by bluecoats.

Cornelius believed that this brutality, coupled with talk of perjury charges by the court, explained why Ross C., William P., and Reginald P. changed their testimony during the examination; they first denied seeing Aaron F. on June 21, 1943, then placed a rock in his hand before the prostrate body of De Horatiis. Similar harassment by officers and magistrate in the trial accounted for Reginald P.'s contradictory, frightened testimony, which only a private visit to the judge's chambers resolved in favor of Aaron F.'s guilt. Cornelius concluded that authorities committed "a fundamental error" by dismissing as lies the initial truthful statements of these youths. He also pointed out earlier that Fred M. merely claimed to have seen the defendant among those who threw missiles at De Horatiis's coupe, as opposed to his having been the physician's lone executioner. Hence only Cleveland R. presented a consistent story, albeit tainted by his grudge against F. and his inability to recognize anyone else in the crowded thoroughfare. And Cleveland R., hinted Cornelius, might have conspired with lawmen against the defendant.[9]

Conversely, Cornelius recognized as truthful the "disinterested witnesses" who advanced F.'s innocence and identified De Horatiis's killer. He described again Henry and Johnel Daniels, Maggie Mitchell, Anna Mae Woods (a second cousin to Reginald P.), and Mary Lou Young, who lived respectively with, across the hall, one floor below or next door to Beatrice B. and her family. All of them reported having seen Aaron F. looking out his front window at the time rioters waylaid the physician. Cornelius pressed even more forcefully the testimony of those, Anna Matthews and Ruby O'Neill, who observed the death blow delivered by "a tall, brown-skinned colored fellow" about "thirty-five years of age." "I know Aaron F.," summarized Carrie Woods who also saw the killer, "it was not him."[10]

Cornelius bolstered the court transcript with affidavits from Gertrude Grayson and Carter B. Nelson, eyewitnesses discovered after the first trial by the Michigan Detective Bureau. Standing with several other tenants on the front porch of 442 Hendrie Street, Grayson and Nelson watched as rock throwers caused the crash of De Horatiis's Chevrolet and a broad-shouldered man fitting the above description buried a piece of concrete in the Italian physician's face. They knew the suspect only as "Chi," reiterated Cornelius. Grayson recognized him as one who visited friends in the building and occasionally bought ice cream for a little girl who lived there, while Nelson verified his frequent presence around the apartment and thought he resided further north in the Brush-Medbury vicinity. Perhaps most startling, Nelson further depicted "Chi" as "a notorious character who lives in the sporting world," a fact seemingly ignored by Cornelius who focused on the existence—rather than the character—of a killer other than his client. Most important, five east siders, four of whom knew Aaron F., swore under oath that someone else killed the doctor.[11]

In addition to marshaling evidence of innocence, Cornelius stressed F.'s character and questioned the jury's motives. He described the defendant's education, religious faith, industrious work habits, and clean police record, someone incapable of the depravity necessary to strike a dazed victim in cold blood. Such a possibility, he contended, seemed "utterly incompatible and unbelievable" in light of Aaron F.'s personality and reputable eyewitness accounts. Against the testimony of "worthless and unreliable" prosecuting witnesses, these factors "should have been sufficient to create a reasonable doubt" in the minds of jurors. That they did not, asserted Cornelius, reflected the all-white jury's race prejudice: "an attitude that somebody must be punished for this race riot and it might just as well be Aaron F. as any other nigger."[12]

If prejudgment doomed his client in the first trial, Cornelius knew that only evidence would free him. He sought testimony supporting further the issue of untrustworthy and coerced witnesses for the prosecution. Hearing that Fred M. had lied in court, he visited F.'s accuser, who was serving a lengthy term in the State Reformatory at Ionia for armed robbery. He knew M. had looted during the riot and, after incarceration for that crime, had committed twenty-five additional thefts in his one month of freedom before being captured again. Now in late July 1945 Cornelius heard M. admit having testified falsely against Aaron F., a person he had never seen during the attack on De Horatiis. The lawyer's success in coaxing the seventeen-year-old recidivist to recant trial testimony greatly supported the motion for a new trial, all the more so in that Fred M. was induced to confess before a prosecuting attorney assigned to evaluate the motion. Like the affidavits of new witnesses, Fred M.'s disavowal gave prosecutors and magistrates much to consider.[13]

Nearly five months later, in mid-December, Cornelius's motion for a new trial received favorable action. Aaron F. was transferred from state prison to county jail, and community efforts coalesced for a speedy trial date.[14] Three months into 1946, Cornelius entered the Recorder's Court of Judge Gillis. There, armed with nearly two years of painstaking research and an array of new, sometimes surprising witnesses, he defended Aaron F. and discredited his accusers—including police investigators.

In pretrial briefs, Cornelius urged jurors to dismiss testimony of the first trial when prosecuting witnesses "willfully and intentionally testified falsely" and consider carefully forthcoming statements by those who perjured themselves earlier. Specifically, he noted that Ross C. and William P. contradicted themselves at the examination, while Reginald P. did so both there and at the first trial. Only the earlier testimony of Fred M., Cleveland R., and Raymond T., which simply placed Aaron F. on the scene as one of many participants, deserved reconsideration. And it, Cornelius knew, would be recanted during the new trial.[15]

Significantly, Cornelius also alerted jurors to the backgrounds of witnesses and the coercion they endured before testifying in the original case. Fred M. and Cleveland R. were only seventeen-years-old when they testified, while Ross C., William P., and Reginald P. did so at even younger ages. More "amenable and subject to fear" than adults—and all of them delinquents in official custody except Reginald P.—they gave in to police coercion and, said Cornelius, lied about having seen Aaron F. stone De Horatiis. Hence those then being held for other crimes—Ross C., William P., and Cleveland R.—later admitted having been threatened with prosecution should they refuse to identify Aaron F. as the killer. Fred M., Cornelius knew from firsthand experience, had undergone similar treatment. And, though he was not a wrongdoer himself, Reginald P. had been treated like one.[16] Approached by police after F.'s arrest, he told them of having seen the defendant looking out of his window at the time of the stoning. He then found himself labeled a liar, placed in the Juvenile Detention Home—where beatings were apparently common—and the following day questioned and paddled by detectives. He remained in custody three more days, browbeaten by investigators who refused to release him until he told the "truth" and threatened to make him a defendant in the case if he did not cooperate. When he balked on the witness stand during both the examination and the first trial, he endured further police harassment and finally, fearing for his own "personal liberty," testified against Aaron F. He perjured himself, repeating the tale spun for him by lawmen.[17]

While several police officers were coercing Reginald P. and his cowitnesses, forty-two-year-old Detective Lt. Charles Buckholdt was heading up the investigation of De Horatiis's murder. Perhaps, as a longtime resident of the city, he felt official and community pressure to solve the mystery and punish someone for the riot. Perhaps, as an eighteen-year-veteran of the Detroit Police Department, he sought to restore pride to fellow officers maligned for their handling of the riot. Perhaps, as a native Texan, he found Aaron F. fitting his Southern expectations of black criminality. Hence he identified Aaron F. as De Horatiis's killer within days of the crime, but released him for lack of witnesses.[18] Buckholdt continued the investigation into October when he apparently raised Aaron F.'s name with Ross C. (himself charged with stealing from the victim). He and fellow detectives then pressured Fred M., William P., Cleveland R., and Raymond T. to incriminate Aaron F. or face dire consequences. He employed outright coercion and evidently prompted Cleveland R. to tackle Fred M. about testifying against F.[19] Needing a non delinquent witness to corroborate the testimony of five delinquents, Buckholdt apprehended, isolated, and threatened Reginald P. until he signed a statement matching those already on file. In fact, he read the depositions to Reginald P., thereby ensuring agreement of all witnesses.[20]

Buckholdt and, wittingly or not, court officials shored up the people's case whenever prosecuting witnesses recanted such testimony. During the examination, Ross C. and William P. denied having seen Aaron F. on the day of De Horatiis's death, but Buckholdt and prosecuting attorney John W. Gilmore threatened them privately with perjury and recalled them publicly to retract such testimony. Their actions, if not tactics, received the support of Judge Christopher E. Stein, despite his having heard William P. testify to having given deposition "under force."[21] Similarly Buckholdt prevented Reginald P. from testifying in the examination, because he intended to contradict his own written statement. Only after threatening to hold the teenager indefinitely and charge him with De Horatiis's slaying did Buckholdt permit P. to testify. He repeated these heavy-handed tactics during Aaron F.'s first trial, for P. again expressed pangs of conscience. When P. testified to the defendant's innocence, Buckholdt reiterated the earlier threats and sent him to the judge's chambers, where Judge Gillis explained the charge of perjury, commenting on Reginald P.'s already being on probation and, if convicted of lying, subject to time at the Lansing School for Boys. Gillis also advised P. to tell what police called the "truth," and "more than likely" he would be released.[22]

Possibly detectives and magistrates alike considered corporal punishment of juveniles an accepted method of persuasion, one necessary for inducing them to tell the truth. Or perhaps they sought retribution for the disorder, knowing that Aaron F. and five of the six prosecuting witnesses both participated in and resembled those "hoodlums" responsible for it. More puzzling than police who paddled witnesses or prosecutors who informed jurors of F.'s Belle Isle activity, Judges Stein and Gillis accepted testimony from three witnesses who contradicted themselves (Reginald P. having done so in both examination and jury trial), while disregarding family and friends testifying for the defendant.[23] Ironically Stein meted out lenient sentences to participants in the Sojourner Truth Homes disturbance of 1942, and Gillis ran an unsuccessful mayoral campaign criticizing police excesses in 1941, possibly additional reasons for their hard-nosed roles in one of the most grisly riot killings.[24]

Although police and court officials rushed to judgment, Cornelius soon embarrassed and divided them and forced the release of Aaron F. on bail. He visited the Juvenile Delinquent Camp on

Cassidy Lake shortly before the new trial and interviewed Ross C., who admitted lying about F. and himself. He heard the now familiar story of police coercion: beating and threatening Ross C. and William P. to "come clean," admit their theft of De Horatiis, and finger F. as his killer. He heard also the equally familiar plea of innocence, for C. denied having robbed the doctor or seen the defendant on that fateful day. In order to substantiate C.'s disavowal of previous testimony, Cornelius also spoke with William P., who was no longer in custody. He listened as P. reiterated having neither been on the scene of De Horatiis's death nor having seen Aaron F. on June 21. Also like Ross C., William P. told of "days of riding and browbeating" by police, on one occasion Buckholdt twisted his arm so violently that "he suffered great pain." Relief came to C. and him only after they falsely admitted their own guilt and that of Aaron F., "what the officers claimed was the truth."[25] Cornelius knew that similar, though less legally binding renunciation came from Cleveland R., who approached Beatrice B. in the courthouse prior to the new trial and apologized for having lied about her son earlier; he did not see Aaron F. on the day in question, and had testified against him because of police threats.[26] Given these and the previous recantations of Reginald P. and Fred M., then, Cornelius possessed affidavits challenging every one of the testimonies that incriminated his client.

Perhaps because of the delinquent status of most prosecuting witnesses and the possibility of their disavowals being self-serving, Judge Gillis focused the new trial on Buckholdt's failure to present witnesses two years earlier. Yet the judge must have realized that Cornelius's investigations, however indirectly, brought his own handling of the first trial into question. He had seemed aware of—if not in cooperation with—Buckholdt's tactics; he had ignored Reginald P.'s complaints of police harassment and displayed no concern over the truthfulness or selfishness of delinquents willing to condemn Aaron F., often in return for their release from prosecution for riot-related crimes.[27] Moreover, Gillis now knew that Cornelius had uncovered witnesses—Carter B. Nelson and Gertrude Grayson—who described someone other than F. as the killer, and sought independent corroboration of their testimony.

As certainly Gillis must have felt betrayed by Buckholdt, for he interrupted the new trial on March 23, 1946, in its third day. He charged that the detective had withheld testimony by an eyewitness in the original case in order to "get a conviction" and now to prevent its overturn. The eyewitness was Arthur Johnson, whom Gillis himself had traced in one short hour, Buckholdt, the judge pointed out, had failed to do so in nearly two years and thus deprived both trials of "the best witness to be found." Gillis elaborated on Johnson's qualifications: a married, "all around honest American citizen," who had won a Distinguished Service Cross in World War I and, unlike most of the prosecuting witnesses, possessed no police record. Judge Gillis had also discovered that, five days after De Horatiis's death, Johnson had viewed a police lineup and told Buckholdt and a prosecuting attorney that Aaron F. was not the killer. Moreover, Johnson, while subpoenaed as a witness in the first trial, was never called to testify. At the time the judge had told Buckholdt how unfortunate it was that "we could not find any decent witnesses" (apparently forgetting friends and family who had testified to Aaron F.'s innocence), and noted now that Johnson had come forth in spite of the detective. "This case has smelled to high heaven all the way through," he blamed Buckholdt, declaring what blacks had been saying all along (though probably with Gillis in mind as much as the police officer). Shortly thereafter, he resumed the trial.[28]

Gillis presided over only one more day of trial, as startling testimony affirmed both Aaron F.'s innocence and Buckholdt's perfidy. Johnson, who had lived on Hendrie Avenue during the riot, joined Gertrude Grayson, Carter B. Nelson, and Chester A. Harris, a thirty-four-year-old black serviceman home on furlough during the riot, as principal witnesses. They, and other east siders, described De Horatiis's killer as tall, probably around six feet, broad-shouldered, and light-skinned, whom Harris identified on the scene as police arrived only to be threatened by the murderer: "Shut up, or I'll give you what I gave the doctor." In contrast Johnson pointed out that Aaron F. stood only 5 feet 7 inches and appeared dark-complexioned, while Grayson and Nelson again recognized the killer as "Chi." Others like Ira Grover "could identify him today," remembering vividly the heartless determination with which he killed De Horatiis. Just as significant for Aaron F.'s verdict, Reginald P., William P., and Fred M. testified to having been strong-armed by Buckholdt.[29] Their testimony acquired even greater impact when Sam T., father of Aldo T., the convicted assailant of black defense worker Moses Kiska, testified that during the first trial he overheard Buckholdt admonish one of the juveniles about to take the witness stand and identify Aaron F. as De Horatiis's killer: "Say what I told you." Sam T. recalled asking the detective, "Didn't you have time to school him before?" Buckholdt responded by turning "red in the face."[30]

Such courtroom drama climaxed on March 26, less than a week into the retrial. On that day Gillis forced Buckholdt to acknowledge his failure to locate Johnson and his "mistake" in waiving the witness's testimony, wrongly telling prosecutors that the east sider stood two blocks from where De Horatiis died, whereas he was actually only 200 feet away. Gillis ignored Buckholdt's claim that officers sent to subpoena Johnson had made a "diligent" effort to do so; he repudiated the detective's contention that the witness's original statement of Aaron F.'s innocence had been given to defense attorney Cornelius, saying, "I never heard it . . . and I was in on that conference." Following his rebuke of Buckholdt, Gillis accepted the acquittal of F. by an unanimous jury of eleven white and one black women, who deliberated a mere twenty minutes and contended that the black youth "never should have been convicted in the first place."[31]

Aaron F.'s freedom came in the wake of a crusade by "interested friends" and, said black journalists, "particularly the efforts of Judge Gillis."[32] No doubt supporters and magistrate merited some credit, yet Aaron F.'s mother and attorney were the ones truly responsible for his release. Beatrice B. labored to save money and retained both private eye and attorney, never doubting her son's innocence. In Cornelius, she chose a devoted, seasoned lawyer, who persuaded prosecuting witnesses to bare their souls and located east siders willing to challenge existing testimony. She hired someone who built on previous investigations and, without having been paid in full, pressed the case as "a public duty."[33]

Gillis well might have displayed similar motives in the retrial, but it was Cornelius who forced the issue and laid open to view the judge's questionable role in the first trial. In pretrial motions, he demonstrated how Gillis pressured prosecuting witnesses, insinuating that they might be imprisoned for perjury should their testimonies stray from statements given the police. Cornelius, for example, noted that in open court Gillis intimidated an uncooperative Reginald P.; rather than permit the high school student to renege on his sworn word, the judge threatened "to take some action."[34] Similarly, and long before Gillis discovered Johnson, his wife, and five other witnesses during the retrial, Cornelius presented the depositions of several, previously ignored eastsiders who declared Aaron F.'s innocence and described De Horatiis's killer. In fact, Cornelius seemed to have brought Johnson's presence to Gillis's attention during the second trial, thereby saving his client and condemning Buckholdt further. As paramount, he provided Gillis the opportunity to save face by interrupting the trial to locate Johnson and lambast Buckholdt. He stepped back as Gillis addressed newsmen, posed for photographers, told the public of his personal search for Johnson, and after the trial charged that Buckholdt "relied upon the testimony of hoodlums" to obtain the first conviction.[35] Popular perception of Gillis aside, Cornelius more than anyone deserved the credit for freeing Aaron F.

And Buckholdt emerged as both culprit and scapegoat, bearing the burden for prosecutors and magistrates who should have been more critical and questioning themselves. He soon faced a police department inquiry, tainting further the reputation of officers already besmirched by their mishandling the riot.[36] Meanwhile, his methods in the Aaron F. suit provided Aldo T.'s attorneys reason to request a retrial for their client. Buckholdt, they claimed, used the same tactics in both cases. Certainly he acted unprofessional enough for Circuit Court Judge Sherman D. Callender to release Aldo T. from prison on $2,500 bond and provide him with an opportunity for adjudication "comparable to that worked out in the Aaron F. case."[37] Buckholdt probably experienced bitter irony as Aldo T.'s lawyers now prepared evidence for the forthcoming hearing on a motion to dismiss his case.

The T. family sensed that the time was ripe for Aldo T.'s conviction to be overturned also. Since his capture—along with Robert C., Armando M., Anthony S., and Ralph T.—in July 1943, they had pressed litigation to prove him innocent of having gunned

down Kiska. Their fight originated in the face of public anger over
the riot and press reports of T.'s unrepentant confession and delinquent life-style. Family members also encountered the possibility of his being charged for the murder of Charles Grundy, a pros-
pect raised publicly by officials who spoke of the similarities of
both homicides and the confiscation of possible murder weapons.[38]
They squirmed, no doubt, as fact and fiction combined with sensa-
tionalism and speculation to condemn Aldo T. and his "hoodlum"
friends long before legal proceedings began; they read editorials
calling for the enactment of capital punishment legislation. In
taking Kiska's life so unthinkingly, contended the Detroit *News* editor, T. and company acted "as though morals and law—Michigan
law—did not exist"; deliberate killers respected only one punishment: "the death penalty."[39]

Given this climate of opinion, the outcome of the preliminary
examination in August was predictable. Robert Hicks, who had
witnessed Kiska being shot, identified Aldo T. as the shooter, and
Buckholdt summarize his confession: wanting to "help the white
people," piling into the Ford, firing one shot, and hitting the victim, he believed, "in the leg."[40] These testimonies, reinforced by
those of medical examiners and others, bound Aldo T. over for
trial.

Five months later, in January of 1944, Aldo T. and his family
faced their ordeal again, albeit with much more hope. They knew
now that neither of the rifles among the belongings of Aldo T. and
his codefendants proved to be the weapon that had killed Grundy
or—more importantly given eyewitness accounts—Kiska; officials
thereupon reduced the charges against T. and his band from first
degree murder to manslaughter. Still, defendant and family encountered prosecutors intent on establishing an unlawful "conspiracy" among the Italian youths "to get negroes." They watched
as testifiers again incriminated T. and attorneys, even without ballistics evidence, re-created his exhorting others to "go out" and assail blacks, scouring the east side for targets, and "inflicting mortal
wounds" on Kiska.[41] Despite defense challenges to the validity
of T.'s and Armando M.'s much publicized confessions—those
"forced from the mind by the flattery of hope or the torture of
fear"—and the "overzealous" tactics of Buckholdt and fellow de-

tectives, T. and his parents soon realized the futility of their efforts. Nor did they benefit from defense arguments that the bullet fired into Kiska's body came from a yet-to-be-found revolver, thus breaking the chain of circumstantial evidence and creating reasonable doubts of guilt. Likewise, their expectations that Aldo T.'s "good character" and "life of unblemished integrity" might even establish his innocence were dashed by twelve disbelieving white jurors.[42]

On January 27, 1944, eleven women and one man found Aldo T., Armando M., and Ralph T. guilty. Tussling with reasonable doubt, jurors deliberated for nearly forty hours, certainly raising defendant hopes. They must have responded to some defense arguments, for Robert C. and Anthony S. were both acquitted because of insufficient evidence. Robert C. had never accompanied the gang of killers, although his sedan served as the death car; and Anthony S., a minor who incriminated himself through an illegal and questionable conversation with detectives, might not even have been in the vehicle.[43] By contrast jurors accepted the validity of Aldo T.'s and Armando M.'s confessions, and Ralph T.'s less formal but no less incriminating admittance of guilt before family and police.[44] Jurors returned several times for instructions from Recorder's Court Judge Thomas M. Cotter before rendering final judgment, an indication of the difficulty of discovering and reconciling individual truth with community justice.[45]

Judge Cotter wrestled with no such doubt and in mid-February sentenced the guilty trio to the State Prison of Southern Michigan at Jackson. Aldo T. and Armando M. received lengthy sentences, respectively five and one half and two and one half to fifteen years, and Ralph T. three months to fifteen years without recommendation for the earliest possible releases. He considered trigger man Aldo T. "most culpable" for Kiska's senseless death and old enough to know better despite his youth. Reflecting both public opinion and its impact on the case, Cotter described the riot as "disgraceful" for Detroit and said that all residents simply desired that "justice be done."[46]

Even before Judge Cotter pronounced sentence, weeping and emotionally distraught relatives and friends of the murderers were removed from the room. Within a month, however, Aldo T.'s parents and lawyer, Cosimo M. Minardo, filed for a new trial. They, along with the additional counsel of Walter M. Nelson and Isaac M. Smullin, then spent eighteen months maneuvering the motion through the Recorder's Court.[47] They challenged the jury's verdict on several legal fronts, the first being Aldo T.'s constitutional rights. Attorneys contended that neither their client nor they themselves had received notice of the prosecutor's change of the original charge from first degree murder to conspiracy for harming black people, which effectively denied them the knowledge necessary to prepare a proper defense. They also maintained that the judge had erred in admitting evidence in support of the conspiracy charge and trying Aldo T. for "two separate and distinct offenses." Cotter permitted testimony regarding the "atrocities and horrors" of the race riot, but failed to apprise Aldo T. that this material would be connected with Kiska's death. Defense counselors asserted further that these judicial actions both confused jurors about their options and, in the face of public demand for punishment of all rioters, prejudiced them against Aldo T. Moreover, they claimed that no direct evidence linked their client to Kiska's killing and, with the jury having dismissed the so-called conspiracy theory, he must be set free. Instead, they protested, judge and jury disregarded the rule of double jeopardy and reached "a compromise verdict based on speculation" and "calculated to satisfy public pressure."[48]

Between March 1944 and September 1945, Minardo, Nelson, and Smullin raised the questions of direct evidence and riot influence. Kiska, they repeated, was wounded fatally by a single bullet fired from a weapon other than the gun found on Aldo T. Although no one knew exactly how the black defense worker had died or by whose hands, prosecutors had to demonstrate categorically that he was killed by Aldo T. and his friends—and no one else. This they failed to do, contended defense lawyers, and thus conceived of a broad, sweeping conspiracy theory, using Kiska's murder as one overt act of collusion without making it the lone or direct incident upon which to prove guilt. T.'s lawyers further alleged that jurors exhibited enough conscience to deny the conspiracy theory but not enough to dismiss the manslaughter charge. At a time when the nation was denouncing Detroit for the riot and "public indignation" was demanding retribution, jury members fed T. and his codefendants to revenge-minded citizens. Had the defendants known that prosecutors and jurors intended to inject the riot and race prejudice into the trial, concluded T.'s lawyers, they would have sought a change of venue and selected jurors differently. Instead the defendants fell prey to preconceived opinion that "sacrificed" them in order to preserve "the reputation of our great metropolis." Simply put, Aldo T. and his friends were railroaded by the court—prosecutors, jury, and judge—and consequently denied their constitutional rights necessary for an adequate defense.[49]

Prosecuting attorneys, of course, denied any miscarriage of justice. They dismissed the contention that Aldo T. and his companions became the victims of adverse public reaction to the disorder, or appeared before the court without knowledge of the charges against them. From the case's inception, argued prosecutors, all defendants knowingly stood accused of murdering Kiska, a charge that need not, according to state statutes, set forth "the manner in which" or "the means by which" the death occurred. Hence the conspiracy theory constituted neither a new charge against them nor double jeopardy, but served the people as acceptable legal strategy. Prosecutors claimed commitment to their conspiracy strategy long before ballistics evidence ruled out T.'s rifle as the murder weapon. They also discounted defense claims that jurors were confused by the collusion thesis and, lacking a firearm, the homicide offense: Jury members alone knew what was in their minds during the trial. Surely lawyers for the prosecution referred to the "deplorable race riot" in which Kiska's killing occurred and the "blot" of racial disturbance on Detroit, statements of obvious fact. If T.'s attorneys thought otherwise, concluded prosecutors, they should have shown cause to change venue and challenge prospective jurors.[50]

Judge Cotter died in the fall of 1944, so Recorder's Court Judge Paul E. Krause heard arguments for and against the new trial motion and, on September 10, 1945, denied it.[51] He agreed with prosecutors that Aldo T. and his codefendants had received adequate information regarding their charges and the people's conspiracy theory, both of which appeared in the preliminary examination.

He also deemed the prosecuting strategy proper and the reference to citywide racial violence as part of the circumstances surrounding Kiska's death nonprejudicial. In summary, Krause judged the trial fair and the evidence sufficient to sustain a verdict of manslaughter.[52]

Aldo T.'s lawyers appealed this ruling to the Michigan Supreme Court. They may have suspected prejudice (Krause had been Mayor Jeffries's University of Michigan roommate, law partner, and corporation counsel),[53] but their official claim was of "irregularities" in the original trial.[54] Summarizing earlier arguments, the defense lawyers presented Aldo T. as a minor charged belatedly with conspiracy "to get negroes" and found guilty of a crime "he never committed." They resketched their contention that the jury had been confused by the charge of collusion—a crime peculiar to the state but unknown to common law—and prejudiced by a judge who implied that conviction could result without direct evidence (of the killing) or on evidence of an entirely different offense. They once more portrayed T. as victimized by prosecutors, who were seeking a scapegoat for the riot and by jury members, who, in bowing to public pressure, reached a "compromise verdict": innocent of conspiracy, guilty of manslaughter. Because of this "miscarriage of justice," the defense also criticized Krause for denying the motion for a new trial and requested a complete examination of the case by state magistrates.[55]

In response, Krause provided the court with a statement of proceedings and facts from the trial transcript. He quoted the prosecuting attorney's specific reference to Kiska's death as a crime in itself and the court's equally precise caution against mention of the disorder as "very dangerous ground." He quoted further the prosecutor's explanation of the conspiracy theory and the judge's instruction to the jury: "If two or more persons enter into an illegal agreement . . . to commit a crime," all participants are equally guilty. He cited also the magistrate's position that, whether or not jurors determined the existence of a conspiracy, they could convict defendants for any of the enumerated crimes. Without elaboration, Krause noted that his hearing of the defense motion for a new trial was continued seventeen times before being denied.[56]

Since Minardo, Nelson, and Smullin expected the state court to take the same amount of time, or more, before acting on their appeal, they pressed for Aldo T.'s release on $3,500 bond. This effort was backed up by family friends and supporters, none more crucial than the Rev. J. S. Coogan, University of Detroit sociologist and Roman Catholic priest. T. T. Brumbaugh of the Detroit Council of Churches agreed with them and local NAACP officials promised not to cause "a difficulty" over Aldo T.'s release.[57] Most forcefully Coogan, "an experienced teacher of criminology," recounted T.'s age, twenty-six months of incarceration, and "model conduct" in both the county jail and state reformatory. He stressed the possibility of T.'s innocence and the importance of his wages for "a poor family" impoverished by trial expenses.[58] Together, Coogan and attorneys persuaded the prosecuting attorney and, in turn, Judge Krause to release Aldo T. in October of 1945.[59]

Aldo T. returned home, and his lawyers awaited state action. In mid-January of 1946, they received word that supreme court justices had denied the defense appeal against Krause's ruling and Aldo T. was behind bars again. Their legal efforts seemed spent. However, attorneys and client found new hope in the proceedings and outcome of Aaron F.'s retrial.

In the wake of Aaron F.'s acquittal in March 1946, Minardo, Nelson, and Smullin moved quickly. They once more obtained Aldo T.'s release on bail and filed a motion to dismiss his case. Pointedly they shifted strategy, now blaming Detective Lt. Buckholdt rather than prosecutor, judge, and jury for the travesty of justice. Like Aaron F.'s lawyers, they rolled back on the detective's witnesses and brought his methods into question, resurrecting T.'s chances for freedom by impugning Buckholdt's reputation further.

Minardo and his fellow counselors located Attilio C., one of three witnesses for the prosecution who had identified Aldo T. as the person who shot Kiska. He recanted his trial testimony of the previous year, admitting that he had never been at the scene of the shooting or seen the defendant on June 21, 1943. He, along with Frank C. and Fred S. now serving overseas in the armed forces, received everything they knew about the killing from Buckholdt. If Attilio C. and his friends refused to "squeal" on T., the detective told them, they would be tried for the killing. Threatened and tutored by Buckholdt to "stay away from everybody" and not discuss their testimony, they did as they were told. Attilio C. even recalled that Buckholdt instructed him to bring his story into line with ballistic evidence: "Don't mention any rifle." He speculated that the detective cornered him, Frank C., and Fred S. because the latter, having heard of a reward for information leading to the conviction of Kiska's murderer, bragged that he and his buddies had seen it all; they soon attracted Buckholdt's attention and wrath.[60]

Shrewdly, defense lawyers stressed the methods employed by Buckholdt that had recently set Aaron F. free. He threatened and coerced "three minor boys"—Attilio C., Frank C., and Fred S.— into giving "false and illegal testimony." He made up their stories and orchestrated their courtroom performances, assisted by fellow officers who admonished the teenagers to cooperate or "be in trouble for life." He worked closely with the prosecutor, who, along with Judge Cotter, appeared to have pressed witness less vigorously than their counterparts had done in the Aaron F. case. As in that fiasco, however, Buckholdt had produced inadmissable testimony that wrongly convicted an innocent youth. Without the detective's illegal activities and intimidated witnesses, contended the defense, Aldo T. "could not have been convicted of any crime."[61]

Despite the defense's request for an immediate new trial (because Attilio C.'s military induction seemed imminent), the Recorder's Court moved slowly.[62] Finally in early January 1947, Minardo and company again appeared before the bench and moved to dismiss the complaint against Aldo T.[63] This time they did so with the consent of prosecuting attorneys, police officials (including Buckholdt), and all judges, who dismissed the case "without prejudice," discharged the defendant, and canceled his bond.[64]

Like Aaron F., Aldo T. gained from having a loving and loyal family, important friends, competent lawyers, and ultimately public opinion. Soon after his trial and conviction in January 1944, Father Coogan approached the Greater Detroit Interracial Fellowship about the case and, in highly empathic terms, suggested inquiry into the "over punishment for inadvertent victims of the riot."[65] While Beatrice B. was taking steps to free her son, Coogan continued to press his victimization theory, and in the summer of 1945, as the state considered Aldo T.'s appeal, sought bail for the young man. His plea could have fit Aaron F.: a teenage boy from a good family who, like thousands of other citizens, "lost his head on the most exciting day in the long history of Detroit."[66] The court's denial of the defense request for a new trial was a setback, but meanwhile the Aaron F. case was revealing overzealous police tactics, thus making Aaron F. a cause célèbre and, by implication, raising questions about the treatment of Aldo T. Perhaps, unknown to Father Coogan and Beatrice B., Buckholdt reminded many people of strong-arm police tactics during the riot. In any event, as Cornelius's revelations surfaced, public anger over participants began to wane.

Hence, by early 1946 Aaron F.'s and Aldo T.'s supporters had closed ranks and combined Father Coogan's victim thesis with Beatrice B.'s "railroad" charge. Earlier Coogan had received black assurances that their leaders would cause no difficulty over Aldo T.'s bail, and later several priests supported Aaron F.'s retrial. (As was pointed out earlier, Aldo T.'s father testified for the defense.) Thereafter, black ministers demanded a new trial for Aldo T., and Aaron F.'s mother appeared in his behalf. In addition, police-court reporters Frances D'Hondt of the *Times* and Marguerite Gahagan of the *News* (a member of the Catholic Women's Interracial Council) organized a crusade favoring the youths. Aldo T. appeared in court for final bail in March 1946 and for final discharge in January 1947 with Aaron F. at his side. Both "boys," concluded Father Coogan, perhaps the person most responsible for orchestrating the interracial, interdenominational campaign, were "victims of riot hysteria and . . . convicted on much the same dubious evidence."[67]

Who then, Detroiters might have asked, killed Dr. Joseph De Horatiis and Moses Kiska? The physician's killer, testified reliable witnesses, was an underworld figure called "Chi," whose age and physical features bore no resemblance to Aaron F. Kiska's murderer, verified ballistic experts, fired a weapon other than the rifle in the possession of Aldo T. and remained unknown, possibly even unaware that he had slain the defense worker. T.'s lawyers speculated that the gunman might have been someone in a nearby mob who fired a .22 caliber pistol wildly and hit Kiska in the abdomen by accident.[68] Whoever were the assailants of De Horatiis and Kiska, they remained at large, as did several other mysterious riot slayers.

Although innocent of murder, Aaron F. and Aldo T. nevertheless committed riot acts of lesser criminal consequence. Despite Aaron F.'s testimony that "no trouble" occurred on Belle Isle while he frolicked there until 9:00 P.M. on June 20, 1943, or that he never saw Charles L. on the Sunday of disorder, he had served as one of "Little Willie's" marauders and also, said witnesses, as one of Gus Niarhos's attackers.[69] Belated alibi notwithstanding, F. seemed to have participated in the upheaval until 11:00 P.M. and probably originated the rumor that whites had tossed a black mother and her child from the Belle Isle bridge.[70] Prosecutors in the De Horatiis case emphasized his participation in the disturbance even though they dropped charges against him for the attack on Niarhos.[71]

Like Aaron F., Aldo T. was much less angelic than portrayed by family and friends. He admitted to the shooting as described by Armando M., Ralph T., and Anthony S.—that is, he aimed and fired the rifle but failed to hit his human target—and in spite of Buckholdt's tactics, much of their testimony carried the ring of truth: Twenty-year-old Armando M. appeared more boastful than afraid, and Ralph T. confessed in the presence of his mother and elder brother.[72] Moreover, Aldo T.'s staunchest supporters, like Father Coogan, originally challenged the harshness of his sentence, not the question of his guilt, and virtually admitted that guilt when they were seeking T.'s release on bond.[73] Aldo T., then, did not fire the weapon that killed Kiska, but he and his band of vigilantes entered the east side intending "to get some negroes" and, in fact, shot *at* Kiska—or at some other unknown black man.[74] Having been victimized in the deaths of De Horatiis and Kiska, Aaron F. and Aldo T. also victimized others during the riot.[75]

Certainly Aaron F. and Aldo T. paid a price for their criminal acts, but so did their cohorts, who received little concern from crusaders or court officials. Perhaps because Ralph T. served only one and a half years in prison, for having been Aldo T.'s chauffeur, before being paroled in January 1945, he attracted few do-gooders.[76] His early release may have strengthened Aldo T.'s legal appeals. Long after Ralph T. and Aldo T. were enjoying freedom, however, Armando M. languished behind bars. In a pretrial motion he had denied being implicated in the murder, because he had attempted "to prevent the commission of any crime"—that is, he had contended that he had tried to stop Aldo T. from shooting Kiska.[77] This failed to convince the Recorder's Court judge, who quickly denied his motion for dismissal and no appeal was later entered against his conviction.[78] Given his age, twenty, his brash confession printed by the press, and absence from military duty, Armando M. evoked little public sympathy. He was moved from one correctional facility to another, ignored publicly even though his conviction was based on the same dubious evidence and heavy-handed tactics as Aldo T.'s and his sentence nearly as stiff. So did Charles L. and Leo T., doubtlessly riot participants convicted in another case partly because of Fred M.'s testimony.[79] They drew little attention, despite common knowledge that Buckholdt had handled their cases and Fred M. had perjured himself in Aaron F.'s first trial. As those blamed most by officials and residents for igniting and spreading the riot, Charlie L. and Leo T. fared no better than Armando M. In the wake of Aaron F.'s dismissal, no one thought of providing them a chance for comparable adjudication. Apparently, Judge Callender's belief that "such opportunity should be given to all persons sentenced under the riotous conditions" pertained only to Aldo T.[80]

Aldo T. and Aaron F. served over two years in prison for riot crimes they did not commit and came out of the upheaval both as victims and perpetrators. Yet their ordeals and the riot itself soon faded from public memory, largely replaced by Detroit image building and only recalled in vague terms twenty-four years later when Detroit exploded again. Unsurprisingly, the next generation of participants shared personal characteristics and riot patterns with their predecessors, and revealed much about collective violence in historical perspective. Their outburst of 1967 occurred, as did that of wartime rioters, in layers of escalating violence, but shifted from Hastings to Twelfth Street.

SIX

From Hastings to 12th Street

Until the second Detroit riot of 1967, the 1943 outburst exhibited the greatest destruction of any urban disorder in twentieth-century United States. Hence its participants, when compared to those of the later eruption, lent themselves to a more complete understanding of who rioted in each upheaval and what links existed between them. They delineated the interaction of crises and change, gauged the limits of race relations, and signaled attitudinal, demographic, and socioeconomic shifts over time. From Hastings Street in 1943 to 12th Street in 1967, Detroiters demonstrated various rioter portraits and distinct riot phases, each adding weight and intensity—layered violence—to the rampages.

Both clashes came in summer months, covered sizable portions of the city and—usually at the hands of lawmen and guardsmen—claimed substantially more black than white lives. Both disturbances occurred when the nation was fighting wars abroad, when blacks at home were pressing for equality in unprecedented ways, and when racial tensions permeated society. Both upheavals exploded despite recent socioeconomic gains for some blacks and, particularly in the second civil disorder, significant support from some whites. Both disorders came at a time of rising expectations and blocked opportunities, further accentuated by some participants—members of both races in 1943—sensing relative deprivation in housing and employment. Both outbursts happened against a backdrop of strained police–community relations, caused in part by undermanned and prejudiced police departments. Both riots came in periods of optimism and moralism, respectively during a war for democracy and a movement for racial equality, and represented hope in the future of race relations and urban living. Large segments of both races had not yet given up the dream of integration, and even as whites fled to the suburbs, most blacks believed the city retrievable. Both explosions comprised part of the clusters of violence that besieged 1943 and 1967, and served to propagate bloodshed, however less serious, elsewhere. And, despite important distinctions between them—such as preriot mayoral racial policies—Detroit's conflicts sprang from the same violent heritage.

Detroit had been experiencing heightened racial tensions since 1915, as recently arrived Southern blacks and their already established brethren competed with native whites and European ethnics. Numbering 40,838 in 1920, blacks challenged the color line, and whites, regardless of class, religion, and ethnic differences, protected it. Only in mid decade, in the face of a Ku Klux Klan-backed mayoral candidate, did blacks, Catholics, and the foreign-born close ranks to defeat a common enemy. More often they contested one another, particularly over living space. In a celebrated 1925 case, when Dr. Ossian Sweet, prominent black gynecologist, moved beyond the ghetto into southwest Detroit, he was attacked by largely Polish mobs and allegedly killed one assailant. Sweet was freed but his experience presaged future housing clashes. Meanwhile blacks, whose numbers grew to 120,066 in 1930, found themselves devastated by the Great Depression and terrorized by the nefarious Black Legion, a secret society of local racists. Conflict continued in the late 1930s, when blacks fortunate to hold jobs in the automobile industry sided with management in union conflicts.[1]

With the advent of World War II, racial rivalries intensified as black ranks swelled to nearly 150,000 persons, 9.2 percent of 1,623,452 Detroiters, and faced increased indignities amidst a war. Blacks resented discrimination in restaurants, segregation in housing (already in short supply because of the war), violence by police, and mistreatment of their sons serving in Southern military camps. By early 1942, they had clashed with Polish residents over federally built defense homes in northeast Detroit, resulting in 220 arrests and forty injuries. Blacks, assisted by Double V rhetoric ("Victory at home, Victory abroad")—the wartime call for racial justice made popular by the *Pittsburgh Courier*—white liberals, and official escort, ultimately occupied the Sojourner Truth Homes. Meantime, approximately 450,000 white newcomers and, increasingly after the housing disorder, 35,000 Southern blacks flooded the city looking for defense work and overtaxed its already inadequate living conditions and social services. By the summer of 1943, the metropolitan population had soared to over 2 million. Blacks pushed for more housing, job upgrading, and recreational opportunities, and whites, in some cases with mayoral and police support, opposed these initiatives. Black and white clashed regularly for stakes in the rapidly changing, promising world: in neighborhoods, on shop floors and streetcars, at amusement parks. A series of racial confrontations broke out on several DSR cars. Most seriously in early June 1943, tensions were raised in a "hate strike" at Packard Motor Company, and the races spilled each other's blood at Eastwood Park. Their animus elevated as race riots swept Mobile, Beaumont, and Los Angeles.[2]

While a later observer labeled Detroit "one of the nation's most segregated, if not bigoted, northern cities," blacks and whites considered it worth fighting for.[3] Their competition bespoke hope, despite "boom town" conditions and uprooted populations. Although some residents imagined the city "a mining town in Michigan rather than in Montana," they also thought of it as a "creative environment" in which to live rather than an "ecological malaise," as a later writer called it, sparking racial violence.[4] Detroit emerged as both dynamic and dynamite.

Small wonder that riot erupted at Belle Isle on Sunday, June 20, 1943. Strain, hostile beliefs, and precipitating incidents mobilized

Detroiters of both races. Against the background of historical cleavage, inadequate policing, and ineffective channels of redress, black and white Belle Isle patrons responded aggressively. Clearly the strain they experienced varied, blacks like Charles L. and Aaron F. doubtless smarting over their ousting from Eastwood Park and white sailors mindful of fellow seamen having been beaten by blacks.[5] Their breaking point, as well as that of numerous others, came in the wake of several "tension-heightening incidents."[6] Soon blacks and whites were exploding in what appeared to be senseless acts of retribution. Blacks saw their opportunities for better housing, jobs, and—in Charles L.'s case—recreation blocked by whites, and whites, in turn, saw "cocky" black teenagers and young adults stepping well beyond their ascribed place.[7] Facing one another in a public park on a sweltering Sunday, blacks mobilized their attacks easily, while whites responded in kind. Their original altercations appeared "wild and furious," as those in Harlem six weeks later were described, yet marked by "primitive organization."[8]

These were precipitating incidents, climaxing in pitched battle along the Belle Isle bridge. Hostile beliefs were channeled into rumor—crystallized and spread.[9] Aaron F. reached Jefferson Avenue and accused whites of hurling a black mother and her child into the Detroit River. This message founds its way to Leo T. and thence to Forest Club patrons already predisposed to believe the worst about white society. Once in the east-side street, black club goers spread out, searching for whites. One of them apparently phoned area bars, mobilizing additional black participants. Thereafter word surfaced among whites along Woodward Avenue and just above the black west side that black men had attacked, raped, and in some versions killed white girls at Belle Isle, and that carloads of black soldiers from Fort Custer and black residents from Chicago were headed for the city.[10] Hence, by 4:00 A.M. on June 21, black and white rioters, separated by ecological and police lines, controlled their respective turfs and assailed racial enemies in their midst. From then until the arrival of federal troops late that evening, communal and commodity disorders raged side-by-side.

For one tense period, between 6:00 P.M. and 9:00 P.M., whites endeavored to penetrate the east side. They gathered in large numbers at Woodward Avenue and Vernor Highway, facing an equally sizable group of blacks assembled a block or so away, between John R and Brush Street. Whites, "milling, shouting, surging back and forth across Vernor Highway," terrified blacks watching from buildings beyond the police line. In this charged atmosphere, snipers began to fire from windows and roofs, provking "massive law enforcement" retaliation and putting an end to the siege stage.[11] Predictably, black deaths and injuries, both at the Frazer Hotel and northward throughout the ghetto, jumped during this three-hour time span.[12]

Whether at Belle Isle, inside Paradise Valley, or on Woodward Avenue, the rioters formed into mobs and coordinated common interests. Crudely formed, they communicated with one another and, experiencing both anonymity and moral righteousness, acted out impulses that they would have suppressed under normal circumstances. Their actions grew out of racial friction and race-related grievances and represented—however symbolically—the struggle for power. What began as a series of brawls on Belle Isle was transposed to outright upheaval in Detroit.[13] Essentially the Sunday activities of blacks and whites set in motion a "pattern of progression" leading to wholesale destruction.[14]

Once the breakdown in social order had occurred, "different kinds of deviance" and additional participants came forth.[15] Hence the crowd that emptied the Forest Club transformed itself into a Hastings Street mob, assailing whites, smashing store windows, and ultimately looting businesses.[16] White rioters, also organized, counterattacked long before sunrise on Monday. On Woodward Avenue they gathered in sizable groups, armed themselves with brickbats and pipes, broke streetcar windows, halted the vehicles, and beat black riders senseless. Occasionally they divided up these tasks—for example some among them pulled the trolley's pole from electric contact while others cut the cord.[17]

Certainly some rioters knew one another and operated in gangs of acquaintances. Charles L.'s marauders and armory sailors fought on the island and its bridge as loosely organized combat

units. Similarly other blacks, and whites drawn to Belle Isle early
Monday morning, came in groups prepared for race war. Walter
H. and seven black adults jammed into a Ford carrying razors
and knives, while Walter J. and five white teenagers rode in an
Oldsmobile with knives and a wrench; all appeared on Jefferson
Avenue for more than the stated reason of curiosity.[18] With one
exception, those in Walter H.'s sedan lived far from one another
and even farther from Belle Isle, yet three of them were related,
and seven of them were employed as laborers—relationships of
kin and class. These eight black adults, twenty-three to thirty-five
years of age, five of them married, probably met through work
and resented white opposition to upgrading and, given the lone
soldier among them, mistreatment of servicemen.[19] The white
teenagers in Walter J.'s car also resided significant distances from
one another and were apparently brought together by their age,
unattached status, and possibly parochial-school affiliation. Several
such vehicles arrived at Belle Isle packed with white youths, and
this provides additional indication of some organization.[20] Perhaps
their actions stemmed from recreational conflicts or, as in the case
of Aldo T., sociopsychological resentment.

The site where rioters did their organizing before entering the
riot zones varied. Charles L. gathered his band at the Belle Isle
playground, while Aldo T. did so at the local poolroom. Woodward Avenue toughs like Erving M. and four comrades used soda
fountains and similar establishments along the thoroughfare as
staging areas for their activity.[21]

Other participants denied being members of clubs or even acquainted with each other. Several blacks arrested and held in the
Piquette Armory, for instance, neither belonged to gangs nor were
ever asked to join them.[22] Among those placed on probation, many
more blacks than whites acted alone, a small majority of whites
having been part of a group.[23] And some east siders apprehended
in the same store—such as Albert V. and Leophys T.—proved to
be total strangers.[24] Nor could J. C. G., a white participant who
stripped a black-owned Ford on Woodward Avenue, identify the
soldier who instructed him in the thievery.[25]

When crude gangs existed, however, so did spontaneous leadership, itself a requirement for riots.[26] Charles L. mobilized and directed younger east siders on their rampages of Belle Isle. Others led ghetto dwellers in their attacks on white targets, though less was revealed about them. The police—not to mention fear—barred newspaper photographers and others from the east side during the crucial hours.[27]

In contrast, reporters, prominent figures, and many more everyday citizens witnessed the role of mob leaders both downtown and on Woodward Avenue. On Park Avenue early Monday morning, Martin P. and Mike F. led twenty-five club-wielding rioters in pursuit of Robert Lee Smith, a longtime black resident of Detroit and veteran employee of Ford Motor Company.[28] P. threatened Smith with an ice pick before being arrested and received from one to five years in Jackson State Penitentiary for carrying a concealed weapon, whereas Mike F., unarmed, drew ninety days in the Detroit House of Correction for disturbing the peace.[29] Martin P. lived beyond the western edge of Paradise Valley on McDougall Avenue, two and one-half miles from the crime scene. Born in nearby Clarkston, unmarried, educated through the eighth grade, and working for the past six weeks at Aeronautical Products, he came into Detroit "off and on" to earn $40 a week.[30] Mike F., in contrast, resided just below the ghetto in the 2300 block of John R and within a quarter mile of the assault. A native of Italy, married, literate, and employed as a laborer, he fought on home ground and apparently did not know Martin P.[31]

White leaders also ran rampant on Woodward Avenue, sometimes with police countenance and assistance.[32] Robert M. chatted with bluecoats at 11:00 A.M., then led a mob that halted vehicles and chased after passengers and pedestrians. He struck black men with an iron pipe and ordered white women to bash a lone "colored lady." Later in the day he paraded up and down the boulevard and, along with George F., incited further violence.[33] That afternoon another unidentified ringleader led a bottle-hurling mob against blacks on lower Woodward Avenue. Wearing a white handkerchief around his head, he seemed "very calm, cold and calculating." And, without trepidation, he reappeared on Woodward Avenue four days later.[34]

Observing "several young boys leading groups of adolescents,"

Dr. Lowell S. Selling of the Recorder's Court Psychopathic Clinic considered them "ragamuffins under sixteen who were just out for the sheer love of brawling."[35] His observations provided only one view, for the ages of those at the head of black or white mobs varied: Charles L. twenty, Mike F. twenty-six, Robert M., George F., and the handkerchief wearer in their early thirties.

The motives of riot leaders also differed and were occasionally multidimensional. Charles L., Aldo T., and Martin P., all of small stature, seemed antisocial and delinquent, having brushed with the law previously. Going on eighteen years of age, for instance, Martin P. stood only 5 feet 2½ inches in height, weighed around 130 pounds, and following a school break-in served three years probation.[36] And three months before the disorder, he entered a Pontiac warehouse unlawfully for the purpose of larceny. He appeared to be on his own, drifting in and out of the city, heading toward complete alienation. Indeed, when this earlier felony was discovered, Martin P. found his riot sentence increased substantially.[37] Mike F. also bore previous arrest for lesser offenses, and as an immigrant living in the lower east side—the city's traditional port of entry for newcomers—expressed anomie.[38]

Robert M., more decidedly criminal, quit his job as taxi driver on the first day of rioting, when he and George F. became "principal aggressors, assaulting negroes." Earlier Robert M. had spent five years in the federal penitentiary for transporting prostitutes across state lines, and George F. committed larceny while awaiting trial for assault and battery during the riot. Both felons were identified from photographs of their riot activity, the *Free Press* alone printing pictures of Robert M. in four separate acts of mob violence.[39]

Riot leaders, then, evidenced serious economic and cultural strain. Generally single outcasts, in some cases criminals, they seized the moment to declare war on larger black or white society. Delinquents Aldo T. and recidivists Martin P., Robert M., and George F. probably brutalized blacks for more than racist reasons. Aliens within their own white society, they rioted to promote white supremacy and feelings of solidarity, but also to displace their own aggression. Using blacks as scapegoats, they compensated for their own marginality.[40] Certainly—as in the example of Charles L. who recalled eviction from Eastwood Park by white youths, or the handkerchief-headed white who noted his brother's car having been burned by blacks—some of the vanguard professed race-related grievances. If Aldo T. and, especially, Martin P., Robert M., and George F. fit Selling's hoodlum thesis, Charles L. and the handkerchief wearer more accurately represented the great majority of participants, black and white, who fought for or against the color line.

Despite the transient nature of ringleaders like Martin P. and George F., or a handful of participants in general, few of those who rioted were outsiders. Occasionally someone like nineteen-year-old Willie L. of Port Huron, Michigan, entered the city as it was bursting and found himself stopped at DuBois and Macomb streets, just southeast of Paradise Valley and slightly above the river front—for violating the curfew. Since he was carrying a small ax, he received a prison term of six months to five years. A single, unemployed youth, he might have come to fight; but since he had neither a police record nor anywhere to stay, he could as easily have come looking for work and carried the ax for protection.[41] Regardless of Willie L.'s motivation, he represented very few rioters. Ninety-seven percent of all black and white male and 100 percent of all black female arrestees claimed Detroit as their residence.[42] And rumors of black multitudes surging in from Flint, Michigan, Chicago, and elsewhere proved false.[43]

Nor did saboteurs explain the upheaval. No domestic or international intrigue was ever proved,[44] and local and federal investigators dismissed all conspiracy theories, interpreting Detroit's upheaval instead as "the product of spontaneous combustion in a highly explosive community." They traced the disturbance to a backlog of racial animosity and wartime tensions, aware that Klansman and Japanese agents only added to the already charged atmosphere.[45] Bureau members deemed the KKK too small and unimportant "to be responsible for a riot of this sort."[46] Likewise, military intelligence operatives uncovered "no organization backing" unsuccessful efforts of 1,500 blacks from Toledo to enter the Detroit disorder.[47]

And participants themselves denied knowledge of plans for violence. Even M. C. M., who accompanied Charles L. to Belle Isle, claimed that none of the youths he met spoke about participating in such an outbreak, much less "any fight."[48] Similarly, over 160 black males cleared from east-side streets told Michigan State Troopers that they knew of no "outside instigation" for the outburst, which "just started."[49]

Once it did, additional individuals entered the fray and, partly in response to police activity, shifted their attacks from one object to another.[50] On Woodward Avenue, sizable crowds of whites, numbering upward of 15,000 persons, and "several thousand" blacks along east-side thoroughfares between Vernor Highway and Forest Avenue rioted throughout Bloody Monday.[51] Before the disorder petered out, Mayor Edward J. Jeffries, Jr., estimated that 100,000 people had participated in it.[52] More white males and probably white females (as observed by witnesses) participated in the communal outburst, traditionally "a men's affair," than in all previous pogroms save possibly Chicago in 1919. Their numbers reflected war-related population increases and racial antagonisms that also expanded, isolated, and mobilized blacks in the commodity disorder.[53] White Detroiters climaxed past reactions to assaults on the color line, while black ghetto dwellers, following the lead of Harlemites in 1935, reintroduced the so-called property riots that became common in the 1960s.

Within each outburst numerous Detroiters became spectators. Some of them, purportedly "the better elements of both races," gave the impression of being "completely detached and disinterested in what was occurring."[54] Others, such as twenty-one-year-old black west sider William Lee B., said they "just stopped and watched" the mobs without participating. Arrested for disturbing the peace, they might have been innocent of throwing rocks and wrongly sentenced to ninety days in the house of correction. But— young, single, employed in defense industry, living at home, and frequenting Hastings Street in search of entertainment—their presence in unruly crowds created problems for outnumbered patrolmen. Everyone on the street—including William Lee B. who came from a stable family of seven, had enlisted in the Navy only to receive a medical discharge, and possessed no arrest record— seemed riotous to policemen clearing the area of humanity.[55]

Most rioters and spectators of riots shared similar feelings,

though the "carnival air" so evident in the initial stages of commodity riots was less apparent in Detroit.[56] The upheaval racially
divided Detroiters yet emotionally liberated and unified them in
respective rampages of common purpose, "powerful identity," and
"righteous indignation."[57] "On nearly every street corner" of Paradise Valley, reported the *News* of June 21, knots of blacks assembled, while whites gathered west of the ghetto.[58] The criminal
actions of some notwithstanding, blacks and whites annihilated
one another, destroyed environments, and looted property whenever possible for far more than "fun and profit."[59] Desiring opposite goals—blacks sought change while whites repulsed it—they
struggled to resolve long-standing grievances.

Others of both races refused to enter the conflict. Prominent
black and white leaders meeting with Jeffries on the first day of
violence, for instance, issued separate statements condemning the
spilling of blood, on the one hand assuring whites that "the Negro
people" were their friends and on the other assuring everyone
that "the overwhelming majority of Detroiters" wanted "no part of
these enemy-aiding disturbances."[60] Spokesmen also served as
counterrioters; the Rev. Horace A. White, for one, rode a sound
truck urging east siders to end the rioting.[61] Their courage was duplicated by everyday residents: White women hid black males
while aboard Woodward Avenue streetcars, and "Chinese fellows"
endeavored to protect another black DSR passenger from mobsters.[62] Inside Paradise Valley, blacks assisted innocent victims
wounded by brutal patrolmen and protected white-owned stores,
Jewish and gentile, from vandals and looters.[63]

Forty-eight-year-old Thomas F. emerged a tarnished hero. Born
in Tennessee, orphaned as a child, and raised by relatives in Chicago and Detroit, he worked for Ford Motor Company before becoming tubercular and acquiring a kidney ailment. He had lived in
the city for well over twenty years, served a short sentence for
fighting, and settled into a common-law marriage. For a livelihood,
he supervised rooming houses and occupied an apartment above
Ben Levine's dry-goods store in the 3800 block of Hastings Street,
and he and his wife Susie, a hospital employee, had saved $800.
Once the looting started, he phoned Levine of the disorder and

began boarding up the store's rear windows, but discovered a fire in the building. He warned his wife, escaped to the street himself—and ironically faced charges of rioting. He denied participating in the disturbance, but spent time in Piquette Armory before being released for lack of evidence. Older and more incapacitated than most black rioters, Thomas F. represented those who deemed the upheaval and its participants "foolish."[64]

The activities of rioters bore a decidedly racial and interracial character. Race more than any other factor underscores the most frequent, most intense physical violence in this and earlier riots.[65] Living amidst wartime uncertainty, and competition over class, power, and the color line, they fought as racial entities for racial ends.[66] Hence Charles L. and his band attacked whites for having won an interracial clash at Eastwood Park. Racial rather than class, ethnic, or other epithets were hurled at enemies. Shouts of "Goddamned nigger" and "white mother-fucking son of a bitch" punctuated the night air of Belle Isle and, soon enough, Woodward Avenue and Hastings Streets. Even policemen deliberately provoked pedestrians: "Where are you going, nigger?"[67] Equally telling, all rumor mongers spread stories of racial abuse, often with sexual overtones, emphasizing longtime hostile beliefs.[68] Forest Club revelers struck at any white face within reach and east siders later assaulted light-skinned blacks in mistake for whites, displaying the enormous potential for all-out race war. So did signs of racial identity hung by store owners in Paradise Valley and home owners across Grand Boulevard in the Owen-Oakland-Westminster districts.[69] Ultimately other blacks destroyed and looted black establishments, yet the primal instincts of rioters exhibited racial grievances and focused on racial targets. Their resentment was greatest against "members of the white race," manifesting itself in emblematic attacks on white-owned businesses and direct confrontations with white patrolmen.[70] Significantly some Jewish and gentile merchants later inspected their stores with police guards, all white outsiders invading black province.[71]

Meanwhile, whites beyond the ghetto single-mindedly mobbed blacks in automobiles, aboard trolleys, and on foot, clearly going far beyond simply engaging in "retaliatory action" for earlier attacks by blacks. Whites along Woodward Avenue struck blacks for incidents on crowded DSR lines where social distance had eroded steadily—traumatically for some.[72] Their assaults on public and private vehicles reversed months of humiliation and symbolized the reestablishment of white dominance and proper racial etiquette. Knowing the "customary community patterns"—that blacks were to be shunned in most social situations—and immersed in the racism of larger society, natives like Martin P. and ethnics like Mike F. reflected the aggressive behavior that shaped their prejudices.[73] Surely some whites like Aldo T. entered the riot bearing personal burdens that magnified their racial animus. Hence they came substantial distances, from communities where few blacks resided, driven by a desire—in Armando M.'s chilling words—to "kill us a nigger."[74] The riot, commented Police Commissioner John H. Witherspoon on its interracial character, "has been in the air for a long time."[75]

Whites, most notably patrolmen armed with weapons and authority, seemed more bent on taking black lives than vice versa. Historically whites employed violence as a means of social control, exposing blacks to ever-present threats and terror.[76] Blacks reacted aggressively at times, yet they rarely used deadly force—perhaps because they possessed few firearms and faced armed police as defenseless civilians. Black participants like those who cornered Officer William Long on Forest Avenue retreated in the face of drawn revolvers.[77] Still whites and blacks intended to harm one another, the former—also lacking firepower—beat several blacks senseless and frequently expressed the desire to kill.[78] And surely black and white community leaders understood the specter of race war.[79]

In fact, during the first day of riot, they endeavored to negotiate its end. As early as 8:30 A.M. on June 21, black members of the Citizens Committee for Jobs in War Industries visited Jeffries and requested that he call in soldiers. He refused. Thereafter Rev. White, a committeeman and housing commissioner, toured the east side with the mayor, returned to entreat rioters, and later with the assistance of other committee members distributed 50,000 handbills, urging the cessation of violence. At noon the Citizens

Committee sponsored an emergency meeting, where Jeffries met with black and white leaders, including NAACP Pres. Dr. James J. McClendon, union executive R. J. Thomas, and State Senator Stanley Nowak. They criticized antiblack police activity and advocated deputizing 200 black counterrioters to operate in Paradise Valley. Yet they disagreed over the need to employ federal troops. Conferees also encouraged Jeffries to consider a radio address, identifying subversives as those responsible for the outburst. Significantly, they endorsed delegates to confer with Justice Department officials and Wayne County Prosecutor William E. Dowling about investigating "Fifth Column activity against Negroes in this vicinity" and sought legal defense for "the innocent now arrested."[80] Finally they elected a steering committee to formulate public statements.

These negotiations resulted in Jeffries deploying black counterrioters and broadcasting an appeal that castigated saboteurs. Additional entreaties occurred throughout the day as clergy, labor leaders, and youth advisers exhorted Jeffries to press Gov. Harry F. Kelly for martial law. Meanwhile steering committeemen issued their peace statements, pushing again the charge of subversion. And influential Detroiters like R. J. Thomas called together UAW shop stewards and neighborhood residents to counter the bloodshed.[81] The admirable efforts of these peacemakers notwithstanding, that evening Jeffries and Kelly finally requested federal soldiers because of mounting disorder.

In the wake of upheaval, Jeffries created the Mayor's Interracial Committee, the nation's first permanent municipal body that worked into the 1960s to avert riot.[82] By that decade 482,229 blacks, comprising 28.9 percent of 1,670,144 Detroiters, had benefited from the civil rights movement and liberal politicians. Some earned good wages and held significant union positions in the automobile industry; others—40 percent—owned homes throughout the city, and in 1967 most admitted that their situation had improved during the previous three years. Moreover blacks had supported Jerome Cavanagh's 1961 mayoral election and thereafter applauded his police commissioner appointments and his ability to attract Model Cities and antipoverty funds. They considered Detroit "the best city in the world to live in" and cooperated with Cavanagh, gaining Detroit national reputation as the model city for harmonious race relations.[83]

Nevertheless, black Detroiters also endured significant strain. Along with elder, retired whites, they confronted increasing tax problems as younger, affluent whites fled to surrounding suburbs. They earned less than whites, enjoyed fewer white collar jobs, experienced greater levels of unemployment—particularly among young males—and poverty, yet rented apartments and purchased goods from mostly white, absentee proprietors. They also realized fissure along several sociopolitical lines, for white flight contradicted the myth of progressive integration, and councilmen and policemen represented a near lily-white government. Blacks, in fact, resented white lawmen, who comprised 95 percent of the force and charged them with harassing east-side youths and sparking the Kercheval incident, a small disorder in 1966. Aware of their deprivation and limited opportunities, blacks heard militants describe ghettos as colonies and whites as imperialists. They knew, too, that nationalists considered rioters of the 1960s to be "revolutionary guerrillas . . . waging war in the belly of the beast." Black Detroiters felt the agitation of an age that televised its violence: Vietnam war abroad, race riots at home.[84]

And as happened in other major riot cities—Tampa, Cincinnati, Atlanta, and especially Newark—Detroit erupted over a police incident. In the early morning of July 23, 1967, when bluecoats raided an after-hours bar—a blind pig—at 12th and Clairmount streets, black partygoers honoring a couple of Vietnam soldiers fought back. Word spread grapevine fashion, and the confrontation expanded into riot all along 12th Street and its more respectable surrounding neighborhood. When police followed the policy of restraint that proved so successful in the Kercheval incident, it failed to work. Blacks from various socioeconomic strata, as well as handfuls of whites, carried the disorder beyond the west side and into large sections of the city. In typical commodity format, they eventually turned on black-owned establishments and homes in "a spirit of carefree nihilism" before spending themselves four days later. Meanwhile, their death and injury toll rose as humiliated and resentful police and inexperienced, frightened guardsmen (brought into a state of emergency the evening of July 23) replaced the "walk softly" approach with indiscriminate, deadly force.[85]

Too numerous for patrolmen and troopers, rioters finally forced local, state, and federal authorities—in a shameless replay of the political upmanship of 1943—to commit combat-tested paratroopers. Very late on the second day of upheaval, regular soldiers quickly restored peace. In the original riot zone west of Woodward Avenue, however, snipers continued to engage police and guardsmen in an escalated version of violence. They quit only after three more days of mayhem, leaving behind forty-three dead, over 600 injured, and $40 million worth of property damage. Unlike World War II rioters, they scarcely affected war production; like them, they participated in the worst of several nationwide disturbances—164 during the first nine months of 1967—and acted more out of hope than despair. They also disclosed the limitations of officials, whose political in-fighting exacerbated bloodshed, and they fostered creation of the first National Advisory Commission on Civil Disorders.

Like their predecessors of 1943, then, contemporary Detroit rioters experienced strain and shared hostile beliefs. Before exploding, they inundated Cavanagh's administration with continuous complaints, which ran the gamut from inadequate housing facilities to unemployment. Despite advances in some of these areas, they expressed relative deprivation in comparison with segregated white residents—one of "the most frequent forms of strain"—and showed perennial, racial divisions. They smarted most over police behavior, which had improved since World War II yet lagged far behind the expectations of civil rights-minded black Detroiters. Rioters knew of the previous summer's Kercheval disturbance and had heard rumors of police beating one prostitute in April and killing another in July. Many of those who triggered the outburst represented the major victims of abusive police power—streetwalkers and pimps, gamblers and vagrants—and reacted on 12th Street, scene of the rumored brutality.[86]

Hence, participants from the underworld considered the police raid fraught with "racial and symbolic significance." So did the middle and working-class rioters, also present in the crowd of 200, having been attracted from nearby neighborhoods or while en route to work. They channeled general beliefs into specific griev-ances for which there seemed no redress; they resented police disrespect, illegal search, unnecessary detention, and especially violence.[87]

In muggy, summer weather, when night life spilled into Sunday morning and sleeping proved uncomfortable, participants gathered on the major thoroughfare.[88] They stood for an hour as bluecoats loaded eighty-five blind-pig occupants into patrol wag-ons, increasingly incensed by the action and swelling in numbers as time wore on. Responding to a bottle hurled at the last police vehicle to leave the arrest area, they erupted into riot, smashed windows and, by 6:00 A.M., had looted stores along 12th Street. They also spread the rumor that a patrolman had beaten "a preg-nant Negro woman," the transgression of a strongly held racial proscription.[89]

By early afternoon, hearing that police had bayoneted a black man, they became more belligerent. Soon thousands of rioters ex-tended beyond 12th Street and entered the second phase of dis-order. Between 5:00 P.M. and 6:00 P.M., they covered twenty-five miles of the city, extending east to west from Connor Street to Livernois Street and north to south from Seven Mile Road to the Detroit River by midnight. They centered in the west side, where sniper fire first occurred shortly after 9:00 P.M. on July 23, every-where over the next ten days repeating acts of destruction. Ulti-mately their wholesale devastation and sporadic guerrilla war-fare—which peaked during the early hours of July 25—were quelled by federal troops, local police, and state guardsmen.[90]

Their black predecessors of 1943 reacted to an incident free of direct police involvement, covered a decidedly smaller portion of the city for a much shorter period of time, and engaged in little sniper fire. The pattern of 1967 was somewhat different. Rioters mocked patrolmen and rampaged without interference for nearly seventeen hours, only to be brutally repressed afterward. Twenty-four years earlier their counterparts engaged no less deadly police but faced few state troopers. Neither generation of participants lost many lives to Army personnel, who killed no one in the first riot and only one in the second. Still the overall riot death tolls (thirty-four in 1943 and forty-three in 1967) set successive records for all twentieth-century disorders. The larger death toll in 1967 probably resulted from greater levels of police frustration, the presence of guardsmen and availability of firearms, black awareness, and consequently sniper activity (which took few deaths but reinforced a siege mentality among lawmen).[91]

Also like the previous generation of Detroit rioters, those of 1967 drew others into their activity, operated in mobs demonstrating "clear role definition," and established new "notions of right and wrong." Blacks outside the blind pig interpreted bluecoat activity as everlasting grievance.[92] Representing both bar scene and respectability, they formed gangs and surged along 12th Street, smashing windows, looting stores, and by early morning setting fires. They entered burned-out homes that afternoon and sacked white-owned businesses at will, extending their wrath to black establishments by nightfall (despite window signs of "Very, Very, Very, Very Black"). Looters came in waves of street hustlers, teenagers, and young adults, representing all sections of the community, as well as normally law-abiding citizens and habitual thieves. Some doubled as arsonists; youthful, allegedly organized snipers, kept police and firemen from extinguishing the fires. By late evening rioters appeared well beyond 12th Street, many of them entering the tumult in response to the initial phase of police repression.[93]

Some Detroit rioters of 1967, again like their wartime counterparts, knew one another and worked in units. "As if on signal," recalled a journalist on West Grand Boulevard, one group of black youths smashed store windows, a second group tore down metal gratings, and a third group, including both teenagers and young men, rushed the violated building and picked it clean. Even more familiar with one another and calculated in their modus operandi, a gang of thieves repeatedly rode through the riot scene and "methodically" looted several stores.[94]

More black rioters, like their 1943 predecessors, neither knew other participants well nor sought mere self-aggrandizement. No doubt some street people, teenage boys, factory workers, and even lawful residents rioted in company with acquaintances. Yet only about one third of those rioters interviewed by federally sponsored researchers learned of upheavals from relatives and friends or met companions at the outburst.[95] And, contrary to the motives of criminals and hoodlums, most participants spilled into the streets to protest racial inequality. In fact, Detroit Urban Leaguers found rioters (rather than nonrioters) leaning more strongly toward "traditional American beliefs." Whether comprised of those who brushed with the law frequently or not at all, crowds adjusted their activities to the behavior of police, guardsmen, and soldiers.[96]

In this respect, everyday participants followed—as had their forerunners in 1943—impromptu leaders forged from the violence. Of these, Mr. Greensleeves—so-called because of his attire—came forth as the most conspicuous. Incensed by the rough treatment of those arrested in the blind pig, he exhorted the original 12th Street crowd to kill the police. He shouted "Black Power," but turned out to have no ties with radical groups and had only one conviction, for carrying an unregistered gun. A twenty-two-year-old, longtime Detroit resident, high-school dropout, and automobile worker, he harbored deep-seated resentment toward lawmen as "whitey motherfuckers" and outside intruders. Michael L., as he was identified later, resembled the age, background, and, most significantly, hostility of Charles L. Unlike L., he escaped conviction. Lesser known spontaneous leaders also rallied mobs, such as the son of one of the blind-pig owners and unidentified young militants.[97] However, the identity and personal traits of most 1967 ringleaders remain unknown, though again like their ancestors of World War II they had probably experienced greater strain than their followers and represented those more prone to violence.

Ringleaders or adherents, the great majority of rioters claimed long-term residence in Detroit, even longer than those who stayed clear of violence. More likely to have been Northerners, born in the city or having lived there for at least six years, they belied the supposition that participants represent "atypical elements in the ghetto population." Those of Southern origin had lived in Detroit

at least ten years and came from urban backgrounds.[98] Outsiders—participants who arrived in Detroit by automobiles bearing out-of-state license plates, ranging from California to New
York—proved more real than those rumored to have participated
in the 1943 disorder.[99] Still, their meager presence suggested only
the impact of rapid communications and increased black militancy.

Despite some widespread belief in "the devil theory,"[100] Communists and Black Nationalists, who wanted the credit for such
"national revolutions," hardly seemed responsible for the disorder.[101] Very few participants attributed the trouble to "agitators"
or conspirators. Nor, most importantly, did local, state, or law-
enforcement agencies, though they identified more group activity
than had been present a generation earlier.[102]

Rioters, in fact, needed little encouragement from subversives.
Eleven thousand persons filled Detroit streets by midnight on the
first day of disturbance, nearly 75 percent of them in the original,
west-side riot area. Many more blacks than whites and many more
males than females participated, although increasing numbers of
black women, products of greater racial awareness and changing
gender roles, followed the 1943 example of Goldie W. Before the
disorder subsided, 11 percent of those blacks over fifteen years of
age and living in the zones of upheaval—almost 17,000 persons—
had taken part in the lawlessness.[103] Their proportion in the de-
cisive 12th Street corridor rose to 33 percent, according to one
survey.[104] Participants, regardless of race, gender, or residence,
focused on police and property targets and rioted side by side
rather than in opposition to one another, as did the 1943 participants. Those in each outburst represented historically significant
portions of their total populations.[105]

More sizable and equally important numbers of city dwellers,
particularly blacks, watched the mayhem. In riot neighborhoods,
they comprised between 20 and 25 percent of blacks fifteen years
and older. They formed huge crowds and, as in 1943, created
problems for frustrated lawmen.[106] Hence some onlookers became
arrestees. Unlike wartime sightseers, these crowds contained a
greater cross section of blacks. Everybody, contended one rioter,
was "pissed off": "Chicks," including Parent Teacher Association

board members, flashed the Black Power sign, while "Toms" cried in approval of the protest.[107]

Initially spectators, like the early participants, acted carefree. Those who gathered outside the blind pig mocked arrestees and cheered when someone smashed the rear window of a police car. From that moment until the police toughened their stance several hours later, they bantered with patrolmen, destroyed, looted, and ignited property in what Cavanagh called "a carnival spirit."[108] They struck at those—real, imagined, and symbolic—responsible for their oppressed lives, exhibiting the unity and purpose shared by Detroiters in 1943. Unlike them, however, contemporary revelers soon engaged in sheer nihilism, destroying anything for pleasure.[109]

Small numbers, especially community leaders, did seek to check the upheaval and restore order. Celebrity or commoner, counterrioters tended to be better educated, more affluent, more likely to be Southern born and reside in a stable, integrated neighborhood.[110] At the initiation of Hubert G. Locke, Police Commissioner Ray Girardin's administrative assistant, several 12th Street spokesmen toured the major riot zone, urging everyone to clear the streets. They drew jeers from the crowds during the first morning of violence.[111] Lesser known citizens also acted as peacemakers in numerous, sometimes dangerous ways, such as fighting blazes and assisting victims. Mostly, they guarded their property, signaling their stake in society and opposition to violence as redress.[112]

Some counterrioters became victims of the turbulence, as had those in 1943. Fifty-five-year-old Julius L. Dorsey, a black security officer who kept would-be looters at bay by discharging his pistol into the air, died of indiscriminate shots fired at the thieves by National Guardsmen.[113] Other peacemakers no doubt sustained injuries and even found themselves, like Thomas F. a generation earlier, incarcerated as rioters.

Even greater than the counterrioters—who comprised 16 percent of the black residents over fifteen years of age residing in the disturbance area—were individuals who simply avoided the conflict, approximately half of those in the same survey. They, as well as those in other studies, considered such devastation the futile work of undesirable, irresponsible, or criminal elements. Many of these naysayers represented middle-class stakeholders benefiting from postwar socioeconomic and civil rights gains.[114]

Unlike the riot of 1943, when black and white Detroiters battled over the color line, rioters in 1967 generally protested an abusive system. Unquestionably a black woman cursing "whitey" and a white man shooting a black youth were exhibiting interracial passions. Nevertheless most black and white participants attacked white lawmen and firemen or white-owned property, convinced that they shared the same fight. Blacks, argued investigators and historians, alerted society to its unacceptable exploitation. If whites, comprising only 12 percent of those arrested, also wanted "a change of norms," they articulated their purpose much less clearly.[115] Still, black and white Detroit rioters of 1967 completed the transition from communal to commodity violence begun by their forebears; less interested in interracial combat, they fought more along class lines.

Black and white rioters rarely fought one another, but they did take three lives—a minuscule figure in comparison with the toll taken by law enforcers, who killed thirty of the forty-three casualties. Heavily armed, anxious police and guardsmen often fired without judgment. Perhaps most tragic was the Algiers Motel incident, where local enforcers sought out snipers. Three blacks were killed in cold blood and several other patrons, including white prostitutes whose presence with black males enraged patrolmen, were terrorized. None of the victims proved to have been snipers; their deaths and the abuse of others were vicious, bigoted acts of retribution.[116]

Long before this incident, blacks and whites moved to end the outburst. In addition to the efforts of Locke's mediators on the first morning of riot, several dozen community, political, and youth leaders and 12th Street representatives met with Mayor Cavanagh that afternoon. All believed that additional force would be needed to crush the disturbance. Meanwhile numerous municipal agencies and private organizations, for example the Mayor's Committee for Human Resources Development, worked to keep schoolchildren at home. Throughout the second day of conflict, as Cavanagh and

Gov. George Romney negotiated with presidential aides for federal troops, black and white leaders pressed the point. They expressed relief as paratroopers secured the east side late that evening.[117]

Almost uncannily, the Detroit riot of 1967 resembled its wartime predecessor—in community leadership, official response, and federal intervention. So, too, did the reactions of many city residents and the reconstruction efforts of municipal leaders. Governmental bodies were set up—the Governor's Fact-Finding Committee and the National Advisory Commission on Civil Disorders—and, in addition, Cavanagh sought the assistance of private enterprise and laid the basis for the New Detroit Committee.

Investigative bodies identified very similar characteristics among 1943 and 1967 rioters, but they often interpreted these traits differently. The Governor's Committee dismissed the 1,893 mostly black rioters as hoodlums—a minority of youthful, unattached, uprooted, and unskilled misfits within an otherwise law-abiding black community. It based these conclusions solely on police reports which received some support from municipal and state investigators. Had certain irresponsible black leaders and journalists not provoked militant behavior in 1943, commiteemen believed, the City of Detroit would have resolved its racial problems peacefully.

The National Commission, in contrast, deemed black rioters viable protesters and their actions a significant comment on minority life in urban America. Focusing on the 7,231 mostly black Detroit participants, it described them as being much like non-rioters: neither uneducated nor alienated, Detroit born and bred, hopeful, politically active, and aware that racial conditions had improved in recent years.[118] It even extended these characteristics to all black rioters of the 1960s, considering them, in the words of a commission investigator, "the cream of urban Negro youth in particular and urban Negro citizens in general."[119] It visualized "new" ghetto men as noble and righteous, and accorded them a legitimacy never enjoyed by earlier generations of rioters, black or white.[120]

The National Commission in 1967 seemed as intent on discrediting the hoodlum-riffraff thesis as the Governor's Committee had been in advancing it a generation earlier. It knew that a state-appointed committee, which had accepted the riffraff theory for the Los Angeles riots, had drawn scathing criticism from reform-minded academicians like Robert M. Fogelson of MIT.[121] Thus, it made Fogelson's critique required reading for all staff members and asked the MIT scholar to assist them.[122] While Fogelson and Robert Hill of Columbia University worked independently, the commission issued its official report with an a priori commitment to the protest image of rioters. It made the rioters as one-dimensional as their earlier counterparts: aggrieved victims turning to violence, the last redress.[123] It soon gathered support from Fogelson and Hill, who considered the participants of 1967 "fairly representative of the ghetto residents, especially of the young adult males."[124]

Subsequent investigations of the 1967 riot challenged this paramount yet exclusive view. Researchers Elliot Luby of Wayne State University and James Hedegard of the University of Michigan found both riffraff and, in smaller quantities, New Ghetto Man characteristics among their random sample of those arrested. They profiled individuals who reacted to social injustice and those who were merely sparked by the "carnival of excitement."[125] Similarly, sociologists Benjamin D. Singer and Richard W. Osborn of the University of Western Ontario and James A. Geschwender of the State University of New York–Binghamton concluded from their accidental sample of arrestees that potential rioters were more readily to be found among the less educated and those of lower occupational status, income, and employment.[126] Stressing diversity of another kind, Robert A. Mendelsohn of Wayne State University identified arrestees—without describing his data base—as comprising an "important segment" of the black working class: predominantly young, employed, and unattached males, lacking ideological slants and organizational memberships, but sparked by "racial consciousness" and rising expectations.[127]

Collectively these scholars expanded the view of who participated in the Detroit riot of 1967. Benefiting from theories, methodologies, and resources unknown to their wartime counterparts, they identified in broad, faceless terms a multifaceted group, driven by diverse motivations. By pressing one concept—for example, anomie, New Ghetto Man, or relative deprivation—over another, they advanced knowledge of those rioters who had been arrested. Still, they could not identify all rioters categorically.[128]

Therefore, University of Michigan historian Sidney Fine found the rioters—who had sparked the most ruinous upheaval of the century—to be neither riffraff nor "the cream of the crop among blacks in the city." Synthesizing the contemporary works, he characterized them as less well educated, politically aware, civil-rights oriented, and economically accomplished than nonrioters, yet more recent residents, socially isolated, and frequently unemployed than nonrioting Detroiters. Although he identified only a minority of all participants as true militants, Fine nevertheless refrained from interpreting the specific motivations of most rioters. He acknowledged, but did not detail, the "variety of reasons" for rioters' behavior. He also summarized the very scant information on female and white rioters, noting that some of the latter shared "the resentment of black rioters" while others sought "nothing more than personal gain." He recapitulated the somewhat more extensive findings on juveniles—typical adolescents whose daily encounters with oppression and personal desires for self-respect accounted for their involvement. So did peer pressure, though surprisingly not socioeconomic status. Like other researchers, Fine looked for a monolithic portrait of who rioted without finding one, and reinforced Fogelson's view of violence as protest; Detroit rioters called attention to their conditions but did not seek to restructure the political power.[129]

Despite differences, the 1967 surveys provide profiles of the rioters that are strikingly similar to those of 1943, revealing relationships between individuals of each generation who entered the streets and suggesting patterns for all twentieth-century participants. Overwhelmingly blacks dominated the disorders, comprising 78 percent of all arrestees in 1943 and 88 percent of them in 1967; their upswing in participation was fostered by increasing ghetto numbers and isolation, as well as the climate of increased racial awareness.[130]

Age was another important factor, most rioters in both disorders being teenagers or young adults. The median age of those in the 1943 upheaval stood at twenty-six years, while that of their 1967 counterparts remained the same or dropped slightly to twenty-four years or somewhat lower, depending on the study.[131] Female rioters in both eras resembled the ages of their men, though slightly older in 1943. In that earlier riot, white male participants were considerably younger than the blacks, and in 1967 they were considerably older. In 1943, teenagers comprised 50 percent of all white participants; they lived closer to the black ghetto than did their 1967 counterparts and experienced greater threats to the racial status quo; in 1943, teenagers represented their parents and invaded black turf. In both riots, black participants, who lived in the riot zones, represented a more complete cross section of their community than did whites.[132] In riot as in war, youngsters of whatever race served their communities as soldiers. They were more physically fit and had fewer obligations or inhibitions than their elders, and they seemed to harbor greater anger toward the police.[133]

Although being male, too, characterized the rioters, female rioters did appear more in evidence than was indicted by arrest records in 1943, and they increased their involvement in the 1960s. Their proportions grew from 4.5 percent (1943) to 12 percent (1967), revealing the steady erosion of female passivity and police chivalry. No doubt fewer women rioted during the earlier conflict, in part because they had been "taught to focus on personal matters"; besides, few of them attracted police attention, which was concentrated on potential male aggression. In 1967, both females and police—in the face of increased racial and gender awareness—acted more aggressively. Perhaps the growing number of female-headed families also placed more women in the public arena. As a result, although only black women were arrested in 1943, the later riot saw both black women and white women arrested.[134]

Whatever the era or the race, more females engaged in riot and looting than was recorded, and they shared many socioeconomic traits with male arrestees. They experienced higher jobless rates than the men, and in 1943 what jobs they had—especially black women—were as service workers or domestics. Small wonder that females in both disorders committed theft, more than any other crime and expressed normally "inhibited aggressive impulses."[135]

Regardless of gender, all participants were longtime Detroiters. Data on black female residency in 1943 has been destroyed by court officials, but that for male probationers stood at nine and one half median years (black) and seventeen median years (white). Those who rioted in 1967—both races and genders—reported having been born in Detroit or raised there for at least ten years.[136] They demonstrated that it took "some time in the city to develop the inclination to riot" and that it remained for the community to look at itself, rather than Southerners or newcomers, for the "root causes" of bloodshed.[137] Rioters were socialized—increasingly so among the young and from one disorder to another—toward greater instead of less collective violence.[138] Ironically, in 1943 several years of residence was viewed by officials as recent arrival, while a similar period of residency in 1967 was seen as "unequivocally" homegrown.[139]

Backed by federal statistics, residents and officials made much of the hoodlum thesis in 1943, while their counterparts a generation later generally ignored such an interpretation.[140] This change in outlook occurred despite a higher percentage of police records among the 1967 rioters: Nearly 50 percent of those arrested already knew the Detroit Police Department booking procedure. Nevertheless only 31 percent of all whites and 11 percent of all blacks canvassed in the postriot period said criminals caused the upheaval. No doubt expanded ghetto boundaries, greater urban socialization toward violence, and increased community–police strain meant a higher percentage of police records among the general community. Yet 1967 rioters who had previous trouble with the law, at least black arrestees, possessed records comparable to those of equivalent age groups in the total black population, and fully half of these previous arrests had never resulted in convictions.[141] Furthermore the percentages of previous arrestees in Detroit (1967) stood only slightly above those of previous arrestees involved in the Newark disorder and well under those for Watts. Participants of both Detroit riots displayed some degree of criminality, but that carries questionable historical significance. Their involvement simply lent disproportionate weight to the hoodlum-riffraff thesis.

Other traits, such as birthplace, provided more important distinctions between two generations of Detroit rioters. Among black male probationers for whom 1943 information exists, only 2.4 percent were born in the city as compared to their white male counterparts with 52.9 percent. No data for black female participants of that period endured, but in 1967 the National Commission study, which combined black men and black women, established native rioters at 59.4 percent. Other surveys of only black males reduced this figure to 35.4 percent. In either case, native-born black males rioting in larger proportions during the second outburst signified the delayed impact of wartime in-migration. Predictably, more black male participants of 1943 than of 1967 were of Southern upbringing: 64.7 percent versus 25.6 percent. Nevertheless, the length of residence of the 1943 rioters challenged the theory that it was newcomers who were rioting, while the birthplaces of the 1967 rioters confirmed that it was *urban living* that predisposed youngsters to collective violence.[142]

Perhaps marital status signified even bigger differences among participants. In 1943 black male arrestees registered marriage rates of 62.9 percent, fully 25 percent greater than their 1967 counterparts. Instead of being young, detached hooligans, they tended to be mature adults: married, employed, with little previous police contact. Most black female and white male participants, in contrast, recorded much lower marital percentages of 35.7 and 28.1. However, nearly one third of all the women identified themselves as separated, divorced, or widowed, indicating that marital characteristics replicated race and age patterns: attached black adults, single white teenagers. Essentially black rioters, male and female, belied the speculation that irresponsible youths comprised black participation in the 1943 disorder.[143]

In the second Detroit outburst, nearly 50 percent of the black male arrestees identified themselves as unattached, a much higher percentage than found in the postriot community sample. The unmarried seemed more likely to riot than married men.[144] White male rioters reported single rates very similar to those for white men in 1943: 71 percent.[145] Curiously, female participants were not asked their marital status.

The marital status discrepancy between black Detroiters of 1943 and 1967 occurred because of different riot patterns and possibly interpretations. During the first disorder, black males acted alone in their home communities while white youngsters traveled long distances in groups to threaten the ghetto. Presumably many married men entered the fray to strike at these unattached marauders, at white lawmen, and at property owners. In this context, black husbands and fathers participated in violence for the same reason that their counterparts avoided doing so twenty-four years later, when the one-sided commodity riot kept them at home to defend wives and children. Rioters in the 1967 disturbance might have possessed greater familial responsibility than is obvious in the single-versus-married statistics; separated, divorced, and widowed categories might have shown a different story. Combining National Commission statistics of the married and the previously married resulted in a larger figure—51.4 percent—than that for the unattached. Separated, divorced, and widowed rioters did not carry the full responsibility of married participants, yet they were hardly without family obligations. They and married rioters combined in percentages very similar to those of single participants, and suggest that attached and unattached shared similar stakes—or that marital status was not a significant factor in a commodity riot.[146]

Employment rates for participants of each generation also varied, though they shared similar occupational statuses. World War II rioters registered different work percentages, depending on age and gender. Older, married black males benefited from the wartime boom and enjoyed near full employment of 97 percent. Younger, single white men fared less well, dropping to 89.6 percent. Most striking, because of the economic expansion, unattached black women in their midtwenties experienced a very low 69 percent job rate.[147] Conversely, in 1967, a time when the city-wide rate stood at 93.8 percent, employment rates for black males, the only rioters surveyed on this variable, plummeted to 78.2 percent—far below that of older black or younger white male rioters and closest to black female participants in 1943. Their *unemploy-*

ment rates dramatically exceeded those for black men nationally and for black Detroiters living in the riot zones: 8.2 percent and 11 percent.[148] Somewhat younger and more unattached than their 1943 counterparts, they faced problems of race, class, and ability in a shifting, sophisticated economy that had little place for poorly skilled ghetto dwellers.[149]

Ironically, this occurred at a time when rioters had completed more years of education than those in World War II. Black and white male participants placed on probation in 1943 had received eight and nine years of schooling, respectively, while black female probationer levels remain unknown.[150] Twenty-four years later, black male rioters upped their schooling: at least 75 percent had completed some high school, and 23 percent had graduated.[151] Yet their schooling might have been inferior at the very time that the work place was starting to require more than rudimentary skills.[152]

Comparisons of those who rioted, in short, revealed both similarities and differences, but hardly one-dimensional profiles. As demonstrated in 1943, those involved constituted various segments of the larger black and white communities, acted for diverse reasons, and in distinct layers of expanding violence. They also revealed much about the experiences of nonrioters in their midst, and of city dwellers who lived elsewhere yet shared similar industrial settings and racial competition before, during, and long after the war. In historical terms, wartime Detroiters struck well beyond the narrow confines of Hastings Street and placed collective violence in even broader perspectives.

SEVEN

Broader Perspectives

Layered violence, of course, occurred elsewhere long before and shortly after the Detroit upheavals of midtwentieth century. Beyond comparisons within their own municipality and among their own descendants, Motor City rioters of 1943 offer insights into the motives of earlier and later riot participants in other cities, suggesting from whose ranks they sprang and from whose numbers future rampagers might rise. They stepped out of the larger population and shared characteristics with fellow residents who did not riot, and this proves valuable for understanding other perpetrators of collective violence. They impacted on the urban populations of Chicago, New York, and other major cities, revealing much about the social order in a national context and the efforts to preserve it. Moreover, Detroit rioters of 1943 reveal ties to western heritage: violent protest among European peoples in urban settings.

Prior to the 1960s, European scholars of collective violence in England and France followed the lead of Gustave Le Bon.[1] They characterized early rioters as criminal, maladjusted, and riffraff, unstable persons fulfilling emotional needs and selfish, apolitical aims. Lacking quantifiable evidence and drawing on psychological interpretations, they posited breakdown and contagion theories: Urbanization and industrialization promoted antisocial behavior in some individuals, and these misfits exploded, drawing others into a "mental unity" of excitement, destruction, and anonymity.[2]

Le Bon's theory is still quite popular with some officials and private citizens, but it began losing its credibility among scholars in the early 1960s. Some, like E. J. Hobsbawm and E. P. Thompson, resurrected and revised Karl Marx's solidarity theory, and interpreted collective violence as the struggle of working-class people for political power. Non-Marxist historians also explained riot as protest and participants as ordinary people seeking redress.[3] Perhaps most influential is George Rudé's synthesis of preindustrial crowds, which posits violence as collective behavior evolving through a precise set of determinants. Rudé presented history from the bottom up and suggested similarities between food rioters and political rebels. He also encouraged further investigation of the mob in other eras and locales as a "living and many-sided historical phenomenon."[4] Slightly more than a decade later, a comparative history of upheavals in England, France, and Germany between 1830 and 1930 by Charles Tilly, Louise Tilly, and Richard Tilly extended the revised history of collective violence into modern times and suggested parallels for the recent civil disorders in the United States.[5]

Indeed, by 1975, several interpretations of race riots in Watts (1965), Detroit (1967), and elsewhere had pinpointed who had rioted and presented "violence as protest."[6] Despite continued adherence to Le Bon's thesis by local officials, historians and sociologists, as well as the National Advisory Commission on Civil Disorders, found mobs comprised of young, under- and unemployed black males, between the ages of fifteen and twenty-four, somewhat better educated than their peers and decidedly more politically aware and active, racially proud, and hostile.[7] They deemed the "mental unity" of crowds the results of real grievances, ranging from relative deprivation and blocked opportunities to racial pride and political identity.[8] Their research presented the "New Ghetto Man" in the United States, just as that of Rudé and the

Tillys indicated new self-images and political purposes among riotous Europeans of earlier eras.[9]

Still, some other interpreters of the 1960s disorders advanced convergence theories, stressing sociopsychological characteristics that predisposed certain individuals to gather about violent activity. They emphasized the impact of environmental circumstances and reiterated or modified Le Bon's breakdown theory, postulating hypotheses about riffraff, underclass, family, youth, and newcomers. In certain instances, they denied or diminished the political motivation of rioters.[10] Instead, they implied pathology, and in some cases envisioned blacks as bearers of bloodshed rather than victims of racism.[11] Nevertheless, most scholars reinforced Rudé rather than Le Bon and in the process also identified communal and commodity patterns associated with twentieth-century urban race riots in the United States.

Researchers noted that riots occurring between 1900 and the early 1920s grew out of intergroup competition, ultimately exacerbated by wartime in-migration, expanding ghettos, and black awareness: forays initiated by whites to protect the racial status quo in employment, housing, and recreation. In contrast to these early communal disorders, violence in the 1960s resulted from a lag in civil rights gains for working-class and poor blacks, sparking assaults on white-owned property and white police officers. Given the composition of black inner cities and white suburbs, blacks in New York, Los Angeles, and elsewhere lashed out at racist symbols in these commodity riots—so-called because of wholesale looting. Meantime, disorders in the Great Depression and World War II marked the transition from communal to commodity disturbances, remnants of both patterns being most identifiable in the Detroit upheaval of 1943.[12]

Yet only impressionistic descriptions exist for those who rioted before 1960: in Atlanta, New Orleans, and Brownsville (1906), East St. Louis and Houston (1917), Chicago (1919), Tulsa (1921), New York (1900, 1935), Mobile, Beaumont, and Los Angeles (1943). East St. Louis and Chicago rioters of both races, for example, appeared to be unattached teenagers and young men from the working and lower classes (long-standing white residents and second generation Irish, respectively) protecting their turf against oncoming black migrants. In contrast, Tulsa rioters "came from all economic and social classes." White spectators everywhere probably represented several socioeconomic strata and definitely intensified the level of violence, and black victims retaliated, especially in Chicago. Less is known about blacks in Harlem who rioted in 1935; the triggering incident was an erroneous rumor that police had beaten a shoplifter to death, and in revenge the rioters assaulted officers and looted stores, perhaps sparing white passersby and properties of whites who hired blacks because of efforts by Communist Party members of both races. Crowds of rioters "constantly changed their make-up," and besides criminals, looters included youngsters "in the spirit of adventure" and law-abiding adults expressing their resentment against discriminatory economic practices. However, none of the participants in these disturbances, or those in Elaine, Arkansas, during 1921 and Columbia, Tennessee, twenty-five years later, surfaced in aggregate profiles.[13]

Nor did rioters of World War II, the exception being the Detroiters of 1943. Investigators presented fuller, but largely one-dimensional portraits: uneducated black ruffians with few redeeming qualities who fit easily into the Le Bon thesis. Of these inquiries, the Governor's Fact-Finding Committee opinion dominated all mention of the rioters in later histories of the upheaval.[14]

Writing in 1959, sociologist Allen D. Grimshaw advanced a synthesis of previous rioters and those of wartime Detroit. He challenged the characterization of all participants in past riots as criminals, noting the presence of servicemen, middle-class blacks, and females of varying age and status. He questioned also the validity of interpreting rioters solely on the basis of those caught. But he neither provided original data on the participants nor contested all aspects of Le Bon's breakdown thesis.[15]

Working from sketchy data, historians writing after Grimshaw compared World War I and Harlem rioters of 1943 with those of the most recent upheavals. One of these found the preponderance of participants in the first war and in the 1960s to have been unmarried males, teenagers, and young adults harboring "fewer inhibitions and responsibilities than their elders" and great contempt for lawmen. Another identified Harlem participants as predominantly lower-class teenage boys and young men, housewives, and children from various social strata, who compared favorably with the age, class, employment, and long-standing residency of their counterparts in the 1960s.[16] Yet their general, tentative findings neither furnished individual and aggregate profiles of the rioters nor sought out patterns that would connect one generation of rioters with the next.

Most recently, however, Roberta Senechal provided the first profile of white rioters in an early twentieth-century communal disorder: Springfield, Illinois, in 1908. She identified the rioters as single, Illinois-born, semiskilled males in their midtwenties, largely from the working class; they were acquainted with one another and with many of their black victims. Prevented by authorities and a prominent businessman from lynching two black arrestees, an alleged murderer and an alleged rapist, they attacked the major areas of black business and housing, seeking to annihilate all blacks and punish influential whites for hiring black workers, servicing black customers, and vying for black political support. They perceived these racial advances as challenges to their own status and, accordingly, assaulted some white establishments. Some members of the Springfield elite had supported the riot initially as a symbol of needed municipal reform, but when rioters carried their violence to excess, they denounced it. Although they were led by a handful of so-called undesirables, most of those arrested or injured came from the general population, and their participation revealed the socioeconomic diversity of racist thinking and behavior. In the aftermath they and the very whites they had challenged during the riot closed ranks, and no rioter faced serious fine or imprisonment. Ultimately white solidarity cut across class, gender, and ethnic lines.[17]

Lacking data for comparable sketches of white female and black rioters, Senechal's study suggested links between white male participants in Springfield and their wartime successors thirty-five years later. Like them, white Detroiters in 1943 tended to be single, Northern born, even younger laborers, representing a working class threatened by black socioeconomic advances; their ranks also contained small, but significant numbers of ethnics. They too sought to obliterate blacks, sometimes with police assistance. In the aftermath of riot, they drew criticism from some officials and influential whites who dismissed them as hoodlums. Unlike Springfieldians, however, white Detroit rioters experienced social strain and several preriot incidents brought on by war, as well as perceived shifts in black status, and they encountered more racially aware and competitive blacks. The ethnics among them were predominantly second generation Italians and Poles, rather than historically antagonistic Irish-Americans. White Detroiters knew neither one another nor their victims and, once arrested, faced more justice-minded whites and received sentences more equal to those of their black adversaries. Despite differences due to changing demographic characteristics, racial attitudes, and urban structure after 1908, however, successive generations of white participants bore more similar traits and motivations than diverse ones.

In fact, the Detroit rioters of 1943 provided the necessary example for understanding successive generations of white and black participants in riots dating back to the turn of the century and, particularly for blacks, forward to the 1960s. Taken together and allowing for distinctions of time, place, and riot patterns, Springfield and Detroit profiles have dashed officials' self-serving descriptions of earlier white rioters as riffraff and raised anew the possibility that rioters in other cities—Tulsans, for instance—represented several classes and ethnic groups. While additional research is needed of all those who erupted before World War II, Detroiters and Springfieldians came from the general populace and shared certain traits with them.

Indeed, participants in the 1943 Detroit outburst desired greater participation in society. White rioters felt threatened and their black counterparts resentful, for members of both races had made enough gains to want much more. Unlike more successful residents, they were too impatient to mark time amid democratic rhetoric and wartime change. Younger, more energized, and less influential than those who avoided violence, they sought redress in the streets; they rioted to improve rather than destroy the system. They came forth as neither mainstream nor misfit, but as desperate people seeking respectability through protest that shed blood and ironically reinforced their disrepute in the eyes of the public.

Census data for 1940 provides even further insights into the rioters. It permits an overall view of the Detroit populace and a detailed look at specific tracts—smaller areas of "fairly homogeneous population"—within the city.[18] An analysis of the tracts where most black and white rioters lived revealed the relationship of participants to peaceful neighbors and to their environment, while that for the entire city indicated the broader context out of which the rioters emerged.

Hence, in conformity with the uniquely youthful populace of 1940, rioters—particularly if white—were younger than other Detroiters who resided in the same census tracts.[19] They also reflected the ethnic patterns of the census tracts, Italians and Poles constituting small yet ample percentages of residents and rioters. Like their nonethnic counterparts, they were long-term residents, for the number of foreign-born had been reduced significantly over the previous quarter century by world wars and immigration legislation.[20]

Regardless of age or ethnicity, male rioters of both races had attained approximately one more year of education than that reported in their census tracts. Their youth probably accounted for these somewhat higher levels of schooling, elder blacks and whites traditionally having left school at earlier ages.[21]

Black and white rioters, like nonrioters, nevertheless found their employment affected more by race and circumstance than by education. In 1943, black male participants recorded nearly full employment because of the war boom; this rate far exceeded the roughly 89 percent for all Detroiters three years earlier. Enigmatically, only 70.7 percent of black female rioters were employed when arrested as compared to 80.6 percent of black women throughout the city. This unusually high jobless rate probably indicated pervasive discrimination against black women in the automobile industry, their own lower class status, or even police disinterest when writing tickets. White male troublemakers also reported lower rates of work than black males, but this relatively depressed employment probably resulted both from their youth and student status. Indeed, pupils and retirees combined made up only 30,000 of 625,000 additions to the labor force during the period 1941–1944.[22]

Black male participants benefited from wartime expansion and wages, especially in defense industries, where weekly salaries jumped from under $40 to over $50 between the 1940 census and the 1943 riot, for they held more jobs, percentagewise, than all laborers had held in 1940. But both black and white rioters were listed on arrest tickets chiefly as "laborer," evidence either of low police expectations for black men and white youths, or their indifference to occupation detail that census takers recorded more precisely. No doubt black males faced discrimination in upgrading, and white teenagers held entry-level jobs. But both should certainly have held more diverse jobs than is suggested by the catchall term "laborer."[23]

Perhaps nowhere did rioters share characteristics with nonrioters more closely than in living accommodations. Most Detroiters rented, though blacks to a greater degree than whites. They also experienced more congestion than residents in other parts of the municipality. A year after the disturbance a study found that it would have required 19,000 additional dwellings to house all black families in less crowded units, pointing up the impact of housing shortages on the lives of rioters and nonrioters alike. Blacks also lived in quarters worth considerably less money and needing many more repairs than those of whites. Altogether black and white rioters, reprsenting their neighborhoods, encountered pressures and competition unknown in the more affluent, home-owning areas of the city.[24]

Therefore, in 1943, longtime Detroiters responded to well-known racial conflicts exacerbated by three years of war migration. They observed the steady influx of newcomers seeking work in the Arsenal of Democracy, straining already overtaxed living space and municipal services. Nearly 500,000 additional people increased competition for resources and job opportunities throughout the city, and their influx was often bitterly resented—especially that of Southern whites and perhaps as many as 35,000 blacks.[25] For reasons of class and regionalism, denizens of both races viewed the oncoming hordes from Dixie as embarrassments and threats to their own well-being. Native white Detroiters, including some Old Southerners, never embraced the white newcomers, but Northern blacks ultimately recognized that, however backward their Southern cousins, the racial struggle could ill afford class or culture bias against them.[26] Ironically, the race issue made longer-term residents feel as alien as their recently arrived brethren.[27]

The wartime housing shortage exacerbated the newcomer problem. Rental premises were already scarce, exorbitant, and dilapidated. Detroiters dug in—sometimes refusing accommodations to white Southerners who penetrated their sections of the city, and always forcing black migrants into prescribed, primarily eastside areas. White owners feared the depreciation of their property and neighborhoods, more so when black migrants spilled over ghetto boundaries and joined white Southerners in search of dwellings. Black natives—resentful that new buildings, private and government-sponsored, were white-only—doubled up with black migrants, in apartments, garages, even stables, and winced as the newcomers ignorantly dumped refuse in halls and out windows.[28]

Throughout 1940 and 1941, blacks pressed local authorities to investigate high rents, enforce sanitary codes, and challenge restrictive covenants, but both organizational efforts by State Sen. Charles C. Diggs and court cases by individual residents faltered before deep-seated racism and relentless migration. They soon realized that overcrowding lay at the core of all housing problems, including a disproportionately high rate of tubercular deaths and other health issues, and concentrated on federal defense projects for relief. They formed the Sojourner Truth Citizens Committee under the leadership of the Rev. Charles A. Hill and, despite Polish opposition, secured the occupancy of 200 units. This impressive victory raised tensions considerably between residents of both races, and on February 28, 1942, it provoked a riot that resulted in 200 arrests and forty injuries. Bitter memories of this clash no doubt helped set the stage for worse violence.

Whites groused because Mayor Jeffries vacillated on the question of black occupancy, and then supported it with police force; blacks smarted because he soon adopted a law that forbade the construction of additional public housing in contested neighborhoods and thus prevented blacks from moving beyond the ghetto or, given the lack of sites, building more homes in it. With most black and many white migrants still to come, black Detroiters attacked and white Detroiters supported a mayoral policy that unrealistically sought to avert further bloodshed by maintaining an outdated status quo in housing. Protest continued, and conditions worsened throughout 1942 and 1943, increasing racial animosity, but the black community remained unable to break this impasse. Ultimately it pushed many long-standing residents into the streets.[29]

So, too, did the question of employing and in particular upgrading black men. As preparedness began in mid-1940, Detroiters moved from relief rolls of the depression to shop floors of the converted automobile industry. Whites, of course, led the way in defense employment and government training opportunities. Blacks, facing perennial discrimination, left the dole much more slowly and found livelihoods in services and municipal jobs vacated by whites, facilitated by mayoral policy, and supported by municipal unions. By mid-1941, they had picked up a few white leavings, yet some remained on welfare, and few benefited from either the Fair Employment Practices Committee forced on Pres. Franklin D. Roosevelt by A. Philip Randolph or the many local protests by officials of the NAACP and the UAW. Instead, black workers augmented their original prewar numbers in manufacturing only after white labor sources petered out in mid-1942. By November, they accounted for 33,500 positions, mostly foundry work, in 185 defense plants, less than 7 percent of the total work force.

Actually, black women fared the worst of all workers throughout the war. They remained the last hired, both because white workers insisted on segregated facilities for supposedly unsanitary, diseased females and because federal officials gave their equal treatment a very low priority. They also suffered from the emphasis that both black and white societies placed on male employment, and society's habitual relegating of black females to unskilled, non-industrial jobs. Ultimately, they were permitted to enter the most important defense industries, since black leaders and unionists pressed FEPC officials and auto makers to engage black females. There were few black Rosie the Riveters, however. Black women made only token inroads, mostly as matrons, sweepers, and stock handlers, though a minuscule number did set precedent by advancing to production lines. In January 1943, they comprised merely 1.5 percent or 990 of 66,000 females working in the fifty leading war plants, automobile or otherwise; in fact, black females found work in only nineteen of these factories. By spring, small gains occurred in several area industries, but one month after the riot, 28,000 black women constituted the "largest neglected source of labor" in metropolitan Detroit. Their long history as breadwinners and contributors to the economic survival of Afro-America notwithstanding, black women in the Motor City encountered unyielding race, gender, and class discrimination amid the wartime boom.[30]

Black males moved more quickly onto the shop floor, only to be denied promotion by manipulative managers seeking control over equally power-minded union leaders, and by racist laborers fearing physical closeness to blacks and economic competition from them. They experienced several white walkouts or "hate strikes" throughout 1941 and mid-1942, before UAW leadership, federal officials, and labor needs reduced these stoppages drastically and brought larger numbers of blacks into defense industries. Once in the plants and the unions, however, black men sought upgrading, which triggered a new wave of wildcat strikes during the first six months of 1943. Sometimes black workers retaliated in kind and refused to work, as in the worst preriot showdown at the Packard Motor Company that began on May 24; after white workers had walked out over the advancement of three blacks on the teardown-reassembly lines, blacks too exited the plant. Blacks then made up 5,000 of the more than 25,000 Packard strike force and drew inspiration from the militancy of earlier protests and frustration from recent setbacks. They, and white opponents, returned to work on June 3, avoiding both bloodshed and threatened reprisals (from union leaders and federal representatives). Sidestepping violence in this and the dozen or so other hate strikes, more short-lived and less well-supported, black and white workers expressed deep-seated resentments that would surface brutally within three weeks. As coworkers and union members bound by the same work-place relationships, the same familiar stewards, and the same powerful government officials, they behaved with some circumspection in the Packard stoppage. As rioters they could act anonymously and therefore more boldly.[31]

Long before the riot explosion, incidents in restaurants intensified racial antagonisms. Blacks in the depression felt the sting of being refused service in eateries, prompting State Senator Diggs to sponsor successful civil rights legislation in 1937. Many white owners flouted it and avoided prosecution or conviction because of difficult-to-prove violations and biased white juries. As blacks advanced in the growing economy and sought meals en route to work, on lunch breaks, and after hours, resentment at this treatment grew. Aware of the law and militant about their rights, black Detroiters seethed at this reminder of their second-class citizenship. White newcomers reinforced the bigotry of native restaurateurs and pressured others (who used to serve black customers) to stop. White Southerners, natives, and ethnics overcame their dislike for one another to close ranks racially, as they did in housing and employment. Black residents of many years experienced higher prices, back door service at large establishments or none at all—most insultingly Greenfield Restaurant directly adjacent to the ghetto and even more recently in small cafés throughout the city. Their rejection by the latter implied that "they were not even good enough for a second-rate restaurant." From 1940 through 1942, they pressed for civil rights through protest, litigation, and confrontation, as their white counterparts, increasingly bolstered by recently arrived Southerners, denied them equal access to one third of all restaurants. Nor did things improve as the numbers of black migrants and black servicemen increased the following year. Lawsuits against Greenfield's and, on the eve of riot, a restaurant near Belle Isle failed.[32]

Public school facilities evoked similar animosities among youngsters of both races, sometimes touching off violence. All schools were overcrowded as tight depression budgets reduced construction and curricula, but pupils in the older sections of Detroit, such as the black east side, where the lowest educational levels and greatest educational need existed, received the least financial support. Hemmed in and neglected, ghetto youth turned inward and vented anger on each other, and in January 1943 150 members of "the Brewster Street gang" entered Norvell School in southeast Detroit and beat teachers of both races for shielding a black girl who refused to join their ranks. Even before the crush of numbers and unsupervised children of working parents gave rise to this kind of outburst, black and white children had clashed in schools beyond the east side where status-minded whites drew racial lines. They rioted at Northwestern High School in 1940, when whites wrongly perceived that black students, roughly 700 of 4,000 and many from the middle-class, were increasing in numbers too fast, and at Lincoln High School in 1941 and 1942, when 600 whites resented the presence of eighty black teenagers in their previously lily-white district. Biracial efforts, particularly among municipal officials, civil leaders, and parents of Northwestern High School, moved to avert further incidents through plans for black counselors, democratic materials, and sensitivity training. On the eve of race riot in 1943, however, black and white students citywide continued to clash and awaited implementation of the Northwestern program.[33]

In part, this reflected the steady rise of deviant behavior among youngsters under seventeen years of age. Nationally, juvenile delinquents appeared in both urban and rural areas; locally and throughout the state, they continued a trend dating back at least twenty years and accelerated in the face of war-induced pressures on families. Their ranks grew steadily between 1940 and 1942, then exploded in 1943 as full employment neared, couples worked, and their children went unsupervised in a tension-filled, under-policed martial atmosphere. Greater percentages of whites than blacks, males than females, and longtime residents than migrants comprised the delinquents of Detroit, but the high proportion of blacks fed racist stereotypes. In 1943, as more children under ten years of age and more female offenders encountered juvenile authorities, blacks comprised approximately 10 percent of the Detroit population and almost 25 percent of its delinquents.[34] Most of them lived within Grand Boulevard, the oldest municipal sector, where marginal economic status and social instability fostered the highest indices of juvenile offenses and crimes against persons.[35] Their transgressions became standard copy for journalists of both races, and no doubt heightened racial anxiety and prepared the ground for rumors that would feed the riot.[36]

Despite mayoral and gubernatorial plans to address juvenile crimes in early 1943, Detroit youths increased their activities in "startling" and "more vicious" ways during the first half of the year. Blacks, particularly males running in gangs, attacked innocent, mostly white victims—said biased observers whose opinions were echoed by the Governor's Committee as the primary cause for upheaval on June 20. They instigated these assaults, supposedly agitated by older leaders charging race discrimination where none existed. Presumably their continuous provocations drew little retaliation until the outburst, when white teenagers "spearheaded" forays into the east side.[37]

Black adult offenders also raised public concern. They constituted alarming percentages of police statistics and dominated offenses against the person, including homicide, assault, rape, and robbery. They attracted sensational news coverage that reinforced white fears and often ignored the fact that most victims were also black. Most of these offenders, especially those prosecuted before 1943, had probably resided in Detroit for some time and definitely appeared somewhat older than those young adults who participated in interracial clashes. Like black juveniles, they also inhabited the east side and projected the very images that evoked racial animosities beyond the ghetto.[38]

Longtime residents, black and white, most notably within the highly congested area bounded by Grand Boulevard, also competed for inadequate recreation facilities. Under 5 percent of the city's entire acreage constituted space for play, and no major facility existed inside the ghetto. In fact, blacks had less space to picnic and play ball than to bury their dead. They overtaxed facilities

within their communities, segregated by demography and enduring racist policy in quasi-public YMCAs and private roller-skating
rinks. In racially-mixed areas blacks fought for much coveted playgrounds and athletic fields, a significant prelude for the disorder
at Northwestern High School in 1940 and, later that summer, the
disturbance at Belle Isle. That ruckus between blacks and police sparked angry white reactions, as the city's largest park became "Nigger Island." Black and white picknickers, their numbers
rapidly expanding as newcomers settled in the city, continued to
patronize the island and annoy one another, despite failed at-
tempts by a mayoral committee to improve both police and race
relations.[39]

Grievances from past incidents were carried onto public conveyances. Old-time black and white Detroiters came together daily
and intimately on the Detroit Street Railway (DSR), as greater employment, migration, and gas and tire rationing limited private
transportation and upped numbers of bus and trolley fares by 42
percent between May 1940 and May 1943. At first, as blacks filled
motorman positions vacated by whites, white drivers expressed
their backlash by exchanging verbal insults with black passengers.
After mid-1942, racial altercations escalated; by then blacks were
operating 30 percent of all DSR vehicles and constituted heavy
percentages of passengers. Nerves frayed, particularly in and
about the ghetto, and "incidents" grew more frequent. Younger
blacks led the way, sometimes with drawn knives, often damaging
streetcars. DSR white employees and passengers also provoked retaliation along racial lines. Subsequently, blacks seemed "more aggressive and insulting" than whites, in May spitting on a white
woman and stabbing a white teenager. Nevertheless, both races
fostered the climate of hate on the transit system: whites repulsed
by close physical contact with blacks and troubled by the erosion of
their own superior status; blacks alienated by white contempt for
their humanity and enraged by the opposition to their socioeconomic aspirations.[40]

Essentially, racial clashes on buses and streetcars were the outward manifestations of innumerable affronts, arguments, and altercations that had occurred for years in neighborhoods and

schools, on shop floors, and at parks. Depression-wracked Detroiters jousted for improved lives amidst the hope and anxiety of war, their competition defined by race and, increasingly, sharpened by newcomers. Both races swore, spat, and slashed at one another on DSR vehicles, or witnessed such blood-boiling incidents between others. However, neither the successful nor the migrant among them entered the foray in large numbers on June 20, 1943. Rather, the action was dominated by young black men on the make, but not yet arrived, and teenage white boys defending the race of their working parents.

These rioters took center stage against the backdrop of war, and in part because of the circumstances it unleashed. As early as 1940, black Detroiters fought for inclusion in the armed forces and, once admitted the following year, sought fair treatment. Indeed, they found themselves in segregated Army units, severely humiliated, and often brutalized by white civilians, police, and fellow soldiers. In 1941, they encountered segregation in the theaters of Fort Custer, Michigan, and savage beatings at Camp Robinson, Arkansas, where nearby townsfolk and state police assaulted, cursed, and intimidated unarmed members of the 94th Engineer Battalion (Second Army). Incredibly, some of them faced court-martial for fleeing to the safety of Michigan. Although they survived these charges, another black soldier from Detroit confronted the death penalty a year later for having been involved in the alleged rape of a white waitress at Camp Livingston, Louisiana; he plead not guilty, but was convicted and sent to prison. Throughout 1942 and into 1943, black Detroit servicemen clashed with whites in Southern camps, and, most shockingly, one of them was shot dead in broad daylight by the commander at Selfridge Field, only a few miles north of Detroit. That was only six weeks before the riot in June. Between these bloody episodes, black pilots of the 332nd Fighter Group, stationed in Oscoda, a small community northeast of Detroit, faced the ostracism of local officials, who petitioned military authorities to remove them; the Army refused.[41]

In Detroit, black residents knew of the humiliation and physical abuse heaped on their fighting men and, by implication, their entire race. Shortly after the bombing of Pearl Harbor, they protested the American Red Cross's refusal to accept blood from black donors and its subsequent Jim Crow compromise. They attended meetings and donated money in support of NAACP investigations of mistreated black Detroiters. Like blacks nationally, Detroiters expressed bitterness over "the whole military service issue" and well understood the "symbolic significance" of being asked "to die for a country" that accepts unproven aliens in the armed forces and "segregates Negroes with long records of loyalty."[42]

Detroit whites no doubt shared the national ignorance that a so-called "Negro Problem" existed in the war effort. Many probably questioned black patriotism and soldiering ability.[43] They allowed blacks to be affronted in the city and restaurateurs refused service to black military personnel; occasionally patrolmen assailed blacks without provocation. White soldiers and sailors also fought with black youths several times before the Belle Isle incident. Whites constantly reminded black citizens that their presence was unwanted even in a war for democracy. This prompted one federal investigator to suggest, six months before the disorder, that racial violence would depend upon the success or failure of "the United Nations concept among whites in Detroit."[44]

Endeavoring to advance that belief, NAACP officers scheduled a massive spring rally for Detroit to challenge the hypocrisy of whites preaching democratic war aims while practicing race discrimination. Dramatically, they intended to alert "America and the world" that nonwhite people universally would no longer stand "for continued exploitation and insult based on color." Aggressively, they resolved to check "the forces of reaction in Congress" and throughout the country that spread Jim Crow patterns and brutalized black servicemen.[45]

Thereafter, black and white Detroiters hosted the Emergency War Conference from June 3 to June 6. Walter White opened the meeting and set its militant tone by castigating those who jeopardized the war effort. Subsequent speakers and discussion leaders reinforced his Double V message, and 25,000 persons attending the final session at Olympia Stadium incorporated it in a "Statement to the Nation"; they supported the Four Freedoms wholeheartedly, but criticized "weak-kneed" gradualists opposing legitimate protest, federal officials permitting undemocratic treatment of black soldiers and defense workers, and journalists and other image makers stereotyping blacks as "intellectually, socially, and biologically inferior." Most sensational, they heard William H. Hastie, who six months earlier resigned in protest as civilian aide to the Secretary of War, lambaste the government's racist military policy, and UAW President R. J. Thomas charge the Ku Klux Klan with fomenting the Packard hate strike then in progress.[46]

How many Motor City residents of either race actually considered NAACP conference speakers "inflammatory and seditious," as did military intelligence operatives, can never be known, but other, more volatile events happened in their wake and before the riot two weeks later. Besides participation in the work stoppage, which dominated private conversations of the conferees, several blacks and whites brawled at Inkster, Eastwood Park, and throughout Detroit the week prior to June 20.[47] It is not known whether some, all, or none of these battlers and later rioters might have been moved by the rhetoric of the Emergency War Conference.

It has been impossible to determine church, civic or other affiliations of the rioters, but they must have experienced the militancy of black institutions, the reaction of white organizations, and the failure of officials. Black leaders pressed for racial equality, often with the support of white liberals, leftists, and laborites, increasing their assertiveness as the war evolved; they focused on ethical principle rather than their individual ideology, even when aligned with Communists—despite federal allegations to the contrary In housing, the Rev. Hill headed the Sojourner Truth Citizens Committee, transforming it in the wake of that bloody victory into the Citizens Committee for Jobs in War Industries. Executive secretary Gloster B. Current directed the local NAACP on several fronts, especially that of housing, and expanded the branch's membership to record numbers of 12,356 in 1942 and over 20,000 in 1943.[48] Horace Sheffield, Shelton Tappes, and other unionists drew UAW leadership more directly into the fight for employment and promotion rights. Editor Louis E. Martin enlisted the Michigan *Chronicle* in the name of these spokesmen and their struggles, relentlessly pushing Double V rhetoric before readers. So did the

Rev. Horace A. White from his pulpit at the Plymouth Congregational Church and his seat on the Detroit Housing Commission.
Assisted by Common Councilman George C. Edwards, Civil
Rights Federation of Michigan Executive Secretary Jack Raskin,
and UAW Pres. R. J. Thomas, among others, they carried the fight
to prejudiced white home owners and unionists, but found little
backing from several council members, the mayor, and police
commissioner.[49]

Despite Governor's Committee charges that the NAACP and the
Chronicle alone fomented trouble, all the above leaders challenged
the discrimination that blacks experienced and reaffirmed the
racial equality that they sought. They did so in assertive protest
and often fiery language, having abandoned the more moderate
approaches of John C. Dancy of the Urban League, J. Edward
McCall of the Detroit *Tribune,* several ministers, and interracial religious organizations. Yet their militancy appeared no greater than
that of the Rev. Hill, numerous black unionists, or, for that matter,
white racists. In the wake of the Sojourner Truth disturbance,
three whites but no blacks were indicted by a federal grand jury
for inciting riot; white unionists, including local officials, and white
plant managers instigated the walkout at Packard Motor Company; white students initiated the fighting at Northwestern High
School; white toughs drew first blood at Eastwood Park; white
newsmen of the Detroit *Times* advocated a social conservatism that
sometimes advanced racial intolerance. Black Detroiters grew increasingly exasperated as mayor and council became less receptive
to demands for basic civil rights and public housing. NAACPers
and *Chronicle* personnel knew that police, both higher-ups and patrolmen, proved more antagonistic than protective, and thus gave
racists leeway when dealing with blacks.

Blacks also found organizations to blame for the tension: National Workers League provocations in the Sojourner Truth controversy and Ku Klux Klan subversions in the Packard stoppages.
If they exaggerated the puny influence of home-grown fascists,
they did so much less than self-serving white opponents, who
claimed, with even less evidence, that Communists directed the
black protesters. Both sides accepted allies without much discre-

tion, but neither fell under the spell of reactionary or leftist ideology. And, their supporters aside, blacks embraced the very democracy that the nation was founded upon and that racists—despite the patriotic bombast of some—steadfastly subverted. For politics of another kind and for reasons of race, the Governor's Committee placed greatest blame on blacks, especially their leaders and editors, for a catastrophe triggered by specific members of both races.

Whatever the role of black or white protestors, the largest majority of rioters were unlikely to be affiliated with civil rights or reactionary organizations. Their profiles and statements make it plain that they were not active as members of some group or conspiracy or even in accordance with a plan.[50] Except for juveniles, for whom information is sketchy, rioters surfaced as longtime residents: blacks struggling for a stake in society; whites fighting to hold onto tenuous socioeconomic positions in the face of wartime anxiety and black gains.[51] Black and white participants exploded in the face of pressures that migrants and more established Detroiters dealt with nonviolently.

Of central importance, the Detroit experiences influenced efforts to avert large-scale outbursts in other sizable cities. Some outbreaks did occur prior to the Detroit riot: shipbuilders in Mobile, denizens in Beaumont, Texas, sailors and youths in Los Angeles; but none brought into the open fear of widespread interracial clashes.[52] Participants in Alabama on May 25 and Texas on June 15 depicted archetypical Southern outbursts, while those in California on June 3 displayed communal riot and supposed criminal repression: invading Mexican-American neighborhoods and clearing out "zoot suiters" from downtown.[53] Only Detroiters demonstrated the potential for unlimited race war in the defense production centers; unless defused by presidential intervention, predicted an Office of Facts and Figures investigator immediately after the Sojourner Truth outburst, "havoc" would occur "in the working force of every Northern industrial city" where newcomers and blacks competed.[54] The potential for destruction loomed large as Double V-minded blacks in Pittsburgh marched on a police station, protested the arrest of loiterers, and chanted, "Do you want another Detroit?" Local and county officials, themselves mindful of the Detroit riot, deployed bluecoats and conciliated blacks, and disorder—whether for that reason or not—did not occur.[55]

Detroiters induced even greater fear in Chicago, where memory of 1919 and recent frictions produced one of the most constructive municipal responses. Mayor Edward J. Kelly quickly calmed law-abiding citizens and warned racial troublemakers. He also issued "emergency police procedures," including efforts to separate the races in areas of known conflict, and met with civic leaders in an Emergency Citizens' Conference. Bending to pressure from the conferees and subsequent private endeavors to improve race relations, he created the Mayor's Committee on Race Relations. Kelly, and numerous blacks and whites who goaded him, placed his city and state in the forefront of what became a "national riot prevention movement": over thirty municipalities and several states creating interracial bodies within the year.[56]

The Detroit riot prompted similar concern in New York City, where Mayor Fiorello H. La Guardia staved off disorder momentarily, but failed to prevent its occurrence six weeks after Detroit's outburst. While irate black editors plastered their newspapers with headlines and photographs of the Detroit cataclysm and urged retaliation should white mobs form in Gotham, La Guardia acted even quicker than Mayor Kelly in Chicago. He too called for calm, promised protection of both races, and warned "snakes" against instigating trouble; he also took pains to instruct police and mayoral aides to be very careful handling interracial incidents. He went further than Kelly initially, receiving firsthand reports on the Detroit riot from Walter White, personal friend and NAACP officer, and from New York police observers sent to that upheaval while it still raged. Thereafter, he prepared the New York Police Department (NYPD) in riot control, attempting to guard against the racial prejudice and tactical errors of bluecoats in the Motor City. Into July, he worked closely with black and white citizens, leaders, and ministers; he even considered forming a race relations committee, but nixed the idea, believing that tensions were easing and that civilian boards challenged mayoral authority.[57]

Nevertheless, La Guardia was hit by an upheaval in Harlem on August 1, triggered by an altercation between a white patrolman and a black soldier plus the false rumor that the serviceman had died protecting his mother. This incident occurred at a time when Harlem was ready to explode, outraged by traditional police brutality and recent beatings of Harlem sons stationed in Southern military camps. New York police drew praise for quelling the outburst, holding the death toll to six persons, and snuffing out the rampage within twenty-four hours. But they also fed the animosity that had ignited Harlemites in the first place.

La Guardia's careful preparations came too late to eradicate the racial affronts of national policy, the recent example of Detroit, or the militancy that permeated Harlem. Harlem was the home of fiery minister and councilman Adam C. Powell, Jr., and New York City the headquarters of the NAACP, the March on Washington Committee, and other nationally known Double V organizations. It was also an area of abject living conditions that predate the Great Depression and a series of recent mayoral slights, such as the closing of the Savoy Ballroom for allegedly immoral activities in May. It is moot that even an agency like Kelly's in Chicago could have kept the lid on potential rioters.

Even presidential advisers wrung their hands at the specter of Detroitlike participants advancing racial violence city by city, endangering unity and threatening war production further. Jonathan Daniels, FDR's adviser on race relations, considered Detroit the culmination of a near "epidemic of racial tensions" that had not yet run its course; and, in the wake of the June rising, he urged the President to make a public statement to check further violence. Nor did Attorney General Francis Biddle regard the rage of Detroiters "an isolated case," expressing concern for similar upheaval in Los Angeles, Chicago, Washington, D.C., and elsewhere, and identifying "the hot season up to Labor Day" as "the period of greatest danger." He too recommended executive action—but largely bureaucratic, indirect, and short of an "unwise" presidential broadcast. Roosevelt himself believed many blacks were poised for militant response and was concerned about alienating whites further, perhaps even sparking more bloodshed, and he heeded Biddle's advice, remaining silent in public. He did create an interdepartmental committee, loosely coordinated by Daniels, to exchange information and devise recommendations. Amid a full-scale war, FDR vacillated over Detroit and did so again in the aftermath of the Harlem riot.[58]

Unlike all previous rioters, Detroiters gave everyone pause. Wrongly or not, they appeared to officials and citizens as black hoodlums or migrants and white Southerners brought to the surface by economic change and especially the strain of congested housing, transportation, and recreation. Biddle, for one, created a furor by suggesting a moratorium on black newcomers whose "physical limitations or cultural background" prevented their being absorbed into local communities: "No more Negroes should move into Detroit."[59] The influx of migrants (both races) and war-induced conditions did exacerbate long-standing grievances.[60] Why they—and Harlemites—crossed that threshold while Pittsburghers, Chicagoans, and others did not puzzled many.

Incontestably Detroit rioters shared numerous social conditions with Harlem residents. Both experienced more occupational competition, had fewer black store owners and black police officers, and less governmental representation than typical nonrioting black city dwellers elsewhere.[61] Despite some distinct differences in their municipalities, such as greater migration to Detroit than to New York and Detroit's official designation as a war production center, both endured several tension-heightening occurrences involving the violation of important mores, one of which eventually detonated. They also encountered a vacillating mayor in Jeffries and a fair, but self-assured one in La Guardia, who cut short his riot prevention efforts too soon; and police forces renowned for heavy-handed and biased treatment of blacks. They erupted for similar, though scarcely identical reasons (for no disorder, then or later, was typical in all characteristics).[62] Moreover, white rioters in Detroit enraged black New Yorkers and contributed to the explosion of Harlem six weeks later.

While these outraged black urbanites were venting their emotions, others—perhaps most surprisingly Chicagoans—refrained from violence. Chicago experienced some of the same localized tensions, generalized war strain, and racial showdowns as Detroit: the Francis Cabrini Homes and location of additional black projects (Sojourner Truth housing controversy); the placing of blacks in defense jobs and paying them wages equal to white laborers (the Detroit struggle for industrial opportunities minus the numerous hate strikes); the conflict between black customers and white merchants in ghetto neighborhoods (Paradise Valley competition between residents and largely absentee Jewish shopkeepers); the Double V campaign (the protest of Detroit editors), plus awareness of racial violence nationally and witnessing daily wrongs on the local scene. And yet, despite the questionable killing of a sixteen-year-old youth by white policemen in the spring of 1943, no riot came to Chicago. "When Detroit exploded, Chicago jumped"—but its residents, black and white, did not swing.[63]

However, Chicagoans did lack some of the underlying conditions that most lent themselves to wartime violence. Chicago did not experience "a mass invasion of new and strange people" during the war—not a riot preventative in itself, but surely a deterrent especially given the city's history of absorbing large numbers of blacks and, during the war, few white Southern in-migrants. Chicago underwent neither "rapid expansion of the Black Belt" toward white neighborhoods nor intensification of racist attitudes toward black employment. Lack of a labor surplus also checked tensions.[64] Consequently, whites in Chicago were more satisfied with black war efforts than whites in Detroit, and far fewer white Chicagoans advocated the segregation of blacks on public conveyances or shop floors; blacks in Chicago were less dissatisfied than blacks in Detroit about their opportunity to "help win the war." As late as March of 1943, then, although Chicago residents registered "above normal" racial temperatures in opinion surveys, these were nowhere near as high as those of Detroiters. Even after Detroit "boiled over," they registered only "somewhat tense" readings.[65]

Moreover, Chicago municipal officials had taken action to ensure peace long before Detroiters rioted. During the previous summer, white sailors were barred from the Black Belt, and the recent spring police shooting resulted in a grand-jury investigation, and in spite of its failure to indict, charges were brought against the patrolmen by the police commissioner as soon as he heard of the

Detroit upheaval. Chicagoans well might have erupted over that interracial killing or the interracial miniriot at the Cabrini homes in April.[66] They did not, in part because officials—"external control" agents—gave the impression of being responsive, if not even-handed, and because blacks still considered themselves part of the larger community's "social and political fabric"; moreover, Chicago blacks and whites lacked the level of militant ideology, which was needed to transform normally law-abiding residents into rioters. They perceived municipal authorities and their own avenues of redress somewhat positively, and thus never saw "institutional malfunctioning" or experienced the depths of frustration that fostered riot.[67] Significantly, between the Cabrini miniriot of April and the Detroit holocaust of June, racial tensions in Chicago actually eased. Chicagoans responded favorably to the newly formed Mayor's Committee on Race Relations and either endorsed the committee's summer-long program to thwart disorder or—if they were mischief-makers—were cowed by the city's clear intention to move forthwith and firmly against rioters.[68]

Just as Detroit rioters represented potential protestors in other urban centers, Chicagoans exemplified the nonrioters. Lacking the dramatic interplay of underlying conditions, weak government, militant ideology, and inciting episode, they demonstrated the dynamics also lacking in Pittsburgh and any number of other industrial metropolises. Milwaukeeans, for example, also benefited from a Socialist presence, smaller size, and "lower percentage of blacks in the total industrial labor force."[69] They and others averted violence because of the absence of some factors and the presence of others. None of these factors, by itself, was enough to cause a riot; small size fostered peace in Milwaukee but could not prevent a riot in Chester, Pennsylvania.

Predictably, much about the sociocultural environment experienced by the Detroit rioters in 1943 signaled conditions that would spark future outbursts and serve as backdrop to them. Like those in riot-torn cities of the 1960s, they inhabited densely populated areas of a large municipality in which a high proportion of nonwhites lived and where their influx disrupted "the on-going social order" and created or accentuated "existing problems in the black community." They also occupied deplorable housing, usually as tenants, while working in a diversified manufacturing economy that restricted black employment opportunities. They further suffered from environs exhibiting "signs of social and economic decay," and functioned under a less responsive mayor–council form of government. With the stage set by these underlying conditions, Detroit rioters experienced "a very specific [triggering] incident" that united individuals into crowds of violence. Detroit rioters erupted from conditions "rooted in the context" of their city.[70]

And, like their successors in the 1960s, they belonged to communities that lacked extensive social participation or clear social identity in the larger municipality. Their east side and Woodward Avenue neighborhoods were settings conducive to riot: little informal social interaction, especially among recent arrivals, black and white; scant participation in voluntary associations; greater attribution of their problems to outside sources.[71] Additionally, Detroit rioters of 1943, again like those of 1967, represented "neither the poorest nor the most prosperous" of city dwellers and resided in neighborhoods where congestion worsened just when their lives began to improve.[72]

The social and historical circumstances that these two generations of Detroiters have shared suggest much about rioters in more contemporary situations. Looters in New York City during the 1977 blackout seemed a throwback to Le Bon's criminals and misfits, stealing for purely selfish reasons. At first glance, they might have appeared as the "truly disadvantaged," who had benefited little from the civil rights gains of the previous decade and inhabited ghetto neighborhoods bereft of diverse classes, vibrant institutions, social participation, and employable skills.[73] Criminals in their twenties initiated the theft of the most valuable items, followed by alienated youngsters and poorly educated adults, while more stable and better-off residents joined in for a once-in-a-lifetime spree. Evolving from "a deliberate pursuit of goods" to a "chaotic scramble" for leavings, their violence lacked "racial rage and anger," black-white confrontations, ideology, and animus against the police. They took advantage of an accidental power outage to erupt throughout large portions of all five boroughs and steal.[74]

Nevertheless, blackout participants shared characteristics with 1943 and 1967 rioters in Detroit. They came from somewhat similar neighborhoods of congestion and poor housing, and they formed mobs of traditional composition, looting in well-known patterns. Of 3,076 arrestees, blacks, women, and juveniles comprised respectively 65.3 percent, 6.7 percent, and .06 percent, while whites constituted 4 percent, and slightly over half of those apprehended either fell between sixteen and twenty-five years of age (52 percent) or had previous records (56.1 percent). Despite the expansive geographic area and Hispanic involvement (30.3 percent), they duplicated the basic traits of 1943 and 1967 rioters in race, gender, and age.[75] Perhaps professional thieves and the very poor were overrepresented among the looters, but their actions protested life as they lived it—lacking the goods and minor luxuries that make life bearable. Never sensing real possibilities for change by means of their own power made them less political, but no less dissident than the Detroiters who preceded them. And they acted as racial units in separate neighborhoods.

Rioters in the 1980s, more categorically race-related and connected with past violence, both repeated traditional patterns and charted a new archetype. In Miami, Florida, in 1980, for example, they revealed profiles and motivations somewhat similar to those of wartime Detroiters. They—and presumably their successors in 1982, 1984, and 1989—appeared as overwhelmingly black, teenagers and young adults, without police records, and in some cases making ends meet. In short, "the good people of the ghetto" rioted in substantial numbers, many of them "willing to commit criminal acts and expose themselves to arrest." They did so, again like black Detroiters in 1943, because their political and socioeconomic aspirations for advancement in the city were being blocked by most Miamians. In spite of civil rights victories nationally, they experienced underrepresentation among Miami government leaders, police officials, and business and professional people. Although other factors partly account for their plight—such as apathy among some youth and negative effects of integration on black-owned businesses—they blamed it on the majority. When black insurance agent Arthur McCuffie was brutally beaten to death by white policemen, who were then acquitted of murder, Miami blacks exploded, tearing their neighborhoods apart.[76]

Black Miamians rioted in somewhat different ways and for somewhat different reasons from those of black Detroiters in 1943 (or 1967). They "set out to kill white people," rather than concentrate solely on the symbols of racism: white police and white-owned stores; and they did so in the economically expanding sunbelt, instead of the rustbelt of Northern industrial centers. By targeting whites, they reversed the assaults on blacks that occurred early in the century and extended the aggression of ghetto dwellers—in depression-wracked Harlem (1935), wartime Detroit (1943), and numerous postwar municipalities (1967)—beyond police and realty.[77] By "white," they most often meant Cubans, with whom they competed for jobs, political power, and residential space. Beginning in the 1960s, they had been losing ground to Spanish-speaking newcomers, who "leap-frogged over them." After thirty years, better educated, more acculturated Hispanics, mostly Cubans, made up 60 percent of Miami's populace, endured far less unemployment than blacks, dominated the offices of mayor, manager, and commissioner, and comprised 43 percent of the police force. Blacks rioted several times to protest this steady erosion of prosperity and power. In 1980, the precipitating incident involved white lawmen; in 1989, it was Hispanic policemen. (Hispanic police were considered brutal as a result of their experience with authoritarian governments of Latin America—a view somewhat analogous to that held by black Detroiters in 1943 of supposedly Southern patrolmen.) Black Miamians lumped together Hispanics and non-Hispanic whites, who constituted only 11 percent of the population in 1989, much as wartime Detroiters had considered native-born whites, foreign-born whites, and Southern migrant whites as a single enemy.[78]

In the North, black teenagers and white ethnics duplicated patterns of violence prevalent in wartime Detroit. In 1989, seven East Harlem youngsters, fourteen- and fifteen-year-olds, some from caring families and none with criminal records, savagely raped and left comatose a white female jogger. On a cool evening, about one month into spring, they entered Central Park as part of a loosely organized group of thirty-two schoolboys; separating into the smaller "posse," they accosted two white male runners, a couple on a tandem bicycle, and a lone white man picnicking before they descended on the woman banker. Like Charles L., whose Belle Isle "wilding" led to mayhem forty-six years earlier, they seemed angered by the discrepancies of wealth between themselves and affluent whites just south of their neighborhood; unlike him, they came from a drug-infested environment that enhanced power, machismo, and violence among young males. Their random terrorism was made even more ferocious because it lacked the regulation and leadership of formal gangs. They enjoyed power within their own community, where elders were cowed by fear, and sometimes benefited from drug profits, a phenomenon absent from east-side Detroit in 1943. Yet they failed to ignite riot. Rather, most blacks and whites viewed their senseless rampage with confused horror. Nevertheless, these teenagers both reestablished previous black-white definitions and blurred ethnic lines, since some of them were Hispanic.[79]

Reversing the races of assailant and victim, however, New York youths killed black males who entered white enclaves of Howard Beach (1986) and Bensonhurst (1989). In the Howard Beach tragedy a gang of whites set upon three black men in the neighborhood, who had been seeking assistance for their disabled vehicle, and chased one of them into oncoming high-speed highway traffic, where he was hit by a car and killed. Their violence seemed a reversion to interracial combat in wartime Detroit.[80] Even more devastating, when sixteen-year-old Yusef Hawkins ventured into Bensonhurst, Brooklyn, to inquire about a car for sale, neighborhood youths shot him to death at point-blank range. This was six months after the black wilding in Manhattan and exhibited once more, as did the Howard Beach incident, the ethnic dimension of interracial bloodshed.[81]

The Italian-American youths who confronted Hawkins seemed to have stepped out of the past. Like the Poles in the Sojourner Truth housing controversy of 1942, they came from a tightly knit, Old World working-class community, closed to all newcomers except recent immigrants, who comprised nearly half of the Italian-

American population (which itself made up 65 percent of the white section). Also like the Poles, the youths were protecting their physical and cultural turf from outsiders. Like Aldo T. in the Detroit riot of 1943, they carried deadly weapons—mostly baseball bats—and "a macho code" to defend family, neighborhood, and church; like him also, they proved most intolerant of black people. Unlike earlier Polish or Italian rioters, Bensonhurst youths also alighted on the black teenagers because a local girl, who dated blacks and Hispanics despite neighborhood taboos, announced boldly that she would bring dark-skinned friends into Bensonhurst. The killers believed that Hawkins and the three friends who accompanied him were intruding at her request, thus affronting community mores: outside invasion, ethnic impurity, interracial sex, and personal jealousy. Primarily teenagers, without police records and from solid families, the killers resembled most of the ethnics caught up in wartime Detroit's interracial competition and the riot it sparked.[82]

Neither wilding nor brutal murder touched off riot in New York City, but black collegians ignited Virginia Beach, Virginia, during the 1989 Labor Day Greekfest. They descended on the city, as they had every year for a decade, 30,000 students from thirty east-coast colleges celebrating the end of summer. Perhaps they recalled the previous year's confrontations with predominantly white policemen and merchants, or had brooded over well-publicized racial incidents like Bensonhurst and closer-to-home cross burnings. Provoked by an unknown event, students became rock-throwing mobs, disorganized vandals, and opportunistic looters. They raged for two evenings, injuring fifty persons and plundering 125 stores before being quelled by the combined forces of local police, state police, and national guardsmen. Students constituted most of the 650 arrestees, although the looters seemed to be black males younger than college age and possibly from the surrounding area.[83]

Virginia Beach students engaged in a commodity disorder that resembled 1943 Detroit only tangentially. They represented those with far greater stakes in society, and they destroyed a neighborhood other than their own. Black, young, well-educated, and no doubt lacking police records, they attributed the mayhem to insen-

sitive municipal officials, overbearing patrolmen, and price-goug-
ing storekeepers. They resented deeply such bigoted, long-standing treatment, although investigators blamed a combination of
nonracial factors for the upheaval, including failure of leadership
and "the unlawful actions of a small percentage of the crowd."
Also unlike the Detroit rioters of 1943, they faced more restrained
lawmen, manifesting less than deadly intent, and sparked neither
retaliatory violence by white citizens nor verbal backlash by official
investigators.[84]

Virginia, Florida, and New York rioters hinted at both traditional and new characteristics, linking them with earlier Detroiters
and, more than likely, future participants. Miami rioters affirmed
that urban residence continues to promote a "riot orientation"
among increasingly racially aware, yet politically and economically
deprived blacks; East Side wilders showed that drug infestation
imposes an "urban shock" quite different and more violence-producing than that experienced by 1943 Detroit.[85] Not all of the
Miami rioters or the East Side youths seemed members of the underclass, but they revealed how values of the disadvantaged per-
vaded their communities and how class conflict—"an issue of
haves and have-nots" as much as race—prompted their outbursts.[86]
Virginia Beach rioters appeared even more class conscious, mostly
upwardly mobile sons and daughters of accomplished blacks, resentful of being treated like second-class citizens of a bygone era.
When merchants deny "certain black people" entrance to their
stores or charge them higher prices, accused a Howard University
student, "you get offended."[87] And, among other stereotypes,
Bensonhurst's working-class ethnics surely looked with askance at
the presumably shiftless—in derogatory southern Italian dialect—
mulignans.[88]

Such name calling displays the cultural differences that also
affected many rioters. Virginia Beach students seemed least influenced by how their ways of life differed from those they fought,
and Bensonhurst ethnics most. Between these limits, East Side
youths assailed the Yuppie phenomenon, and Miami blacks attacked the Cuba life-style. Bensonhurst ethnics and East Side wilders also possessed exaggerated codes of machismo and honor,

another cultural distinction and one conducive to violence. Recent lawbreakers, like their 1943 Detroit counterparts, probably encountered varying degrees of cultural alienation with cleavage along racial lines, sharpening hostile beliefs and justifying bloodshed, its influence accentuated by stark contrasts in culture and lengthy periods of competition.[89]

Overlapping black-and-white class and culture traits notwithstanding, aggressors reacted most to race. Miami rioters exploded over racial grievances and lashed out at white people, many more of whom would have fallen had they been accessible. On this point, they resembled black and white Detroiters of 1943. Many observers tried to play down the racial dimension of wilding, but the East Side youths were all black or Hispanic, and their victims all white; raping the white jogger exhibited extreme forms of power, sexism, and revenge, an explosive display of machismo and clear evidence of sexual dynamics being most pronounced in racial conflicts.[90] Surely Bensonhurst ethnics opposed all outsiders, yet Yusef Hawkins's blackness and his purported association with an Italian girl intensified their fears. "This wasn't racial," contended one neighborhood resident, but added, "White people should stick together."[91] And Virginia Beach students certainly considered race prejudice (of the police and proprietors) as the underlying cause for their disorder, though municipal officials disagreed, pointing instead to problems of crowd control. Black students might have received similar treatment regardless of race, as had several rowdy white fraternity members who sparked violence during a July 4th celebration at New York City's Jones Beach (where 20,000 persons from several northeastern colleges gathered for the third consecutive year).[92] Yet, once the fracas began at Virginia Beach, race became for both students and police "a way to differentiate potential friends and foes."[93]

Though other factors remain significant as determinants of violence, race loomed large in intergroup conflict, and will continue to generate antagonisms in a highly competitive society facing fewer socioeconomic opportunities and scarce resources. This is most likely where achieving groups challenge and interact with one another as in Miami. Given the physical separation of both races and the civil rights gains of middle-class blacks, few white ethnic communal or black student commodity disorders lie ahead. Conversely, black city dwellers enduring slum conditions and drug traffic or sharing little political influence, economic chance, and social status are also capable of sparking catastrophic upheaval. More often than wilding or rioting, their violence has been and might continue to be turned inward, perpetrators and victims alike representing the poor and chronically jobless of "superexploited sections."[94] White urban residents facing similar constraints might also explode along racial lines.

Ironically, violence might well continue to occur in the future, as it has since World War II, amidst "a troubling paradox" of improvements for some individuals and deterioration of race relations generally. Miami blacks and Virginia Beach students jousted respectively with Cubans for power and with white authorities for recognition made possible by the civil rights movement and the black revolution. East Harlemites, lacking the skills necessary to benefit socioeconomically and politically from these gains, languished in the ghettos left by better-prepared inhabitants; they grew more resentful and angry, partly as a result of militant conscious-raising campaigns, and lashed out at both white society and white women in a spontaneous, opportunistic fit of violence.[95] A black youth felt free to enter Bensonhurst, a white ethnic enclave, and a girl from an Italian-American neighborhood felt equally free to date nonwhite males, neither of which would have been permitted before the crusades for race and gender equality of the 1960s. Other interracial, interethnic conflicts await where groups sense their way of life threatened, their chance for advancement blocked, or their ability for successful redress limited. In the words of one Bensonhurst resident (speaking long before the Hawkins slaying), they tend to see prejudice not "as a cancer, but as a way of maintaining the status quo."[96]

Future tragedy might be averted if policy-makers realized the limitations of past responses to collective violence. In 1943 the Governor's Committee focused only on black young male rioters, labeled them criminal, mentally defective, or culturally backward, and accordingly denied their outburst any legitimacy; in 1967 the

National Commission again concentrated solely on black young male participants, identified them as normal—no one dared to suggest measuring their intelligence or examining their sexual health as had been done to wartime rioters—and consequently recognized their violence as redress. To be sure, 1943 committeemen stressed the supposed pathology of rioters while 1967 commissioners emphasized their socioeconomic characteristics, and suggested large-scale programs in employment, education, welfare, and housing. Yet, in a final analysis, both generations of authorities failed. The 1943 committeemen recommended changing those who rioted rather than the system or the disorder-producing conditions, and 1967 commissioners never witnessed full commitment to their far-reaching programs. In part the conditions underlying one riot carried over to the next outburst. Because 1943 officials disregarded the violence as a sign that Detroit's political, social, and economic orders were malfunctioning for many black and some white residents, bloodshed recurred twenty-four years later. Similarly, the recent racial outbursts in Miami and elsewhere reveal that 1967 officials, despite their call for radical action, concentrated more on rehabilitating riot participants than on addressing the dysfunctional structures of society.[97]

In sum, rioters of past Detroit generations, like more recent purveyors of violence in other cities, represented both the diversity within black and white societies and the diversities between them. Evolving from long, historical lines, marked by racial antagonisms, violent eruptions, and predictable patterns, they protested actual and imagined transgressions. Hardly anomalies, they and all other twentieth-century rioters manifested the presence of class, culture, ethnic, gender, and especially race competition. Black or white, their actions represented much more than abnormal behavior in an otherwise orderly, progressive social order. Only by understanding this reality, identifying those in the crowd, and their layers of increasing violence, as well as concentrating on the societal context that fosters such behavior, can there be objective analysis of collective racial violence—or hope for racial justice and interracial harmony.

APPENDIX A: *Resources and Strategies*

Since we recognized the generally spontaneous and fleeting nature of disorders and the difficulty of identifying rioters who entered the streets forty-eight years ago, our study of the Detroit rioters of 1943 took advantage of numerous data and methods—each permitting a distinctive approach and insight and, in combination with one another, broadened perspective, refined analysis, and strengthened interpretation.[1] Among the most fruitful sources on the Detroit riot and its rioters were local newspapers. Through picture and story, they charted events, identified rioters, and, better than any other resource, reflected "the broad aspects of the social climate."[2]

Organizations also documented the riot and the rioters. The National Association for the Advancement of Colored People collected affidavits from those who envisioned themselves more victim than perpetrator. Likewise the Civil Rights Federation of Michigan recorded accounts from primarily black Detroiters who spoke of police brutality. While those in authority usually disregarded the personal experiences of individuals who by chance or choice joined the fray, these eyewitness testimonies defined their reality: views of violence "from the bottom up."[3]

In addition, officials—the Governor's Committee, Recorder's Court Psychologist Lowell S. Selling, and State Penitentiary personnel Elmer R. Akers and Vernon Fox—identified the participants collectively. Widely distributed, often cited, and largely accepted, these authorized evaluations advanced distorted views of the rioters and indicated the sociopolitical exigencies that influenced them. Only State Child Welfare Bureau supervisor C. F. Ramsay presented a more objective, albeit one-dimensional profile.[4]

All of these investigations dealt with those arrested, detained, imprisoned, or otherwise officially identified for alleged or real riot participation. The Governor's Committee assembled a series of thirty-two exhibits, prepared by the police department, which identify participants and victims. In contrast Selling, Akers and Fox, and Ramsay chose samples conveniently rather than scientifically. Given their data selection and monolithic, sometimes prejudiced interpretations, we reconsidered every official's findings.

Of the available data, police arrest tickets specified the rioters most inclusively. Though collected by patrolmen during a crisis, they like other archival resources, proved viable when assessed within their "situated context."[5] They served as the core for an array of additional data, rather than as a single, perfect source. They permitted quantitative summaries and analyses, indispensable knowledge beyond the reach of purely qualitative, impressionistic data.[6]

The riot wound down on Monday evening, June 21, and petered out the following day, June 22. Although other apprehensions followed, 1,350 (71.3 percent) of the 1,893 arrests occurred during that forty-eight-hour period. Therefore, we defined the riot population as those arrested on these two days and randomly chose 270 (20 percent) arrest tickets from among them. Of those arrestees selected, 246 were deemed riot-related and yielded a .90 confidence level—plus or minus .06 margin of error—for prediction and generalization. Matching our sample with commensurate data reported by the Governor's Committee revealed that comparable variables fall within plus or minus 6 percent of the actual population proportions. Representative of the population of rioters our sample provided the basis for the generalizations and rioter vignettes in Chapter 1.[7]

White males and both white and black females comprised few

participants when compared with black males. In order to establish a more definitive study, we selected—in a subsequent drawing of arrest tickets—all females and white men arrested for riot-related offenses on June 21 and June 22. Their profiles were developed more fully in Chapter 2 and elsewhere.[8]

The arrest tickets revealed personal and demographic information, as well as previous and current arrest records. Additional adjudication data came from the Recorder's Court Misdemeanor Calendar. And every felon was traced through the Recorder's Court Files, which—although sometimes incomplete—contain all examinations and some probation records.[9] A few psychiatric evaluations also appear among these legal papers, but the Recorder's Court Psychiatric Clinic declined to open its official holdings. These evaluations, and those of Dr. Selling, were appraised by Dr. Clifford I. Whipple, professor of psychology, Southwest Missouri State University.

The General Register of Prisoners identified the name, age, gender, race, offense, and record of every rioter sent to the Detroit House of Correction, while the Criminal Calendar listed the legal motions of those who came before the Recorder's Court. Probation Records furnished extensive personal and family information, as well as progress reports for rioters placed on probation.[10] Revealing both idiosyncratic detail and generalized patterns, this combination of narrative documents and statistical records yielded as complete a profile as possible for each rioter.

For female and juvenile rioters, information was especially sketchy. Except for the data recorded by arrest tickets, Misdemeanor Calendar, General Register of Prisoners, and Recorder's Court Files, other records for women have been destroyed. So have the official records of juveniles. Although a handful of their files did surface in our search of the adult collections, teenager identities and stories generally appeared only in newspaper accounts or the Governor's Committee exhibits.[11] Indeed, we only managed to accumulate the sources for females and juveniles through the diligent help of archivists and public officials, plus some luck.[12]

The riot that occurred in wartime Detroit demolished large

areas. In 1943 ghetto store owners incurred the heaviest losses of entrepreneurs. Their identification was established by the arrestee records, and their home addresses and store addresses by the local telephone directory. Comparison of the two disclosed the degree of absentee ownership in the riot area. The ethnicity and race of the store owners were determined with the assistance of knowledgeable individuals.[13] Jewish and non-Jewish proprietors of both races and community attitudes toward them, before and after the outburst, appeared in the studies of Donald C. Marsh and his students. An overall assessment of economic loss, as well as the kinds of businesses looted, damaged, or destroyed, was summarized by the Governor's Committee.[14]

In the final analysis, police identified the participants. They were on the streets and as close to the action as the rioters themselves, so on June 21 and June 22 their judgments and actions defined the riot population. Examining lawmen provided insights into how they did their jobs. Information on Detroit Police Department personnel was recorded in the Police Force Books, which served as the bases for a random sample.[15] They contain personal and demographic data for each officer, and a brief summary of his or her career.

Michigan State Troopers arrived in force on the morning of June 22. Some of them interviewed forty-three black males detained in the Piquette Armory. Troopers reported excerpts of these statements, which never became part of official police records. Nonetheless, these interviews reflected the detainees' instant perceptions of violence and thus enhanced the resource base of participants.[16]

Demographic data pinpointed the distance between the rioters' places of residence and places of arrest, which came chiefly from police tickets. Only one of our nearly 350 subjects appeared to have given a false home location. Census information for 1940 identified the origins of participants for the map of Detroit at the front of our manuscript.

The participants of 1943 take on added significance when they are compared with the rioters of 1967. The official account of the second Detroit outbreak by the National Advisory Commission on

Civil Disorders analyzed the data of self-avowed participants and riot-related arrestees. It reflected a different sociopolitical environment and a more sophisticated handling of the data than occurred twenty-four years earlier.[17] Utilizing the commission's findings, then, we explored intergenerational linkages between the rioters of 1943 and 1967.

In order to locate central trends and patterns, we quantified and aggregated the data with basic statistical measures, such as percentage, mean, median, and mode. These tendencies, helpful in constructing overall profiles for rioters, nonetheless masked variation and diversity.[18] Noting such distinctions added breadth to the analysis and suggested the multidimensional character of the participants. Still the humanity of those generating the statistics sometimes became lost. Other cases were so few or so incomplete they could not be studied statistically. For everyone involved, however, the richness of the qualitative data animated the numbers, shed light on the unusual, and broadened the interpretations advanced by statistical analysis alone.[19]

In an effort to interpret history accurately, our strategies—known as unobtrusive research—utilized an array of records. These documents, provided by people with different aims, motivations, and perspectives, raised questions of validity and reliability, which have been reduced significantly through corroboration and triangulation: the use of multiple sources and multiple methodologies. The end result has been a realistic, multidimensional portrayal of those who rioted.

APPENDIX B: *Tables*

TABLE 1

Comparison of Sample with Governor's Committee Report [1]

	SAMPLE (N = 246)		GOVERNOR'S COMMITTEE	
	#	%	#	%
			Exhibit 24 [2]	
Arrested				
June 21	177	72.0	958	71.0
June 22	69	28.0	392	29.0
Race				
Black	216	87.8	970	82.1
White	30	12.2	212	17.9
Gender				
Male	235	95.5	1173	93.7
Female	11	4.5	120	6.3
17 to 20 Years				
Black	42	17.1	242	20.5
White	18	7.3	111	9.3

Table 1 (*continued*)

	SAMPLE (N=246)		GOVERNOR'S COMMITTEE	
	#	%	#	%
			Exhibit 13[3]	
Charge				
Misdemeanor	113	45.9	597	48.7
Felony	133	54.1	630	51.3
Specific Offense				
Weapons	73	29.7	315	25.7
Looting	63	25.6	286	23.1
Conduct	107	43.5	597	48.7
			Exhibit 14[4]	
Arrest Precinct				
13	103	41.9	719	39.6
9	38	15.4	200	11.0
1	24	9.8	246	13.5

1. Percentages in this table that do not add up to 100 indicate missing data or categories too small to warrant inclusion.

2. Exhibit 24 indicates that 1,893 arrests were recorded for the riot period—June 21 to June 30. Of these arrests, 1,182 were prosecuted, the others being discharged after investigation. Day of arrest and gender are calculated from total arrests, while race and age are reported in terms of prosecuted arrests.

3. Exhibit 13 identifies the specific charges for the dates June 21 through June 26. Warrants were issued for 1,227 of the total arrests (1,844) recorded.

4. Exhibit 14 identifies the precinct of arrest for 1,817 arrests between June 20 and June 26.

TABLE 2

Detroit Rioters, 1943: Profile of Rioters and Behavior

Characteristics	BLACK MALES (N=205) #	%	WHITE MALES (N=30) #	%	BLACK FEMALES (N=11) #	%	TOTAL SAMPLE (N=246) #	%
Black	205		—		11		216	87.7
Male	205		30		—		235	95.5
Median age	27 years		19 years		28 years		26 years	
Range of ages	16 to 64		17 to 41		17 to 38		16 to 64	
Married	129	62.9	11	36.7	4	36.4	144	58.5
Laborer	176	85.9	16	53.3	1	9.1	193	78.5
Employed	197	96.1	28	93.3	6	54.5	231	93.9
Resident pre- cinct 3,9,13	150	73.2	10	33.3	10	90.0	170	69.1
Detroit resident	199	97.1	27	90.0	11	100.0	237	96.3
No previous arrest	124	60.5	21	70.0	11	100.0	156	63.4
Riot Behavior								
Felony	115	56.1	12	40.0	6	54.5	133	54.1
Misdemeanor	90	43.9	18	60.0	5	45.5	113	45.9
Weapon	59	28.8	13	43.3	1	9.1	73	29.7
Looting	55	26.8	1	0.03	7	63.6	63	25.6
Conduct	88	42.9	16	53.3	3	27.3	107	43.5
Arrested in home precinct	126	61.5	7	23.3	5	45.5	138	56.1
Arrested within ½ mile of home	106	51.7	7	23.3	9	81.8	122	49.6
Arrested in precinct 1,3,9,13	158	77.1	16	53.3	8	72.7	182	74.0

Table 2 (*continued*)

Additional Characteristics[1]	BLACK MALES (N = 68)		WHITE MALES (N = 5)		PROBATION RECORDS (N = 73)	
	#	%	#	%	#	%
Home state in South[2]	59	86.8	2	40.0	61	83.6
Acted alone	49	72.1	2	40.0	51	69.9
No children	41	60.3	2	40.0	43	58.9
Protestant	66	97.1	3	60.0	69	94.5
Median education	8 years		9 years		8 years	
Median length of residence	9.5 years		14 years		12 years	
Median length of present employment	1 year		1 year		1 year	
Median weekly salary	$50.00		$50.00		$50.00	

1. These additional data are drawn from the probation records that could be located for male felons.

2. South includes the lower South (South Carolina, Mississippi, Louisiana, Alabama, Georgia, Texas, and Florida), upper South (Tennessee, Virginia, Arkansas, and North Carolina), and border states (Kentucky and Missouri).

TABLE 3

Detroit Rioters, 1943: All White Males and Black

Females and Sampled Black Males[1]

	BLACK MALES (N=205)		WHITE MALES (N=96)		BLACK FEMALES (N=42)	
	#	%	#	%	#	%
Median age	27 years		20 years		24.5 years	
Range of ages	16 to 64		17 to 54		17 to 45	
Married	129	62.9	27	28.1	14	33.3
Employed	197	96.1	86	89.6	29	69.0
Skilled/semiskilled	18	8.8	27	28.1	1	2.4
Laborer	176	85.9	54	56.3	8	19.0
Service/domestic	2	.01	1	1.0	18	42.9
Detroit resident	199	97.1	93	96.9	42	100.0
Paradise Valley resident (Precincts 3,9,13)	150	73.2	28	29.2	38	90.5
No previous arrests	124	60.5	74	77.1	33	78.6
Arrest day/time						
6/21 12 A.M.– 5:59 A.M.	27	13.2	14	14.6	6	14.3
6:00–11:59 A.M.	17	8.3	7	7.3	7	16.7
12 noon– 5:59 P.M.	42	20.5	9	9.4	10	23.8
6:00–11:59 P.M.	58	28.3	38	39.6	10	23.8
6/22 12 A.M.– 5:59 A.M.	15	7.3	15	15.6	1	2.4
6:00–11:59 A.M.	13	6.3	2	2.1	4	9.5
12 noon– 5:59 P.M.	17	8.3	3	3.1	2	4.8
6:00–11:59 P.M.	9	4.4	8	8.3	2	4.8
Distance traveled to riot						
¼ mile of home	71	36.4	13	13.5	20	47.6
½ mile of home	35	17.1	7	7.3	7	16.7
¾ to 2 miles of home	58	28.3	28	29.2	9	21.4
More than 2 miles	30	14.6	39	40.6	3	7.1

Table 3 (*continued*)

	BLACK MALES (N=205)		WHITE MALES (N=96)		BLACK FEMALES (N=42)	
	#	%	#	%	#	%
Precinct of arrest						
1	16	7.8	25	26.0	2	4.8
5 (Belle Isle)	14	6.8	19	19.8	1	2.4
13	93	45.4	21	21.9	14	33.3
Street of arrest						
Oakland	16	7.8	0	0.0	7	16.7
Woodward	3	1.5	28	29.2	1	2.4
Hastings	50	24.4	0	0.0	11	26.2
Hastings/St. Antoine/ Beaubien/Brush	96	47.8	4	4.2	19	45.2
Arrested in home precinct	126	61.5	24	25.0	26	61.9
Arrested for						
Misdemeanor	90	43.9	65	67.7	18	42.9
Felony	115	56.1	31	32.3	24	57.1
Arrest charge						
Weapon	59	28.8	31	32.3	5	11.9
Knife	26	12.7	7	7.3	2	4.8
Firearm	15	7.3	14	14.6	0	0.0
Looting	54	26.3	2	2.1	21	50.0
For food	11	5.4	0	0.0	4	9.5
For clothes/shoes	12	5.9	0	0.0	9	21.4
Median value of goods	$9.70				$15.80	
Conduct	88	42.9	59	61.5	15	35.7

1. Percentages in this table that do not add up to 100 indicate missing data or categories too small to warrant inclusion.

TABLE 4

Rioters With Probation Records [1]

	BLACK MALES (N=68)		WHITE MALES (N=17)	
	#	%	#	%
Median age	27.8 years		19 years	
Range of ages	17 to 51		17 to 50	
Married	43	63.2	5	29.4
Employed	67	98.5	15	88.2
Skilled/semiskilled	4	5.9	5	29.4
Laborer	61	89.7	10	58.8
Detroit resident	66	97.1	17	100.0
Precinct of residence				
3	11	16.2	3	17.6
9	11	16.2	1	5.9
13	32	47.1	2	11.8
Home state in South	59	86.8	3	17.6
Home state is Michigan	5	7.4	9	52.9
No children	41	60.3	12	70.6
Protestant	66	97.1	5	29.4
Catholic	1	1.0	12	70.6
Median education	8 years		9 years	
Median length of residence	9.5 years		17 years	
Median length of present employment	1 year		11.5 months	
Median weekly salary	$50.00		$50.00	
Acted alone in riot	49	72.1	8	47.1
No previous arrests	46	67.6	12	70.6

Table 4 (*continued*)

| | BLACK MALES (N = 68) | | WHITE MALES (N = 17) | |
	#	%	#	%
Arrest day/time				
6/21 12 noon– 5:59 P.M.	14	20.6	1	5.9
6:00–11:59 P.M.	22	32.4	8	47.1
6/22 12 A.M.– 5:59 A.M.	4	5.9	0	0.0
Arrested 6/21/43	50	73.5	12	70.6
Rioted within ½ mile of home	36	52.9	3	17.7
Arrested in home precinct	45	66.2	4	23.5
Precinct of arrest				
1	4	5.9	6	35.3
5 (Belle Isle)	3	4.4	1	5.9
13	39	57.4	5	29.4
Street of arrest				
Oakland	1	1.5	0	0.0
Woodward	0	0.0	10	58.8
Hastings/St. Antoine/ Beaubien/Brush	38	55.9	0	0.0
Arrest Charge				
Weapon	33	48.5	15	88.2
Knife	20	29.4	3	17.6
Firearm	6	8.8	7	41.2
Looting	33	48.5	1	5.9
Food/clothes/shoes	14	20.6	0	0.0
Liquor	8	11.8	0	0.0
Median value of goods	$9.99		—	—

1. Percentages in this table that do not add up to 100 indicate missing data or categories too small to warrant inclusion.

TABLE 5

Juveniles, Age 10 to 16, Arrested June 21 and 22 [1]

	BLACK MALES (N=64)		WHITE MALES (N=33)	
	#	%	#	%
Median age	14.9 years		15.6 years	
Range of ages	10 to 16		14 to 16	
Resident precinct				
13	15	23.4	1	3.0
9	14	21.9	5	15.6
3	14	21.9	4	12.1
6	10	15.6	0	0.0
5	0	0.0	9	27.3
Arrest precinct				
9	17	26.6	0	0.0
3	11	17.2	0	0.0
13	9	14.1	1	3.0
1	4	6.3	12	36.4
5	3	4.7	10	30.3
Arrested in home precinct	42	65.6	11	33.3
Arrested June 21	46	71.9	15	45.5
Arrested June 22	18	28.1	18	54.5

Table 5 (*continued*)

	BLACK MALES (N=64)		WHITE MALES (N=33)	
	#	%	#	%
Offense				
Misdemeanor	20	31.3	22	66.7
Felony	44	68.7	10	30.3
Arrest charge				
Weapon	10	15.6	7	21.2
Assault	7	10.9	2	6.1
Looting	28	43.8	0	0.0
Conduct	19	29.7	22	66.7
Ethnicity of surname[2]				
Polish			1	3.0
Italian			5	15.2
French			2	6.1

1. Governor's Committee, *Factual Report,* Part II, Exhibit 15, BHC. Percentages in this table that do not add up to 100 indicate categories too small to warrant inclusion.
2. Determined by the authors.

Notes

ABBREVIATIONS

ALUA   Archives of Labor and Urban Affairs, Walter P. Reuther Library, Wayne State University, Detroit, Michigan

BHC   Burton Historical Collection, Detroit Public Library, Detroit, Michigan

CUA   Catholic University Archives, Mullen Library, The Catholic University, Washington, D.C.

DPDR   Detroit Police Department Records, Detroit Police Department, Detroit, Michigan

DULP   Detroit Urban League Papers, Microfilm Edition

FBIF   Federal Bureau of Investigation Files, U.S. Department of Justice, Washington, D.C.

FDRL   Franklin D. Roosevelt Library, Hyde Park, New York

FHLP   Fiorello H. La Guardia Papers, Municipal Archives and Records Center, New York, New York

HLIP   Harold L. Ickes Papers, Library of Congress, Washington, D.C.

MHC   Michigan Historical Collections, Bentley Historical Library, University of Michigan, Ann Arbor, Michigan

MSA   Michigan State Archives, Lansing, Michigan

MSPR   Michigan State Police Records, Michigan State Police, Lansing, Michigan

NAACP National Association for the Advancement of Colored People Papers, Library of Congress, Washington, D.C.

NARS   National Archives and Records Service, Washington, D.C.

NUL   National Urban League Papers, Library of Congress, Washington, D.C.

RCR   Recorder's Court Records, Frank Murphy Hall of Justice, Detroit, Michigan

WNRC   Washington National Records Center, Suitland, Maryland

FROM *FACTUAL REPORT OF THE GOVERNOR'S COMMITTEE TO INVESTIGATE THE RIOT OCCURRING IN DETROIT ON JUNE 21, 1943*

Exhibit 19: Detailed report of Det. Lt. George R. Branton, DPD Homicide Squad, to Chief of Detectives Paul H. Wencel of riot deaths and injuries, with synopsis of each death and injury
    (a.) Dead and injured due to rioting, June 20–22, 1943
    (b.) Death and injuries by hours due to rioting, June 20–22, 1943
    (c.) Synopsis of deaths due to rioting
    (d.) Death and injuries to police officers during rioting
    (e.) People killed and injured as result of rioting on June 20–23, 1943

PREFACE

    1. Nathan S. Caplan, "The New Ghetto Man: A Review of Recent Empirical Studies," *Journal of Social Issues* 26 (Winter 1970): 59–73.
    2. Roberta Senechal, *The Sociogenesis of a Race Riot: Springfield, Illinois, in 1908* (Urbana, 1990).
    3. August Meier and Elliott Rudwick, "Black Violence in the 20th Century," in *Violence in America: Historical and Comparative Perspectives*, Vol. 2, eds. Hugh D. Graham and Ted R. Gurr (Washington, D.C.,

1969), pp. 307–16; Morris Janowitz, "Patterns of Collective Racial Violence," in *Violence in America,* Vol. 2, pp. 317–39.

4. Clark McPhail, "Civil Disorder Participation: A Critical Examination of Recent Research," *American Sociological Review* 36 (Dec. 1971): 1059–71; Dominic J. Capeci, Jr., and Martha Wilkerson, "The Detroit Rioters of 1943: A Reinterpretation," *Michigan Historical Review* 16 (Spring 1990): 56–58. While some of these rioters appear undeserving of arrest and innocent of crimes, very few of them falsified personal information. Nor do they overrepresent those considered riffraff—the unattached, unemployed, unskilled, or criminal group usually willing to admit participation and apprehended by class-conscious police. They portray a broad spectrum of those rioting: inciters, combatants, looters, and lesser offenders who came in their wake.

5. Elliot D. Luby, "A Comparison Between Detroit Negro Riot Arrestees and a Riot Control Sample," paper presented at the American Political Science Association Conference, Washington, D.C., Sept. 3–7, 1968, for the quotation; Joe R. Feagin and Harlan Hahn, *Ghetto Revolts: The Politics of Violence in American Cities* (New York, 1973), p. 48.

CHAPTER 1: *Riot and Reconstruction*

1. Herbert J. Rushton, William E. Dowling, Oscar Olander, and John H. Witherspoon, *Factual Report of the Governor's Committee to Investigate the Riot Occurring in Detroit on June 21, 1943,* 11 Aug. 1943, Part II, Exhibit 24, p. 1, BHC (hereinafter cited as Governor's Committee, *Factual Report*).

2. Walter White, "What Caused the Detroit Riots?" n.d., pp. 1–2, Box 2574, FHLP; Alan Clive, *State of War: Michigan in World War II* (Ann Arbor, 1979), pp. 130–57; Dominic J. Capeci, Jr., *Race Relations in Wartime Detroit: The Sojourner Truth Housing Controversy of 1942* (Philadelphia, 1984), pp. 75–99.

3. Neil J. Smelser, *Theory of Collective Behavior* (New York, 1962), p. 236.

4. "Detroit Is Dynamite," *Life,* 17 Aug. 1942, p. 15.

5. Arrest Ticket 901, 21 June 1943, Duplicate Arrest Tickets, Reel 85, DPDR (herein cited as Arrest Ticket plus number, the date being 21 June 1943 unless noted otherwise); Michigan *Chronicle,* 30 Oct. 1943, p. 2 (herein cited as *Chronicle*), for biographical information in this and the following paragraph.

In order to gain access to arrest tickets and probation files, the authors agreed to protect the identity of riot participants by citing only their first names and last initials and by assigning bogus numbers to their arrest tickets. This is done whenever information was obtained from the Detroit Police Department and the Detroit Recorder's Court.

6. "Diagrammatic Map of the City of Detroit," in Philip Brezner, "Vernor-McClellan-Van Dyke and Jefferson Avenue Area Rehabilitation," Feb. 1945, Box 10-B, Schermer Collection, ALUA; Federal Home Loan Bank Board, "Greater Detroit: Summary of an Economic, Real Estate, and Mortgage Finance Survey," Area Description 31, 38, 20 Oct. 1939, Box 18, RG 195, NARS (hereinafter cited as Federal Home Loan, "Greater Detroit: Summary," Area D-plus number).

7. Governor's Committee, *Factual Report*, Part II, Exhibit 24, p. 1; President's Committee for Congested Production Areas, "Report: Detroit, Michigan," p. 1, and Federal Coordinating Committee for Michigan, Minutes, 14 Oct. 1943, p. 2, Box 48, RG 212, NARS.

8. Detroit *News*, 31 July 1943, p. 2 (hereinafter cited as *News*), for the quotation of Dr. Lowell S. Selling; David O. Sears and John B. McConahay, *The Politics of Violence: The New Urban Blacks and the Watts Riot* (Boston, 1973), p. 33, for the theory that "mainstream socialization" in Northern ghettos advances collective violence.

9. Examination, 28 July 1943, pp. 12–13, Recorder's Court File A-35070, BHC (hereinafter cited as Examination, date, RFC plus number).

10. Governor's Committee, *Factual Report*, Part II, Exhibit 3.

11. Kenneth B. Clark and James Barker, "The Zoot Effect in Personality: A Race Riot Participant," *Journal of Abnormal and Social Psychology*, 40 (1945): 143–48, for a participant in the Harlem riot of 1943 who is analogous to Charles L.

12. John J. Considine, "A Summary of Recreational Activities and Facilities Available to the Citizens of Detroit," n.d., p. 4, Detroit Committee on Community Relations Collection, ALUA.

13. Federal Bureau of Investigation, "Detroit Riots, June 20–22, 1943," 28 June 1943, p. 1, FBIF (hereinafter cited as FBI, "Detroit Riots"). See Box 18, RG 319, WNRC, for an unexpunged copy of this document.

14. Kenneth J. Creagh to Thomas M. Cotter, 22 Mar. 1944, RCF A-35069, BHC.

15. Governor's Committee, *Factual Report*, Part I, pp. 3, 4, 7, for the quotations, and Part II, Exhibit 9, pp. 1–3; Examination, 28 July 1943, pp. 3, 12–13, RCF A-35070, BHC; Robert Shogan and Tom

Craig, *The Detroit Race Riot: A Study in Violence* (Philadelphia, 1964), pp. 35–39.

16. Governor's Committee, *Factual Report,* Part I, pp. 7, 8, for the quotations, and Part II, Exhibit 9, p. 2.

17. Memorandum for the Attorney General (from C. E. Rhetts), 12 July 1943, pp. 3–4, Box 213, HLIP (hereinafter cited as Rhetts Memorandum); Alfred M. Lee and Norman D. Humphrey, *Race Riot* (New York, 1943), pp. 26, 27 for the quotations; John H. Witherspoon to the Common Council, City of Detroit, 28 June 1943, *Journal of the Common Council* (Detroit, 1944), p. 1855 (hereinafter cited as Witherspoon Statement).

18. Thurgood Marshall, "Report Concerning Detroit Police Activities During the Riots," 26 July 1943, p. 4, Box 1, NAACP Collection, ALUA (hereinafter cited as Marshall, "Report").

19. Shogan and Craig, *The Detroit Race Riot,* p. 42, for the black statistics and, by contrast, nineteen whites arrested and eight whites injured; Lee and Humphrey, *Race Riot,* p. 26.

20. Examination, 12 Aug. 1943, p. 38, RCF A-35288, BHC, for the possibility of Harper M. being the messenger; Detroit *Tribune,* 14 Aug. 1943, p. 1, and 16 Oct. 1943, p. 1 (hereinafter cited as *Tribune*) for his questioning and release; File Jacket, RCF A-35228, BHC, for Charles L.'s conviction—probably wrongful—for inciting riot at the Forest Club.

21. David A. Levine, *Internal Combustion: The Races in Detroit, 1915–1926* (Westport, Conn., 1976); Morris Janowitz, "Black Legions on the March," in *America in Crisis: Fourteen Episodes in American History,* ed. Daniel Aaron (reprint ed., Hamden, Conn. 1971); pp. 305–307; Capeci, *Race Relations.*

22. Arrest Ticket 902, 28 July 1943; *Chronicle,* 2 Oct. 1943, p. 2; Governor's Committee, *Factual Report,* Part I, p. 11, n. 38; *Tribune,* 7 Aug. 1943, p. 1.

23. Governor's Committee, *Factual Report,* Part I, p. 10; Rhetts Memorandum, p. 4; Examination, 12 Aug. 1943, p. 29, RCF A-35288, BHC, for the first and third quotations; Leo G. Mack and Milton Swingle to Commanding Officer, Special Investigation Squad, 3 July 1943, Jesse Stewart Personnel File, DPDR (hereinafter cited as Stewart File), for the second quotation. We thank Mr. Stewart for permission to consult his personnel file.

24. James P. Comer, "The Dynamics of Black and White Violence," in *Violence in America: Historical and Comparative Perspectives,* eds. Hugh D. Graham and Ted R. Gurr, Vol. 2 (Washington, D.C., 1969), p. 349.

25. Governor's Committee, *Factual Report*, Part I, p. 10; Tamble Whitworth, Statement, 30 July 1943, Stewart File, DPDR.

26. Terry A. Knopf, *Rumors, Race, and Riot* (New Brunswick, 1975), pp. 145, 154; Stanley Lieberson and Arnold H. Silverman, "The Precipitants and Underlying Conditions of Race Riots," *American Sociological Review* 30 (Dec. 1965): 888.

27. William Lang, Statement, 17 Sept. 1943, Stewart File, DPDR; Edward J. Jeffries, Jr., to the Common Council, City of Detroit, 29 June 1943, *Journal of the Common Council* (Detroit, 1944), p. 1829 (hereinafter cited as Jeffries Statement); *Chronicle*, 23 Oct. 1943, p. 2; Fred Stephan to Chief of Detectives, "Riot at Forest and Hastings," 21 June 1943, in Donald S. Leonard, "Detroit Race Riot," n.d., Box 7, Leonard Papers, MHC; Lee and Humphrey, *Race Riot*, p. 28.

28. Justin Driscoll, Statement, 15 Sept. 1943, Stewart File, DPDR; Joseph Boskin, "Violence in the Ghettos," *New Mexico Quarterly* 37 (Winter 1968): 318.

29. Governor's Committee, *Factual Report*, Part II, Exhibit 19b, p. 1; Shogan and Craig, *The Detroit Race Riot*, p. 45.

30. Witherspoon Statement, p. 1856.

31. Governor's Committee, *Factual Report*, Part I, p. 13, n. 46; Arrest Ticket 27.

32. See the Appendix for explanation of the data and methodology. All the profiles of rioters in this chapter are drawn from a representative random sample (N=246) of all available riot-related arrest tickets on June 21 and 22, 1943. Participants like John T. are selected because they match as closely as possible the aggregate characteristics of the particular rioters under consideration. For example, thirteen were arrested on Oakland Avenue on June 21: all black, ten male, seven married, ten employed (seven as laborers), with a typical age (the middle 20 percent) between twenty-one and twenty-four years; John T.—black, married, employed, and twenty-four years old—was arrested on Oakland Avenue, June 21, at 3:55 A.M. for a misdemeanor. August Meier and Elliott Rudwick, *Black Detroit and the Rise of the UAW* (New York, 1979), pp. 162–74.

33. August Meier and Elliott Rudwick, "Black Violence in the 20th Century," in *Violence in America*, Vol. 2, p. 312.

34. FBI, "Detroit Riots," p. 7; Governor's Committee, *Factual Report*, Part II, Exhibit 19a.

35. Dominic J. Capeci, Jr., "Black-Jewish Relations in Wartime Detroit: The Marsh, Loving, Wolf Surveys and the Race Riot of 1943,"

Jewish Social Studies 47 (Summer/Fall 1985): 225; Rhetts Memorandum, p. 4, n. 2; FBI, "Detroit Riots," p. 4.

36. Lee and Humphrey, *Race Riot,* pp. 28–29; Federal Home Loan, "Greater Detroit: Summary," Area D-37.

37. Elliott M. Rudwick, *Race Riot in East St. Louis, July 2, 1917* (Carbondale, Ill., 1964), pp. 52, 67, 217; Lee and Humphrey, *Race Riot,* p. 117.

38. William E. Guthner, "Commander's Estimate of the Situation, June 20–24, 1943," 26 June 1943, pp. 1–3, RG 79-10, MSA (hereinafter cited as Guthner, "Commander's Estimate"); Shogan and Craig, *The Detroit Race Riot,* pp. 66–73; Harvard Sitkoff, "The Detroit Race Riot of 1943," *Michigan History* 53 (Fall 1969): 191–96.

39. Anonymous, "Joint Meeting of Citizens Committee and Other Civic and Labor Groups," 21 June 1943, passim and p. 11 for the quotation, Box 70, Civil Rights Congress of Michigan Collection, ALUA (herein cited as Citizens Committee, "Joint Meeting"). The Sojourner Truth Citizens Committee, organized in December of 1941 to obtain black occupancy of the government-financed housing named for the famed black abolitionist-feminist—a successful campaign. The committee shifted its focus in the spring of 1942 to black defense employment—and renamed itself the Citizens Committee for Jobs in War Industries. A biracial committee of church, civic, labor, and leftist organizations, as well as an unaffiliated individuals, it carried on the struggle for racial equality throughout the war, and eventually it became known simply as the Citizens Committee. Capeci, *Race Relations,* pp. 75–99.

40. Governor's Committee, *Factual Report,* Part II, Exhibit 19b; Memorandum for the Inspector General (from Joel R. Burney), 30 June 1943, p. 1, Box 1789, RG 389, NARS (hereinafter cited as Burney Memorandum).

41. Witherspoon Statement, pp. 1856–57; FBI, "Detroit Riots," pp. 2–3.

42. Leonard, "Detroit Race Riot," p. 4; Report for Charles Mahoney (from Thurgood Marshall), 10 July 1943, pp. 4–6, Box 1 NAACP Collection, ALUA.

43. Of N=246, seventy-nine were arrested June 21 in the east-side ghetto (John R, Brush, Beaubien, St. Antoine, and Hastings streets): all black, seventy-eight male, forty-eight married, and seventy-two employed as laborers, their typical age fell between twenty-four and twenty-eight years.

44. Federal Home Loan, "Greater Detroit: Summary," Area D-31 and D-38; George W. Beatty, "The Background and Causes of the 1943 Detroit Race Riot," unpublished senior thesis, Princeton University, 1954, pp. 12–14.

45. Arrest Ticket 118; Wayne County Probation Services, Case 17, RCR (herein cited as Probation Case plus member); Lowell S. Selling, "A Study of One Hundred Offenders Who Were Apprehended During the Disturbances of June 20th and 21st in Detroit, Michigan," n.d., p. 39, Box 9, Mayor's Papers (1943), BHC, for the Southern knife-carrying tradition. In comparison to the average weekly wage of $58.28 in June of 1943 for workers in the automobile industry (i.e., defense production), Rudolph M. earned $35. United Automobile Workers, "Employment, Hours and Earnings," n.d., p. 4, Box 89, UAW Research Department Collection, ALUA.

46. Meier and Rudwick, "Black Violence," p. 312; Louis H. Masotti, et al., A Time to Burn? An Evaluation of the Present Crisis in Race Relations (Chicago, 1969), p. 129; H. Otto Dahlke, "Race and Minority Riots—A Study in the Typology of Violence," Social Forces 30 (May 1952): 421.

47. Arrest Ticket 81; Examination, 25 June 1943, pp. 6, 7, 10, RCF A-34730, BHC; Probation Case 76.

48. Russell Dynes and E. L. Quarantelli, "What Looting in Civil Disorders Really Means," Trans-Action 5 (May 1968): 13–14; Comer, "Black and White Violence," p. 347.

49. Edward C. Banfield, The Unheavenly City: The Nature and Future of Our Urban Crisis (Boston, 1970), p. 185, for the quotation.

50. Examination, 23 June 1943, p. 3, RCF A-34545, BHC, for the inference that Rudolph M. did not know the proprietor of Paul's Drug Store; Examination, 25 June 1943, pp. 2–3, RCF A-34730, BHC, for verification that Roy S. did not know the Jewish owner of the grocery store he looted; Capeci, "Black-Jewish Relations," p. 228, for the "white caste" quotation by Donald C. Marsh.

51. Jeffries Statement, pp. 1827–28; Guthner, "Commander's Estimate," pp. 4–8; Lee and Humphrey, Race Riot, pp. 33–37, 36, for the quotation; Shogan and Craig, The Detroit Race Riot, pp. 74–79; Sitkoff, "The Detroit Race Riot," p. 193.

52. Leonard, "Detroit Race Riot," p. 4.

53. Arrest Ticket 577; Probation Case 75. Of N=246, eight were arrested June 21 on Woodward Avenue: five white, eight male, six married, eight employed (three laborers, three skilled, two semi-

skilled), with the median age of twenty-two years and five without previous arrests.

54. Examination, 28 June 1943, passim, RCF A-34583, BHC.

55. Governor's Committee, *Factual Report,* Part II, Exhibit 19b, pp. 6–9.

56. Jeffries Statement, p. 1828; Lee and Humphrey, *Race Riot,* p. 39, for the presence of only thirty-two immobile troppers being on duty at Piquette Armory at this time.

57. Guthner, "Commander's Estimate," p. 10.

58. Governor's Committee, *Factual Report,* Part II, Exhibit 14.

59. Arrest Ticket 42; Capeci, *Race Relations,* p. 12; Hubert M. Blalock, Jr., *Toward a Theory of Minority-Group Relations* (New York, 1967), pp. 51–72. Of N=246, eight were arrested June 21 in the black west side (bounded by Tireman, 24th, Warren, and Livernois streets): eight black, eight male, five married, eight employed (six laborers), with a median age of thirty-eight years and six without previous arrests.

60. Of N=246, five were arrested June 21 in Precinct 11-SW (east of Highland Park and north Hamtramck): all black, all male, three married, four employed (laborers), with a median age of twenty-one years and three without previous records.

61. Arrest Ticket 79; P. H. Doyle to Whom It May Concern, 2 Aug. 1943, Green Davis to Chief Probation Officer, 2 Aug. 1943, Kenneth J. Creagh to Thomas N. Cotter, 9 Aug. 1943, and File Jacket, RCF A-34617, BHC; Probation Case 37. Harding D. lived at 13132 Greeley, beyond the city's slum area. "Diagrammatic Map of the City of Detroit," Box 10-B, Schermer Collection, ALUA.

62. Guthner, "Commander's Estimate," pp. 10–11; Shogan and Craig, *The Detroit Race Riot,* pp. 80–82; Allen D. Grimshaw, "Factors Contributing to Colour Violence in the United States and Great Britain," and "Actions of Police and the Military in American Race Riots," in *Racial Violence in the United States,* ed. by Allen D. Grimshaw, (Chicago, 1969), pp. 268 and 286; Morris Janowitz, *Social Control of Escalated Riots* (Chicago, 1968).

63. Guthner, "Commander's Estimate," pp. 11–12; *News,* 23 June 1943, p. 2; *Tribune,* 26 June 1943, pp. 1, 2, for the information in this paragraph unless cited otherwise.

64. Thomas Colladay, "Report on Mobilization, Concentration, Tour of Duty in Detroit and Duty Mobilization of Michigan State Troops, June 21 to July 6, 1943," 10 July 1943, p. 2, Box 74, Kelly

Papers, MSA (hereinafter cited as "Report of Mobilization").

65. Lee and Humphrey, *Race Riot*, p. 44.

66. Governor's Committee, *Factual Report*, Part II, Exhibit 19b, p. 13. Before this death, seven others occurred between 9:00 P.M. and 10:30 P.M. on June 21.

67. Of N=246, sixty-nine were arrested June 22 in all riot areas: sixty black, sixty-four male, thirty-six married (thirty single), sixty-six employed (fifty-five laborers), with a median age of 29.5 years for those married (19.5 years for those single) and forty without previous arrests. Married rioters perpetrated twenty-three felonies and thirteen misdemeanors; single participants committed fourteen felonies and sixteen misdemeanors.

68. Arrest Ticket 256, 22 June 1943; Examination, 24 June 1943, pp. 1–4, 5, for the quotation, RCF A-34635, BHC; Probation Case 41.

69. Lee and Humphrey, *Race and Riot*, p. 69; Guthner, "Commander's Estimate," p. 12.

70. Governor's Committee, *Factual Report*, Part II, Exhibit 19a; Anonymous, "Receiving Hospital Statistics on the Riot of June 21, 1943," n.d., Box 18, Detroit Committee on Community Relations Collection, ALUA; Colladay, "Report of Mobilization," pp. 2, 4; *News*, 27 June 1943, p. 17.

71. *News*, 24 June 1943, p. 2, for the quotations; Winifred Raushenbush, "How to Prevent Race Riots," *American Mercury* 57 (Sept. 1943): 302.

72. Governor's Committee, *Factual Report*, Part II, Exhibit 19a, for the statistics and the indication that six whites were killed by unknown black assailants and five blacks were slain by unknown persons.

73. Governor's Committee, *Factual Report*, Part II, Exhibit 15, for the juvenile data and Exhibits 24, 26, and 29 for the information on adults.

74. White, "What Caused?" pp. 14, 16; Marshall, "Report," passim. See also Walter White and Thurgood Marshall, *What Caused the Detroit Riots?* (New York, 1943) for the published version of these reports and Walter White, *A Man Called White* (New York, 1948), pp. 224–32.

75. John H. Witherspoon to Herbert F. Robb, 18 Oct. 1943, Box 9, OF 4245-G, FDRL.

76. Rhetts Memorandum, pp. 7–9; Memorandum to the Police Commissioner (from Edward M. Butler and Emanuel Kline), 28 June 1943, pp. 1–5, Box 2574, FHLP, for the criticism from representatives of the United States Justice Department and the New York Po-

lice Department.

77. *PM* (New York), 22 June 1943, p. 3, for the quotation.

78. Editorial, "We Must Have Order," *News*, 22 June 1943, p. 18, for an example; Citizens Committee, "Joint Meeting," pp. 7–8, and Josephine Gomon to Dear Kids, 22 June 1943, Box 1, Gomon Collection, MHC, for Jeffries's concern over a Detroit *Times* story and subsequent management of press coverage during the riot.

79. Gerald L. K. Smith, "Race Riot! An Interpretation," *The Cross and the Flag* 2 (July 1944): 233, for the quotation of the Reverend Mr. White.

80. Citizen to Jeffries, n.d., Box 8, Mayor's Papers (1943), BHC.

81. Citizens Committee, "Joint Meeting," p. 8.

82. Jeffries Statement, p. 1828; Witherspoon Statement, pp. 1856, 1858.

83. Anonymous to Norman Thomas, n.d., and Taxpayer to Jeffries, 22 June 1943, Box 9, Mayor's Papers (1943), BHC.

84. Philip P. Bruno to Jeffries, 26 June 1943, Box 8, ibid.

85. Richard Deverall to Clarence Glick, 28 June 1943, Box 9, OF 4245-G, FDRL; John Wood, "I Cover the Town," *Chronicle*, 3 July 1943, p. 7.

86. William E. Guthner, "Summary of Events and Commander's Estimate, June 27, 1943," 2 July 1943, p. 5, RG 79–10, MSA.

87. George Gallup, "America Speaks," *News*, 28 July 1943, p. 10; *Tribune*, 21 Aug. 1943, p. 1, for the quotation of Judge Maher.

88. Sophie M. Eckman, "Incident Report to Inter-racial Committee," 28 July 1944, Box 3, Detroit Committee on Community Relations Collection, ALUA.

89. Memorandum for the NAACP (from P. W.), 26 June 1943, p. 7, Box 1, NAACP Collection, ALUA, for the quotation of an elderly white witness (hereinafter cited as P. W. Memorandum).

90. *News*, 22 June 1943, p. 2.

91. Raushenbush, "How to Prevent," p. 307.

92. *Chronicle*, 26 June 1943, p. 4; A. M. Smith, "Better Recreation Facilities Needed," *News*, 9 July 1943, p. 12, for the quotations of Eleonore L. Hutzel, chief, DPD Women's Division.

93. Lee and Humphrey, *Race Riot*, pp. 37–38; J. H. Reichert to Jeffries, 13 June 1943, Box 9, Mayor's Papers (1943), BHC.

94. Governor's Committee, *Factual Report*, Part II, Exhibit 3 and Exhibit 8; P. W. Memorandum, pp. 9, 10, 13; Smith, "Better Recreation Facilities Needed," p. 12.

95. Zoot-Suiters, Twelve of Them, to the Editor, *News*, 12 July 1943, p. 14; One of the People to the Editor, *News*, 19 July 1943, p. 14.

96. Editorial, "Look Into Their Minds," *News*, 24 June 1943, p. 24.

97. *News*, 24 June 1943, p. 1.

98. Ibid., 25 June 1943, p. 30; Shogan and Craig, *The Detroit Race Riot*, p. 100.

99. America First Party of Detroit, Resolution, 28 June 1943, Box 10, Smith Papers, MHC.

100. Ralph McGill telegram to Jeffries, 22 June 1943, Box 8, Mayor's Papers (1943), BHC.

101. "The Commentator," *News*, 22 June 1943, p. 18.

102. "Are We a Fighting People?" *The Civic Searchlight*, July/Aug., 1943.

103. George Gallup, "America Speaks," *News*, 28 July 1943, p. 10.

104. *News*, 24 June 1943, p. 1.

105. Josephine Gomon to Dear Kids, 25 June 1943, Box 1, Gomon Papers, MHC; P. W. Memorandum, p. 6, for the evaluation of a sixty-year-old white foreman.

106. Richard Deverall to Clarence Glick, 28 June 1943, Box 9, OF-4245, FDRL.

107. Sheridan A. Bruseaux Investigation to Horace A. White, "Investigation of Recent Detroit Riots," 12 July 1943, p. 2, Box 8, Mayor's Papers (1943), BHC (hereinafter cited as Bruseaux, "Investigation"); Federal Home Loan, "Greater Detroit: Summary," Area D-37.

108. Clive, *State of War*, pp. 173–84.

109. Josephine Gomon to Dear Kids, 25 June 1943, Box 1, Gomon Papers, MHC.

110. Jim Burgess to the Editor, *News*, 25 June 1943, p. 18. See also D.A.S. to the Editor and Z.E. to the Editor, *News*, 2 July 1943, p. 18.

111. Alice Jordan to the Editor, *News*, 25 June 1943, p. 18.

112. E Pluribus Unum to the Editor and A Reader to the Editor, *News*, 2 July 1943, p. 18.

113. Mrs. Penihouse to Mr. and Mrs. Charles B. Morgan, 7 July 1943, Anonymous to Charles B. Morgan and Wife, n.d., and Anonymous, 7 July 1943, Box 1, NAACP Collection, ALUA.

114. W. F. Carr to Jeffries, 30 June 1943, Box 8, Mayor's Papers (1943), BHC.

115. Jeffries to W. F. Carr, 8 July 1943, ibid.

116. W. P. Clark to Jeffries, 26 June 1943, ibid.; Maury Maverick to Donald Nelson, 29 July 1943, Box 1017, RG 179, NARS.

117. Estelle M. Reid to Kelly, 24 June 1943, Box 75, Kelly Papers, MSA.

118. Charles E. J. Newman to Director of Intelligence, Second Service Command, 9 July 1943, Box 18, RG 389, NARS.

119. Federal Bureau of Investigation, "Survey of Racial Conditions in the United States," 1944, p. 13, Box 44, OF 10-B, FDRL (hereinafter cited as FBI, "Survey of Racial Conditions"); Bruseaux, "Investigation," pp. 2–3; Memorandum for the Attorney General (from Francis J. Haas), 5 July 1943, p. 2, Box 45, Haas Papers, CUA; Ulysses W. Boykin, "Pastor Foresees New KKK Hold," *Tribune*, 26 June 1943, p. 16, for the quotation of the Rev. Claude Williams.

120. FBI, "Survey of Racial Conditions," p. 6, for the fifty-three Hamtramack arrests: fifteen blacks and thirty-eight whites (presumably mostly Polish-Americans).

121. W. Kucharski to Jeffries, 21 July 1943, Box 8, Mayor's Papers (1943), BHC.

122. *Chronicle*, 26 June 1943, p. 3; Editorial, "The Bitter Fruit," *Chronicle*, 26 June 1943, p. 1.

123. Verne C. Piazza to Jeffries, 21 June 1943, Box 9, and Martin Darvin to Jeffries, 28 June 1943, Box 8, Mayor's Papers (1943), BHC.

124. Harold Johnson, et al., to Kelly, 14 July 1943, Box 75, Kelly Papers, MSA; Dorothy Bokas (Ferndale, Michigan) to the Editor, *News*, 25 June 1943, p. 18.

125. Editorial, "A Nation Divided," *Chronicle*, 26 June 1943, p. 7.

126. A. R. Braunlich, Jr., to the Editor, *News*, 4 July 1943, Sec. II, p. 10.

127. *PM*, 22 June 1943, p. 4, for the rumors in "nearly all of the outbreaks."

128. Frank J. McCarthy to Kelly, 21 July 1943, Box 75, Kelly Papers, MSA.

129. Beulah T. Whitby, Oral History, p. 26, Blacks in the Labor Movement, ALUA; Paul A. Adler, "Local, International Plot Clues Plentiful," *News*, 25 June 1943, p. 1.

130. Sol Lumberg to the Editor, *News*, 24 June 1943, p. 24; G. L. to the Editor, *PM*, 29 June 1943, p. 17.

131. *Tribune*, 3 July 1943, pp. 1, 2.

132. Harold Mulbar to Oscar G. Olander, 29 July 1943, p. 5, Case 6152, MSPR (hereinafter all MSPR citations refer to Case 6152).

133. Beatty, "The Background and Causes," p. 81.

134. Citizens Committee, "Joint Meeting," pp. 2, 4, 10; Citizens Committee, "Remarks of R. J. Thomas, et al.," 21 June 1943, pp. 1,

10, Box 70, Civil Rights Congress on Michigan Collection, ALUA (hereinafter cited as Citizens Committee, "Remarks").

135. Citizens Committee to Citizens of Detroit, n.d., Box 70, Civil Rights Congress of Michigan Collection, ALUA.

136. Civil Rights Federation of Michigan, "Action," 23 June 1943, pp. 1, 2, ibid. (hereinafter cited as Civil Rights Federation, "Action"); Capeci, *Race Relations*, pp. 84, 111, 134, 150; Communist Party of Michigan, "Statement of the State Committee," n.d., Box 70, Civil Rights Congress of Michigan Collection, ALUA; Adreline Kohl to Kelly, 25 June 1943, Box 75, Kelly Papers, MSA, for the quotation of the executive secretary, Young Communist League of Michigan. The Civil Rights Federation of Michigan was allegedly a Communist front organization with influential members on the Citizens Committee.

137. *Tribune*, 3 July 1943, p. 7; Lester B. Granger telegram to John C. Dancy, 21 June 1943, and Lester B. Granger to Executive Secretaries of Affiliated Organizations, 24 June 1943, Reel 10, DULP.

138. Lester B. Granger, et al., telegram to Franklin D. Roosevelt, 22 June 1943, Box 14, NULP for the quotation; National Urban League, "Report of the Detroit Race Riots and Recommendations for a Program of Community Action," 28 June 1943, p. 5, Reel 10, DULP.

139. Margaret Collingwood Nowak, Diary, 21 June 1943 entry, Box 5, Nowak Collection, ALUA; Donald Thurber and Arthur Bowman, "A Statement to Detroit Youth," n.d., Box 70, Civil Rights Congress of Michigan Collection, ALUA.

140. *News*, 30 June 1943, p. 10.

141. Editorial, "Who Is to Blame?" *Tribune*, 26 June 1943, p. 8.

142. *Chronicle*, 26 June 1943, p. 2.

143. Ibid., 3 July 1943, p. 12, for the quotation of R. J. Thomas; FBI, "Survey of Racial Conditions," pp. 8–10, for the Bureau's suspicions.

144. Capeci, *Race Relations*, pp. 47, 70–74, 100, 113, 115–17, 120, 126–27, 151, 152.

145. John Tebbel to Malcolm Bingay, 24 June 1943, Folder 1, Bingay Papers, BHC; John Roy Carlson [Avedis Derounian], *Under Cover* (New York, 1943), pp. 321–36; Philip A. Adler, "Under Cover Man Digs Up a Political Underworld," *News*, 17 July 1943, p. 19.

146. Editorial, "Who Is to Blame?" *Tribune*, 26 June 1943, p. 8, for an example.

147. America First Party, Press Release, 24 June 1943, Box 10, Smith Papers, MHC; Glen Jeansonne, *Gerald L. K. Smith: Minister of*

Hate (New Haven, 1988), pp. 80–100, for Smith's wartime ideology and activities (which focus on national issues).

148. Gerald L. K. Smith, "Statement: The Detroit Race Riots," 28 June 1943, Box 10, Smith Papers, MHC.

149. Civil Rights Federation, "Action," 23 June 1943, p. 2; Philip A. Adler, "Shadow of Fascism Seen on Race Riots," *News*, 1 July 1943, p. 20; Carlson, *Under Cover*, passim; Mary Smith to Jeffries, 1 Aug. 1943 (postmark), Box 8, Mayor's Papers (1943), BHC, for the local resident example, which also expressed anti-Catholicism.

150. Sixty Soldiers to Jeffries, 22 June 1943, Box 10, Smith Papers, MHC, for the quotation; Jack D. Rennie to Jeffries, 30 June 1943, Box 8, Mayor's Papers (1943), BHC.

151. Gerald L. K. Smith to Gerald L. K. Smith, Jr., 1 July 1943, Box 10, Smith Papers, MHC.

152. L. A. Lowenstein to H. R. Kibler, 25 June 1943, Box 18, RG 319, WNRC.

153. *Republican-Tribune* (Sandusky, Michigan), 1 July 1943, Box 12, Kelly Papers, MSA; M. Shipman to Kelly, 22 June 1943, Box 75, Kelly Papers, MSA.

154. Philip A. Adler, "Planning Indicated in City Race Riots," *News*, 24 June 1943, p. 1.

155. *News*, 21 June 1943, p. 2; Francis J. Haas, Notebook, 2 July 1943 entry, Haas Papers, CUA.

156. *News*, 21 June 1943, p. 2, 22 June 1943, p. 2, and 29 June 1943, p. 1; J. Edgar Hoover to Marvin H. McIntyre, 23 June 1943, Box 10-B, FDRL.

157. Telephone transcript: Allen W. Gullion and Henry S. Aurand, 22 June 1943, Box 1789, RG 389, NARS.

158. Harold Mulbar to Oscar G. Olander, 8 July 1943, for the quotation, and 29 July 1943, MSPR; *News*, 8 July 1943, p. 2; FBI, "Survey of Racial Conditions," p. 27; J. D. Murray, Meeting with Representatives of the Department of Justice (Criminal Division), 8 July 1943, Box 200, RG 107, NARS; Burney Memorandum, pp. 6, 7.

159. *News*, 8 July 1943, p. 2.

160. Editorial, "Keep Troops at Hand to Maintain Order," *News*, 23 June 1943, p. 22.

161. Louis R. Halgren to the Editor, *News*, 11 July 1943, II, p. 10; *News*, 25 June 1943, p. 30.

162. William H. Baldwin to Board Members and Executive Secretaries of Affiliated Organizations, 6 July 1943, p. 3, Reel 10, DULP; Editorial, "The Riots," *Crisis*, July 1943, p. 199.

163. Larry Yost, "Racing for Riches Causes Races to Disagree," *Ford Facts*, 15 July 1943, p. 5-A; Edward B. Davis to Jeffries, n.d., Box 8, Mayor's Papers (1943), BHC, for the quotation.

164. Gail Winters, "Ku Klux Klan Works Underground, Whips Up White Lunatic Fringe," *Chronicle*, 3 July 1943, p. 6.

165. Albert Deutsch, "Whose Riots?" *PM*, 25 June 1943, p. 11.

166. FBI, "Survey of Racial Conditions," pp. 8–10.

167. C. F. Ramsay to Kelly, 2 Aug. 1943, Box 74, Kelly Papers, MSA.

168. *Chronicle*, 31 July 1943, pp. 1, 2; *Tribune*, 7 Aug. 1943, p. 1.

169. *News*, 27 July 1943, pp. 1, 2.

170. Lee and Humphrey, *Race Riot*, pp. 68, 69, for the first quotation; Sitkoff, "The Detroit Race Riot," pp. 203–204; Governor's Committee, *Factual Report*, Part I, p. 13, for the third, fourth, and fifth quotations, p. 15, for the second and sixth quotations, and Part III, p. 2, for the seventh quotation, p. 6 for the eighth quotation.

171. W. K. Kelsey, "The Commentator," *News*, 23 June 1943, p. 22; *News*, 25 June 1943, p. 30.

CHAPTER 2: *Of Hoodlums and Hillbillies*

1. George Rudé, *The Crowd in History: A Study of Popular Disturbances in France and England 1730–1848* (New York, 1964), p. 195.

2. Press Report, 23 June 1943, Box 74, Kelly Papers, MSA; Detroit *News*, 23 June 1943, p. 1, and 24 June 1943, p. 2 (hereinafter cited as *News*). Among the conferees were Jeffries, Police Superintendent Louis L. Berg, Chief of Detectives Paul H. Wencel, State Police Captain Donald S. Leonard, Michigan State Troops Adjutant General LeRoy Pearson, Chief Assistant State Prosecutor Julian G. McIntosh, and State Assistant Attorney General Thomas A. Kenney.

3. Herbert J. Rushton, et al., to Kelly, [25] June 1943 and "Progress Report of Governor's Fact-Finding Body," 6 July 1943, Box 74, Kelly Papers, MSA, for the quotation; *News*, 24 June 1943, p. 2, 25 June 1943, p. 1, and 26 June 1943, p. 1. The Federal Bureau of Investigation, U.S. Army, and U.S. Navy Intelligence, Michigan State Police, Wayne County Prosecutor's Office, and Detroit Police Department were the agencies.

4. *News*, 27 July 1943, p. 2, for the first and third quotations; Michigan *Chronicle*, 31 July 1943, p. 1, for the second quotation (hereinafter cited as *Chronicle*).

5. *News*, 28 July 1943, pp. 1, 10; Editorial, "Mr. Dowling Speaks

Out," *News*, 28 July 1943, p. 18; *Chronicle*, 31 July 1943, pp. 1, 3; Detroit *Tribune*, 7 Aug. 1943, p. 1 (hereinafter cited as *Tribune*); Alfred M. Lee and Norman D. Humphrey, *Race Riot* (New York, 1943), pp. 64–65.

6. *News*, 11 Aug. 1943, pp. 1, 2; Herbert J. Rushton, William E. Dowling, Oscar Olander, and John H. Witherspoon, *Factual Report of the Governor's Committee to Investigate the Riot Occurring in Detroit on June 21, 1943*, 11 Aug. 1943, Part I, p. 15, and Part II, Exhibits 4–8, BHC (hereinafter cited as Governor's Committee, *Factual Report*).

7. William M. Graves and Gloster B. Current, Minutes of Legal Redress Committee, 5 July 1944, Detroit, Michigan, 1942, folder, Branch File, NAACP, for an example; *Chronicle*, 14 Aug. 1943, p. 1.

8. Governor's Committee, *Factual Report*, Part I, pp. 2–15; Harvard Sitkoff, "The Detroit Race Riot of 1943," *Michigan History* 53 (Fall 1969): 203–04; George W. Beatty, "The Background and Causes of the 1943 Detroit Race Riot," unpublished senior thesis, Princeton University, 1954, p. 116.

9. Governor's Committee, *Factual Report*, Part I, p. 15, n. 54, for the quotations, released juveniles, and detained females, Part II, Exhibit 15, for the male juveniles, and Exhibits 24, 26, and 29, for the adult arrestees. Of those placed in detention, three were black females and one was a white female; none of the fifty-eight released juveniles were identified by race.

10. *New York Times*, 25 June 1943, p. 8, for the quotation; *News*, 24 June 1943, p. 1.

11. *News*, 25 June 1943, p. 30; *Chronicle*, 3 July 1943, p. 12; C. F. Ramsay to Kelly, 2 Aug. 1943, Box 74, Kelly Papers, MSA (hereinafter cited as Ramsay to Kelly, 2 Aug. 1943); Memorandum: Statements of Negro Prisoners Taken at the Piquette Armory, June 24th, 1943, to Thomas Colladay (from Leo M. Wendell), 24 June 1943, pp. 1–22, RG 79-10, MSA, for earlier questioning by local police, federal agents, and county prosecutors (hereinafter cited as Wendell Memorandum). The Council of Social Agencies included numerous members, such as the Detroit Community Fund.

12. Ramsay to Kelly, 2 Aug. 1943; *News*, 11 Aug. 1943, p. 1.

13. C. F. Ramsay, "Analysis of Interviews Made with Prisoners Taken in the Detroit Race Riot," 2 Aug. 1943, pp. 1–14, Box 74, Kelly Papers, MSA, for the information in this and the following two paragraphs unless cited otherwise (hereinafter cited as Ramsay, "Interviews"). The white rioters are analyzed in Chapter 3.

14. Ibid., p. 11; Ramsay to Kelly, 2 Aug. 1943, for the quotation.

15. Ramsay, "Interviews," p. 12. Of N=314 blacks, 171 (54.5 percent) claimed not to know the cause for the riot, sixty-two cited rumors, fifty-two hoodlums, twenty-two subversive activity, nine discrimination, three lack of education.

16. Ramsay to Kelly, 2 Aug. 1943, for the latter percentage, which includes white rioters whose scant numbers indicate that most of the illiterate were black.

17. Ramsay, "Interviews," p. 7, Table 8; Ramsay to Kelly, 2 Aug. 1943. Of N=314 blacks, sixteen (5.1 percent) reported venereal disease and three (1 percent) reported tuberculosis; of twenty-six whites, none reported either illness. Of N=340 prisoners, including twenty-six whites, only ten (2.9 percent) were identified by psychiatrists as exhibiting signs of "mental deviation"; of the ten so diagnosed, Ramsay did not reveal their race.

18. Editorial, "Look into Their Minds," *News*, 24 June 1943, p. 24.

19. Military Intelligence Division (U.S. Department of War), "Riot and Investigation: Detroit, Michigan," 23 July 1943, Box 18, RG 319, WNRC.

20. Lowell S. Selling, "A Study of One Hundred Offenders Who Were Apprehended during the Disturbance of June 20th and 21st, 1943, in Detroit, Michigan," n.d., pp. 2–3, 6, 9–10, 18, 31–33, Box 9, Mayor's Papers (1943), BHC (hereinafter cited as Selling, "One Hundred Offenders,").

21. *Chronicle*, 27 Nov. 1943, p. 1; Selling, "One Hundred Offenders," pp. 11, 53, 66–67, 81–87, Tables III and IV.

22. Selling, "One Hundred Offenders," p. 22, for the quotation, pp. 21–24, 40–41, 44–45, 48–49, 59–63, 70–75, Tables IV and VIII, for examples of individual cases. Alabama, Georgia, and Mississippi natives accounted for seventeen, fifteen, and nine rioters respectively.

23. Selling, "One Hundred Offenders," pp. 36–50, 42, for the first quotation, p. 50 for the second quotation, pp. 68–70, Tables I, VI, and IX. Four of five white rioters scored very low in the intelligence scale; twenty-two offenders were diagnosed as psychopathic.

24. Selling, "One Hundred Offenders," p. 52, for the quotation, pp. 50–55, Table V.

25. Ibid., pp. 55–63, 52, 55, 57, and 63, for the respective quotations, Table V.

26. Elmer R. Akers and Vernon Fox, "The Detroit Rioters and Looters Committed to Prison," n.d., pp. 1–2, Box 1, NAACP Collection, ALUA (hereinafter cited as Akers and Fox, "Rioters"). See *Jour-*

nal of Criminal Law and Criminology 35 (1944): 105–11, for a briefer version of the original manuscript.

27. Akers and Fox, "Rioters," 6–7. Forty-six convicts had venereal disease, while only four were or had been drug addicts.

28. Ibid., pp. 3–4, 5–10. Fifty-four convicts (51.4 percent) entered or looted stores, while thirty-seven prisoners (35.2 percent) carried concealed weapons.

29. Governor's Committee, *Factual Report*, Part II, Exhibit 24, for 958 arrests on June 21, but no mention of the number held and prosecuted.

30. Selling, "One Hundred Offenders," pp. 12–13, 77–79; Ramsay to Kelly, 2 Aug. 1943; Akers and Fox, "Rioters," p. 1.

31. Allen D. Grimshaw, "A Study in Social Violence: Urban Race Riots in the United States," unpublished Ph.D. dissertation, University of Pennsylvania, 1959, p. 248. The impression given by Selling and Akers and Fox, as well as Grimshaw, is that Selling's sample contained only felons. In fact, samples of all researchers were unrepresentative rather than numerically insufficient.

32. Selling, "One Hundred Offenders," pp. 54, 79, for recognition of these limitations.

33. Ibid., pp. 9, 34; Ramsay to Kelly, 2 Aug. 1943; Robert Shogan and Tom Craig, *The Detroit Race Riot: A Study in Violence* (Philadelphia, 1964), p. 100, for the quotation of Ramsay staff member Agnes McCreery.

34. Akers and Fox, "Rioters," p. 1; Selling, "One Hundred Offenders," p. 4, 64, Tables III, IV, VII. Seventy-eight percent of the rioters and 74 percent of the murderers scored below average in intelligence quotients, indicating that slightly more participants than killers were of low intelligence (though Selling provided no statistics on how this characteristic was measured); 27 percent of the rioters and 18.2 percent of all criminals were between twenty and twenty-four years old.

35. Akers and Fox, "Rioters," p. 5, for the quotation, and p. 9.

36. Grimshaw, "A Study in Social Violence," p. 250, n. 73, pp. 251–53.

37. Alfred Cassey, "Political Observations," *Tribune*, 10 Aug. 1940, p. 12, and 19 Oct. 1940, p. 12; *Tribune*, 10 Aug. 1940, p. 1, 2 Nov. 1940, p. 16, 4 Jan. 1941, p. 1, and 24 Oct. 1942, p. 3.

38. Dominic J. Capeci, Jr., *Race Relations in Wartime Detroit: The Sojourner Truth Housing Controversy of 1942* (Philadelphia, 1984), pp. 15–27, 100–105, 126; *Tribune*, 14 Mar. 1942, pp. 1, 2, and 21 Mar. 1942, p. 2; *News*, 28 May 1943, p. 14.

39. Editorial, "Negro 'Radicals,'" *Chronicle,* 19 June 1943, p. 6; Lee and Humphrey, *Race Riot,* pp. 64–65, 68–69.

40. Horace A. White, "The Facts in Our News," *Chronicle,* 7 Aug. 1943, p. 6.

41. Editorial, "The Famous Report," *Chronicle,* 21 Aug. 1943, p. 6.

42. Anonymous, "Information for Committee on Candidates," July, 1940, Candidates File, Box 9, Detroit Citizens League Papers, BHC, for Dowling's honesty, fairness, "good legal mind" and "judicial attitude." See also Letter to W. P. Lovett, 14 Sept. 1940, ibid., for the unsolicited opinion of an unidentified attorney who characterized Dowling as duplicitous and "dangerous."

43. Sitkoff, "The Detroit Race Riot," p. 204; Ramsay to Kelly, 2 Aug. 1943, for the quotation.

44. *News,* 24 June 1943, p. 1.

45. Selling, "One Hundred Offenders," p. 56.

46. Grimshaw, "A Study in Violence," p. 254; William Ryan, *Blaming the Victim* (New York, 1971), for that theory; interview with Dr. Clifford I. Whipple (Springfield, Missouri, 25 Apr. 1989). How Selling measured the intelligence of his subjects is unknown, yet the tests available to him during this period were "verbally loaded" and would have been very difficult for blacks with only eighth grade educations and living in ghetto conditions. Adjusting for these factors, Selling's rioters probably represented people of average intelligence.

47. Selling, "One Hundred Offenders," pp. 56, n. 14, 83–85.

48. Arrest Ticket 54, 21 June 1943, Duplicate Arrest Tickets, Reel 85, DPDR (hereinafter cited as Arrest Ticket plus number, the date being 21 June 1943 unless noted otherwise); File Contents, Lowell S. Selling to Thomas M. Cotter, 10 Nov. 1943, Green Davis, Report, n.d., and Kenneth J. Creagh to Thomas M. Cotter, 12 Nov. 1943, Recorder's Court File A-34496, BHC (hereinafter cited as File Contents, date, RCF plus number).

49. Arrest Ticket 134; File Contents and Lowell S. Selling to Donald Van Zile, 26 Aug. 1943, RCF A-34511, BHC.

50. Selling, "One Hundred Offenders," pp. 77–78; Robert M. Fogelson, *Violence as Protest: A Study of Riots and Ghettos* (Garden City, 1971).

51. David O. Sears and John B. McConahay, *The Politics of Violence: The New Urban Blacks and the Watts Riot* (Boston, 1973), pp. 17–33, for a summary of theories posited in the 1960s; Edward C. Banfield, *The Unheavenly City: The Nature and Future of Our Urban Crisis* (Boston, 1970), p. 187, for the quotation.

52. Nathan Caplan, "The New Ghetto Man: A Review of Recent Empirical Studies," *Journal of Social Issues* 26 (Winter 1970): 59–73, for the theory of protest; Sears and McConahay, *The Politics of Violence*, p. 33, for the theory of socialization.

53. Kelly to Robert H. MacRae, 2 July 1943, Box 75, Kelly Papers, MSA.

54. Thomas A. Kenney to William E. Dowling, 26 Aug. 1943, Box 74, Kelly Papers, MSA.

55. See the clippings from numerous newspapers, for example, the Ionia *Sentinel-Standard* and the Flint *Journal*, Folder 11, Box 74, Kelly Papers, MSA; John M. Carlisle, "Official Report on Riot," *News*, 11 Aug. 1943, pp. 1, 2; Editorial, "Race Riots Analyzed," *News*, 12 Aug. 1943, p. 22.

56. *News*, 12 Aug. 1943, p. 5, for Jeffries's views and Kelly's quotations.

57. Frank A. Roberts to Kelly, 13 Aug. 1943, Box 75, Kelly Papers, MSA, for an example.

58. William P. Lovett to Charles B. Van Dusen, 18 Aug. 1943, and William P. Lovett to Charles G. Oakman, 18 Aug. 1943, Correspondence Files, Box 40, Detroit Citizens League Papers, BHC; John D. Dixon to Kelly, 13 Aug. 1943, Box 75, Kelly Papers, MSA; Capeci, *Race Relations*, pp. 46, 59, for Dixon's earlier letters and dislike for established black leaders.

59. Editorial, "Judge Hastie's Error," *News*, 21 Aug. 1943, p. 8.

60. *Chronicle*, 14 Aug. 1943, p. 1, and 21 Aug. 1943, p. 1; *Tribune*, 28 Aug. 1943, p. 15, for the respective statements of the Negro Youth Council for Victory, Socialist Party, and Citizens Committee.

61. *Ford Facts*, 15 Aug. 1943, p. 3-A for the quotation of Tappes; Sam Milgram to Kelly, 14 Aug. 1943, Box 74, Kelly Papers, MSA.

62. Lee and Humphrey, *Race Riot*, p. 69.

63. Walter White to Alfred M. Lee, 20 Aug. 1943, Box 478, General Office Files (1940–1955), NAACP; *Tribune*, 14 Aug. 1943, p. 2.

64. *Tribune*, 28 Aug. 1943, p. 15.

65. Nelson Williams, Jr., to Kelly, 13 Aug. 1943, (received), Box 74, Kelly Papers, MSA.

66. Editorial, "The Famous Report," *Chronicle*, 21 Aug. 1943, p. 6, for the quotation; T. T. Brumbaugh, "Truce in Detroit," *Christian Century*, 11 Aug. 1943, p. 13.

67. *Tribune*, 21 Aug. 1943, p. 14; Socialist Party, Press Release, 11 Aug. 1943, Reel 10, DULP.

68. *Tribune*, 14 Aug. 1943, p. 15.

69. Editorial, "Race Riots Analyzed," *News*, 12 Aug. 1943, p. 22.

70. Walter White telegram to Kelly, 25 June 1943, for the quotation, and Walter White to Kelly, 17 Aug. 1943, Box 74, Kelly Papers, MSA; N. E. Aronstam to Kelly, 16 Aug. 1943 (received), Box 75, Kelly Papers, MSA.

71. Anthony M. Platt, *The Politics of Riot Commissions, 1917–1970: A Collection of Official Reports and Critical Essays* (New York, 1971), p. 14, Table 3; Editorial, "Something More Is Needed," *Tribune*, 21 Aug. 1943, p. 8.

72. W. K. Kelsey, "The Commentator," *News*, 12 Aug. 1943, p. 22.

73. Detroit Chapter, National Lawyers Guild, "Analysis of the Report of the Governor's Fact-Finding Committee," 9 Sept. 1943, p. 7, Box 70, and Civil Rights Federation, Press Release, 18 Aug. 1943, p. 1, Box 88, Civil Rights Congress of Michigan Collection, ALUA.

74. Clarence W. Anderson to Jeffries, 12 Aug. 1943, Box 8, Mayor's Papers (1943), BHC.

75. Platt, *The Politics of Riot Commissions*, pp. 44–46; Michael Lipsky and David J. Olson, *Commission Politics: The Processing of Racial Crisis in America* (New Brunswick, 1977), p. 57; Herbert Shapiro, *White Violence and Black Response: From Reconstruction to Montgomery* (Amherst, 1988), p. 317.

76. Lee and Humphrey, *Race Riot*, p. 69.

77. Nelson Williams, Jr., to Kelly, 13 Aug. 1943 (received), Box 74, Kelly Papers, MSA.

78. Robert F. Moylan to Thomas A. Kenney, 23 Sept. 1943, and Thomas A. Kenney to Robert F. Moylan, 28 Sept. 1943, ibid.

79. H. P. Breitenbach, "Speech of William Dowling," Adcraft Club, 1 Oct. 1943, Additional Papers, Box 14, Detroit Citizens League Papers, BHC; Jewish Community Council, Minutes: Executive Committee, 22 Nov. 1943, Box 22, Jewish Welfare Federation Papers, BHC; Earl Brown, "The Truth About the Detroit Riot," *Harper's Magazine* 187 (Nov. 1943): 488–98.

80. [Samuel J. Lieberman], "William Dowling's Speech on the Race Riot," Kiwanis Club, 27 June 1944, Box 70, Civil Rights Congress of Michigan Collection, ALUA.

81. Gloster B. Current to Walter White, 1 July 1944, and 8 July 1944, Box 479, General Office Files (1940–1955), NAACP; Walter White to Gloster B. Current, 20 July 1944, ibid.

82. William E. Dowling to Gerald L. K. Smith, 22 Sept. 1943, Box 10, Smith Papers, MHC, for an example of the prosecutor's political shift.

83. J. Edward McCall, "Survey Shows Unbiased Study," *Tribune*, 27 Nov. 1943, p. 1; Editorial, "Dr. Selling Discloses Anti Riot Plan," *Chronicle*, 27 Nov. 1943, pp. 1, 4; Selling, "One Hundred Offenders," pp. 31–32, 82–83; Lee and Humphrey, *Race Riot*, pp. 120–35, for the possible source of Selling's municipal bureau recommendation.

84. Fred Hart Williams, "The Evening Hour," *Tribune*, 4 Dec. 1943, p. 16.

85. Arthur E. Gordon to Jeffries, 27 Nov. 1943, Box 8, Mayor's Papers (1943), BHC.

86. *Tribune*, 15 Jan. 1944, p. 1.

87. *Chronicle*, 15 Jan. 1944, p. 1, for an example; Tyrone Tillery, *The Conscience of a City: A Commemorative History of the Detroit Human Rights Commission and Department, 1943–1983* (Detroit: Wayne State University Center for Urban Studies, 1983), pp. 3–6, for the creation of the Mayor's Peace Committee and its restructuring as the Mayor's Interracial Committee early in the new year.

88. J. Edward McCall, "Survey Shows Unbiased Study," *Tribune*, 27 Nov. 1943, p. 1.

89. W. K. Kelsey, "The Commentator," *News*, 25 June 1943, p. 18.

90. *Tribune*, 3 July 1943, p. 16; *News*, 24 June 1943, p. 1, for Selling's original press statement regarding the rioters.

91. Editorial, "Dr. Selling Discloses Anti Riot Plan," *Chronicle*, 27 Nov. 1943, p. 4 for the quotation of Selling.

92. Selling, "One Hundred Offenders," pp. 83–87; Editorial, "Call the Doctor," *Chronicle*, 21 Aug. 1943, p. 6. Shortly after the riot, Biddle suggested to Pres. Franklin D. Roosevelt that the federal government curtail black migration to Northern war industry centers as a means to avert future racial violence. He received the suggestion from his special assistant, C. E. Rhetts, who met with several municipal officials, including Jeffries and Dowling, and might have heard of Sellinglike opinions on black migration from one of them. (Perhaps the Wayne County prosecutor passed the idea on to Selling.) Rhetts also might have been influenced by the racial tension in Detroit. In any case, Rhetts's recommendation and Biddle's confidential endorsement of it quickly became public knowledge, drew intense criticism from black and white libertarians, and forced the Attorney General to evade the issue entirely. Subsequently, Selling's call for federal supervision of in-migration fell on deaf ears. See Memorandum for the President (from Francis Biddle), 15 July 1943, Memorandum for the Attorney General (from C. E. Rhetts), 12 July 1943, and Francis Biddle to Harold L. Ickes, 22 July 1943, Box 213, HLIP; Dominic J. Ca-

peci, Jr., *The Harlem Riot of 1943* (Philadelphia, 1977), pp. 91–98, and Charles W. Eagles, *Jonathan Daniels and Race Relations: The Evolution of a Southern Liberal* (Knoxville, 1982), Chapter 5, for the Biddle proposal, the controversy over it, and Roosevelt's overall response to the Detroit riot.

93. Editorial, "Proper Procedure," *News*, 25 June 1943, p. 18.

CHAPTER 3: *Faces in the Crowd*

1. Our study, drawn from the police files of those arrested between the time police reported the outburst on June 21 and the time soldiers quelled it forty-eight hours later, contains 205 black men, ninety-six white men, and forty-two black women. Of these 343 subjects, black males represent a random sample, white males and black females depict complete populations. Probation records were located for eighty-five felons (sixty-eight black men and seventeen white men); unfortunately identical data does not exist officially for women, and only sketchy data of any kind (that compiled by the Governor's Fact-Finding Committee) survives for arrestees under sixteen years of age. Nor can significant analysis be made of white women, for none were arrested for riot-related offenses during the first two days of the riot.

2. See Appendix B, Tables 3 and 4, for information in this and the following paragraph.

3. Seventy-three rioters were sixteen to eighteen years of age. Of these, sixty-seven (91.8 percent) were single; forty-eight (65.8 percent) committed misdemeanors; eighteen (24.7 percent) were arrested on June 21 between 12:00 midnight and 5:59 A.M.; twenty (27.4 percent) were apprehended on Belle Isle and ten (13.7 percent) on Woodward Avenue. Sixty-two rioters were thirty-eight to sixty-four years of age. Of these, forty (64.5 percent) were married; thirty-nine (62.9 percent) committed felonies; thirty-one (50 percent) were arrested on June 21 between 12:00 noon and 11:59 P.M.; twenty-nine (46.8 percent) were apprehended on Hastings, St. Antoine, Beaubien, and Brush Streets.

4. See Appendix B, Table 3.

5. See Appendix B, Tables 3 and 4.

6. Of the 115 black male felons, sixty-eight (59.1 percent) had probation records that could be located. A Chi Square test of significant differences between felons with and felons without probation rec-

ords indicated no significant demographic or socioeconomic distinctions. Nor were there important differences between probated felons and misdemeanants—except for age: Elders were overrepresented among the felons and youth among the misdemeanants. Hence inferences drawn from black male felons with probation records seem representative of black male rioters in general. Appendix B, Table 4.

7. Arrest Ticket 23, 21 June 1943, Duplicate Arrest Tickets, Reel 85, DPDR (hereinafter cited as Arrest Ticket plus number, the date being 21 June 1943 unless cited otherwise); File Contents, Recorder's Court File A-34582, BHC (hereinafter cited as RCF plus number); Wayne County Probation Services, Probation Case 84, RCR (hereinafter cited as Probation Case plus number).

8. Arrest Ticket 133; File Contents and Examination, 23 June 1943, RCF A-34580, BHC; Probation Case 33; Examination, 23 June 1943, RCF A-34559, BHC for the 3-inch legal length of knives.

9. Lowell S. Selling, "A Study of One Hundred Offenders Who Were Apprehended during the Disturbance of June 20th and 21st, 1943, in Detroit, Michigan," n.d., p. 78, Box 9 Mayor's Papers (1943), BHC (hereinafter cited as Selling, "One Hundred Offenders,"); "C. F. Ramsay to Kelly, 2 Aug. 1943, Box 74, Kelly Papers, MSA (hereinafter cited as Ramsay to Kelly, 2 Aug. 1943); Appendix, Table 3. Of N=205 black males, 124 (60.5 percent) had no previous arrest; thirty-four (16.6 percent) had one previous arrest; forty-five (22 percent) recorded two or more previous arrests.

10. Selling, "One Hundred Offenders," pp. 38–40; Appendix B, Table 3. Of N=205 black male rioters, 115 (56.1 percent) were felons and, of these, fifty-nine (28.8 percent) were arrested for weapon offenses, twenty-six of them (44.1 percent) knives; of N=205 black male rioters, 126 (61.5 percent) were apprehended less than one mile from home, sixty-eight (33.2 percent) were caught one mile or more from home.

11. Of N=205 black males, seventy-nine (38.5 percent) were repeat offenders: fifty (63.3 percent) married, seventy-five (94.9 percent) employed, seventy-six (96.2 percent) Detroit resident, fifty-one (64.6 percent) arrested on June 21. Arrest Tickets 65 and 122; Probation Cases 3 and 7; Examination, 24 June 1943, RCF A-34673, BHC.

12. Arrest Ticket 184; Probation Case 35; Examination, 23 June 1943, and Frank P. Finn to Arthur E. Gordon, 14 Aug. 1944, RCF A-34512, BHC.

13. Of N=205 black male rioters, fifty-four (26.3 percent) were arrested for looting and, of these, thirty-four (63 percent) were ap-

prehended on Hastings Street; of N=205, three black males (1.5 percent) were charged with assault.

14. Of N=68 black male felons with probation records, fourteen (20.6 percent) had arrived in the past two years, seventeen (25 percent) had been in Detroit for two to five years, thirty-seven (54.4 percent) had been in Detroit six or more years. Bureau of Agricultural Economics (USDA), "The Ethnic Axis: Southerners," c. 1943, pp. 1, 3, Box 9, and "The Social Dynamics of Detroit," 3 Dec. 1942, pp. 8–9, 37–39, Box 10, Likert Papers, MHC; David O. Sears and John B. McConahay, *The Politics of Violence: The New Urban Blacks and the Watts Riot* (Boston, 1973), pp. 32–33, for the respective theories.

15. Of N=68 black male felons with probation records, fourteen (20.5 percent) were newcomers—those with less than two years of residence in Detroit—and, of these, thirteen (92.9 percent) were of Southern origins: six from the lower states (the black belt) of Alabama, Georgia, Louisiana, Mississippi, and South Carolina, five from the upper states of Arkansas and Tennessee, two from the border states of Kentucky and Missouri. Of N=14 newcomers, ten (71.4 percent) were in their twenties (the median age of twenty-five years), nine (64.3 percent) were married, seven (50 percent) had eight years or more of education, twelve (85.7 percent) worked as laborers and ten (71.4 percent) in defense industries; of N=14 newcomers, six (42.8 percent) were arrested within one-half mile of home and seven (50 percent) from three-fourths mile to more than two miles beyond their residences; eleven (78.6 percent) were apprehended throughout the day on June 21, nine (64.3 percent) for weapons charges and ten (71.4 percent) without previous records.

16. Arrest Ticket 247, 22 June 1943; File Contents and Examination, 23 June 1943, RCF A-34559, BHC; Probation Case 49; Detroit *News*, 24 Aug. 1943, p. 4 (hereinafter cited as *News*). Everyone in the vehicle was placed on probation except the driver, who received one year in prison for carrying concealed weapons.

17. Bureau of Agricultural Economics (USDA), "The Ethnic Axis: Old Americans," c. 1943, p. 13, and "The Ethnic Axis: Negroes," c. 1943, pp. 3, 11, Box 9, Likert Papers, MHC.

18. Of N=205 black male rioters, twenty (9.8 percent) were white collar and skilled (five had probation records indicating that three, or 80 percent, had lived in Detroit more than sixteen years); of these, seventeen (85 percent) were married, thirteen (65 percent) were apprehended within half a mile of their homes, twelve (60 percent) were

in their twenties (the median age being twenty-eight years) and thirteen (65 percent) were arrested for felonies. Arrest Ticket 64; Examination, 2 July 1943, RCF A-34794, BHC.

19. Arrest Ticket 28; Examination, 24 June 1943, RCF A-34639, BHC; Probation Case 20.

20. Herbert J. Rushton, William E. Dowling, Oscar Olander, and John H. Witherspoon, *Factual Report of the Governor's Committee to Investigate the Riot Occurring in Detroit on June 21, 1943*, 11 Aug. 1943, Part I, pp. 2–4, 6, BHC (hereinafter cited as Governor's Committee, *Factual Report*); Franz Prattinger to Frank P. Finn, 21 Mar. 1944, Lowell S. Selling to Thomas M. Cotter, 21 Mar. 1944, and Kenneth J. Creagh to Thomas M. Cotter, 22 Mar. 1944, RCF A-35069, BHC.

21. Of N=96 white male rioters, sixty-one (64.2 percent) were less than twenty-three years old and fifty (52.1 percent) resided in precincts 1, 3, 5, 7, and 13; of N=205 black male rioters, sixty-seven (32.7 percent) were less than twenty-three years old. Appendix B, Table 3.

22. Of N=96 white male rioters, seventeen (17.7 percent) had probation records (one misdemeanor and sixteen felonies); fifteen of the sixteen felons were weapons offenders and, of these, eleven (73.3 percent) were single, ten (66.7 percent) were twenty-two years old or younger, nine (60 percent) were laborers, thirteen (86.7 percent) were employed and eleven (73.3 percent) were without previous arrests. Bureau of Agricultural Economics, "The Ethnic Axis: Southerners," pp. 1, 2; Alan Clive, *State of War: Michigan in World War II* (Ann Arbor, 1979), pp. 170–84.

23. Arrest Ticket 558, 21 June 1943, and Arrest Ticket 634, 22 June 1943; Examination, 28 June 1943, and Roy T. Doherty to W. McKay Skillman, 27 Jan. 1944, RCF A-34498, BHC; Examination, 28 June 1943, and Roy T. Doherty to Donald Van Zile, 24 July 1944, RCF A-34584, BHC; Probation Cases 26 and 15.

24. Of N=96 white male rioters, sixteen felons possessed probation records; of these, fourteen (87.5 percent) had lived in Detroit for six or more years. Appendix B, Table 3.

25. Arrest Ticket 574; Examination, 24 June 1943, RCF A-34568, BHC; Probation Case 95.

26. Of N=96 white male rioters, forty-seven (49 percent) were identified as Anglo-Saxon, seventeen (17.7 percent) as Italian, and twelve (12.5 percent) as Polish. Their ethnicity was determined by circulating a list of all white male rioters to individuals who represented

the respective ethnic groups and know the history of them in Detroit. Appendix A, n. 14.

27. Dominic J. Capeci, Jr., "Black-Jewish Relations in Wartime Detroit: The Marsh, Loving, Wolf Surveys and the Race Riot of 1943," *Jewish Social Studies*, 47 (Summer/Fall 1985): 221–42; Appendix B, Table 4.

28. Will Herberg, *Protestant-Catholic-Jew: An Essay in American Religious Sociology* (New York, 1960), pp. 27–45.

29. George M. Fredrickson, *White Supremacy: A Comparative Study in American and South African History* (New York, 1981), pp. 87, 161 for the theory of racial self-interest among whies.

30. Dominic J. Capeci, Jr., *Race Relations in Wartime Detroit: The Sojourner Truth Housing Controversy of 1942* (Philadelphia, 1984), passim, for Polish efforts to preserve ethnic integrity rather than mere white dominance.

31. Arrest Tickets 570, 571, 573, 574, 575, and 576.

32. Nineteen of forty-seven Anglo-Saxon rioters (40.4 percent), eight of seventeen Italians (47.1 percent), and four of twelve Poles (33.3 percent) were in the fourteen- to eighteen-year-old age group; nine of twenty ethnically unidentified white male rioters (45 percent) also fell into this age group.

33. Walter White, "What Caused the Detroit Riots?" n.d., 10–11, Box 2574, FHLP. Defense workers were determined by place of work—for example a rioter working at the Packard Motor Car Company or the Briggs Manufacturing Company; hence, of sixty-eight blacks and seventeen whites with probation records, forty-six (67.6 percent) and five (29.4 percent) respectively were identified as defense workers.

34. Of N=46 black defense workers, twenty-eight (60.0 percent) were married, forty-two (91.3 percent) were employed as laborers, forty-four (95.7 percent) were Detroit residents, thirty-five (76.1 percent) were without previous records, fourteen (30.4 percent) acted on June 21 between 6:00 P.M. and 11:59 P.M. Arrest Ticket 18; File Jacket, RCF A-34766; BHC; Probation Case 59; a Protestant and thirty-six years old, Henry G. was caught within one-quarter mile of his residence; he was a native of Georgia.

35. Arrest Ticket 634, 22 June 1943; Examination, 28 June 1943, and Roy T. Doherty to Donald Van Zile, 24 July 1944, RCF A-34584, BHC; Probation Case 15.

36. Interview with Donald C. Marsh (Detroit, Michigan, 6 June

1978); interview with Eleanor P. Wolf (Detroit, Michigan, 12 June 1978); Earl Raab and Seymour Martin Lipset, "The Prejudiced Society," in *Racial Conflict: Tension and Change in American Society*, ed. Gary T. Marx (Boston, 1971), pp. 33–34, for the frame of reference theory.

37. Governor's Committee, *Factual Report*, Part II, Exhibit 9, p. 2.

38. William E. Guthner, "Commander's Estimate of the Situation, June 20–24, 1943," 26 June 1943, p. 1, RG 79-10, MSA (hereinafter cited as Guthner, "Commander's Estimate"); Examination, 23 June 1943, RCF A-34551, BHC. Of N=205 black male rioters and N=96 white male rioters, one (.5 percent) and one (1 percent) respectively were members of the military; eleven others—ten (4.9 percent) blacks and one (1 percent) white—had their charges or sentences dismissed because they had joined the military before the riot or agreed to be inducted.

39. Arrest Ticket 578; File Jacket, RCF A-34585, BHC; Probation Case 27. Donald S. possessed a ninth-grade education and came from Indiana.

40. Arrest Ticket 121; Examination, 24 June 1943, and File Jacket, RCF A-34651, BHC; Probation Case 9.

41. Guthner, "Commander's Estimate," p. 2; Alfred M. Lee and Norman D. Humphrey, *Race Riot* (New York, 1943), p. 43.

42. Capeci, *Race Relations*, pp. 56–57.

43. See note 38 above for the percentages of soldiers, black and white, among the rioters; Arrest Ticket 252, 22 June 1943; Examination, 23 June 1943, and File Jacket, RCF A-34605, BHC; Probation Case 56.

44. Arrest Ticket 105; Examination, 28 June 1943, and File Jacket, RCF A-34587, BHC; Probation Case 21.

45. See note 38 above for the percentages of black and white soldiers among the rioters.

46. Of N=96 white male rioters, thirty-nine (40.6 percent) traveled more than two miles to riot and thirty-one (32.3 percent) were arrested on weapons charges; of seventeen white male probationers, nine (52.9 percent) acted in groups of two or more.

47. Of N=205 black male rioters, ninety-three (45.5 percent) were arrested in Precinct 13, thirty-three (16.1 percent) in Precinct 9, sixteen (7.8 percent) in Precinct 5, and sixteen (7.8 percent) in Precinct 3; of N=95 white male rioters, twenty-five (26 percent) were apprehended in Precinct 1, twenty-two (22.9 percent) in Precinct 5,

twenty-one (21.9 percent) in Precinct 13 and twelve (12.5 percent) in Precinct 7; Appendix B, Table 3, for all other comparisons.

48. Governor's Committee, *Factual Report*, Part II, Exhibit 17, p. 1, for the arrest and prosecution of one white female—Lula F.—who was drunk and disturbed the peace west of Woodward Avenue on June 21 at 12:10 A.M.; since this took place long *before* the disorder spread to mainland Detroit, her violation was unrelated to the riot; Arrest Ticket 501; Misdemeanor Calendar, vol. 277, 86712, RCR (hereinafter cited as Misdemeanor Case plus number). Of N=42 black female rioters, fourteen (33.3 percent) had never married; Appendix B, Table 3. Since only a handful of black female probation records are in existence—those located in the Burton Historical Collection—their places of birth, lengths of residence, numbers of children, levels of education, and weekly salaries are unknown.

49. Appendix B, Table 3.

50. Miriam F. Hirsch, *Women and Violence* (New York, 1981), p. 154, for the theory of female theft; of N=42 black female rioters, eight (19 percent) had no occupation, twenty-three (54.8 percent) were employed and apprehended for the first time in their lives, and twenty-one (50 percent) were arrested for looting: nine (42.9 percent) stole clothing and shoes, while four (19 percent) took food; of the establishments looted by black females, eleven were identified: five clothing and/or shoe stores and three food stores; of the eleven store owners identified, all were white. Appendix B, Table 3; Memorandum for the Attorney General (from C. E. Rhetts), 15 July 1943, p. 4, note 2, Box 213, HLIP (hereinafter cited as Rhetts Memorandum); Richard R. Lingeman, *Don't You Know There's A War On? The American Home Front, 1941–1945* (New York, 1970), pp. 234–70, for rationing, which began in earnest with the Emergency Price Control Act of January 1942; Russell Dynes and E. L. Quarantelli, "What Looting in Civil Disturbances Really Means," *Trans-action*, 5 (May 1968): 13, for the stages of looting and the quotation.

51. Arrest Ticket 630, 22 June 1943, and Arrest Ticket 564; Examination, 30 June 1943, and File Jacket, RCF A-34601, BHC; Vemba M. Dunlap to John J. Maher, 27 Sept. 1943 and 28 Sept. 1945, RCF A-34601, BHC, for information in this and the following paragraph. Although misdated as June 22, Goldie W.'s arrest occurred the previous day.

52. Arrest Tickets 648 and 648B, 22 June 1943; Vemba M. Dunlap to Joseph A. Gillis, 13 Aug. 1943, RCF A-34801, BHC, for the infor-

mation in this and the following paragraph unless cited otherwise.

53. File Jacket and Vemba M. Dunlap to Joseph A. Gillis, 13 Aug. 1943, RCF A-34801, BHC; Detroit House of Correction, General Register of Prisoners, p. 69, BHC.

54. Detroit *Tribune*, 14 Aug. 1943, p. 1 (hereinafter cited as *Tribune*).

55. Arrest Tickets 631 and 238, 22 June 1943; Examination, 23 June 1943, and Roy T. Doherty to Chester P. O'Hara, 11 April 1944, RCF A-34514, BHC; Probation Case 43.

56. Appendix B, Table 3, for the information in this and the following paragraph.

57. Appendix B, Table 5. The Juvenile Detention Home was located at Forest and Rivard Streets in the black east side.

58. Appendix B, Tables 3 and 5, for the information in this and the following paragraph.

59. Ramsay to Kelly, 2 Aug. 1943.

60. Appendix B, Table 5; Governor's Committee, *Factual Report*, Part II, Exhibit 15, p. 3, for the targets of juveniles.

61. Arrest Ticket 160; Kenneth J. Creagh to Christopher E. Stein, 8 Sept. 1943, and File Jacket, RCF A-34792, BHC; Probation Case 104.

62. Selling, "One Hundred Offenders," p. 50; Sears and McConahay, *The Politics of Violence*, p. 33.

63. Governor's Committee, *Factual Report*, Part II, Exhibit 15 for the males, and Part I, p. 15, note 54, for the females.

64. Governor's Committee, *Factual Report*, Part I, pp. 4, 6, 7; Examination, 28 July 1943, and Abner A. Tatken, Motion to Reduce Bail of Mattie Mae B., 7 Oct. 1943, RCF A-35070, BHC.

65. Of N=15 black seventeen-year-old rioters, eight (53.3 percent) had previous police records, six (40 percent) were arrested on Brush, Beaubien, St. Antoine, or Hastings streets, four (26.7 percent) were apprehended on Oakland Avenue, ten (66.7 percent) were caught between 12:00 A.M. and 6:00 P.M. on June 21, six (40 percent) traveled three-fourths to two miles to riot, twelve (80 percent) committed misdemeanors, three (20 percent) looted, none carried weapons; of N=28 white seventeen-year-old rioters, four (14.3 percent) had previous police records, eight (28.6 percent) were arrested on Woodward Avenue, and eight (28.6 percent) in Precinct 5 (Belle Isle), nineteen (67.9 percent) were apprehended between 6:00 P.M. and 11:59 P.M. on June 21 and 12:00 midnight to 5:59 a.m. on June 22, thirteen

(46.4 percent) traveled more than two miles to riot, nineteen (67.9 percent) committed misdemeanors, and nine (32.1 percent) perpetrated felonies—all weapons charges.

66. Arrest Tickets 19 and 589; Misdemeanor Cases 86848 and 87328; Detroit House of Correction, General Register of Prisoners, pp. 31, 36, BHC.

67. See note 64 above for the information in this and the following two paragraphs unless cited otherwise.

68. Appendix B, Tables 3 and 5.

69. Arrest Ticket 903, 19 July 1943.

70. Asher L. Cornelius, Brief for a New Trial, n.d., pp. 8–10, 12, and Petition to File for a New Trial, 28 Mar. 1945, RCF A-36135, BHC, for the information in this and the following paragraph.

71. Ibid., p. 2, for fights that occurred after the riot but indicate their regular occurrences in the black east side.

72. Governor's Committee, *Factual Report*, Part II, Exhibit 3; Charles Denby, *Indignant Heart* (Boston, 1978), p. 110.

73. Governor's Committee, *Factual Report*, Part I, pp. 2, 3, 4, 6, and 8, for the quotation, and Part II, Exhibit 9, p. 2; Examination, 28 July 1943, RCF A-35070, BHC.

74. Affidavit: Mrs. Marion Grier, 24 Aug. 1943, Box 1, NAACP Collection, ALUA; Examination, 6 Dec. 1943 and 7 Dec. 1943, RCF A-36135, BHC; Michigan *Chronicle*, 11 Mar. 1944, pp. 1, 2 (hereinafter cited as *Chronicle*); Governor's Committee, *Factual Report*, Part II, Exhibit 19, p. 7; Julian G. McIntosh, Motion of Nolle Prosequi, 22 Mar. 1944, RCF A-35069, BHC.

75. See Chapter 5 for the further history of Aaron F.

76. Arrest Ticket 904, 21 July 1943; George C. Parzen, Motion to Quash Information and Discharge Defendant, 6 Nov. 1943, and J. E. Coogan to Gerald K. O'Brien, 20 Sept. 1945, RCF A-35189, BHC.

77. "Foreign-Born White by Country of Birth for the Detroit Metropolitan District and for the City of Detroit, 1940 Census," n.d., unprocessed material, Marsh Collection, ALUA.

78. George W. Beatty, "The Background and Causes of the 1943 Detroit Race Riot," unpublished senior thesis, Princeton University, 1954, p. 126, n. 1; John McManus, "It Couldn't Happen, But It Did," *News*, 31 July 1943, p. 1.

79. Agricultural Economics Bureau (USDA), "The Ethnic Axis: The Foreign Born," pp. 1, 5–7, 10–12, 28 Oct. 1943, Box 9, Likert Papers, MHC, for the representative attitudes of foreign-born ethnics.

80. Agricultural Economics Bureau (USDA), "The Ethnic Axis: Second Generation Foreigners," pp. 3, 7–10, 28 Oct. 1943, Box 9, Likert Papers, MHC, for the representative examples of second-generation ethnics: Gilbert Osofsky, *Harlem: The Making of a Ghetto* (New York, 1966), pp. 45–46, for racism as one aspect of Americanization.

81. Morton Barnett, Ralph Kernkamp, and Lowell S. Selling to State Hospital Commission, 7 Sept. 1943, RCF A-35189, BHC.

82. Beatty, "The Background and Causes," 1943 p. 126, note 1; Morton Barnett, Ralph Kenkamp, and Lowell S. Selling to State Hospital Commission, 7 Sept. 1943 (two reports) and 8 Sept. 1943 (two reports), RCF A-35189, BHC, for independent evaluations of Robert C., Armando M., Anthony S., and Ralph T. respectively; Kenneth B. Clark and James Barker, "The Zoot Effect in Personality: A Race Riot Participant," *Journal of Abnormal and Social Psychology* 40 (1945): 143–48, for the theory applied to a Harlem rioter of 1943.

83. Arrest Ticket 904, 21 July 1943, for Aldo T.'s stature: 5 feet 6½ inches and 142 pounds; McManus, "It Couldn't Happen," p. 1, for Aldo's T.'s "average" size; Clive, *State of War*, pp. 207–13, for juvenile delinquency during the war.

84. *News*, 30 July 1943, p. 1, McManus, "It Couldn't Happen," p. 1, for Armando M.'s story, which erroneously says Aldo T. steered the car and Robert C. rode in it, and fails to mention Ralph T.'s role as driver; Examination, 17 Aug. 1943, RCF A-35189, BHC, for police and eyewitness accounts correcting these errors and sometimes referring to Ralph T. by his middle name, Rudolph.

85. Governor's Committee, *Factual Report*, Part II, Exhibit 19, p. 7; Examination, 17 Aug. 1943, RCF A-35189, BHC.

86. *Tribune*, 7 Aug. 1943, p. 1.

87. Joseph L. Bannigan, People's Supplemental Requests to Charge, n.d., RCF A-35189, BHC; *Tribune*, 21 Aug. 1943, p. 1; *Chronicle*, 19 Feb. 1944, p. 1. Armando M. received two and one-half years to fifteen years in the state penitentiary; Ralph T. drew fifteen months to five years.

88. Examination, 17 Aug. 1943, RCF A-35189, BHC, for Robert C. not being in the car. Controversy surrounding the prosecutor's case also accounts for the leniency shown Anthony S. See Chapter 5.

89. McManus, "It Couldn't Happen," p. 1, for the quotation; *News*, 30 July 1943, pp. 1, 4, and 31 July 1943, p. 1.

90. Ibid.; Arrest Ticket 905, 22 June 1943, for Robert C.'s concealed-weapon offense.

258 NOTES TO PAGES 83-85

91. *Tribune,* 15 Jan. 1944, p. 1, for the exception.

92. Arrest Ticket 904, 21 July 1943; Arrest Tickets 906, 29 July 1943, 907 and 908, 30 July 1943, 909, 3 Aug. 1943, Duplicate Arrest Tickets, Reel 86, DPDR.

93. McManus, "It Couldn't Happen," p. 1.

94. Morton Barnett, Ralph Kenkamp, and Lowell S. Selling to State Hospital Commission, 7 Sept. 1943 (three reports) and 8 Sept. 1943 (two reports), RCF A-35189, BHC, for independent evaluations of Robert C., Armando M., Aldo T., Anthony S., and Ralph T., respectively.

95. *Chronicle,* 19 Feb. 1944, p. 1, for the paraphrase of Recorder's Court Judge Thomas M. Cotter.

96. *News,* 31 July 1943, p. 2; J. S. St. Clair, "Report: Race Riot in Detroit, Michigan," 2 Aug. 1943, Case 6152, MSPR.

97. Appendix B, Table 3, for the percentage of rioters without previous arrest records. Of N=42 black female rioters, none were arrested more than once during the riot; of N=205 black male rioters, two (1 percent)—Charles L. and Aaron F.—were arrested twice; of N=96 white male rioters, two (2.1 percent)—Robert C. and J. C. G.—were arrested twice.

98. Arrest Tickets 8 and 566; Examination, 23 June 1943, and File Jacket, RCF A-34551, BHC; Probation Case 22.

99. Of N=343 rioters (205 black males, ninety-six white males and forty-two black females), seventy-two (21 percent) were incarcerated in the Detroit House of Correction and, of these, sixty-two (86.1 percent) were released early; seventy-six (22 percent) were placed on probation and, of these, fifty-four (71.1 percent) were discharged with improvement. Eight arrestees had served previous time in the Detroit House of Correction, and one other escaped from that facility after being incarcerated for a riot-related offense; eight probationers violated the terms of their sentences. Of these seventeen rioters, fifteen (88.2 percent) were black, thirteen (76.5 percent) were male, nine (52.9 percent) were married, sixteen (94.1 percent) were employed; their ages ranged from eighteen to fifty-four, with twenty-eight years being the median.

100. Arrest Tickets 126 and 651; Examination, 24 June 1943, File Jacket, and Roy T. Doherty to John P. Scallen, 23 May 1945, RCF A-34639, BHC; File Jacket, and Roy T. Doherty to Arthur E. Gordon, 17 Nov. 1945, A-34809, BHC; Probation Cases 20 and 83.

101. Governor's Committee, *Factual Report,* Part I, p. 15, and Part II, Exhibits 4-8.

102. Lee and Humphrey, *Race Riot,* p. 117, for the kick-blacks-back paraphrase, of Walter White, executive secretary of the NAACP.

103. See, for example, Capeci, *Race Relations;* August Meier and Elliott Rudwick, *Black Detroit and the Rise of the UAW* (New York, 1979); Clive, *State of War.*

CHAPTER 4: *And Victims, Too*

1. Herbert J. Rushton, William E. Dowling, Oscar Olander, and John H. Witherspoon, *Factual Report of the Governor's Committee to Investigate the Riot Occurring in Detroit on June 21, 1943,* 11 Aug. 1943, Part II, Exhibit 19a, BHC (hereinafter cited as Governor's Committee, *Factual Report*); Detroit *News,* 27 June 1943, p. 17 (hereinafter cited as *News*).

2. Anonymous, "Joint Meeting of Citizens Committee and Other Civic and Labor Groups," 21 June 1943, p. 7, Box 70, Civil Rights Congress of Michigan, ALUA (hereinafter cited as Citizens Committee, "Joint Meeting").

3. Walter White, "What Caused the Detroit Riots?" n.d., p. 14, Box 2574, FHLP; Editorial, "The Police in Riots," *Crisis,* Aug. 1943, p. 231.

4. Thurgood Marshall, "Report Concerning Detroit Police Activities During the Riots," 26 July 1943, Box 1, NAACP Collection, ALUA, and "The Gestapo in Detroit," *Crisis,* Aug. 1943, pp. 232–47; Detroit Chapter, National Lawyers Guild, "Executive Board Statement on the Recent Disorders in Detroit," 26 June 1943, p. 3, for the quotation, and "Analysis of Report of Governor's Fact Finding Committee," 9 Sept. 1943, p. 3, Box 70, Civil Rights Congress of Michigan, ALUA.

5. Ibid.; Governor's Committee, *Factual Report,* Part I, p. 12, note 45; John H. Witherspoon to Dr. Herbert F. Robb, 18 Oct. 1943, Box 9, OF 4245-G, FDRL.

6. Alfred M. Lee and Norman D. Humphrey, *Race Riot* (New York, 1943), p. 27; Affidavit: Edward Grace, 24 June 1943, and Affidavit: Benjamin Holston, 4 Oct. 1943, Box 1, NAACP Collection, ALUA (hereinafter all affidavit citations refer to Box 1, NAACP Collection, ALUA).

7. Affidavit: Henry Griggs, 4 Aug. 1943, and Affidavit: Henry Montgomery, 6 July 1943; P.H.H. to Jack Raskin, 23 June 1943, Box 70, Civil Rights Congress of Michigan Collection, ALUA.

8. Milton Swingle and James Van Landegend, "Report," 9 Aug.

1943, Case 6152, MSPR (hereinafter all MSPR citations refer to Case 6152); Marshall, "The Gestapo in Detroit," p. 232.

9. John H. Witherspoon to the Common Council, City of Detroit, 28 June 1943, *Journal of the Common Council* (Detroit, 1944), pp. 1854, 1857, and 1858, for the quotation (hereinafter cited as Witherspoon Statement).

10. Governor's Committee, *Factual Report*, Part II, Exhibit 19c, p. 9, and Exhibit 19d, p. 53.

11. Lawrence A. Adam entry, Police Force Book, vol. X, p. 139, BHC. DPD personnel statistics are based on a random sample of every tenth officer drawn from approximately 3,000 entries in Police Force Books I, J, N, Q, W, X, and Z for intermittent periods from August 1917 to September 1945. Although females comprised approximately 3 percent of all entries in the force books, none of them appeared in the random sample. Hence of N=309 male police officers, 307 (99.4 percent) were white, nearly 70 percent were married, and over 50 percent were parents. Of N=205 midwesterners, 30 percent came from Detroit, 23 percent from elsewhere in Michigan, and 41 percent from surrounding states.

12. *News*, 1 July 1943, p. 1, for the quotation; Robert Shogan and Tom Craig, *The Detroit Race Riot: A Study in Violence* (Philadelphia, 1964), p. 78, for the death by tetanus.

13. Governor's Committee, *Factual Report*, Part II, Exhibit 19d, p. 10, for the information in this paragraph unless cited otherwise.

14. Ibid., Exhibit 19c, p. 2.

15. Ibid.

16. Affidavit: Henry Griggs, 4 Aug. 1943; Affidavit: Benjamin Holston, 4 Oct. 1943.

17. Governor's Committee, *Factual Report*, Part II, Exhibit 19a and Exhibit 19c, passim.

18. Ibid., Exhibit 19c, pp. 6, 9, 11; *News*, 28 June 1943, p. 2; Mamie T. to Jeffries, 28 Oct. 1943, Box 10, Mayor's Papers (1943), BHC.

19. Governor's Committee, *Factual Report*, Part II, Exhibit 19c, for the source upon which this evaluation was made.

20. Michigan *Chronicle*, 26 June 1943, p. 1 (hereinafter cited as *Chronicle*); Governor's Committee, *Factual Report*, Part II, Exhibit 19c, p. 5, for the quotation. Temporarily living in Birmingham with their grandmother, Hackworth's children were to have joined her shortly. Two of her sisters lived in Detroit, and two of her brothers served in the armed forces.

21. Paul Keen, "Between the Headlines," *Chronicle*, 3 July 1943, p. 1; Charles A. Hill, Oral History, p. 16, Blacks in the Labor Movement, ALUA.

22. Carol Crater to Gloster B. Current, n.d., Box 1, NAACP Collection, ALUA.

23. Governor's Committee, *Factual Report*, Part II, Exhibit 19e, p. 35.

24. Dominic J. Capeci, Jr., *Race Relations in Wartime Detroit: The Sojourner Truth Housing Controversy of 1942* (Philadelphia, 1984), p. 29.

25. Examination, 17 Aug. 1943, pp. 4–8, 12–18, 19, for the quotation, Recorder's Court File A-35189, BHC (hereinafter cited as Examination, date, RCF plus number); *News*, 30 July 1943, p. 1, and 31 July 1943, p. 1.

26. Governor's Committee, *Factual Report*, Part II, Exhibit 19c, p. 9; *News*, 31 July 1943, p. 1, for the quotation and 2 Aug. 1943, p. 2.

27. Affidavit: Travis Brunt, 9 July 1943, for the quotation; Affidavit: Opal McAdoo, 9 July 1943.

28. Governor's Committee, *Factual Report*, Part II, Exhibit 19d, passim.

29. Examination, 6 Dec. 1943, p. 1, RCF A-36135; *News*, 23 June 1943, p. 6, contains erroneous information regarding De Horatiis's route and his being on foot.

30. *News*, 25 June 1943, p. 1.

31. Examination, 6 Dec. 1943, pp. 6–8, 48, 52–53, RCF A-36135; *News*, 21 June 1943, p. 1, for the quotation.

32. Shogan and Craig, *The Detroit Race Riot*, p. 51; *News*, 25 June 1943, p. 1, for the quotation of Father Hector Saulino of Blessed Sacrament Church.

33. *News*, 26 June 1943, p. 2; Governor's Committee, *Factual Report*, Part II, Exhibit 19c, p. 10.

34. Governor's Committee, *Factual Report*, Part II, Exhibit 19c, p. 8.

35. Citizens Committee, "Joint Meeting," p. 8; Witherspoon Statement, p. 1857.

36. Govenror's Committee, *Factual Report*, Part II, Exhibit 18. Of the assaulted patients, sixty-four of 101 (63 percent) were black; of the assaulted who died from their wounds, fourteen of sixteen (83 percent) were black; of the injured women, seventeen of thirty (57 percent) were black, 40 percent white and 3 percent (one person) Indian; of the emergency treatment patients over thirty years of age, sixty-five (38 percent) were black and 105 (62 percent) were white.

37. "The Social Front," *Race Relations: A Monthly Summary of Events and Trends* 1 (Aug. 1943): 6; Capeci, *Race Relations,* pp. 39−41. Apparently other municipal hospitals—most notably Herman Kifer and Mayberry Sanatorium—received few if any riot victims.

38. W. Roderick Brown to George Baehr, 28 July 1943, pp. 3−4, Box 11, OF 4245-G, FDRL; *News,* 22 June 1943, p. 6. With the exception of black-owned Parkside Hospital, these private facilities received the overflow of casualties from Receiving Hospital; whites also were treated at these—except for Parkside—and a handful of other institutions.

39. Governor's Committee, *Factual Report,* Part I, pp. 1−5, and Part II, Exhibit 9, p. 1; Harold Mulbar to Oscar G. Olander, 5 July 1943, MSPR.

40. William Lang, Statement, 17 Sept. 1943, Jesse Stewart Personnel File, DPDR (hereinafter cited as Stewart File).

41. Governor's Committee, *Factual Report,* Part II, Exhibit 19e, pp. 2−3, 9, 16.

42. *News,* 21 June 1943, p. 2; Governor's Committee, *Factual Report,* Part II, Exhibit 19e, p. 19.

43. Examination, 29 June 1943, RCF A-34550; Detroit *Tribune,* 28 Aug. 1943, p. 1 (hereinafter cited as *Tribune*); Governor's Committee, *Factual Report,* Part II, Exhibit 19e, p. 54.

44. Lee and Humphrey, *Race Riot,* pp. 26−27; *Tribune,* 26 June 1943, p. 1; Governor's Committee, *Factual Report,* Part II, Exhibit 19e, p. 2.

45. Affidavit: Samuel Mitchell, 7 July 1943; Shogan and Craig, *The Detroit Race Riot,* pp. 58−59.

46. Affidavit: Henry Griggs, 4 Aug. 1943.

47. Affidavit: John Bell, n.d.

48. John Paul Riney, Statement, 15 Sept. 1943, Stewart File.

49. Examination, 23 June 1943, RCF A-34551, BHC.

50. Claribel Wright to Jeffries, 8 July 1943, Box 9, Mayor's Papers (1943), BHC.

51. Affidavit: Henry Powers, 9 July 1943; Governor's Committee, *Factual Report,* Part II, Exhibit 20, pp. 1−4, and Exhibit 25, p. 1, for 145 automobiles damaged by 126 black, four white, and fifteen unknown perpetrators, none of these incidents involved injuries to the owners or their passengers. Only five of the 145 vehicles were located on Woodward Avenue, and only four of them were owned by blacks. Given Witherspoon's official report to the Common Council that

"Many cars were damaged and burned by the whites on Woodward Avenue," these statistics are open to question. Witherspoon, Statement, p. 1857.

52. Jeffries to Claribel Wright, 13 July 1943, Box 9, Mayor's Papers (1943) BHC.

53. Affidavit: James L. Moon, n.d.

54. George W. Stark, "Town Talk," *News*, 23 June 1943, p. 12.

55. Examination, 2 July 1943, pp. 2–5, RCF A-34783, BHC. Levine lived on Pasadena Avenue.

56. Of N=53 looted and/or vandalized stores, twenty-nine (54.7 percent) were located on Hastings Street; forty-three (81.1 percent) on other east-side locations—between Woodward Avenue and St. Aubin Street, from Vernor Highway to Grand Boulevard; three (5.7 percent) on Oakland Avenue. Of N=53 establishments, fifteen (28.3 percent) were grocery stores, eight (15.1 percent) clothing and/or shoe marts, five (9.4 percent) liquor outlets or beer gardens, four (7.5 percent) pawnshops. Of N=53 stores, seventeen (32.1 percent) suffered multiple attacks; e.g., Isadora Cohen's clothing mart on Hastings Street sustained four assaults.

57. Of N=47 identified store owners, all were white, forty (85.1 percent) male, thirty-two (68.1 percent) Jewish; forty (85.1 percent) lived outside the ghetto, and thirty (63.8 percent) resided in police Precinct 10. Appendix A, note 13, for the method of identifying store owners; Examination, 28 June 1943, pp. 2–8, 3, for the quotation, RCF A-34786, BHC.

58. Examination, 30 June 1943, p. 3, RCF A-34730, BHC; Examination, 9 July 1943, p. 3, RCF A-34702, BHC; Examination, 30 June 1943, p. 3, RCF A-34680, BHC.

59. Examination, 2 July 1943, p. 2, RCF A-34794, BHC; *Chronicle*, 3 July 1943, p. 2.

60. *News*, 23 June 1943, p. 2, for the first quotation of a representative of the Detroit Retail Merchants Association; Helen Q. Warren to Harry F. Kelly, 23 June 1943, Box 9, Mayor's Papers (1943), BHC, for the second quotation.

61. Examination, 8 July 1943, pp. 2–3, RCF A-34588, BHC.

62. Examination, 1 July 1943, p. 4, RCF A-35699, BHC.

63. Examination, 2 July 1943, p. 10, RCF A-34783, BHC.

64. *News*, 2 July 1943, p. 17.

65. *Chronicle*, 3 July 1943, p. 2.

66. Examination, 30 June 1943, p. 7, RCF A-34730, BHC.

67. Governor's Committee, *Factual Report,* Part II, Exhibit 21, pp. 1–3, and Exhibit 22, pp. 1–9.

68. Examination, 9 July 1943, p. 2, RCF A-34702, BHC; Governor's Committee, *Factual Report,* Part II, Exhibit 21, pp. 1–3.

69. Examination, 1 July 1943, p. 4, and File Contents, RCF A-34699, BHC; Governor's Committee, *Factual Report,* Part II, Exhibit 22, p. 3.

70. Examination, 7 July 1943, pp. 2–3, RCF A-34813, BHC; Examination, 25 June 1943, p. 13, and File Contents, RCF A-34750, BHC; Governor's Committee, *Factual Report,* Part II, Exhibit 22, pp. 1, 7.

71. Examination, 8 July 1943, pp. 3–4, and File Contents, RCF A-34588, BHC; Governor's Committee, *Factual Report,* Part II, Exhibit 22, p. 6.

72. Governor's Committee, *Factual Report,* Part II, Exhibit 21, p. 2, and Exhibit 22, p. 6, for the comparison of Oakland Avenue establishments.

73. Examination, 25 June 1943, p. 5, RCF A-34782, BHC; Governor's Committee, *Factual Report,* Part II, Exhibit 22, p. 3.

74. Examination, 9 July 1943, p. 5, RCF A-34702, BHC; Governor's Committee, *Factual Report,* Part II, Exhibit 22, p. 3.

75. Governor's Committee, *Factual Report,* Part II, Exhibit 22, p. 4, for the example of grocery store entries for 4871 Hastings Street ($5.00 by a specific looter) and 5025 Hastings Street ($550 by unknown thieves).

76. File Contents, RCF A-34601, BHC; Governor's Committee, *Factual Report,* Part II, Exhibit 22, p. 6.

77. Oral Statement of Aaron Shifman (West Bloomfield, Michigan, 14 Mar. 1987); Governor's Committee, *Factual Report,* Part II, Exhibit 22, passim, for the absence of destruction along Woodward Avenue.

78. *News,* 8 Aug. 1943, p. 4, for the example of a case adjudicated after police department tabulations were presented to the Governor's Committee.

79. *News,* 24 June 1943, p. 1; Affidavit: James Townsend Lee, 30 June 1943.

80. James W. McKnight to the Editor, *News,* 1 July 1943, p. 24; Editorial, "Detroit's Moral Responsibility," *Tribune,* 3 July 1943, p. 8; Gentile to Jeffries, 25 June 1943, Box 8, Mayor's Papers (1943), BHC.

81. *News,* 24 June 1943, p. 1, for the quotation.

82. Jeffries to Claribel Wright, 13 July 1943, Box 9, Mayor's Papers (1943), BHC.

83. *News,* 9 July 1943, p. 4, and 20 Aug. 1943, p. 3, for the quotation.

84. James R. Walsh to Mamie T., 15 Nov. 1943, Box 10, Mayor's Papers (1943), BHC.

85. *Tribune,* 24 June 1944, p. 1; *Chronicle,* 24 June 1944, p. 1; Oral Statement of Mendel Shifman (West Bloomfield, Michigan, 14 Mar. 1987) for the recollection that no lawsuit succeeded; however, the outcome of the suit is unknown.

86. Francis J. Haas, Notebook, 1 July 1943 entry, Haas Papers, CUA; John Wood, "I Cover the Town," *Chronicle,* 3 July 1943, p. 7; Philip A. Adler, "Anti-Semitism Cited as a Prelude to Riot," *News,* 29 June 1943, p. 7.

87. Memorandum for the Attorney General (from C. E. Rhetts), 12 July 1943, p. 4, n. 2, Box 213, HLIP (hereinafter cited as Rhetts Memorandum).

88. Gentile to Jeffries, 25 June 1943, Box 8, Mayor's Papers (1943), BHC.

89. Memorandum for the NAACP (from P.W.), 26 June 1943, p. 14, Box 1, NAACP Collection, ALUA.

90. Lucy S. Stewart to P. Phinney, 24 July 1943, Box 9, Smith Papers, MHC.

91. Interview with Donald C. Marsh (Detroit, Michigan, 6 June 1978).

92. Dominic J. Capeci, Jr., "Black-Jewish Relations in Wartime Detroit: The Marsh, Loving, Wolf Surveys and the Race Riot of 1943," *Jewish Social Studies* 47 (Summer/Fall 1985): 221–25; Marshall F. Stevenson, Jr., "Points of Departure, Acts of Resolve: Black-Jewish Relations in Detroit, 1937–1962," unpublished Ph.D. dissertation, University of Michigan, 1988, pp. 15–49.

93. Oral Statement of Aaron and Mendel Shifman (West Bloomfield, Michigan, 14 Mar. 1987).

94. Donald C. Marsh, Alvin D. Loving, and Eleanor P. Wolf, *Negro-Jewish Relationships,* Wayne University Studies in Inter-Group Conflict in Detroit, no. 1, (Detroit, 1944), and "Some Aspects of Negro-Jewish Relationships in Detroit, Michigan," n.d., unprocessed material, Marsh Collection, ALUA, for information in this and the following paragraph; Capeci, "Black-Jewish Relations," pp. 221–42, for the background and analysis of the Marsh, Loving, Wolf surveys.

Given the many drafts, sometimes incomplete, of the Marsh, Loving, Wolf materials in the Marsh Collection, we have assigned them titles for the purpose of identification.

95. Marsh, Loving, and Wolf, "Negro-Jewish Relationships," p. 7, and "Conclusions (Post Riot)," n.d., p. 122, unprocessed material, Marsh Collection, ALUA; interview with Donald C. Marsh (Detroit, Michigan, 13 June 1978).

96. Marsh, Loving, and Wolf, "Post Riot," n.d., pp. 2, 5, unprocessed material, Marsh Collection, ALUA.

97. Examination, 30 June 1943, p. 3, RCF A-34730, BHC; Examination, 25 June 1943, p. 3, RCF A-34782, BHC.

98. Donald C. Marsh, Alvin D. Loving, and Eleanor P. Wolf, "Negro-Jewish Attitude Analysis," n.d., p. 97, unprocessed material, Marsh Collection, ALUA.

99. Marsh, Loving and Wolf, "Post Riot," p. 2.

100. Examination, 24 June 1943, pp. 1–2, RCF A-34633, BHC; Examination, 28 June 1943, p. 4, RCF A-34786, BHC. Examination, 30 June 1943, p. 7, RCF A-34680, BHC, for the exception of Harry Brandt knowing one of those who looted his store.

101. Marsh, Loving, and Wolf, "Some Aspects," pp. 3–4.

102. Marsh, Loving, and Wolf, "Post Riot," pp. 2, 5, and "Some Aspects," p. 122; Donald C. Marsh to Isaque Graeber, 17 Jan. 1944, unprocessed material, Marsh Collection, ALUA for the quotation.

103. Interview with Donald C. Marsh, 6 June 1978; Marsh, Loving, and Wolf, *Negro-Jewish Relationships*, p. 1.

104. Capeci, "Black-Jewish Relations," pp. 228–29, for the limitations—such as nonrandom sampling, overemphasis on grocery stores, and transtolerance responses—of the Marsh, Loving, Wolf surveys.

105. Marsh, Loving, and Wolf, "Attitude Analysis," pp. 73, 74, 75, for the quotations.

106. Ibid., pp. 78, 102, for the quotations.

107. Marsh, Loving, and Wolf, "Conclusions (Post Riot)," p. 122.

108. Interview with Eleanor P. Wolf (Detroit, Michigan, 12 June 1978); Marsh, Loving, and Wolf, "Attitude Analysis," p. 87.

109. Interview with Donald C. Marsh, 13 June 1978.

110. Marsh, Loving, and Wolf, "Some Aspects," p. 1; Oral Statement of Mendel Shifman, 14 Mar. 1987; interview with Eleanor P. Wolf for the quotation.

111. Marsh, Loving, and Wolf, "Attitude Analysis," p. 92, for

speculation about black customer reaction that one Marsh, Loving, Wolf survey failed to measure; Marsh, Loving, and Wolf, "Some Aspects," pp. 6–9, for black youth and black adult responses toward Jews generally and Jewish merchants specifically.

112. Marsh, Loving, and Wolf, "Conclusions (Post Riot), p. 123, for the quotation.

113. Marsh, Loving, and Wolf, *Negro-Jewish Relationships*, pp. 1–7, and "Some Aspects," pp. 1–4.

114. Rhetts Memorandum, p. 4, n. 2.

115. *Chronicle*, 26 June 1943, p. 2.

116. Marsh, Loving, and Wolf, "Post Riot," p. 2, and "Conclusions (Post Riot), p. 122. Approximately 15 percent of the Jewish and white gentile merchants departed the riot area for reasons of financing or fear.

117. Affidavit: J. Cole n.d.

118. Clarence Sharpe, Statement, 30 June 1943, and File Contents, RCF A-34892, BHC.

119. Complaint, 30 June 1943, and File Contents, RCF A-34890, BHC; Wayne County Probation Services, Case 85, RCR (hereinafter cited as Probation Case plus number); *Tribune*, 20 Nov. 1943, p. 1, for the quotation; *Chronicle*, 20 Nov. 1943, pp. 1–2, and 27 Nov. 1943, p. 1, for the information in this and the following paragraph.

120. Governor's Committee, *Factual Report*, Part II, Exhibit, 24, p. 1.

121. Affidavit: Charles K. Scales, n.d.; Affidavit: Louis Gabbins, 6 July 1943; Affidavit: John Smith, 6 July 1943.

122. Affidavit: John Lewis, 28 Sept. 1943; Affidavit: Susie Mae Ransom, 29 June 1943.

123. Affidavit: Cora Lee, 2 July 1943; Arrest Ticket 201, 21 June 1943, Duplicate Arrest Tickets, Reel 85, DPDR for the example of one prostitute (hereinafter cited as Arrest Ticket plus number, the date being 21 June 1943 unless cited otherwise).

124. Of 170 felons, fifty-two (30.5 percent) waived their right to an examination; therefore, no records exist of the circumstances under which they were arrested.

125. Examination, 30 June 1943, pp. 5–6, for the quotations and File Contents, RCF A-34604, BHC.

126. Examination, 24 June 1943, pp. 1–3, and File Contents,

RCF A-34671, BHC; Arrest Ticket 607; Examination, 27 July 1943, pp. 1–7, and Roy T. Doherty to Joseph A. Gillis, 22 Sept. 1943, RCF A-34763, BHC.

127. Examination, 23 June 1943, pp. 1–6, and File Contents, RCF A-34563, BHC; Dorothy E. C. to NAACP Officials, n.d., Box 1, NAACP Collection, ALUA, for the quotation; Affidavit: Samuel P., n.d.; Arrest Ticket 72; Probation Case 82, for the information in this and the following paragraph.

128. Examination, 1 July 1943, pp. 1–2, File Contents, Franz Prattinger, Report, n.d. and Kenneth J. Creagh to John J. Maher, 14 Sept. 1943, RCF A-34803, BHC; Arrest Ticket 154; Probation Case 65, for the information in this and the following two paragraphs unless cited otherwise.

129. Examination, 1 July 1943, p. 4, RCF A-34803, BHC, for the quotation.

130. Kenneth J. Creagh to John J. Maher, 14 Sept. 1943, RCF A-34803, BHC, for the quotations.

131. Lee J. To Gloster B. Current, 6 July 1943, Box 1, NAACP Collection, ALUA, for the quotation; Arrest Ticket 57; Misdemeanor Calender, vol. 277, 86910, RCR (hereinafter cited as Misdemeanor Calender plus number); Detroit House of Correction, General Register of Prisoners, p. 32, BHC.

132. John H. Witherspoon to Jeffries, 8 July 1943, Box 5, Mayor's Papers (1943), BHC, for the first quotation; Shelton Tappes to Jeffries, 26 June 1943, Box 5, Mayor's Papers (1943), BHC, for the second and third quotations: Arrest Ticket 233, 22 June 1943; Misdemeanor Calender 86936.

133. Arrest Ticket 253, 22 June 1943; Examination, 1 July 1943, pp. 2–7, File Contents, and Roy T. Doherty to John P. Scallen, 24 Aug. 1945, RCF A-34532, BHC; Probation Case 46, for the information in this and the following paragraph unless cited otherwise.

134. Examination, 1 July 1943, p. 6, RCF A-34532, BHC, for the quotation.

135. Mamie T. to Jeffries, 28 Oct. 1943, Box 10, Mayor's Papers (1943), BHC; Governor's Committee, *Factual Report*, Part II, Exhibit 19C, p. 11.

136. *News*, 25 June 1943, p. 30, for the quotation; Complaint, 29 June 1943, and File Contents, RCF A-34873, BHC; Probation Cases 78a and 78b, for the information in this and the following two paragraphs unless cited otherwise; *News*, 22 June 1943, p. 1, for the ex-

ample of black stone throwers receiving harsher sentences, albeit from a different judge.

137. Hence the mutes were arrested on June 25 and are not counted among the sample for June 21 and 22.

138. Arrest Ticket 8, 25 June 1943, for James N.'s ethnicity.

139. *News,* 21 June 1943, p. 1, for the quotation.

140. Ibid., 24 June 1943, p. 1, for the quotation.

141. Of N=170 felons, forty (23.5 percent) were referred by Recorder's Court judges to the Psychopathic Clinic for psychological examinations. A handful of these evaluations do exist among other records, but the great majority of them remain closed to researcher scrutiny. Dr. Willie G. Scott (executive director, Psychiatric Clinic, Recorder's Court) to Dominic J. Capeci, Jr., 3 Mar. 1987.

142. Elmer R. Akers and Vernon Fox, "The Detroit Rioters and Looters Committed to Prison," n.d., pp. 6, 7, 10, Box 1, NAACP Collection, ALUA, for no difference among most of these variables between riot and nonriot prisoners (the exception being alleged lower general intelligence of the rioters).

143. Vemba M. Dunlap to Joseph A. Gillis, 13 Aug. 1943, RCF A-34801, BHC.

144. Lowell S. Selling to Chester P. O'Hara, 13 July 1943, and Kenneth J. Creagh to Chester P. O'Hara, 15 July 1943, RCF A-34636, BHC; Lowell S. Selling to Chester P. O'Hara, 14 July 1943, Kenneth J. Creagh to Chester P. O'Hara, 14 July 1943, and John L. Whitehead, Report, n.d., RCF A-34708, BHC.

145. Arrest Ticket 559; File Contents, and Vemba M. Dunlap to John J. Maher, 3 Nov. 1943, RCF A-34690, BHC, for the quotation. Edna A. received three years probation, later discharged with improvement.

146. File Contents, Lowell S. Selling to Thomas M. Cotter, 21 Mar. 1944, and Franz Prattinger, Report, n.d., RCF A-35069, BHC. Without citing a reason, the prosecutor ultimately dismissed the charges against Frank N.

CHAPTER 5: *Causes Célèbres*

1. Arrest Ticket 8, 26 Nov. 1943, Duplicate Arrest Tickets, Reel 87, DPDR; Examination, 6 Dec. 1943, pp. 14–16, 29, for the quotation, p. 37, and 7 Dec. 1943, pp. 53–54, 62, 70, 76, Recorder's Court File A-36135, BHC (hereinafter cited as Examination, date, RCF plus

number); Herbert J. Rushton, William E. Dowling, Oscar Olander, and John H. Witherspoon, *Factual Report of the Governor's Committee to Investigate the Riot Occurring in Detroit on June 21, 1943*, 11 Aug. 1943, Part I, pp. 2–3, note 8, BHC (hereinafter cited as Governor's Committee, *Factual Report*).

2. Russell Costello, John M. Dorsey, and Lowell S. Selling to State Hospital Commission, 7 Jan. 1944, RCF A-36135, BHC.

3. Michigan *Chronicle*, 11 Mar. 1944, p. 1 (hereinafter cited as *Chronicle*); Harold R. Stevens to William E. Dowling, Notice of Alibi, 24 Feb. 1944, and Joseph A. Gillis, Judge's Statement, 15 Mar. 1944, RCF A-36135, BHC.

4. Affidavit: Beatrice B., 3 Mar. 1945, and Affidavit: James W. Leveye, 8 May 1945, RCF A-36135, BHC. Leveye operated the Michigan Detective Bureau.

5. Recorder's Court Criminal Calender, vol. 5-I, pp. 405, 410, 427, 432, 434, BHC, for the chronology of legal proceedings in this and the subsequent paragraphs.

6. Aaron F. (prepared by Asher L. Cornelius) to Joseph A. Gillis, Petition for Leave to File a Delayed Motion for Vacation of Judgment and Sentence and for a New Trial, n.d. [28 Mar. 1945], pp. 1, 2, 3, for the quotation, RCF A-36135, BHC (hereinafter cited as Cornelius, Petition); Affidavit: Asher L. Cornelius, 29 Mar. 1945, RCF A-36135, BHC.

7. Raymond T., who testified at the examination, entered the service before the trial of March 1944.

8. Asher L. Cornelius, Brief and Discussion in Support of Motion for a New Trial, n.d. [22 May 1945], pp. 1–5, 6, for the quotation, RCF A-36135, BHC (hereinafter cited as Cornelius, Brief for a New Trial).

9. Ibid., p. 5, for the quotation; Affidavit: Cornelius L. Asher, 29 Mar. 1945; Examination, 6 Dec. 1943, p. 20, RCF A-36135, BHC, for an earlier indication that Cleveland R. conspired with police; *Chronicle*, 30 Mar. 1946, p. 4.

10. Cornelius, Brief for a New Trial, pp. 7–8, for the quotations.

11. Affidavit: Gertrude Grayson, 25 Apr. 1944, and Affidavit: Carter B. Nelson, 4 May 1944, RCF A-36135, BHC; Cornelius, Brief for a New Trial, p. 7. Later sources sometimes spelled "Chi" as "Shy."

12. Cornelius, Brief for a New Trial, pp. 11–12, for the quotations.

13. Detroit *Tribune*, 10 June 1944, p. 1 (hereinafter cited as *Tribune*); Detroit *News*, 5 Aug. 1945, p. 13 (hereinafter cited as *News*).

14. "The Social Front," *Race Relations: A Monthly Summary of Events and Trends* 3 (Apr. 1946): 267, for the community effort.

15. Asher L. Cornelius, Respondents Request to Charge, n.d., p. 2, for the quotation, RCF A-36135, BHC.

16. Ibid., p. 3, for the quotation; Asher L. Cornelius, Petition to Have Order Entered Holding Certain Witnesses for the Prosecution in Communicado, n.d., pp. 1–5, RCF A-36135, BHC.

17. Affidavit: Reginald P., 20 Oct. 1944, p. 4, for the quotation, RCF A-36135, BHC.

18. Buckholdt's background remains sketchy, because his personnel file is unavailable, and Police Force Book O, which contains his entry, is among several such volumes that are missing. *News*, 23 Mar. 1946, p. 2, for the lack of witnesses immediately after the killing.

19. Examination, 6 Dec. 1943, pp. 19, 20, 23, 32, 36, 43, and 7 Dec. 1943, p. 52, for the chronology of arrests and interrogations, RCF A-36135, BHC; *Chronicle*, 30 Mar. 1946, p. 4. Initially Cleveland R. and Fred M. denied any conspiracy, but later Fred M. admitted to it.

20. Affidavit: Reginald P., 20 Oct. 1944, p. 2.

21. Examination, 6 Dec. 1943, pp. 12, 25, 26, for the quotation, and 7 Dec. 1943, pp. 44, 48–50, 55–56, RCF, A-36135, BHC.

22. Affidavit: Reginald P., 20 Oct. 1944, p. 4.

23. Cornelius, Brief for a New Trial, pp. 14–18.

24. Dominic J. Capeci, Jr., *Race Relations in Wartime Detroit: The Sojourner Truth Housing Controversy of 1942* (Philadelphia, 1984), pp. 48, 109.

25. Affidavit: Asher L. Cornelius, 15 Mar. 1946, p. 2.

26. Affidavit: Beatrice B., 15 Mar. 1946.

27. Julian G. McIntosh, Order of Nolle Prosequi, 22 Mar. 1944, RCF A-35069, BHC; Cornelius, Brief for a New Trial, p. 4, for examples of Raymond T., Ross C., and William P. having been released from prosecution.

28. *News*, 23 Mar. 1946, pp. 1, 2, for the quotations.

29. *Chronicle*, 30 Mar. 1946, p. 4, for the quotations; *News*, 23 Mar. 1946, pp. 1, 2, and 26 Mar. 1946, p. 2. Fred M. signed a deposition.

30. Affidavit: Sam T., 15 Mar. 1946, RCF A-36135, BHC; *News*, 26 Mar. 1946, p. 2, for the quotations.

31. Detroit *Times*, 27 Mar. 1946, p. 3 (hereinafter cited as *Times*).

32. "The Social Front," p. 267; *Chronicle*, 30 Mar. 1946, p. 1, for the quotations.

33. *News*, 4 Aug. 1945, p. 13, for the quotation.

34. Cornelius, Petition, p. 2, for the quotation.

35. *News*, 23 Mar. 1946, p. 2, for Cornelius having spoken to Johnson before Gillis; *Times*, 28 Mar. 1946, p. 4, for the quotation.

36. Robert Shogan and Tom Craig, *The Detroit Race Riot: A Study in Violence* (Philadelphia, 1964), p. 181, for information that the police trial board acquitted Buckholdt of "neglect of duty and conduct unbecoming an officer."

37. *News*, 27 Mar. 1946, p. 4, for the quotation and 28 Mar. 1946, p. 10.

38. *News*, 30 July 1943, pp. 1, 4, 31 July 1943, p. 1, and 2 Aug. 1943, p. 2, for examples.

39. Editorial, "Capital Punishment Needed," *News*, 5 Aug. 1943, p. 26.

40. Examination, 17 Aug. 1943, pp. 19, 41, 43, for the quotations, RCF A-35189, BHC.

41. William E. Dowling, Julian G. McIntosh, and Joseph L. Bannigan, People's Request to Charge, n.d. [26 Jan. 1944], p. 1, for the first quotation, RCF A-35189, BHC; William E. Dowling, Julian G. McIntosh, and Joseph L. Bannigan, People's Supplemental Requests to Charge, p. 3, for the other quotations, RCF A-35189, BHC.

42. Cosimo M. Minardo and Gaeton Urbani, Request to Charge of the Defendant, Aldo T., n.d. [22 Jan. 1944], nos. 20, 21, 23 for the quotations, RCF A-35189, BHC; Alphonse E. Sirica, Defendants' Request to Charge, 22 Jan. 1944, passim, RCF A-35189, BHC (hereinafter cited as Defendants' Request).

43. Examination, 17 Aug. 1943, pp. 45, 58, RCF A-35189, BHC; Sirica, Defendants' Request, n. 24.

44. Examination, 17 Aug. 1943, pp. 47–48, 59, for Ralph T., RCF A-35189, BHC.

45. Tribune, 5 Feb. 1944, p. 1.

46. *Chronicle*, 19 Feb. 1944, p. 4, for the quotation.

47. Cosimo M. Minardo, Motion for a New Trial, 16 Mar. 1944, and Cosimo M. Minardo, Walter M. Nelson, and Isaac M. Smullin, Amended Motion, 18 Oct. 1944, RCF A-35189, BHC; Calendar Entries, Aug. 1943–Sept. 1945, RCF A-35189, BHC.

48. Minardo, Nelson, and Smullin, Amended Motion, 18 Oct. 1944, nos. 13, 21, 26 for the quotations.

49. Cosimo M. Minardo, Walter M. Nelson, and Isaac M. Smullin, Brief in Support of Amended Motion Filed on Behalf of Aldo T., 30 Apr. 1945, p. 7, for the quotations, RCF A-35189, BHC; *Tribune*, 26 May 1945, p. 1, and *Chronicle*, 26 May 1945, p. 2.

50. Gerald K. O'Brien (prepared by Joseph L. Bannigan), People's Answer to Defendants' Brief in Support of an Amended Motion for New Trial, 14 June 1945, pp. 4, 7, for the quotations, RCF A-35189, BHC.

51. *News*, 16 Oct. 1944, pp. 1, 2, for Cotter's death.

52. Paul E. Krause, Statement, 10 Sept. 1945, RCF A-35189, BHC.

53. Karl Sheiffert, "Who's Who and Why," *News*, 26 Oct. 1944, p. 40; Cosimo M. Minardo, Walter M. Nelson, and Isaac M. Smullin, Notice of Hearing, 16 Oct. 1945, RCF A-35189, BHC.

54. T. T. Brumbaugh to George K. O'Brien, 19 Sept. 1945, RCF A-35189, BHC.

55. Cosimo M. Minardo, Walter M. Nelson, and Isaac M. Smullin, Application for Leave to Appeal from an Order of Honorable Paul E. Krause, 16 Oct. 1945, pp. 1, 2, 3, for the quotations, RCF A-35189, BHC.

56. Paul E. Krause, Concise Statement of Proceedings and Facts, 16 Oct. 1945, pp. 4, 5, for the quotations, RCF A-35189, BHC.

57. T. T. Brumbaugh to Gerald K. O'Brien, 19 Sept. 1945, and Aloysius A. Deimel to Gerald K. O'Brien, 20 Sept. 1945, RCF A-35189, BHC.

58. J. E. Coogan to Gerald K. O'Brien, 20 Sept. 1945, RCF A-35189, BHC (hereinafter cited as Coogan Letter).

59. *Chronicle*, 13 Apr. 1946, p. 9, for the chronology of legal proceedings in this and the following paragraph.

60. Cosimo M. Minardo, Walter M. Nelson, and Isaac M. Smullin, Petition to Set Aside Verdict and for a New Trial, n.d., pp. 1–3, RCF A-35189, BHC (hereinafter cited as Petition to Set Aside Verdict); Affidavit: Atilio C., 21 May 1946, pp. 1–3, for the quotations, RCF A-35189, BHC.

61. Ibid., Cosimo M. Minardo, Walter M. Nelson, and Isaac M. Smullin, Motion for Permission to File Petition for a New Trial, 21 May 1946, p. 2, for the quotation, RCF A-35189, BHC.

62. Minardo, Nelson and Smullin, Petition to Set Aside Verdict, pp. 1–3.

63. Cosimo M. Minardo, Motion to Dismiss Complaint and Warrant as to Aldo T., 8 Jan. 1947, pp. 1–2, RCF A-35189, BHC (hereinafter cited as Motion to Dismiss Complaint).

64. John J. Maher, Information for Manslaughter, 10 Jan. 1947, and File Jacket, RCF A-35189, BHC.

65. Minutes, Greater Detroit Interracial Fellowship, 11 Feb. 1944, Box 3, Metropolitan Detroit Council of Churches Collection, ALUA.

66. Coogan Letter.

67. "The Social Front," p. 267, for the quotation; *News,* 28 Mar. 1946, p. 10; *Times,* 11 Jan. 1947, p. 3.

68. Minardo, Motion to Dismiss Complaint, p. 2.

69. Cornelius, Brief for a New Trial, p. 16, for the quotation; Governor's Committee, *Factual Report,* Part I, pp. 6, 8; John J. Jennings, Officer's Statement, n.d., RCF A-35069, BHC.

70. Robert L. Champion, Notice of Alibi, 10 Mar. 1944, RCF A-35069, BHC.

71. Cornelius, Brief for a New Trial, pp. 17–18.

72. Examination, 17 Aug. 1943, pp. 47–48, RCF A-35189, BHC.

73. Coogan Letter.

74. Examination, 17 Aug. 1943, p. 44, for the quotation, p. 53, RCF A-35189, BHC.

75. There is no evidence that either Aaron F. or Aldo T. ever committed another crime.

76. *Tribune,* 3 Feb. 1945, p. 1.

77. George C. Parzen, Motion to Quash Information and Discharge Defendant, 6 Nov. 1943, RCF A-35189, BHC; Recorder's Court Criminal Calender, vol. 5-H, p. 517.

78. Examination, 17 Aug. 1943, p. 53, RCF A-35189, BHC.

79. *News,* 4 Aug. 1945, p. 13.

80. Ibid., 27 Mar. 1946, p. 4, for the quotation.

CHAPTER 6: *From Hastings to 12th Street*

1. Melvin G. Holli, ed., *Detroit* (New York, 1976), p. 271, for these and subsequent demographic statistics unless cited otherwise; Kenneth T. Jackson, *The Ku Klux Klan in the City, 1915–1930* (New York, 1967), pp. 127–43; David A. Levine, *Internal Combustion: The Races in Detroit, 1915–1926* (Westport, Conn., 1976); Norman K. Miles, "Home at Last: Urbanization of Black Migrants in Detroit, 1916–1929," unpublished Ph.D. dissertation, University of Michigan, 1978; Morris Janowitz, "Black Legions on the March," in *America in Crisis: Fourteen Critical Episodes in American History,* ed. by Daniel Aaron (reprint ed., Hamden, Conn., 1971) pp. 305–308; August Meier and Elliott Rudwick, *Black Detroit and the Rise of the UAW* (New York, 1979), pp. 34–107.

2. Dominic J. Capeci, Jr., *Race Relations in Wartime Detroit: The Sojourner Truth Housing Controversy of 1942* (Philadelphia, 1984); Lee Finkle, *Forum for Protest: The Black Press During World War II* (Ruther-

ford, N.J.), pp. 110–113; Herbert J. Rushton, William E. Dowling, Oscar Olander, and John H. Witherspoon, *Factual Report of the Governor's Committee to Investigate the Riot Occurring in Detroit on June 21, 1943,* 11 Aug. 1943, Part II, Exhibit 24, p. 1, for the in-migration statistics, BHC (hereinafter cited as Governor's Committee, *Factual Report*); John H. Witherspoon to the Common Council, City of Detroit, 28 June 1943, *Journal of the Common Council* (Detroit, 1944), p. 1854 (hereinafter cited as Witherspoon Statement); Robert Shogan and Tom Craig, *The Detroit Race Riot: A Study in Violence* (Philadelphia, 1964), pp. 16–33; Charles R. Lawrence, Jr., "Race Riots in the United States, 1942–1946," in *Negro Year Book, 1941–1946,* ed. by Jessie P. Guzman (Atlanta, 1947), pp. 232–57.

3. Hubert G. Locke, *The Detroit Riot of 1967* (Detroit, 1969), p. 53.

4. Office of War Information, Special Memorandum No. 64, 30 June 1943, p. 10, Box 50, RG 212, NARS, for the first quotation; Francis J. Haas, Notebook, 2 July 1943 entry, Haas Papers, CUA, for the second quotation of John L. Lovette, secretary of the Michigan Manufacturers Association; Joseph Boskin, "The Revolt of the Urban Ghettos, 1964–1970," in *Urban Racial Violence in the Twentieth Century,* 2d ed., ed. by Joseph Boskin (Beverly Hills, 1976), p. 155, for the third quotation. Our study challenges Boskin's theory of malaise for the 1960s.

5. Neil J. Smelser, *Theory of Collective Behavior* (New York, 1962), pp. 230–45, for the information in this and the following paragraph unless cited otherwise.

6. Governor's Committee, *Factual Report,* Part I, pp. 1–8, and Part II, Exhibit 9; National Advisory Commission on Civil Disorders, *Report of the National Advisory Commission on Civil Disorders* (New York, 1968), p. 111, for the quotation (hereinafter cited as National Commission, *Report*).

7. Terry Ann Knopf, *Rumors, Race, and Riot* (New Brunswick, 1975), pp. 117–19, 141, 145; Memorandum for the NAACP (from P.W.), 26 June 1943, p. 13, Box 1, NAACP Collection, ALUA, for the quotation (hereinafter cited as P.W. Memorandum).

8. Dominic J. Capeci, Jr., *The Harlem Riot of 1943* (Philadelphia, 1977), pp. 99–108; Harold Orlansky, *The Harlem Riot: A Study in Mass Frustration,* (New York, 1943), p. 21, for the first quotation; Smelser, *Collective Behavior,* p. 255, for the second quotation.

9. Knopf, *Rumors, Race, and Riot,* pp. 78, 154; Smelser, *Collective Behavior,* p. 249.

10. Governor's Committee, *Factual Report,* Part I, pp. 8, 10; Allen

D. Grimshaw, "A Study in Social Violence: Urban Race Riots in the United States," unpublished Ph.D. dissertation, University of Pennsylvania, 1959, pp. 114–15; Charles E. J. Newman, Interview with A. B. Owens, 9 July 1943, p. 1, Box 18, RG 319, WNRC; Michigan *Chronicle*, 26 June 1943, p. 5 (hereinafter cited as *Chronicle*); Sheridan A. Bruseaux Investigation to Horace A. White, "Investigation of Detroit Riots," 12 July 1943, p. 9, Box 8, Mayor's Papers (1943), BHC (hereinafter cited as Bruseaux, "Investigation").

11. Alfred M. Lee and Norman D. Humphrey, *Race Riot* (New York, 1943), p. 40, for the quotation; Joe R. Feagin and Harlan Hahn, *Ghetto Revolts: The Politics of Violence in American Cities* (New York, 1973), p. 160.

12. Governor's Committee, *Factual Report*, Part II, Exhibit 19b, for seven additional deaths and sixty-three more injuries.

13. Robert P. Ingalls, "Lynching and Establishment Violence in Tampa, 1858–1935," *Journal of Southern History* 53 (Nov. 1987): 614, summarizes the theories of George Rudé, Charles Tilly, Louise Tilly, and Richard Tilly; Roger Brown, *Social Psychology* (New York, 1965), p. 754; Lowell S. Selling, "A Study of One Hundred Offenders Who Were Apprehended during the Disturbance of June 20th and 21st, 1943, in Detroit, Michigan," n.d., pp. 25–31, Box 9, Mayor's Papers (1943), BHC (hereinafter cited as Selling, "One Hundred Offenders").

14. Harold Mulbar to Oscar G. Olander, 29 July 1943, p. 5, MSPR (hereinafter all MSPR citations refer to case 6152).

15. Smelser, *Collective Behavior*, p. 257, for the quotation, p. 261.

16. Memorandum for the Attorney General (from C. E. Rhetts), 15 July 1943, pp. 4–5, Box 213, HLIP (hereinafter cited as Rhetts Memorandum); Lee and Humphrey, *Race Riot*, p. 34.

17. Affidavit: Anonymous, n.d., Box 1, NAACP Collection, ALUA (hereinafter all Affidavit citations refer to Box 1, NAACP Collection, ALUA).

18. Examination, 28 June 1943, p. 6, Recorder's Court File A-34587, BHC (hereinafter cited as Examination, date, RCF plus number); Examination, 24 June 1943, p. 5, RCF A-34568, BHC.

19. Arrest Tickets 102, 103, 104, 105, 910, 911, 912, and 913, 21 June 1943, Duplicate Arrest Tickets, Reel 85, DPDR (hereinafter cited as Arrest Ticket plus number, the date being 21 June 1943 unless noted otherwise). One passenger lived one mile from Walter H. and his brother, while another resided two and three-quarter miles and four others resided four and three-quarter miles away.

20. Arrest Tickets 570, 571, 573, 574, 575, and 576. The passengers lived one mile, one and one-quarter mile, two and one-half miles, two and three-quarter miles, and three and one-quarter miles respectively from Walter J.; Examination, 24 June 1943, p. 5, RCF A-34568, BHC.

21. Governor's Committee, *Factual Report,* Part I, p. 2; Detroit *News,* 30 July 1943, p. 1 (hereinafter cited as *News*); Examination, 28 June 1943, p. 3, RCF A-34585, BHC.

22. Memorandum: Statements of Negro Prisoners Taken at the Piquette Armory, June 24th, 1943, to Thomas Colladay (from Leo M. Wendell), 24 June 1943, pp. 10, 14–15, for example, RG 79-10, MSA (hereinafter cited as Wendell Memorandum).

23. Appendix B, Table 4.

24. Wayne County Probation Services, Cases 79 and 80, RCR (hereinafter cited as Probation Case plus number).

25. Examination, 23 June 1943, RCF A-34551, BHC.

26. Selling, "One Hundred Offenders," p. 27.

27. Rhetts Memorandum, p. 6, note 3.

28. Examination, 23 June 1943, p. 3, RCF A-34608, BHC; *News,* 29 June 1943, p. 6; Detroit *Tribune,* 7 Aug. 1943, p. 3 (hereinafter cited as *Tribune*).

29. File Jacket and Examination, 23 June 1943, RCF A-34608, BHC; Misdemeanor Calender, vol. 277, 87053, RCR (hereinafter cited as Misdemeanor Calender plus number); Detroit House of Correction, General Register of Prisoners, p. 38, BHC.

30. Probation Case 28.

31. Arrest Ticket 569.

32. Thurgood Marshall, "The Gestapo in Detroit," *Crises,* Aug. 1943, pp. 232–33, 246–47.

33. Affidavit: Paul Dennie, n.d.

34. Statement of Mildred R., Pearl D., and Miriam W., n.d., Box 70, Civil Rights Congress of Michigan Collection, ALUA.

35. Selling, "One Hundred Offenders," p. 28.

36. Arrest Tickets 901 and 904, 21 July 1943, respectively, for Charles L. (5 feet 4 inches, 145 pounds) and Aldo T. (5 feet 6 1/2 inches, 144 pounds); Arrest Ticket 68; Probation Case 28.

37. Information for Second Felony Conviction, 9 Aug. 1943, RCF A-34608, BHC; *Chronicle,* 7 Aug. 1943, p. 5. Martin P.'s original sentence was one to five years in prison, which was increased to from two years, five and one-half months to seven and one-half years.

38. *Chronicle,* 7 Aug. 1943, p. 5; Olivier Zunz, *The Changing Face of*

Inequality: Urbanization, Industrial Development, and Immigrants in Detroit, 1880–1920 (Chicago, 1982), p. 137; Robert K. Merton, *Social Theory and Social Structure,* rev. ed. (New York, 1967), pp. 131–60.

39. *News,* 21 July 1943, p. 4, and 27 Aug. 1943, p. 1; Arrest Ticket 94, 23 July 1943; Joseph A. Gillis, Judge's Statement, 4 Nov. 1943, RCF A-35386, BHC, for the quotation; Walter White, "What Caused the Detroit Race Riots?" p. 15, Box 2574, FHLP. George F.'s original sentence was one to five years imprisonment, which Gillis changed to five years imprisonment, the maximum penalty.

40. George M. Fredrickson, *White Supremacy: A Comparative Study in American and South African History* (New York, 1981), pp. 70, 87; Jack Levin, *The Functions of Prejudice* (New York, 1975), pp. 42–45.

41. Arrest Ticket 915; Joseph A. Gillis, Judge's Statement, 11 Aug. 1943, RCF A-34713, BHC; Arrest Ticket, 916, 23 June 1943, and Examination, 24 June 1943, RCF A-34614, BHC, for the example of another newcomer Marvel H. from San Francisco, who arrived in Detroit on June 20 and carried a knife for self-defense.

42. Appendix B, Table 3.

43. Vincent Neering, Report, 23 June 1943, MSPR; William Ward, Report, 25 June 1943, MSPR; C. J. Scavarda to Oscar Olander, 29 June 1943, MSPR.

44. Allen D. Grimshaw, "Changing Patterns of Racial Violence in the United States," in *Racial Violence in the United States,* ed. Allen D. Grimshaw (Chicago, 1969), p. 491; Bryan T. Downes, "The Social and Political Characteristics of Riot Cities: A Comparative Study," *Social Science Quarterly* 49 (Dec. 1968): 505.

45. Rhetts Memorandum, pp. 9, 10, for the quotation; Memorandum for the Attorney General (from Francis J. Haas), 5 July 1943, p. 1, Box 45, Haas Papers, CUA; Francis Biddle to Franklin D. Roosevelt, 15 July 1943, Box 213, HLIP; Federal Bureau of Investigation, "Survey of Racial Conditions in the United States," 1944, p. 19, Box 44, OF 10-B, FDRL (hereinafter cited as FBI, "Survey of Racial Conditions").

46. FBI, "Survey of Racial Conditions," pp. 1, 9, for the quotation, pp. 14, 27, for an example.

47. Office of the Provost Marshal General, "Detroit Race Riot," 23 June 1943, p. 3, Box 1789, RG 389, NARS.

48. Franz Prattinger, Report, 21 Mar. 1944, p. 2, RCF A-35069, BHC.

49. Leo M. Wendell to Thomas Colladay, 24 June 1943, RG 79-10, MSA.

50. Smelser, *Collective Behavior*, p. 261; William Ryan, *Blaming the Victim* (New York, 1971), p. 216.

51. William E. Guthner, "Commander's Estimate of the Situation, June 20–24, 1943," 26 June 1943, p. 1, RG 79-10, MSA (hereinafter cited as "Commander's Estimate").

52. Lee and Humphrey, *Race Riot*, p. 87.

53. Affidavit: Paul Dennie, n.d., for an example of several white women rioters; Morris Janowitz, "Patterns of Collective Racial Violence," in *Violence in America: Historical and Comparative Perspectives*, Vol. 2, eds. Hugh D. Graham and Ted R. Gurr (Washington, D.C., 1969), p. 326, for the quotation; Robert M. Brown, *Stain of Violence: Historical Studies of American Violence and Vigilantism* (New York, 1975), p. 215.

54. Bruseaux, "Investigation," p. 7.

55. Arrest Ticket 917; Wendell Memorandum 20. "Picked up twice but never held," William Lee B. came from a family of three sisters and one brother (serving overseas in the U.S. Navy during the riot).

56. Orlansky, *The Harlem Riot*, p. 22, for the quotation; Janowitz, "Patterns," p. 322.

57. Downes, "Social Characteristics," p. 509; Joseph Boskin, "Violence in the Ghettos," *New Mexico Quarterly* 37 (Winter 1968): 318; Boskin, "The Revolt of the Urban Ghettos," p. 165; Joseph Boskin, "Aftermath of an Urban Revolt: The View from Watts, 1965–1971," in *Urban Racial Violence in the Twentieth Century*, p. 182, for the first quotation; Edward C. Banfield, *The Unheavenly City: The Nature and Future of Our Urban Crisis* (Boston, 1970), p. 191, for the second quotation.

58. *News*, 21 June 1943, p. 2.

59. Banfield, *The Unheavenly City*, p. 185.

60. *News*, 22 June 1943, p. 6.

61. *Ibid.*, 21 June 1943, p. 2.

62. White, "What Caused?" p. 15; Affidavit: Walter F. Holland, 3 July 1943, for the quotation.

63. Donald C. Marsh, Alvin D. Loving, and Eleanor P. Wolf, "Conclusions (Post Riot)," n.d., p. 2, unprocessed material, Marsh Collection, ALUA; Affidavit: John Bell, n.d.

64. Wendell Memorandum, 12; Examination, 2 July 1943, p. 2, RCF A-34783, BHC.

65. Richard C. Wade, "Violence in the Cities: An Historical View," in *Urban Violence*, ed. Charles U. Daly (Chicago, 1969), pp. 15, 24; Lewis Coser, "Some Sociological Aspects of Conflict," in *Racial Conflict: Tension and Change in American Society*, ed. Gary T. Marx (Boston, 1971), p. 16.

66. Tamotsu Shibutani and Kian M. Kwan, "Changes in Life Conditions Conducive to Interracial Conflict," and "Scarce Resources and Institutionalized Inequality: The Basis for Realistic Conflict," in *Racial Conflict*, pp. 135–48; Pierre Van Den Berghe, "Paternalistic Versus Competitive Race Relations," in *Racial Conflict*, pp. 132–34.

67. Governor's Committee, *Factual Report*, Part I, pp. 5, 7; Affidavit: James Townsend, 30 June 1943.

68. Marx, "Introduction," in *Racial Conflict*, p. 2.

69. Rhetts Memorandum, p. 4, note 2; *News*, 22 June 1943, p. 6.

70. Selling, "One Hundred Offenders," p. 31.

71. Wendell Memorandum, p. 12.

72. Witherspoon Statement, p. 1856.

73. Earl Raab and Seymour Martin Lipset, "The Prejudiced Society," in *Racial Conflict*, pp. 37–38, 45, for the quotation; Marx, in *Racial Conflict*, "Introduction," p. 3.

74. Lee and Humphrey, *Race Riot*, p. 38.

75. *News*, 22 June 1943, p. 6.

76. Herbert Shapiro, *White Violence and Black Response: From Reconstruction to Montgomery* (Amherst, 1988), pp. xi–xiii.

77. William Lang, Statement, 17 Sept. 1943, Jesse Stewart Personnel File, DPDR (hereinafter cited as Stewart File).

78. Dorothy E. C. to NAACP Officials, 30 June 1943, Box 1, NAACP Collection, ALUA, for an example.

79. Anonymous, "Joint Meeting of Citizens Committee and Other Civic and Labor Groups," 21 June 1943, pp. 8–10, and Citizens Committee, "Remarks of R. J. Thomas, et al.," 21 June 1943, pp. 8–9, Box 70, Civil Rights Congress of Michigan Collection, ALUA (hereinafter cited as Citizens Committee, "Joint Meeting" and Citizens Committee, "Remarks," respectively).

80. *News*, 21 June 1943, p. 2; Citizens Committee, "Joint Meeting," pp. 12, 13, for the quotations.

81. Lee and Humphrey, *Race Riot*, pp. 32, 36; *News*, 22 June 1943, p. 6; Steering Committee, Agenda, 21 June 1943, pp. 1–4, Box 70, Civil Rights Congress of Michigan Collection, ALUA.

82. Sidney Fine, *Violence in the Model City: The Cavanagh Administration, Race Relations, and the Detroit Riot of 1967* (Ann Arbor, 1989), from which this chapter draws heavily for factual information; Tyrone Tillery, *The Conscience of a City: A Commemorative History of the Detroit Human Rights Commission and Department, 1943–1983*, (Detroit, 1983), pp. 3–22.

83. Holli, *Detroit*, p. 271, for the census data of 1960; within ten years blacks had mushroomed to 660,428 persons; with the 1970 population of the city at 1,511,482 this meant a rise from 28.9 percent to 44.5 percent; *Newsweek*, 17 Aug. 1967, p. 18, for the percentage of black homeowners and p. 19, for the quotation.

84. Elliot D. Luby and James Hedegard, "A Study of Civil Disorder in Detroit," *William and Mary Law Review* 10 (Spring 1969): 590–92; Benjamin D. Singer, Richard W. Osborn, and James A. Geschwender, *Black Rioters,: A Study of Social Factors and Communication in the Detroit Riot* (Lexington, 1970), pp. 25–38; Allen J. Matusow, *The Unraveling of America: A History of Liberalism in the 1960s* (New York, 1984), p. 327, for the quotation; John C. Shortell, "A Comparison of the Detroit Race Riots of 1943 and 1967," unpublished senior thesis, University of Notre Dame, 1974, p. 44.

85. National Commission, *Report*, pp. 84–108 and 91, for the first quotation; Sidney Fine, "Chance and History: Some Aspects of the Detroit Riot of 1967," *Michigan Quarterly Review* 25 (Spring 1986): 414, for the second quotation; *Newsweek*, 7 Aug. 1967, pp. 18–27.

86. Fine, *Violence in the Model City*, pp. 39, 70, 93, 136–43, 150–51; Smelser, *Collective Behavior*, p. 245, for the quotation.

87. Fine, *Violence in the Model City*, pp. 96, 155, for the quotation 160, 163; Locke, *The Detroit Riot of 1967*, pp. 24–26; Knopf, *Rumors, Race, and Riot*, p. 145; Singer, Osborn, and Geschwender, *Black Rioters*, p. 99; Detroit Urban League, *The People Beyond 12th Street: A Survey of Attitudes of Detroit Negroes after the Riot of 1967* (Detroit, 1967), pp. 9, 13; U.S. Manpower Administration (U.S. Department of Labor), "The Detroit Riot: A Profile of 500 Prisoners," Oct. 1968, p. 8, Vertical File, ALUA (herein cited as Manpower Administration, "The Detroit Riot").

88. National Commission, *Report*, p. 85.

89. Sheldon J. Lachman and Benjamin D. Singer, *The Detroit Riot of July 1967: A Psychological, Social, and Economic Profile of 500 Arrestees* (Detroit, 1968), p. 5, for the quotation; Stanley Lieberson and Arnold H. Silverman, "The Precipitants and Underlying Conditions of Race Riots," *American Sociological Review* 30 (Dec. 1965): 888. We thank Professor Lachman for providing us a copy of *The Detroit Riot of July 1967*.

90. Locke, *The Detroit Riot of 1967*, pp. 32–33, 41–43; Fine, *Violence in the Model City*, pp. 166–67, 170, 185, 195, 225. Locke identifies the shift in riot phases as having occurred somewhat earlier than does

Fine, though both agree on the second phase's citywide characteristic.

91. Fine, *Violence in the Model City*, pp. 172–80, 196, 236; Janowitz, "Patterns," p. 323.

92. Smelser, *Collective Behavior*, pp. 258–61; Robert A. Mendelsohn, "Profile of the Riot Causes and Participants," in *A City in Racial Crisis: The Case of Detroit Pre- and Post- the 1967 Riot*, ed. Leonard Gordon (Dubuque, 1971), p. 78, for the quotations.

93. Fine, *Violence in the Model City*, pp. 162, 186, 292–93, 364–65; Lachman and Singer, *The Detroit Riot of 1967*, p. 5; *Newsweek*, 7 Aug. 1967, p. 19, for the quotation; John Dotson, "I Don't Care If I Die," *Newsweek*, 7 Aug. 1967, p. 26.

94. Dotson, "I Don't Care If I Die," p. 26, for the first quotation; National Commission, *Report*, p. 91, for the second quotation.

95. Manpower Administration, "The Detroit Riot," pp. 23, 25. Of N=468 subjects, 102 (21.8 percent) and fifty-one (10.9 percent) first learned of the riot from friends and relatives respectively; of N=405 subjects, 151 (37.3 percent) met friends at the riot scene.

96. Detroit Urban League, *The People Beyond 12th Street*, p. 7; Mendelsohn, "Profile of the Riot Causes," p. 78.

97. Fine, *Violence in the Model City*, pp. 160–65. Charles L. resided in Detroit for five years before the 1943 riot, less time than did Mr. Greensleeves prior to the 1967 disorder.

98. Feagin and Hahn, *Ghetto Riots*, p. 10, for the quotation; Manpower Administration, "The Detroit Riot," p. 16; Mendelsohn, "Profile of the Riot Causes," p. 83.

99. Locke, *The Detroit Riot of 1967*, p. 49.

100. *Newsweek*, 7 Aug. 1967, p. 25, for the quotation; Locke, *The Detroit Riot of 1967*, pp. 123–32. Detroit Urban League, *The People Beyond 12th Street*, pp. 8, 13.

101. Matusow, *The Unraveling of America*, p. 364.

102. Manpower Administration, "The Detroit Riot," p. 26, for the quotation; Detroit Urban League, *The People Beyond 12th Street*, pp. 8, 13; Fine, *Violence in the Model City*, pp. 358, 362–65. One quarter (25.9 percent) of the Urban League respondents—albeit more rioters than nonrioters—said that Black Nationalism had "a great deal" to do with the upheaval. Nonetheless, authorities and the riot's leading historian found the evidence of organized rioting at any level by any factions inadequate (contemporary officials being more categorical in their assessment than Fine).

103. Fine, *Violence in the Model City*, pp. 185, 342–43; National Commission, *Report*, p. 128.

104. Feagin and Hahn, *Ghetto Riots*, p. 280.

105. Robert M. Fogelson and Robert B. Hill, "Who Riots? A Study in Participation in the 1967 Riots," in *Supplemental Studies for the National Advisory Commission on Civil Disorders*, ed. National Advisory Commission on Civil Disorders (New York, 1968), p. 231.

106. National Commission, *Report*, p. 128.

107. Tom Parmenter, "Breakdown in Law and Order," in *Ghetto Revolts*, ed. Peter H. Rossi (Chicago, 1970), p. 68.

108. Lachman and Singer, *The Detroit Riot of July 1967*, p. 5; National Commission, *Report*, p. 87; *Newsweek*, 7 Aug. 1967, p. 19, for the quotation.

109. Fine, *Violence in the Model City*, p. 165; National Commission, *Report*, p. 91.

110. National Commission, *Report*, p. 129; Fine, *Violence in the Model City*, p. 347.

111. Locke, *The Detroit Riot of 1967*, pp. 29–31.

112. Fine, *Violence in the Model City*, p. 347; Detroit Urban League, *The People Beyond 12th Street*, p. 13, reported those protecting their property at 32.5 percent and, in the next largest category, those assisting the injured and homeless at 10.3 percent.

113. National Commission, *Report*, p. 98.

114. National Commission, *Report*, p. 128, for the statistics, p. 129; Fine, *Violence in the Model City*, p. 349, for naysayers comprising 65 percent of Elliot D. Luby's community sample.

115. National Commission, *Report*, pp. 89, 96; Locke, *The Detroit Riot of 1967*, p. 38; Fine, *Violence in the Model City*, pp. 341–42, 351–52; Robert M. Fogelson, *Violence as Protest: A Study of Riots and Ghettos* (Garden City, 1971), p. 13, for the quotation.

116. John Hersey, *The Algiers Motel Incident* (New York, 1968).

117. Locke, *The Detroit Riot of 1967*, pp. 26–43; Fine, "Chance and History," pp. 417–23.

118. National Commission, *Report*, pp. 1–2, 127–35, 171–78, for the samples; Detroit Police Department, "Statistical Report on the Civil Disorder Occurring in the City of Detroit, July, 1967," unpublished manuscript, Detroit Police Department, n.d., p. 3. The National Commission used two studies on the Detroit rioters that employed very different methodologies and yet reached similar conclusions: Manpower Administration, "The Detroit Riot," pp. 1–28, involved interviews with arrestees; Nathan S. Caplan and Jeffery M. Paige, "A Study of Ghetto Rioters," *Scientific American*, 219 (Aug.

1968): 15–21, conducted interviews with self-proclaimed rioters who had eluded capture during the disorder.

119. T. M. Tomlinson, "The Development of Riot Ideology among Urban Negroes," *American Behavioral Scientist* 11 (Mar. 1968): 28.

120. Nathan Caplan, "The New Ghetto Man: A Review of Recent Empirical Studies," *Journal of Social Issues* 26 (Winter 1970): 59–73.

121. Robert M. Fogelson, "White on Black: A Critique of the McCone Commission Report on the Los Angeles Riots," *Political Science Quarterly* 82 (Sept. 1967): 337–67. Perhaps the National Commission also hoped to avoid controversy by employing both arrestee and self-proclaimed rioter data.

122. Michael Lipsky and David J. Olson, *Commission Politics: The Processing of Racial Crisis In America* (New Brunswick, N.J., 1977), pp. 181–82.

123. National Commission, *Report*, p. 236.

124. Fogelson and Hill, "Who Riots?" p. 243.

125. Elliot Luby and James Hedegard, "Comparison of the Arrested and Those Who Stayed at Home," in "City in Crisis: The People and Their Riot," unpublished manuscript, Lafayette Clinic, Wayne State University/University of Michigan, n.d., ed. Elliot Luby, p. 8. We thank Dr. Luby for providing us with a copy of "City in Crisis."

126. Singer, Osborn, and Geschwender, *Black Rioters*, p. 22.

127. Robert Mendelsohn, "Arrestee Interpretation of the Riot," in "City in Crisis," p. 1, for the first quotation, and "Profile of the Riot Causes," p. 76, for the second quotation.

128. Merton, *Social Theory;* Caplan, "The New Ghetto Man"; Ted R. Gurr, *Why Men Rebel* (Princeton, 1970).

129. Fine, *Violence in the Model City*, p. 341, for the third and fourth quotations, p. 367, for the first and second quotations.

130. Governor's Committee, *Factual Report*, Part II, Exhibit 17, pp. 34–35; Detroit Police Department, "Statistical Report on the Civil Disorder," p. 4.

131. In part, the discrepancy among the 1967 studies indicates the distinction between data from arrestee and those from self-proclaimed rioters.

132. Appendix B, Tables 3 and 5; National Commission, *Report*, p. 128.

133. Shula Marks, *Reluctant Rebellion* (Oxford, 1970), p. 309; William M. Tuttle, Jr., *Race Riot: Chicago in the Red Summer of 1919*

(New York, 1970), pp. 264–65; C. F. Ramsay to Harry F. Kelly, 2 Aug. 1943, Box 74, Kelly Papers, MSA; Mendelsohn, "Profile of the Riot Causes," p. 83.

134. Appendix B, Table 3; Miriam F. Hirsch, *Women and Violence* (New York, 1981), p. 151, for the quotation.

135. Fine, *Violence in the Model City*, p. 342; Grimshaw, "Changing Patterns," p. 493, for the quotation.

136. Appendix B, Table 3; National Commission, *Report*, p. 130; Fine, *Violence in the Model City*, p. 332.

137. Feagin and Hahn, *Ghetto Revolts*, p. 10, for the first quotation; Karl H. Flaming, *Who Riots and Why? Black and White Perspectives in Milwaukee* (Milwaukee, 1968), p. 16, for the second quotation.

138. David O. Sears and John B. McConahay, *The Politics of Violence: The New Urban Blacks and the Watts Riot* (Boston, 1973), p. 33.

139. Selling, "One Hundred Offenders," pp. 54–59; National Commission, *Report*, p. 130, for the quotation.

140. J. Edgar Hoover to Jonathan Daniels, 22 Oct. 1943, and enclosed page of statistics, Box 17, OF 4245-G, Roosevelt Papers, FDRL. Of 1,182 arrestees tabulated by the FBI, 46.4 percent of the black and 43.9 percent of the white adults had previous records. Their percentages appeared great because the bureau counted only persons held for prosecution. (Black and white juveniles with earlier arrests also registered sizable proportions—34.3 percent each—of 189 participants.)

In fact, data in Table 3 (Appendix B) of this study indicates that repeat adult offenders accounted for much smaller proportions: 36.4 percent for blacks, 22.9 percent for whites. Although many rioters possessed records, they did not dominate the riot. And they lived primarily in neighborhoods where young males, especially if black, ran afoul of suspicious patrolmen early in life. (Juveniles could not be compared with federal statistics because their records are closed.)

141. Fine, *Violence in the Model City*, p. 249, for 48.6 percent of Detroit arrestees lumped together by age, gender, and race, p. 369, for the percentages of self-proclaimed rioters identified only by race; Janowitz, "Patterns," p. 326.

142. Appendix B, Table 4; National Commission, *Report*, p. 173, note 119, p. 174, note 122; Elliott D. Luby, "A Comparison Between Detroit Negro Arrestees and a Riot Area Control Sample," paper read at the American Political Science Association Meeting, Washington, D.C., Sept. 3–7, 1968, p. 7; Manpower Administration, "The Detroit

Riot," p. 16. We thank Dr. Luby for providing a copy of his conference paper.

143. Appendix B, Table 3, for black female rioters of 1943: 33.3 percent single, 33.3 percent married, 31.0 percent separated, divorced, or widowed; Fogelson and Hill, "Who Riots?" p. 235, Table 5, for the black male rioters of 1967: 38.4 percent married.

144. Fogelson and Hill, "Who Riots? p. 235, Table 5: 48.4 percent; Singer, Osborn, and Geschwender, *Black Rioters*, p. 71: 48.7 percent; Luby, "A Comparison," p. 5: 46.5 percent.

145. Elliot D. Luby, "The Detroit Riot," *Sinai Hospital Detroit Bulletin* 16 (Oct. 1968): 137; Appendix B, Table 3. We thank Dr. Luby for providing a copy of this article.

146. Appendix, Table 3; National Commission, *Report*, p. 173, note 117.

147. Ibid.

148. Gerald Wehmer, "Who Was Arrested," in "City in Crisis," p. 4; Fine, *Violence in the Model City*, p. 92.

149. National Commission, *Report*, p. 132, for varying employment rates according to the surveys used: Detroit arrest study (Manpower Administration), 78.2 percent; Detroit survey (Caplan and Paige), 70.4 percent. See also Luby, "A Comparison," p. 5, 76.8 percent, and Sidney M. Willhelm, *Who Needs the Negro?* (Cambridge, Mass., 1970) for the expendability of unskilled black laborers.

150. Appendix B, Table 3.

151. National Commission, *Report*, p. 174, note 126: 76.8 percent (some high school), 23.3 percent (graduated); Caplan and Paige, "A Study of Ghetto Rioters," p. 17: 93 percent (some high school), no percentage given of those who graduated; Luby, "A Comparison," p. 7: 82 percent (some high school), 39 percent (graduated), combining female rioters who no doubt raised the education level; Manpower Administration, "The Detroit Riot," p. 15: 82.3 percent (some high school), 31.8 percent (graduated); Singer, Osborn, and Geschwender, *Black Rioters*, p. 59: 82.1 percent (some high school), 32.1 percent (graduated), 11.2 median years.

152. Fine, *Violence in the Model City*, pp. 45–46, 52–56, for the poor quality of education in Detroit on the eve of riot in 1967.

CHAPTER 7: *Broader Perspectives*

1. Gustave Le Bon, *The Crowd: A Study of the Popular Mind,* (reprint ed., New York, 1960).

2. Roger Brown, *Social Psychology* (New York, 1965), pp. 734–36; Charles Tilly, Louise Tilly, and Richard Tilly, *The Rebellious Century, 1830–1930* (Cambridge, Mass., 1975), pp. 4–6; Le Bon, *The Crowd,* p. 24, for the quotation.

3. Tilly, Tilly, and Tilly, *Rebellious Century,* pp. 7, 273–74: E. J. Hobsbawm, *Primitive Rebels: Studies in Archaic Forms of Social Movement in the 19th and 20th Centuries,* 2d ed. (New York, 1963), pp. 108–25; E. P. Thompson, *The Making of the English Working Class* (New York, 1963), pp. 62–78, 100, 150, 225, 810, 814–15.

4. George Rudé, *The Crowd in History: A Study of Popular Disturbances in France and England, 1730–1848,* rev. ed. (New York, 1981), p. 15; Lewis A. Coser, *The Functions of Social Conflict* (Glencoe, Illinois, 1956); Neil J. Smelser, *Theory of Collective Behavior* (New York, 1963), p. 269, for the value-added sequence of structural conduciveness, structural strain, growth and spread of generalized beliefs, precipitating factors, and mobilization of participants.

5. Tilly, Tilly, and Tilly, *Rebellious Century,* pp. 290–98; Mark Harrison, *Crowds and History: Mass Phenomena in English Towns, 1790–1835* (Cambridge, Mass., 1988), for a historigraphic overview and historical revision of earlier scholars that also expands the analysis of crowds to include those who gathered nonviolently in corporate bodies, meetings, elections, celebrations, and so forth.

6. Robert M. Fogelson, *Violence as Protest: A Study of Riots and Ghettos* (Garden City, N.Y., 1971).

7. National Advisory Commission on Civil Disorders, *Report of the National Advisory Commission on Civil Disorders* (New York, 1968), pp. 128–29 (hereinafter cited as National Commission, *Report*).

8. Ted R. Gurr, *Why Men Rebel* (Princeton, 1971); John S. Adams, "The Geography of Riots and Civil Disorders in the 1960s," *Economic Geography* 48 (Jan. 1972): 24–42; Joe R. Feagin and Harlan Hahn, *Ghetto Revolts: The Politics of Violence in American Cities* (New York, 1973).

9. Nathan S. Caplan, "The New Ghetto Man: A Review of Recent Empirical Studies," *Journal of Social Issues* 26 (Winter 1970): 59–73.

10. David O. Sears and John B. McConahay, *The Politics of Violence: The New Urban Blacks and the Watts Riot* (Boston, 1973), pp. 20–33; James W. Button, *Black Violence: Political Impact of the 1960s Riots* (Princeton, 1978), pp. 4–9.

11. Edward C. Banfield, *The Unheavenly City: The Nature and Future of Our Urban Crisis* (Boston, 1970); William Ryan, *Blaming the Victim* (New York, 1971).

12. Allen D. Grimshaw, "A Study in Social Violence: Urban Race Riots in the United States," unpublished Ph.D. dissertation, University of Pennsylvania, 1959; August Meier and Elliott Rudwick, "Black Violence in the 20th Century," in *Violence in America: Historical and Comparative Perspectives*, Vol. 2, eds. Hugh D. Graham and Ted R. Gurr (Washington, D.C., 1969), pp. 307–16; Morris Janowitz, "Patterns of Collective Racial Violence," in *Violence in America*, Vol. 2, pp. 317–39; Richard M. Brown, *Strain of Violence: Historical Studies of American Racial Violence and Vigilantism* (New York, 1975), pp. 205–35.

13. Charles Crowe, "Racial Violence and Social Reform—Origins of the Atlanta Riot of 1906," *Journal of Negro History* 53 (July 1968): 234–56, and "Racial Massacre in Atlanta September 22, 1906," *Journal of Negro History* 54 (Apr. 1969): 150–73; William Ivy Hair, *Carnival of Fury: Robert Charles and the New Orleans Race Riot of 1900* (Baton Rouge, 1976); Seth M. Scheiner, *Negro Mecca: A History of the Negro in New York City, 1865–1920* (New York, 1965), pp. 113–40; Gilbert Osofsky, *Harlem: The Making of a Ghetto* (New York, 1966), pp. 46–52; James L. Crouthamel, "The Springfield Race Riot of 1908," *Journal of Negro History* 45 (July 1960): 164–81; John D. Weaver, *The Brownsville Raid* (New York, 1970); Ann J. Lane, *The Brownsville Affair: National Crisis and Black Reaction* (Port Washington, 1971); Robert V. Haynes, *A Night of Violence: The Houston Riot of 1917* (Baton Rouge, 1976); Elliott M. Rudwick, *Race Riot in East St. Louis, July 2, 1917* (Carbondale, Ill., 1964), pp. 146, 173, 218, 225; William M. Tuttle, Jr., *Race Riot: Chicago in the Red Summer of 1919* (New York, 1970) pp. 198–99, 264–65; Scott Ellsworth, *Death in a Promised Land: The Tulsa Riot of 1921* (Baton Route, 1982), p. 105, for the first quotation; Chicago Commission on Race Relations, *The Negro in Chicago: A Study of Race Relations and a Riot* (Chicago, 1922), pp. 11, 22–24; Arthur I. Waskow, *From Race Riot to Sit-Ins, 1919 and the 1960s: A Study in the Connections Between Conflict and Violence* (Garden City, N.Y., 1966); Richard Cortner, *A Mob Intent on Death: The NAACP and the Arkansas Race Riots* (Middletown, Conn., 1988); Mayor's Commission on Conditions in Harlem, *The Complete Report of Mayor La Guardia's Commission on the Harlem Riot of March 19, 1935* (New York, 1969), p. 12, for the second quotation, p. 17, for the third quotation; Mark Naison, *Communism in Harlem During the Depression* (Urbana, Ill., 1983), p. 141; Mauricio Mazón, *The Zoot-Suit Riots: The Psychology of Symbolic Annihilation* (Austin, 1984); James A. Burran III, "Racial Violence in the South During World War II," unpublished Ph.D. dissertation, University of Tennessee, 1977.

14. Alfred M. Lee and Norman D. Humphrey, *Race Riot* (New York, 1943), pp. 80–87, 82, also mentions C. F. Ramsay's study; Robert Shogan and Tom Craig, *The Detroit Race Riot: A Study in Violence* (Philadelphia, 1964), pp. 119–20 also cites Alfred M. Lee's and Norman D. Humphrey's account; Harvard Sitkoff, "The Detroit Race Riot of 1943," *Michigan History* 52 (Fall 1969): 183–206, does not describe the rioters.

15. Grimshaw, "A Study in Social Violence," pp. 232–58, omits Ramsay's study; George W. Beatty, "The Background and Causes of the 1943 Detroit Race Riot," unpublished senior thesis, Princeton University, 1954, pp. 118–27, draws on the accounts of the Governor's Committee and C. F. Ramsay to posit similar, though less comprehensive conclusions five years before Grimshaw.

16. Tuttle, *Race Riot*, p. 264; Dominic J. Capeci, Jr., *The Harlem Riot of 1943* (Philadelphia, 1977), pp. 115–33, 177–83; Harold Orlansky, *The Harlem Riot: A Study in Mass Frustration* (New York, 1943), pp. 8–22; Janowitz, "Patterns," p. 321.

17. Roberta Senechal, *The Sociogenesis of a Race Riot: Springfield, Illinois, in 1908* (Urbana, 1990).

18. Though the demographic profiles of Detroiters in the 1940 census do not reflect the impact of immigration between then and the riot three years later, they do provide an overview of the social milieu out of which those rioters who were residents of long-standing came. To identify that environment more accurately, we traced addresses of rioters to the police precincts in which they were located. If a precinct was home to at least 5 percent of the rioters, we selected all tracts in that precinct where a rioter lived; if the tract was 50 percent black it was classified as a black residence tract; otherwise we designated it as white. Hence, twenty black residence tracts were identified: 15, 119, 120, 121, 508, 509, 510, 511, 512, 528, 529, 534, 535, 536, 537, 543, 544, 545, 547, and 558. These tracts are generally clustered in the riot zone, indicating to us that black rioters tended to travel short distances to become involved in the disturbance. The twenty-two white tracts 52, 54, 57, 116, 154, 156, 180, 501, 514, 515, 518, 519, 522, 523, 530, 539, 568, 764, 765, 768, 774, and 776—showed a less concentrated pattern, more outside the riot zone.

The aggregate data from these tracts provided us with a general basis for comparing the rioters with area residents, most of whom refrained from violence. White residence tracts contained 102,372 persons (95.5 percent white), while black tracts comprised 92,718 individuals (84.5 percent black). U.S. Department of Commerce, Bureau of Census, *Sixteenth Census of the United States: 1940. Population and Housing Statistics for Census Tracts, Detroit, Michigan, and Adjacent Area* (Washington, D.C., 1942), p. 2, for the quotation, Table 1, pp. 4–7 (hereinafter cited as *Census Tracts*).

19. We calculated median age from the aggregate data for the tracts: 29.1 years for males in white tracts and 20 years for white rioters; 32 years for males in black tracts and 27 years for black male rioters; 29 years for females in black tracts and 24.5 years for black female rioters. Of N=29 ethnics in this study (seventeen Italians and twelve Poles), probably the sons of immigrants, twenty-two (75.9 percent) were less than twenty-two years old and, of these, twelve (81.8 percent) were eighteen years old or younger. *Census Tracts*, Table 2, pp. 8–68; City Plan Commission, *Master Plan Reports: The People of Detroit* (Detroit, 1944), p. 19.

20. Italians comprised 18.3 percent and Poles 17.9 percent of the whites enumerated in the census tracts; they made up 17 and 12.5 percent, respectively, of the riot precincts. *Census Tracts*, Table 3, pp. 69–150; City Plan Commission, *Master Plan: The People*, p. 19.

21. Median education was 8.7 years for all Detroiters, 8.1 years for those in the white tracts, and 7.2 years for those in the black tracts; median education was 9 years for white rioters and 8 years for black rioters. U.S. Department of Commerce, Bureau of Census, *Sixteenth Census of the United States: 1940. Population*, Vol. II, pt. 3 (Washington, D.C., 1943), Table A-39, p. 894 (hereinafter cited as *Population*); *Census Tracts*, Table 3, pp. 69–150.

22. Employment rate was 97 percent for black male rioters, 70.7 percent for black female rioters, and 89.6 percent for white male rioters. The 1940 employment rate was 89.3 percent for all Detroiters, 88.7 percent for males in the white tracts, 84 percent for males and 80.7 for females in the black tracts. *Population*, Table A-41, p. 895; *Census Tracts*, Table 3, pp. 69–150; Karen Tucker Anderson, "Last Hired, First Fired: Black Women Workers During World War II," *Journal of American History* 69 (June 1982): 85; City Plan Commission, *Master Plan Reports: The Economic Base of Detroit* (Detroit, 1944), p. 19.

23. Laborers made up 62.8 percent of the white male rioters, 87.3 percent of the black male rioters, and 27.6 percent of the black female rioters; domestic or service employees consisted of 1.2 percent white male rioters, 1 percent of black male rioters, and 58.6 percent of black female rioters. In 1940 laborers comprised 12.1 percent of the males

in white tracts, 24.3 percent of the males and 1.3 percent of the females in the black tracts; domestics or service workers constituted 6.8 percent of the males in white tracts, 19.4 percent of the males and 64.3 percent of the females in black tracts. *Census Tracts,* Table 3, pp. 69–150; Robert R. Nathan and Oscar Gass, *National Wage Policy for 1947* (Washington, D.C., 1946), Table 5, p. 25. The overrepresentation of "laborers" among all rioters is the result of most police assigning this designation to arrestees instead of listing their real occupations on the arrest tickets; for example, Ray M., a black welder, and Bedford B., a white machinist, were both written up as "laborers," Arrest Tickets 133 and 558, June 21, 1943, Duplicate Arrest Tickets, Reel 85, DPDR; Wayne County Probation Services, Cases 33 and 26, RCR.

24. Of Detroit's 425,547 occupied dwelling units in 1940, 166,933 (39.2 percent) were owner occupied and 258,614 (60.8 percent) were tenant occupied; the population per occupied dwelling unit for the city was 3.81 persons. Ownership in the white tracts was 36.1 percent; the median value of these units was $3,149; a tenant-occupied unit brought a monthly rent of $28.80; the population density per occupied dwelling unit was 4.02 persons. Of all dwelling units in the white tracts, occupied and vacant, 5.3 percent needed major repairs. Ownership in the black tracts was 14.8 percent; the median value of these units was $2,531; a tenant-occupied unit brought a monthly rent of $24.17; the population density per occupied dwelling unit was 4.3 persons. Of all dwelling units in the black tracts, occupied and vacant, 19.3 percent needed major repairs. *Census Tracts,* Table 1, p. 4, Table 4, p. 158, Table 5, pp. 164–92, Table 6, pp. 193–221; City Plan Commission, *Master Plan: The People,* p. 19.

25. Herbert J. Rushton, William E. Dowling, Oscar Olander, and John H. Witherspoon, *Factual Report of the Governor's Commission to Investigate the Riot Occurring in Detroit on June 21, 1943,* Aug. 11, 1943, Part II, Exhibit 24, p. 1, BHC (hereinafter cited as Governor's Committee, *Factual Report*).

26. Dominic J. Capeci, Jr., *Race Relations in Wartime Detroit: The Sojourner Truth Housing Controversy of 1942* (Philadelphia, 1984), pp. 59–63; Harriet Arnow, *The Dollmaker* (New York, 1954), for a powerful fictional account of the plight of white Southern migrants in wartime Detroit.

27. City Plan Commission, *Master Plan: The People,* p. 19.

28. Bureau of Intelligence (OWI), "Housing Problems in Four Pro-

duction Communities, Part I: Detroit," 8 Oct. 1942, pp. 2, 3, Box 9, Likert Papers, MHC; William K. Divers to John D. Blandford, Jr., 24 May 1943, Box 116, RG 207, NARS; Anonymous, UAW Inter-Office Communication, n.d., p. 1, Box 15, United Automobile Workers Research Department Collection, ALUA.

29. Capeci, *Race Relations*, pp. 33–37, 167–75, for information in this and the following paragraph; Betty Smith Jenkins, "The Racial Policies of the Detroit Housing Commission and Their Administration," unpublished M.A. thesis, Wayne State University, 1950.

30. Capeci, *Race Relations*, pp. 30, 32; August Meier and Elliott Rudwick, *Black Detroit and the Rise of the UAW* (New York, 1979), pp. 136, 153, 154; Anonymous, "Employment of Negroes in Detroit," Jan. 1943, Box 9, UAW Research Department Collection, ALUA, for the January figures, the percentage being given wrongly as 1.6; Memorandum for Joseph D. Keenan (from Anthony Luchek), 14 July 1943, p. 6, for quotation, p. 7, Box 49, RG 212, NARS; Jacqueline Jones, *Labor of Love, Labor of Sorrow: Black Women, Work, and the Family from Slavery to the Present* (New York, 1985).

31. Capeci, *Race Relations*, pp. 69–74; Meier and Rudwick, *Black Detroit*, pp. 162–74. Nearly thirty laborers were suspended for their roles in the Packard strike.

32. Capeci, *Race Relations*, pp. 65–66; Beatty, "The Background and Causes," pp. 61–64, 63, for the quotation; Daniel B. Neusom, "The Michigan Civil Rights Law and Its Enforcement," unpublished M.A. thesis, Wayne State University, 1952.

33. Capeci, *Race Relations*, pp. 21–22, 42–44; City Plan Commission, *Master Plan: The People*, p. 29; Federal Bureau of Investigation, "Survey of Racial Conditions in the United States," 1944, pp. 16, 65, Box 44, OF 10-B, FDRL (hereinafter cited as FBI, "Survey").

34. Philip J. Funigiello, *The Challenge to Urban Liberalism: Federal-City Relations During World War II* (Knoxville, 1978), pp. 136–39; Alan Clive, *State of War*, pp. 207–13; Paul Wiers, "Wartime Increases in Michigan Delinquency," *American Sociological Review* X (Aug. 1945): 515–23.

35. City Plan Commission, *Master Plan: The People*, pp. 29–30.

36. Earl Brown, *Why Race Riots?* (New York, 1944), p. 26.

37. Capeci, *Race Relations*, p. 46; Clive, *State of War*, pp. 210–11; FBI, "Survey," p. 16, for the third quotation, pp. 90–91, for the first and second quotations; Anonymous (USAI), "Clashes Between Whites and Negroes, Detroit, Michigan, 13 June 1943," File 2412, RG 319,

WNRC; Governors' Committee, *Factual Report*, Part I, p. 15, and Part III, pp. 1–7. FBI agents claimed that longtime residents committed "the bulk of the juvenile crimes" for the two and one-half years before the riot; but in regard to crimes committed during the riot, they contended—unconvincingly—that the perpetrators came primarily from the South and had lived "for a comparatively short time" in Detroit. Bureau personnel referred to specific "records," but did not identify them and failed to cite specific statistics or identify rioters by race, gender, or other characteristics. They based the "spearheaded" remark on "personal observation."

38. Detroit Police Department, *Seventy-seventh Annual Report: 1942* (Detroit, 1943), p. 68; Governor's Committee, *Factual Report*, Part III, p. 5, states that, on the basis of cases prosecuted in 1942, blacks comprised 10 percent of the population and committed 71 percent of all major crimes.

39. Department of Parks and Recreation, Property Distribution Chart, 16 Mar. 1944, Box 17, Detroit Committee on Community Relations Collection, ALUA; Rev. Merrill Bates, Speech, n.d., Box 88, Civil Rights Congress of Michigan Collection, ALUA; Capeci, *Race Relations*, pp. 22–24, 44–45; Beatty, "The Background and Causes," pp. 55–59; Edward Gamache to Jeffries, 18 July 1940, Box 12, Mayor's Papers (1940), BHC, for the quotation.

40. Capeci, *Race Relations*, pp. 67–68; Clive, *State of War*, pp. 112–14; Beatty, "The Background and Causes," p. 61; John C. Dancy to Floyd C. Covington, 12 Aug. 1942, Reel 10, DULP; John H. Witherspoon to Jeffries, 17 Dec. 1943, Box, 7, Mayor's Papers (1943), BHC, for the quotation; Memorandum for the Detective Inspector, Homicide Squad (from John R. Machlik), 29 July 1943, Box 2, Detroit Committee on Community Relations Collection, ALUA.

41. Capeci, *Race Relations*, pp. 55–58; Detroit *Tribune*, 15 Aug. 1942, p. 1, 24 Apr. 1943, p. 1, and 15 May 1943, p. 1 (hereinafter cited as *Tribune*); J. A. Ulio to Harry F. Kelly, 17 Apr. 1943, Box 142, Kelly Papers, MSA; Paul Keen, "Behind the Headlines," Michigan *Chronicle*, 15 May 1943, p. 4 (hereinafter cited as *Chronicle*); Bernard C. Nalty, *Strength for the Fight: A History of Black Americans in the Military* (New York, 1986), pp. 125–203, for an overview of black hardships and contributions in World War II.

42. Capeci, *Race Relations*, pp. 58–59; Bureau of Intelligence (OFF), "Preliminary Appraisal of the Present Negro Situation," 9 Mar. 1942, p. 2, Box 9, Likert Collection, MHC, for the quotations; Bureau of

Agricultural Economics (USDA), "The Ethnic Axis: Negroes" (rough copy), c. 1943, pp. 25–26, Box 9, Likert Collection, MHC.

43. Bureau of Intelligence (OWI), "White Attitudes Toward Negroes," 5 Aug. 1942, pp. 2, 13–14, Box 10, Likert Collection, MHC, for a survey of whites "in all parts of the country between June 22 and July 7." Asked if blacks were less patriotic than whites, 14 percent of Northeast and West respondents believed they were less patriotic and 14 percent did not know; asked if blacks would make as good soldiers as whites, 22 percent said no and 16 percent did not know.

44. *Tribune,* 3 Apr. 1943, pp. 1, 3, and 1 May 1943, p. 1; Bureau of Agricultural Economics (USDA), "The Social Dynamics of Detroit," 3 Dec. 1942, p. 37, for the quotation, Box 10, Likert Collection, MHC.

45. Walter White to James J. McClendon, 16 Apr. 1943, Box 248, General Office Files, 1940–1955, NAACP.

46. *Tribune,* 12 June 1943, pp. 1, 2.

47. Military Intelligence Division (USDW), "Negro Conference Prior to Race Riot, Detroit, Michigan," 23 July 1943, Box 18, RG 319, WNRC, for the quotation; Meier and Rudwick, *Black Detroit,* pp. 191–92; Shogan and Craig, *The Detroit Race Riot,* pp. 9–10.

48. NAACP Press Release, 3 Aug. 1942, Box 17 (unprocessed), Detroit Branch File, NAACP; Roy Wilkins to Daisy E. Lampkin, 26 June 1943, Box 566, General Office Files, 1940–1955, NAACP.

49. Capeci, *Race Relations,* passim, for the information in this and the following two paragraphs unless cited otherwise.

50. C. F. Ramsay, "Analysis of Interviews Made with Prisoners Taken in the Detroit Race Riot," n.d., p. 10, Box 74, Kelly Papers, MSA; Memorandum: Statements of Negro Prisoners Taken at the Piquette Armory, June 24th, 1943, to Thomas Collady (from Leo M. Wendall), 24 June 1943, passim, RG 79-10, MSA.

51. FBI, "Survey," 91, for the juveniles; note 36 above.

52. Arnold R. Hirsch, *Making the Second Ghetto: Race and Housing in Chicago, 1940–1960* (New York, 1983), p. 42.

53. Charles R. Lawrence, Jr., "Race Riots in the United States, 1942–1946," in *Negro Year Book,* Jessie Parkhurst Guzman (Atlanta, 1947), pp. 233–37; Burran, "Racial Violence in the South"; Mazón, *The Zoot-Suit Riots.*

54. Nelson Foote, "Special Report on Negro Housing Situation in Detroit," 5 Mar. 1942, p. 1, Box 116, RG 207, NARS.

55. Dennis C. Dickerson, *Out of the Crucible: Black Steelworkers in Western Pennsylvania, 1875–1980* (Albany, 1986), p. 165.

56. Hirsch, *Making the Second Ghetto,* p. 43, for the first quotation, p. 44, for the second quotation. Officers of the Chicago *Defender* first broached the idea for a conference.

57. Capeci, *The Harlem Riot of 1943,* pp. 45–67, 68–90, 82, for the quotation, pp. 134–47, 166–67, for the information in this and the following paragraph.

58. Memorandum for the President (from Jonathan Daniels), 22 June 1943, PPF 1820, FDRL; Francis Biddle to Franklin D. Roosevelt, 15 July 1943, Box 213, HLIP; Capeci, *The Harlem Riot of 1943,* pp. 90–98, 148–56; Charles W. Eagles, "Two 'Double V's': Jonathan Daniels, FDR, and Race Relations During World War II," *North Carolina Historical Review* 59 (Summer 1982): 252–70, *Jonathan Daniels and Race Relations: The Evolution of a Southern Liberal* (Knoxville, 1982), pp. 83–120.

59. Francis Biddle to Franklin D. Roosevelt, 15 July 1943, Box 213, HLIP.

60. Bernard F. Robinson, "War and Peace Conflicts in the United States," *Phylon* IV (1943): 311, 325–27; Warren Schaich, "A Relationship Between Collective Racial Violence and War," *Journal of Black Studies* 5 (June 1975): 375, 385–87, 390–92; Michael Stohl, *War and Domestic Political Violence* (Beverly Hills, 1976), pp. 103–06, 115–117, 121.

61. Stanley Lieberson and Arnold R. Silverman, "The Precipitants and Underlying Conditions of Race Riots," *American Sociological Review* 30 (Dec. 1965): 890–91; Milton Bloombaum, "The Conditions Underlying Race Riots as Portrayed by Multidimensional Scalogram Analysis: A Reanalysis of the Lieberson and Silverman Data," *American Sociological Review* 33 (Feb. 1968): 83.

62. Capeci, *The Harlem Riot of 1943,* pp. 171–75; Alex L. Swan, "The Harlem and Detroit Riots of 1943: A Comparative Analysis," *Berkeley Journal of Sociology* 16 (1971–1972): 75–93; National Commission, *Report,* p. 110.

63. Hirsch, *Making the Second Ghetto,* pp. 45–49, 50, for the quotation; St. Clair Drake and Horace R. Cayton, *Black Metropolis: A Study of Negro Life in a Northern City,* rev. ed., Vol. 1 (New York, 1970), pp. 93, 289.

64. Drake and Cayton, *Black Metropolis,* Vol. 1, pp. 92, 93, for the respective quotations; Lieberson and Silverman, "The Precipitants," p. 893, challenges the premise that "rapid population change accompanies riots"; White, "What Caused?" p. 2.

65. National Opinion Research Center, "A National Barometer of Tension Areas," n.d., Box 1, Detroit Committee on Community Relations, ALUA, for the first and second quotations: among whites, 64 percent in Chicago and 43 percent in Detroit believed that blacks were doing "all that they can to help the war effort"; 40 percent in Chicago and 58 percent in Detroit wanted segregated sections in streetcars and busses; 27 percent in Chicago and 39 percent in Detroit said it would make a difference if a black person was hired to work beside them. Eighty-three percent of the black Detroiters and 72 percent of the black Chicagoans said black people were not "getting chances enough to help win the war effort"; Lee and Humphrey, *Race Riot*, pp. 7, 8, for the third quotation: Earlier in 1943, blacks in Chicago and Detroit registered the same 78 percent response to the question regarding their opportunities; by March of that year, then, black Chicagoans felt less and black Detroiters more discrimination in the war efforts of their respective cities; Memorandum to Lieutenant Colonel Harris (from James F. Perry), 22 June 1943, Box 18, RG 319, WNRC, for the fourth quotation.

66. Drake and Clayton, *Black Metropolis*, Vol. 1, pp. 91–92, contend that "no provocative incident occurred in the Negro community," a reason why Chicago escaped riot; yet they also state that "upon several occasions" disorder "seemed about to happen," and cite the teenager killed by police as one example.

67. Allen D. Grimshaw, "Actions of Police and the Military in American Race Riots," in *Racial Violence in the United States*, ed. Allen D. Grimshaw (Chicago, 1969), p. 286, for the first quotation; Janowitz, "Patterns," p. 319, for the second quotation; Bloombaum, "The Conditions Underlying," p. 90; Lieberson and Silverman, "The Precipitants," p. 898, for the third quotation.

68. Hirsch, *Making the Second Ghetto*, pp. 46, 50–52; Drake and Clayton, *Black Metropolis*, p. 92.

69. Joe William Trotter, *Black Milwaukee: The Making of an Industrial Proletariat, 1915–45* (Urbana, Ill., 1985), p. 229.

70. Bryan T. Downes, "Social and Political Characteristics of Riot Cities: A Comparative Study," *Social Science Quarterly* 49 (Dec. 1968): 511, for the fourth and fifth quotations, p. 513, for the first and second quotations, p. 516, note 30, for the third quotation, p. 520, for the sixth quotation.

71. Donald I. Warren, "Neighborhood Structure and Riot Behavior in Detroit: Some Exploratory Findings," *Social Problems* 16 (Spring 1969): 464–84; Donald C. Marsh, Alvin D. Loving, and Eleanor P.

Wolf, "Some Aspects of Negro-Jewish Relationships in Detroit, Michigan," n.d., pp. 2–3, unprocessed material, Marsh Collection, ALUA, for an example of greater transiency among blacks in the east side than in the west side; C. F. Ramsay, "Analysis of Interviews Made with Prisoners Taken in the Detroit Race Riot," 2 Aug. 1943, p. 10, Box 74, Kelly Papers, MSA, for 227 of 309 black detainees contending that they did not associate with clubs.

72. Adams, "The Geography of Riots," p. 284.

73. William Julius Wilson, *The Declining Significance of Race: Blacks and Changing American Institutions* (Chicago, 1980) and *The Truly Disadvantaged: The Inner City, the Underclass, and Public Policy* (Chicago, 1987); Sidney M. Willhelm, *Who Needs the Negro?* (Garden City, N.Y., 1969).

74. Robert Curvin and Bruce Porter, *Blackout Looting! New York City, July 13, 1977* (New York, 1979), pp. 4–7, 38, for the first quotation, p. 39, for the second and third quotations, pp. 42–43, 86, 112–14.

75. Ibid., p. 86. Given their increased participation from 1943 to 1967, surprisingly fewer women and juveniles attracted police attention during the blackout.

76. Bruce Porter and Marvin Dunn, *The Miami Riot of 1980: Crossing the Bounds* (Lexington, Mass., 1984), p. 115, for the quotations, pp. 110–18, 181–200. Porter and Dunn identify neither gender nor other significant socioeconomic characteristics, but they note that only 32 percent of the rioters had been arrested before and only 24 percent had been convicted of previous crimes; that eighteen to twenty-one-year-olds comprised 23.9 percent of the rioters, twenty-two to twenty-nine-year-olds 42.81 percent, thirty to thirty-nine-year-olds 21.17 percent, and forty-year-olds and older 11.58 percent.

77. *Time*, 2 June 1980, p. 11, for the quotation of Marvin Dunn.

78. Jeffrey Schmalz, "Dreams and Despair Collide as Miami Searches for Itself," *New York Times*, 23 Jan. 1989, p. 1, for the quotation, p. B8; Jeffrey Schmalz, "Miami Tensions Simmering 3 Months After Violence," *New York Times* (national edition), 10 Apr. 1989, p. A8; Raymond A. Mohl, "Ethnic Politics in Miami, 1960–1986," in *Shades of the Sunbelt: Essays on Ethnicity, Race, and the Urban South*, eds. Randall M. Miller and George E. Pozzetta (Boca Raton, Fla., 1989), pp. 149, 151, 155; Alejandro Portes, "From South of the Border: Hispanic Minorities in the United States," in *Immigration Reconsidered: History, Sociology, and Politics*, ed. Virginia Yans-Mclaughlin (New York, 1990), pp. 164–66, 180–81. Miami contains several other Hispanic

groups—including Nicaraguans and Puerto Ricans—plus Haitians, whose competition with both native-born blacks and Cubans provides the potential for violence from another quarter. See *Newsweek*, 17 Dec. 1990, p. 32, for the most recent riot involving Puerto Ricans, whose socioeconomic position most resembles that of blacks.

79. David E. Pitt, "Jogger's Attackers Terrorized at Least 9 in 2 Hours," *New York Times*, 22 Apr. 1989, pp. 1, 30; Craig Wolff, "Attacks Were Planned, Two Park Victims Say," *New York Times*, 22 Apr. 1989, p. 30; Gina Kolata, "Grim Seeds of Park Rampage Found in East Harlem Streets," *New York Times*, 2 May 1989, pp. C1, C13; Michael Oreskes, "Blacks in New York: The Anguish of Political Failure," *New York Times*, 31 Mar. 1987, pp. B1, B4, for the traditional black-Cuban division.

80. George James, "Reports of Racial Assaults Rise Significantly in New York City," *New York Times*, 23 Sept. 1987, pp. B1, B6; Todd S. Purdum, "Acts Linked to Increase in Bias Cases," *New York Times*, 25 Dec. 1987, pp. B1, B8; Steven Erlanger, "After Howard Beach: A New Militancy?" *New York Times*, 27 Dec. 1987, Sec, IV, p. 7.

81. James N. Baker (with Tony Clifton and Kim Fararo), "A Racist Ambush in New York," *Newsweek*, 4 Sept. 1989, p. 25.

82. Ronald Smothers, "Housing Segregation: New Twists and Old Results," *New York Times*, 1 Apr. 1987, p. B4, for Bensonhurst being 93 percent white, Jews comprising 30 percent of that figure; John Kifner, "Bensonhurst: A Tough Code in Defense of a Closed World," *New York Times*, 1 Sept. 1989, pp. 1, B4.

83. R. Drummond Ayres, "Student Gathering in Virginia Turns Violent; 4 Injured," *New York Times* (national edition), 4 Sept. 1989, p. 7; R. Drummond Ayres, "Virginia Beach Is Quiet After Violence," *New York Times* (national edition), 5 Sept. 1989, p. A12; R. Drummond Ayres, "Officials Chided in Virginia on Labor Day Racial Strife," *New York Times* (national edition), 30 Jan. 1990, p. A16; Labor Day Review Commission, *Final Report* (Virginia Beach, Va.: Labor Day Review Commission, 1990), p. 4; Diane C. Roche to Dominic J. Capeci, Jr., 2 July 1990. We thank Ms. Roche of the Labor Day Task Force for providing a copy of the Labor Day Review Commission's *Final Report*.

84. Labor Day Review Commission, *Final Report*, pp. 4, 12. Neither police nor commissioners provide arrestee statistics; the commissioners viewed the only available videotape of participants from one motel.

85. Feagin and Hahn, *Ghetto Revolts*, p. 48, for the first quotation;

Robert A. Mendelsohn, "Profile of the Riot Causes and Participants," in *A City in Racial Crisis*, ed. Leonard Gordon (Dubuque, 1971), p. 83, for the second quotation.

86. Ken Auletta, *The Underclass* (New York, 1982), pp. 46–47; David Gelman (with Peter McKillop), "Going 'Wilding' in the City," *Newsweek*, 8 May 1989, p. 65, for the quotation of psychologist James P. Comer, Yale Child Study Center.

87. Ayres, "Student Gathering," p. 7.

88. Alan Weisman, "Flatbush, 60's; Bensonhurst, 89," *New York Times*, 5 Sept. 1989, p. 19. Literally, *mulignan* means eggplant in Sicilian-American dialect, but its deep purple seemingly black skin also provides Italian-Americans with a pejorative term for black people.

89. Gary T. Marx, ed., *Racial Conflict: Tension and Change in American Society* (Boston, 1971), pp. 1–8.

90. Ibid., p. 7; Lynn A. Curtis, *Violence, Race, and Culture* (Lexington, Mass., 1975), pp. 78–82.

91. Quoted in Kifner, "Bensonhurst," p. B4.

92. *New York Times*, 3 July 1989, p. 23; Sarah Lyall, "After Jones Beach Violence, State Seeks Better Controls," *New York Times*, 4 July 1989, p. 33. Jones Beach students fought with other students, and that brought police to the scene. Other student riots occurred the following year, for example in San Luis Obispo and Chico, California, but they were confined largely to college campuses and lacked a racial focus.

93. Labor Day Review Commission, *Final Report*, p. 5.

94. Samuel G. Freedman, "New York Race Tension Is Rising Despite Gains," *New York Times*, 29 Mar. 1987, p. 28.

95. David Gelman, et al., "The Mind of the Rapist," *Newsweek*, 23 July 1990, pp. 48, 49.

96. Sam Roberts, "The Region," *New York Times*, 3 Sept. 1989, p. 6, for the views of sociologist Herbert J. Gans, Columbia University; CBS, "48 Hours: Simmer in the City," 12 July 1990; Smothers, "Housing Segregation: New Twists and Old Results," p. B4, for the quotation.

97. National Commission, *Report*, pp. 410–83.

APPENDIX A

1. Norman K. Denzin, *The Research Act*, 3d ed. (Englewood Cliffs, N.J., 1989), pp. 234–47, and Eugene J. Webb, et al., *Unobtrusive Measures: Nonreactive Research in the Social Sciences*, 7th printing (Chicago,

1971), pp. 1-34, for advantages of multiple methods (triangulation); Earl Babbie, *The Practice of Social Research*, 5th ed. (Belmont, Cal., 1989), p. 321, for advantages of multiple sources (corroboration).

2. Claire Selltiz, et al., *Research Methods in Social Relations* (New York, 1963), p. 330.

3. William M. Tuttle, Jr., *Race Riot: Chicago in the Red Summer of 1919* (New York, 1970), p. vii.

4. Fred N. Kerlinger, *Foundations of Behavioral Research*, 2d ed. (New York, 1973), pp. 701-03, for potential distortions in secondary sources.

5. Denzin, *The Research Act*, p. 253.

6. Babbie, *The Practice of Social Research*, pp. 313-16, for the questions of reliability and validity when using archival collections.

7. Appendix B, Table 1, for the comparison of variables drawn from the sample with those reported by the Governor's Committee, and Appendix B, Table 2, for the sample itself.

8. Three hundred and forty-three subjects comprised this study: 205 black males drawn in a random selection, 96 white males, and 42 black females. Appendix B, Table 3, for the characteristics of these distinct groups of rioters. Three white females were arrested on June 21 and June 22, one for drunkenness and two for shoplifting, but none for riot-related offenses.

9. Of N=343, 173 misdemeanants were traced in the Misdemeanor Calendar and 170 felons were located in the Recorder's Court Files.

10. Seventy-two rioters (thirty-eight black males, twenty-six white males, and eight black females) were sentenced to the Detroit House of Correction; eighty-five arrestees (sixty-eight black males and seventeen white males for whom probation records exist) were examined. All official probation records for female offenders have been destroyed, though inadvertently a handful survive in the Recorder's Court File.

11. Recorder's Court File A-34601, BHC, for the example of Goldie W.

12. Governor's Committee, *Factual Report*, Part I, pp. 4, 6, for the identification of one female juvenile, Mattie Mae B.

13. Of N=48 owners (seventeen of whose businesses were hit more than once), thirty-two were identified as Jewish, one as black, and seven as female. The ethnic and racial identity of white rioters and all proprietors was made possible by Detroiters: Phillip Applebaum,

president emeritus, Jewish Historical Society of Michigan; Victoria and Judge Elvin L. Davenport (retired); Jerome Kelman, attorney; Alvin L. Kushner, executive director, Jewish Community Council; Benedict Markowski and Margaret Wart (retired), researchers, Burton Historical Collection; Leonard M. Simons, president emeritus, Detroit Historical Commission; and by Louis Wetsman of Southfield, Michigan; Carol Lieberwitz, of Springfield, Missouri; Rabbi David Wulcher of Huntington, West Virginia, and Rabbi David J. Zucker of Aurora, Colorado.

14. Governor's Committee, *Factual Report*, Part II, Exhibits 20 and 21.

15. N=309 for every tenth entry drawn from over 3,000 entries in the Police Force Books, I (8/3/17–9/25/18), J (10/11/18–1/16/20), N (11/1/23–7/31/24), Q (11/1/25–7/5/26), W (3/12/34–6/2/36), X (6/2/37–3/24/41), Y (3/24/41–1/25/43) and Z (1/25/43–9/10/45), BHC.

16. Memorandum: Statements of Negro Prisoners Taken at the Piquette Armory, June 24th, 1943, to Thomas Colladay (from Leo M. Wendell), 24 June 1943, RG 79-10, MSA.

17. National Advisory Commission on Civil Disorders, *Report of the National Advisory Commission on Civil Disorders* (New York, 1968), p. 171, for the data base; Manpower Administration (U.S. Department of Labor), "The Detroit Riot: A Profile of 500 Prisoners" (Mar. 1968), pp. 1–28, Vertical File, ALUA, for the arrestees; Nathan S. Caplan and Jeffery M. Paige, "A Study of Ghetto Rioters," *Scientific American* 219 (Aug. 1968): 15–21, for the self-identified rioters.

18. Babbie, *The Practice of Social Research*, pp. 86–87, for the risks of drawing unwarranted conclusions about individuals when analyzing aggregated data.

19. David Caplovitz, *The Stages of Social Research* (New York, 1983), pp. 161–87, for the role of qualitative data in combination with quantitative data.

Selected Bibliography

MANUSCRIPTS

Archives of Labor and Urban Affairs, Walter P. Reuther Library,
    Wayne State University, Detroit
    Civil Rights Congress of Michigan
    Detroit Committee on Community Relations
    Donald C. Marsh
    Metropolitan Detroit Council of Churches
    National Association for the Advancement of Colored People
    Stanley Nowak
    George Schermer
    United Automobile Workers Research Department
Burton Historical Collection, Detroit Public Library, Detroit
    Malcolm Bingay
    Detroit Citizens League
    Detroit House of Correction, General Register of Prisoners
    Detroit House of Correction, Index to Prisoners' Register
    Jewish Welfare Federation
    Mayor's Papers: Edward J. Jeffries, Jr.
    Police Force Books
    Recorder's Court Criminal Calendar
    Recorder's Court Files
The Catholic University Archives, Mullen Library, Washington, D.C.
    Francis J. Haas

Library of Congress, Washington, D.C.
   Harold L. Ickes
   National Association for the Advancement of Colored People
   National Urban League
Michigan Historical Collections, Bentley Historical Library, University of Michigan, Ann Arbor
   Detroit Urban League (microfilm edition)
   Josephine Goman
   Donald S. Leonard
   Renis Likert
   Gerald L. K. Smith
Michigan State Archives, Lansing
   Record Group 42. Executive Office: Harry F. Kelly
   Record Group 79-10. Department of Military Affairs (Office of Adjutant General)
Municipal Archives, New York, New York
   Fiorello H. La Guardia
National Archives and Records Service, Washington, D.C.
   Record Group 107. Office of Civilian Aide to the Secretary of War
   Record Group 179. War Production Board
   Record Group 195. Federal Home Loan Bank System
   Record Group 207. Department of Housing and Urban Development
   Record Group 212. President's Committee for Congested Production Areas
   Record Group 389. Provost Marshal General
Recorder's Court, Frank Murphy Hall of Justice, Detroit
   Misdemeanor Calendar
   Wayne County Probation Services
Franklin D. Roosevelt Library, Hyde Park, New York
   Franklin D. Roosevelt
Washington National Records Center, Suitland, Maryland
   Record Group 319. War Department Special Staffs

LOCAL, STATE, AND FEDERAL AGENCIES

Detroit Police Department, Detroit
   Duplicate Arrest Tickets, 1943, Reel 85
   Jesse Stewart Personnel File
Federal Bureau of Investigation, Washington, D.C.
   Detroit Riot (1943) File

Michigan State Police, Lansing
    Detroit Riot (1943) File

GOVERNMENT DOCUMENTS

Chicago Commission on Race Relations. *The Negro in Chicago: A Study of Race Relations and a Riot.* Chicago: University of Chicago Press, 1922.
City Plan Commission. *Master Plan Reports: The Economic Base of Detroit.* Detroit: City Plan Commission, 1944.
———. *Master Plan Reports: The People of Detroit.* Detroit: City Plan Commission, 1944.
Detroit Police Department. *Seventy-seventh Annual Report: 1942.* Detroit: Bureau of Records, 1943.
———. "Statistical Report on the Civil Disorder Occurring in the City of Detroit, July 1967." Unpublished report, Detroit Police Department, n.d.
Journal of the Common Council, 1943. Detroit: Inland Press, 1944.
Labor Day Review Commission. *Final Report.* Virginia Beach, Va.: Labor Day Review Commission, 1990.
Mayor's Commission on Conditions in Harlem. *The Complete Report of Mayor La Guardia's Commission on the Harlem Riot of March 19, 1935.* New York: Arno Press & The New York Times, 1969.
Nathan, Robert R., and Oscar Gass. *National Wage Policy for 1947.* Washington, D.C.: Government Printing Office, 1946.
National Advisory Commission on Civil Disorders. *Report of the National Advisory Commission on Civil Disorders.* New York: Bantam Books, 1968.
———. *Supplemental Studies for the National Advisory Commission on Civil Disorders.* New York: Frederick A. Praeger, Publishers, 1968.
Rushton, Herbert J., William E. Dowling, Oscar Olander, and John H. Witherspoon. *Factual Report of the Governor's Committee to Investigate the Riot Occurring in Detroit on June 21, 1943.* Detroit: Wayne County Photostatic Department, 1943.
U.S. Department of Commerce, Bureau of the Census. *Sixteenth Census of the United States: 1940. Population.* Vol. II, pt. 3. Washington, D.C.: Government Printing Office, 1943.
———. *Sixteenth Census of the United States: 1940. Population and Housing Statistics for Census Tracts, Detroit, Michigan and Adjacent Area.* Washington, D.C.: Government Printing Office, 1942.

U.S. Manpower Administration. "The Detroit Riot: A Profile of 500 Prisoners." Unpublished report, Department of Labor, 1968.

ORAL HISTORY

Authors
    Donald C. Marsh, Detroit, 6 June 1978 and 13 June 1978
    Aaron Shifman, West Bloomfield, Michigan, 17 Mar. 1987
    Mendel Shifman, West Bloomfield, Michigan, 14 Mar. 1987
    Clifford I. Whipple, Springfield, Missouri, 25 Apr. 1989
    Eleanor P. Wolf, Detroit, 12 June 1978
Blacks in the Labor Movement Collection, Archives of Labor and Urban Affairs
    Charles A. Hill
    Beulah T. Whitby

MAGAZINES AND NEWSPAPERS

The Civic Searchlight (Detroit)
The Cross and the Flag (Detroit)
The Crisis
Detroit News
Detroit Times
Detroit Tribune
Ford Facts (Detroit)
Michigan Chronicle (Detroit)
New York Times
Newsweek
PM (New York)
Race Relations: A Monthly Summary of Events and Trends

TELEVISION PROGRAMS

CBS, "48 Hours: Simmer in the City," 12 July 1990.

BOOKS

Aaron, Daniel, ed. *America in Crisis: Fourteen Crucial Episodes in American History.* Hamden, Conn.: Archon Books, 1971.
Arnow, Harriet. *The Dollmaker.* New York: Macmillan Co., 1954.

Auletta, Ken. *The Underclass*. New York: Random House, 1982.
Babbie, Earl. *The Practice of Social Research*. 5th ed. Belmont, Cal.: Wadsworth Publishing Co., 1989.
Banfield, Edward C. *The Unheavenly City: The Nature and Future of Our Urban Crisis*. Boston: Little, Brown, & Co., 1970.
Blalock, Hubert M., Jr. *Toward a Theory of Minority-Group Relations*. New York: John Wiley & Sons, 1967.
Boskin, Joseph, ed. *Urban Racial Violence in the Twentieth Century*. 2d ed. Beverly Hills, Cal.: Glencoe Press, 1976.
Brown, Earl. *Why Race Riots?* New York: Public Affairs Committee, 1944.
Brown, Robert M. *Strain of Violence: Historical Studies of American Violence and Vigilantism*. New York: Oxford University Press, 1975.
Brown, Roger. *Social Psychology*. New York: Free Press, 1965.
Button, James W. *Black Violence: Political Impact of the 1960s Riots*. Princeton: Princeton University Press, 1978.
Capeci, Dominic J., Jr. *The Harlem Riot of 1943*. Philadelphia: Temple University Press, 1977.
———. *Race Relations in Wartime Detroit: The Sojourner Truth Housing Controversy of 1942*. Philadelphia: Temple University Press, 1984.
Caplovitz, David. *The Stages of Social Research*. New York: John Wiley & Sons, 1983.
Carlson, John Roy [Avedis Derounian]. *Under Cover*. New York: E. P. Dutton & Co., Inc., 1943.
Clive, Alan. *State of War: Michigan in World War II*. Ann Arbor: University of Michigan Press, 1979.
Cortner, Richard. *A Mob Intent on Death: The NAACP and the Arkansas Race Riots*. Middleton, Conn.: Wesleyan University Press, 1988.
Coser, Lewis A. *The Functions of Social Conflict*. Glencoe, Ill.: Free Press, 1956.
Curtis, Lynn A. *Violence, Race, and Culture*. Lexington, Mass.: Heath Lexington Books, 1975.
Curvin, Robert, and Bruce Porter. *Blackout Looting! New York City, July 13, 1977*. New York: Gardner Press, Inc., 1979.
Daly, Charles U., ed. *Urban Violence*. Chicago: University of Chicago Center for Policy Study, 1969.
Denby, Charles. *Indignant Heart*. Boston: South End Press, 1978.
Denzin, Norman K. *The Research Act*. 3d ed. Englewood Cliffs, N.J.: Prentice-Hall, Inc., 1989.
Detroit Urban League. *The People Beyond 12th Street: A Survey of Atti-*

tudes of Detroit Negroes After the Riot of 1967. Detroit: Detroit Urban League, 1967.

Dickerson, Dennis C. *Out of the Crucible: Black Steelworkers in Western Pennsylvania, 1875–1980*. Albany: State University of New York Press, 1986.

Drake, St. Clair, and Horace R. Cayton. *Black Metropolis: A Study of Negro Life in a Northern City*. rev. ed. 2 vols. New York: Harcourt, Brace, & World, Inc., 1970.

Eagles, Charles W. *Jonathan Daniels and Race Relations: The Evolution of a Southern Liberal*. Knoxville: University of Tennessee Press, 1982.

Ellsworth, Scott. *Death in a Promised Land: The Tulsa Riot of 1921*. Baton Rouge: Louisiana State University Press, 1982.

Feagin, Joe R., and Harlan Hahn. *Ghetto Revolts: The Politics of Violence in American Cities*. New York: Macmillan Co., 1973.

Fine, Sidney. *Violence in the Model City: The Cavanagh Administration, Race Relations, and the Detroit Riot of 1967*. Ann Arbor: University of Michigan Press, 1989.

Finkle, Lee. *Forum for Protest: The Black Press During World War II*. Rutherford, N.J.: Fairleigh Dickinson University Press, 1975.

Flaming, Karl H. *Who Riots and Why? Black and White Perspectives in Milwaukee*. Milwaukee: Milwaukee Urban League. 1968.

Fogelson, Robert M. *Violence as Protest: A Study of Riots and Ghettos*. Garden City, N.Y.: Doubleday & Co., Inc., 1971.

Fredrickson, George M. *White Supremacy: A Comparative Study in American and South African History*. New York: Oxford University Press, 1981.

Funigiello, Philip J. *The Challenge to Urban Liberalism: Federal-City Relations During World War II*. Knoxville: University of Tennessee Press, 1978.

Gordon, Leonard, ed. *A City in Racial Crisis: The Case of Detroit Pre- and Post- the 1967 Riot*. Dubuque, Iowa: William C. Brown, Co., 1971.

Graham, Hugh D., and Ted R. Gurr, eds. *Violence in America: Historical and Comparative Perspectives*. 2 vols. Washington, D.C.: Government Printing Office, 1969.

Grimshaw, Allen, D., ed. *Racial Violence in the United States*. Chicago: Aldine Publishing Co., 1969.

Gurr, Ted R. *Why Men Rebel*. Princeton: Princeton University Press, 1971.

Guzman, Jessie Parkhurst, ed. *Negro Year Book: A Review of Events Affecting Negro Life, 1941–1946*. Atlanta: Foote & Davies, Inc., 1947.

Hair, William Ivy. *Carnival of Fury: Robert Charles and the New Orleans Race Riot of 1900.* Baton Rouge: Louisiana State University Press, 1976.

Harrison, Mark. *Crowds and History: Mass Phenomena in English Towns, 1790–1835.* New York: Cambridge University Press, 1988.

Haynes, Robert V. *A Night of Violence: The Houston Riot of 1917.* Baton Rouge: Louisiana State University Press, 1976.

Herberg, Will. *Protestant-Catholic-Jew: An Essay in American Religious Sociology.* Garden City, N.Y.: Anchor Books, 1960.

Hersey, John. *The Algiers Motel Incident.* New York: Alfred A. Knopf, 1968.

Hirsch, Arnold R. *Making a Second Ghetto: Race and Housing in Chicago, 1940–1960.* New York: Cambridge University Press, 1983.

Hirsch, Miriam F. *Women and Violence.* New York: Van Nostrand Reinhold, Co., 1981.

Holli, Melvin G., ed. *Detroit.* New York: New Viewpoints, 1976.

Hobsbawm, E. J. *Primitive Rebels: Studies in Archaic Forms of Social Movement in the 19th and 20th Centuries.* 2d ed. New York: Praeger, 1963.

Jackson, Kenneth T. *The Ku Klux Klan in the City, 1915–1930.* New York: Oxford University Press, 1967.

Janowitz, Morris. *Social Control of Escalated Riots.* Chicago: University of Chicago Center for Policy Study, 1968.

Jeansonne, Glen. *Gerald L. K. Smith: Minister of Hate.* New Haven: Yale University Press, 1988.

Jones, Jacqueline. *Labor of Love, Labor of Sorrow: Black Women, Work, and the Family from Slavery to the Present.* New York: Basic Books, 1985.

Kerlinger, Fred N. *Foundations of Behavioral Research.* 2d ed. New York: Holt, Rinehart, & Winston, 1973.

Knopf, Terry A. *Rumors, Race, and Riot.* New Brunswick, N.J.: Transaction Books, 1975.

Lachman, Sheldon J., and Benjamin D. Singer. *The Detroit Riot of July 1967: A Psychological, Social, and Economic Profile of 500 Arrestees.* Detroit: Behavior Research Institute, 1968.

Lane, Ann J. *The Brownsville Affair: National Crisis and Black Reaction.* Port Washington, N.Y.: Kennikat, 1971.

Le Bon, Gustave. *The Crowd: A Study of the Popular Mind.* Reprint ed. New York: Viking Press, 1960.

Lee, Alfred M., and Norman D. Humphrey. *Race Riot.* New York: Dryden Press, Inc., 1943.

Levine, David A. *Internal Combustion: The Races in Detroit, 1915–1926.* Westport, Conn.: Greenwood Press, Inc., 1976.

Levine, Jack. *The Functions of Prejudice.* New York: Harper & Row, Publishers, 1975.

Lingeman, Richard R. *Don't You Know There's a War On? The American Home Front, 1941–45.* New York: G. P. Putnam's Sons, 1970.

Lipsky, Michael, and David J. Olson. *Commission Politics: The Processing of Racial Crisis in America.* New Brunswick, N.J.: Transaction Books, 1977.

Locke, Hubert G. *The Detroit Riot of 1967.* Detroit: Wayne State University Press, 1969.

Marks, Shula. *Reluctant Rebellion.* Oxford: Clarendon Press, 1970.

Marsh, Donald C.; Alvin D. Loving; and Eleanor P. Wolf. *Negro-Jewish Relationships.* Detroit: Wayne University Studies in Inter-Group Conflict in Detroit No. 1, 1944.

Marx, Gary, ed. *Racial Conflict: Tension and Change in American Society.* Boston: Little, Brown & Co., 1971.

Masotti, Louis; Jeffrey K. Hadden; Kenneth F. Seminatore; and Jerome R. Corsi. *A Time to Burn? An Evaluation of the Present Crisis in Race Relations.* Chicago: Rand McNally, 1969.

Matusow, Allen J. *The Unraveling of America: A History of Liberalism in the 1960s.* New York: Harper & Row, Publishers, 1984.

Mazón, Mauricio. *The Zoot-Suit Riots: The Psychology of Symbolic Annihilation.* Austin: University of Texas Press, 1984.

Meier, August, and Elliott Rudwick. *Black Detroit and the Rise of the UAW.* New York: Oxford University Press, 1979.

Merton, Robert K. *Social Theory and Social Structure.* Rev. ed. New York: Free Press, 1967.

Miller, Randall, and George E. Pozzetta, eds. *Shades of the Sunbelt: Essays on Ethnicity, Race, and the Urban South.* Boca Raton, Fla.: Florida Atlantic University Press, 1989.

Naison, Mark. *Communism in Harlem during the Depression.* Urbana: University of Illinois Press, 1983.

Nalty, Bernard C. *Strength for the Fight: A History of Black Americans in the Military.* New York: Free Press, 1986.

Orlansky, Harold. *The Harlem Riot: A Study in Mass Frustration.* New York: Social Analysis Report No. 1, 1943.

Osofsky, Gilbert. *Harlem: The Making of a Ghetto.* New York: Harper & Row, Publishers, Inc., 1966.

Platt, Anthony M. *The Politics of Riot Commissions, 1917–1970: A Collection of Official Reports and Critical Essays. New York: Collier Books, 1971.

Porter, Bruce, and Marvin Dunn. *The Miami Riot of 1980: Crossing the Bounds.* Lexington, Mass.: Heath Lexington Books, 1984.

Rossi, Peter H., ed. *Ghetto Revolts.* Chicago: Aldine Publishing Co., 1970.

Ryan, William. *Blaming the Victim.* New York: Vintage Books, 1971.

Rudé, George. *The Crowd in History: A Study of Popular Disturbances in France and England, 1730–1848.* Rev. ed. New York: John Wiley & Sons, Inc., 1981.

Rudwick, Elliott M. *Race Riot in East St. Louis, July 2, 1917.* Carbondale: Southern Illinois University Press, 1964.

Scheiner, Seth M. *Negro Mecca: A History of the Negro in New York City, 1865–1920.* New York: New York University Press, 1965.

Sears, David O., and John B. McConahay. *The Politics of Violence: The New Urban Blacks and the Watts Riot.* Boston: Houghton Mifflin Co., 1973.

Selltiz, Claire; Marie Jahoda; Morton Deutsch; and Stuart W. Cook. *Research Methods in Social Relations.* Rev. ed. New York: Holt, Rinehart, & Winston, 1963.

Senechal, Roberta. *Sociogenesis of a Race Riot: Springfield, Illinois, in 1908.* Urbana: University of Illinois Press, 1990.

Shapiro, Herbert. *White Violence and Black Response: From Reconstruction to Montgomery.* Amherst: University of Massachusetts Press, 1988.

Shogan, Robert, and Tom Craig. *The Detroit Race Riot: A Study in Violence.* Philadelphia: Clinton Books, 1964.

Singer, Benjamin D.; Richard W. Osborn; and James A. Geschwender. *Black Rioters: A Study of Social Factors and Communication in the Detroit Riot.* Lexington, Mass.: Heath Lexington Books, 1970.

Smelsher, Neil J. *Theory of Collective Behavior.* New York: Free Press, 1962.

Stohl, Michael. *War and Domestic Political Violence.* Beverly Hills, Cal.: Sage Publications, 1976.

Thompson, E. P. *The Making of the English Working Class.* New York: Pantheon, 1963.

Tillery, Tyrone. *The Conscience of a City: A Commemorative History of the Detroit Human Rights Commission and Department, 1943–1983.* Detroit: Wayne State University Center for Urban Studies, 1983.

Tilly, Charles; Louise Tilly; and Richard Tilly. *The Rebellious Century,*

1830–1930. Cambridge, Mass.: Harvard University Press, 1975.

Trotter, Joe William. *Black Milwaukee: The Making of an Industrial Proletariat, 1915–45*. Urbana: University of Illinois Press, 1985.

Tuttle, William M. *Race Riot: Chicago in the Red Summer of 1919*. New York: Antheneum, 1970.

Waskow, Arthur I. *From Race Riot to Sit-Ins, 1919 and the 1960s: A Study in the Connections Between Conflict and Violence*. Garden City, N.Y.: Doubleday & Co., Inc., 1966.

Weaver, John D. *The Brownsville Raid*. New York: W. W. Norton, Co., Inc., 1970.

Webb, Eugene J.; Donald T. Campbell; Richard D. Schwartz; and Lee Sechrest. *Unobtrusive Measures: Nonreactive Research in the Social Sciences*. 7th printing. Chicago: Rand McNally & Co., 1971.

White, Walter. *A Man Called White*. New York: Viking Press, 1948.

———, and Thurgood Marshall. *What Caused the Detroit Riot?* New York: NAACP, 1943.

Willhelm, Sidney M. *Who Needs the Negro?* Cambridge, Mass: Schenkman Publishing Co., 1970.

Wilson, William Julius. *The Declining Significance of Race: Blacks and Changing American Institutions*. Chicago: University of Chicago Press, 1980.

———. *The Truly Disadvantaged: The Inner City, the Underclass, and Public Policy*. Chicago: University of Chicago Press, 1987.

Yans-McLaughlin, Virginia, ed. *Immigration Reconsidered: History, Sociology, and Politics*. New York: Oxford University Press, 1990.

Zunz, Olivier. *The Changing Face of Inequality: Urbanization, Industrial Development, and Immigrants in Detroit, 1880–1920*. Chicago: University of Chicago Press, 1982.

ARTICLES

Adams, John S. "The Geography of Riots and Civil Disorders in the 1960s." *Economic Geography* 48 (Jan. 1972): 24–42.

Akers, Elmer R., and Vernon Fox. "The Detroit Rioters and Looters Committed to Prison." *Journal of Criminal Law and Criminology* 35 (1944): 105–11.

Anderson, Karen Tucker. "Last Hired, First Fired: Black Women Workers During World War II." *Journal of American History.* 69 (June 1982): 82–97.

Bloombaum, Milton. "The Conditions Underlying Race Riots as Portrayed by Multidimensional Scalogram Analysis: A Reanalysis of the Lieberson and Silverman Data." *American Sociological Review* 33 (Feb. 1968): 76–91.

Boskin, Joseph. Violence in the Ghettos." *New Mexico Quarterly* 37 (Winter 1968): 317–34.

Brown, Earl. "The Truth About the Detroit Riot." *Harper's Magazine* 187 (Nov. 1943): 488–98.

Brumbaugh, T. T. "Truce in Detroit." *Christian Century*, 11 Aug. 1943, pp. 13–14.

Capeci, Dominic J., Jr. "Black-Jewish Relations in Wartime Detroit: The Marsh, Loving, Wolf Surveys and the Race Riot of 1943." *Jewish Social Studies* 47 (Summer/Fall 1985): 221–42.

———, and Martha Wilkerson. "The Detroit Rioters of 1943; A Reinterpretation." *Michigan Historical Review* 16 (Spring 1990): 49–72.

Caplan, Nathan S., and Jeffery M. Paige. "A Study of Ghetto Rioters." *Scientific American* 219 (Aug. 1968): 15–21.

Caplan, Nathan S. "The New Ghetto Man: A Review of Recent Empirical Studies." *Journal of Social Issues* 26 (Winter 1970): 59–73.

Clark, Kenneth B., and James Barker. "The Zoot Effect in Personality: A Race Riot Participant." *Journal of Abnormal and Social Psychology* 40 (1945): 143–48.

Crouthamel, James L. "The Springfield Race Riot of 1908." *Journal of Negro History* 45 (July 1960): 164–81.

Crowe, Charles. "Racial Massacre in Atlanta September 22, 1906." *Journal of Negro History* 54 (Apr. 1969): 150–73.

———. "Racial Violence and Social Reform—Origins of the Atlanta Riot of 1906." *Journal of Negro History* 53 (July 1968): 234–56.

Dahlke, H. Otto. "Race and Minority Riots—A Study in the Typology of Violence." *Social Forces* 30 (May 1952): 419–25.

"Detroit Is Dynamite." *Life* 13 (17 Aug. 1942): 15–23.

Downes, Bryan T. "The Social and Political Characteristics of Riot Cities: A Comparative Study." *Social Science Quarterly* 49 (Dec. 1968): 504–20.

Dynes, Russell, and E. L. Quarantelli. "What Looting in Civil Disturbances Really Means." *Trans-action* 5 (May 1968): 9–14.

Eagles, Charles W. "Two 'Double V's': Jonathan Daniels, FDR, and Race Relations During World War II." *North Carolina Historical Review* 59 (Summer 1982): 252–70.

Fine, Sidney. "Chance and History: Some Aspects of the Detroit Riot

of 1967." *Michigan Quarterly Review* 25 (Spring 1986): 403–23.
————. "Rioters and Judges: The Response of the Criminal Justice System to the Detroit Riot of 1967." *Wayne Law Review* 33 (1987): 1723–63.
Fogelson, Robert M. "White on Black: A Critique of the McCone Commission Report on the Los Angeles Riots." *Political Science Quarterly* 82 (Sept. 1967): 337–67.
Ingalls, Robert P. "Lynching and Establishment Violence in Tampa, 1858–1935." *Journal of Southern History* 53 (Nov. 1987): 613–44.
Lieberson, Stanley, and Arnold R. Silverman. "The Precipitants and Underlying Conditions of Race Riots." *American Sociological Review* 30 (Dec. 1965): 887–98.
Luby, Elliot D. "The Detroit Riot." *Sinai Hospital Detroit Bulletin* 16 (Oct. 1968): 136–40.
Luby, Elliot D., and James Hedegard. "A Study of Civil Disorder in Detroit." *William and Mary Law Review* 10 (Spring 1969): 586–630.
McPhail, Clark. "Civil Disorder Participation: A Critical Examination of Recent Research," *American Sociological Review* 36 (Dec. 1971): 1058–73.
Raushenbush, Winifred. "How to Prevent Race Riots." *American Mercury* 57 (Sept. 1943): 302–09.
Robinson, Bernard F. "War and Race Conflicts in the United States." *Phylon* IV (1943): 311–27.
Schaich, Warren. "A Relationship Between Collective Racial Violence and War." *Journal of Black Studies* 5 (June 1975): 374–94.
Sitkoff, Harvard. "The Detroit Race Riot of 1943." *Michigan History* 53 (Fall 1969): 183–206.
Swan, Alex L. "The Harlem and Detroit Riots of 1943: A Comparative Analysis." *Berkeley Journal of Sociology* 16 (1971–1972): 75–93.
Tomlinson, T. M. "The Development of Riot Ideology Among Urban Negroes." *American Behavioral Scientist* 11 (Mar. 1968): 27–31.
Warren, Donald I. "Neighborhood Structure and Riot Behavior in Detroit: Some Exploratory Findings." *Social Problems* 16 (Spring 1969): 464–84.
Wiers, Paul. "Wartime Increases in Michigan Delinquency." *American Sociological Review* X (Aug. 1945): 515–23.

UNPUBLISHED DISSERTATIONS, THESES, AND REPORTS

Beatty, George W. "The Background and Causes of the 1943 Detroit Race Riot." Senior thesis, Princeton University, 1954.

Burran, James A., III. "Racial Violence in the South During World War II." Ph.D. dissertation, University of Tennessee, 1977.

Grimshaw, Allen D. "A Study in Social Violence: Urban Race Riots in the United States." Ph.D. dissertation, University of Pennsylvania, 1959.

Jenkins, Betty Smith. "The Racial Policies of the Detroit Housing Commission and Their Administration." M.A. thesis, Wayne State University, 1950.

Luby, Elliott, D., ed. "City in Crisis: The People and Their Riot." Report, Lafayette Clinic (Wayne State University/University of Michigan), n.d.

———. "A Comparison Between Detroit Negro Riot Arrestees and a Riot Control Sample." Paper presented at the American Political Science Association Conference, Washington, D.C., 3–7 Sept. 1968.

Miles, Norman K. "Home at Last: Urbanization of Black Migrants in Detroit, 1916–1929." Ph.D. dissertation, University of Michigan, 1978.

Neusom, Daniel B. "The Michigan Civil Rights Law and Its Enforcement." M.A. thesis, Wayne State University, 1952.

Shortell, John. "A Comparison of the Detroit Riots of 1943 and 1967." Senior thesis, University of Notre Dame, 1974.

Stevenson, Marshall F., Jr. "Points of Departure, Acts of Resolve: Black-Jewish Relations in Detroit, 1937–1962." Ph.D. dissertation, University of Michigan, 1988.

Index

"A Study of One Hundred Offenders," 51. *See also* Selling, Dr. Lowell S.
Aaron F.: case of, 122–33, 139, 140, 141
Aeronautical Corporation, 67, 150
Akers, Elmer A.: rioter study, 39–41, 42, 43, 44, 46–47; biases of, 46–47, 62. *See also* Fox, Vernon
Aldo T.: case of, 122, 133–41, 143; motives of, 151, 152, 156
Algiers Motel incident, 165
Alston, Christopher C., 26
America First Committee, 20. *See also* Smith, Gerald L. K.
America First Party, 22. *See also* Smith, Gerald L. K.
American Red Cross, 190
Anti-lynching bill, 45
Atlanta Constitution, 22
Attilio, C., 139–40

Beatrice B., 78, 123, 125, 130, 132, 140

Beaumont, Texas, 28
Belle Isle Park, 11; described, 5; and riot (1943), 6, 8, 20, 21, 26, 30, 33, 34, 55, 58, 60, 61, 62, 65, 67, 68, 69, 75, 76, 77, 79, 84, 85, 88, 95, 96, 121, 129, 142, 146–48, 149, 150, 155, 190, 202; and riot (1940), 188
Biddle, Francis, 52, 195–96, 247 n92
Birmingham, Alabama, 90
Black Legion, 7, 27, 28, 43, 145
Blacks in Detroit: migrants, 3, 22–23, 24, 52; living area described, 4; westside community, 15, 104, 105, 109; and Jews, 103–09; Eight Mile Road community, 104; merchants, 109–10; history of, 145–46; and the war effort, 146, 189–90; female employment, 183–84; male employment, 184–85; and public accommodations, 185; and public school facilities, 185–86; juvenile delinquency of, 186–87;

crime rates of, 187; and recreation facilities, 187–88; and public transportation, 188–89; leaders of, 191–92. *See also* Detroit; Paradise Valley
Briggs Manufacturing Company, 61, 117
Brown, Earl, 50
Brumbaugh, T. T., 49, 139
Bruno, Philip P., Sgt., 20
Buckholdt, Charles, Det. Lt., 83, 143; and Aaron F. case, 128–33; and Aldo T. case, 133–35, 139–41, 142

Callender, Sherman D., 133, 143
Campbell, Anne, 95
Carlson, John Roy, 28
Carr, W. F., 24
Catholic Women's Interracial Council, 141
Cavanagh, Jerome, 157–58, 159, 164, 165, 166
Chicago, Illinois, 10, 13, 147, 152, 153, 154, 174, 195; racial tension in, 194; and Detroit compared, 196–98. *See also* Riots (United States)
Chrysler Motor Company, 57, 66, 91
Cincinnati, Ohio, 71
Citizens Committee: and riot conference, 10, 25, 26, 29, 157; and Sojourner Truth Homes controversy, 10, 28, 182, 191. *See also* Citizens Committee for Jobs in War Industries; Hill, Charles A.; Sojourner Truth Housing Committee
Citizens Committee for Jobs in War Industries, 91, 156, 191
Civil Rights Federation of Michigan, 28; and conspiracy theory,

27, 30; on Governor's Committee, 50
Cleveland, Ohio, 85
Cleveland R., 123–25, 127–28, 130
Colonial Theater, 9
Columbus, Ohio, 13
Communists, 26, 27, 191, 192–93; fellow travelers of, 28; riot involvement, 20, 21
Communist Party of Michigan: and conspiracy theory, 27; on *Fact Finding Report*, 49
Continental Motors, 84
Coogan, J. S., 139–41, 142
Cornelius, Asher L., 123–30, 132–33, 141
Cotter, Thomas M., 135–37, 140
Council of Social Agencies, 35
Cowans, Russ J., 27
Crater, Carol, 91
Current, Gloster B., 191

Dancy, John C., 192
Daniels, Henry, 78, 125
Daniels, Johnel, 78, 125
Daniels, Jonathan, 195–96
Detroit, 18, 23, 24, 27, 29, 33, 36, 40, 43, 45, 50, 53, 56, 58, 61, 63, 64, 67, 70, 73, 79, 83, 85, 99, 114, 115, 117, 119, 121, 135, 136, 137, 141, 143, 145, 146, 148, 150, 152, 154, 162, 163, 174, 184, 189, 190, 196; migrants to, 3, 22, 23, 181–82; Poles in, 4, 25, 27, 145–46; racial clashes in, 4, 21, 27, 29, 33, 58, 63, 94, 145, 192; housing in, 4, 58, 181, 182, 183; Jews in, 12, 103–05; Housing Commission, 19, 192; Common Council, 20, 52, 193; House of Correction, 41, 43, 72, 76, 84, 117, 150; De-

partment of Recreation, 78; Italians in, 80, 93; government of, 99, 102, 103, 166; and blacks, 103–09; studies of, 105–10; Department of Probation, 120; wartime employment in, 180–81; juvenile delinquency in, 186–87. *See also* Blacks in Detroit; Detroit Police Department (1943); Detroit Police Department (1967); Detroit Street Railway; Sojourner Truth Homes
Detroit Aluminum and Brass Company, 56
Detroit Citizens League, 23. *See also* Lovett, William P.
Detroit Council of Churches, 139
Detroit Free Press, 48, 151
Detroit News, 22, 23, 29, 33, 37, 48, 49, 96, 134, 154
Detroit Police Department (1943): officer killed in riot, 9, 88–89; and riot, 9, 10, 13, 14, 15, 16, 17, 18, 34, 35, 75, 86, 88, 90, 100, 110, 112–13, 114, 115, 117, 150, 155, 156; headquarters of, 9, 11, 35, 112; and rioter deaths, 16, 88; criticism of, 19, 21, 34, 88, 90, 102, 133, 141, 157; defense of, 19, 88; and riot conspiracy, 29; riot reports of, 34, 37, 98, 100–02; composition of, 88; profile of, 89; officers injured in riot, 89–90, 95; estimates of property damages and losses, 100–02. *See also* Buckholdt, Charles, Det. Lt.
Detroit Police Department (1967): composition of, 158; and riot, 159–61, 162, 163, 165, 170
Detroit Retail Grocers Association, 102
Detroit riot (1943): beginning of, 5–6, 79–80, 96; described, 146–48, 150, 154–56; participants in, 18, 19, 20, 21, 23, 31, 32, 53, 54, 84, 119–20, 148–49, 152, 153, 166, 168–73, 189, 193, 196; and rumor, 6, 7–8, 16, 21, 26, 34, 35, 36, 58, 67, 79, 87, 142, 147, 152, 155, 163; victims in, 6, 8, 21, 26, 34, 63, 86, 87, 154–55; injuries in, 8, 18, 87, 91, 94–98; looting in, 8, 9, 10, 11, 12, 115; deaths in, 9, 14, 16, 18, 19, 21, 82, 87, 88–94, 122–23, 134; and subversives, 10, 18, 19, 20, 21, 25–27, 28, 29, 33, 36, 152–53, 157; and weapon bearing, 11, 13, 15, 17; and anti-Semitism, 12, 103, 104, 106, 107, 108; and crowd formation, 13; and liquor sales, 13; state of emergency proclamation, 13; and curfew, 13, 57, 113, 118; area covered, 14, 68, 69, 74; quelled, 15, 17; cost of, 18; and Axis propaganda, 18, 119; and loss of labor productivity, 18, 87; properties damaged or looted in, 18, 60, 70, 71, 87, 98–103, 110, 111, 115, 118, 155; and hoodlums, 19, 20, 21, 22, 34, 36, 37, 39, 40, 45, 46, 49, 53, 65, 70, 74–75, 83, 88, 117, 120, 134; and psychopathy, 22, 38–39, 40, 44, 83, 120; and Southerners, 23–24, 31, 38, 39, 40, 42, 44, 45, 46, 53, 117; spectators of, 25, 26, 153; photos of, 31, 49, 118, 150, 151; and grand jury investigation, 33, 34, 48; and ghetto conditions, 36, 46, 72, 78–79; and previous arrestees, 39, 41, 120; predicted, 43; and riffraff, 45, 46, 53, 117;

and in-migration, 52, 247 n92; and hospitals, 82, 91, 92, 93, 94, 95, 96, 97, 100, 112; sniping in, 89, 113, 148; and municipal compensation, 99–100, 102, 265 n85; and Detroit Riot (1967), 144, 145; background of, 145–46, 181–91, 192; spectators of, 153; counterrioters in, 154, 157, 164; racial character of, 155–56; impact of, 193–96, 197–98. *See also* Akers, Elmer A.; Detroit Police Department (1943); Detroit riot victims (1943); Detroit rioters (1943); Dowling, William E.; Fifth Columists; Fox, Vernon; Governor's Fact-Finding Committee; Jeffries, Edward J., Jr.; Kelly, Harry F.; Ramsay, C. F.; Receiving Hospital; Selling, Lowell S., Dr.

Detroit riot (1967), 175; background of, 157–58; described, 158–59, 161–62; participants in, 158, 159, 161, 163, 166, 167, 168; beginning of, 158, 160; cost of 159; and rumor, 159, 160; deaths in, 159, 161, 164, 165; and state police, 160; area covered, 160; quelled, 160; looting in, 160, 161, 170; and federal troops, 160, 161, 162; arson in, 161; sniping in, 161, 165; and black militants, 162, 163, 164; and national guardsmen, 162, 164, 165; and subversives, 163; spectators of, 163–64; counterrioters in, 164; victims in, 164; nonrioters, 164–65; class characteristics of, 165; racial characteristics, 165. *See also* Cavanagh, Jerome; National Advisory Commission on Civil disorders

Detroit riot streets (1943): Jefferson Avenue, 6, 7, 62, 65, 67, 77, 79, 98, 147, 149; Grand Boulevard, 6, 8, 16, 62, 91, 95, 99, 101, 104, 107, 109, 112, 114, 155, 187; Adams, 8; Dequindre, 8; Hastings, 8, 11, 16, 17, 32, 34, 58, 59, 68, 69, 74, 89, 95, 98, 99, 101, 104, 105, 107, 108, 109, 110, 111, 118, 143, 144, 148, 153, 173; St. Antoine, 8, 11, 57, 58, 74, 95, 99; Forest Avenue, 8, 11, 58, 95, 96, 153, 156; Riopelle, 8, 13; Oakland, 8, 16, 70, 74, 76, 90, 99, 100, 101, 105, 106, 107, 108, 109, 110, 155; John R, 8, 16, 97, 148, 150; Canfield, 8, 23; Westminster, 8, 56, 64, 98, 155; Beaubien, 8, 58, 78, 80, 93, 101, 112, 115, 117, 123; Brush, 8, 71, 89, 91, 99, 110, 112, 126, 148; Rivard, 8, 101; Russell, 8, 72, 80; St. Aubin, 8, 93, 96, 111; Owen, 8, 155; Woodward Avenue, 9, 10, 11, 13, 14, 15, 16, 21, 23, 25, 26, 27, 30, 32, 34, 41, 49, 55, 59, 65, 66, 68, 76, 77, 84, 86, 87, 88, 96, 97, 98, 102, 114, 117, 118, 119, 147, 148, 149, 150, 153, 154, 155, 156, 199; East Ferry, 11; Leland, 11; Hastings, 11, 34; Fort, 13; McNichols Road, 13; Vernor Highway, 13, 14, 23, 65, 66, 89, 95, 113, 117, 148, 153; Ironwood, 14; Tireman, 14; Cadillac Square, 15, 16; Division, 15, 89; Hamilton, 16; Warren Avenue, 16, 60, 105, 106, 107, 108, 109, 110; Elizabeth, 17; Medbury, 17, 126; Peterboro, 21; Grand River Avenue, 23; Delmar, 56; Cass, 62; Field, 62; Helen, 62; Brainard, 65; Willis, 66, 92; Beaufait, 67; Hendrie, 67, 80, 93, 95, 122, 125, 131; Holbrook, 70, 113; Macomb, 72, 152; Kirby, 74; Greeley, 75, 93; Cardoni, 76, 113; Superior, 80, 92; Chene, 82, 91; Mack Avenue, 83, 91; Charlotte, 84; DuBois, 92, 152; Davison Avenue, 93; Alfred, 95; Elliott, 97; Watson, 97; Alexandrine, 99; Winder, 110, 117; Theodore, 111, 115, 116; Brewster, 112; Clinton, 112; Adelaide, 114; Euclid, 114; Van Dyke 114; Hancock, 117; Harper, 114; Davenport, 118; Park Avenue, 150

Detroit riot streets (1967): Twelfth, 143, 144, 158, 160, 161, 162, 165; Clairmount, 158; Woodward, 159; Connor, 160; Livernois, 160; Seven Mile Road, 160; Grand Boulevard, 161

Detroit riot victims (1943): and black-mulatto schism, 90–91; profile of store owners, 98–99; store owners, 98–105, 106, 109–12, 115; aid given, 105, 106, 109, 154; activity of store owners, 106, 107; handicapped, 117–19. *See also* Detroit rioters (1943): as victims; Detroit riot victims (1943)

Detroit riot victims (1943): Niarhos, Gus, 6, 61, 75, 79, 95, 121, 122, 142; Joseph, Joseph B., 6, 79, 95; DeHoratiis, Joseph, Dr., 80, 92–93, 141, 142; Kiska, Moses, 82–83, 91–92, 143; Adam, Lawrence A., Patl.,

88–89, 92; Hartwick, Earnest, Patl., 89; Noot, Fred, Sgt., 89; Reiman, Russell, Patl., 89; Homer E., 89, 90; William H., 89, 90; Hackworth, Carrie, 90, 92; Jackson, Annie, 91; Grundy, Charles, 91–92, 134; McAdoo, William, 92; Holyak, John, 93; Grabowski, Sally, 93, 111–12; Bayock, Earl, 95; Huddleston, Henry, 95; Marchant, Stewart, Patl., 95; Smolinsky, Henry, 95; Williams, John, 95; Stark, George W. 95–96, 98; House, Gladys, 96; Raymond M., 96; Mitchell, Samuel, 96–97; Bell, John, 97; Crawford, Archie, 97; Griggs, Henry, 97; Powers, Henry, 97; Wright, Claribel, 97; Moon, James, 98; Levine, Ben, 98, 100, 154; Bornoty, Harry, 99, 106; Brandt, Harry, 99; Robertson, Jala, 99; Harris, Morris, 99; Cohen, Isadora, 99, 100, 101; Holbrook, Albert, 100, 101; Shifman, Simon, 100, 101; Clover, Abraham, 101; Saad, Baxos, 101; Sorgman, Cecilia, 101; Eiseman, Bernard, 101, 106; Siade, Joseph, 102; Shifman, Aaron, 104–05; Shifman, Mendel, 104–05; Cole, J., 110; Gibbon, S. C., 110; Sharpe, Clarence, 110–11; Napoleon M., 111–12; Gabbins, Louis, 112; Lewis, John, 112; Smith, John, 112; Brooks, Miss, 113; Lee, Cora, 113; Ella Mae H., 113, 114; Samuel P., 114–15; Thomas, Louis, 115; Dee G., 115–16; Isaiah F., 115–16; Howard G., 117; Lee J., 117; James G., 117–18, 121;

Jarrett, John, 118; Virgil G., 118; Edward T., 118–19; Elry T., 118–19; James N., 118–19; Smith, Robert Lee, 150; Thomas F., 155, 164

Detroit rioters (1943): servicemen, 6, 65–68, 112–13; black males, 6–8, 10, 11, 14, 15, 34, 55–61, 75, 85–86; white males, 9, 10, 13, 14, 15, 34, 61–64; and Detroit rioters (1967) compared, 12, 55, 168–73, 206–07; killed, 16, 89; as hoodlums, 19, 20, 21, 22, 31, 34, 65, 70, 83, 84, 152, 170–71; white juveniles, 20, 21, 22, 34, 73–76, 77, 85; black juveniles, 20, 21, 34, 73–76, 77, 86, 168–69; studies of, 22, 32, 33–41; white Southerners, 23, 24, 31, 61–62, 65, 171; origins of, 23, 38, 40, 45, 48, 56, 61, 62, 63, 65, 66, 67, 70, 71, 84, 111, 115, 119, 150, 152, 154, 155–56, 171; black Southerners, 24, 31, 59–60, 67, 70, 171; white ethnics, 24–25, 63–64, 73, 80–81, 83, 96, 119, 134, 150, 151, 156; black females, 34, 69–73, 75–76, 77, 86, 113, 169–72; number of arrestees, 34, 166; profile of, 54–55, 56, 61, 63, 68–69, 73, 76, 116, 168–73, 178–79; employment of, 55, 60, 61, 69, 172–73; felons, 56, 57, 59, 62, 68, 69, 74, 77, 84; marital status of, 56, 59, 60, 61, 69, 171–72; residency of, 56, 59, 61, 62, 73, 170; age of, 56, 61, 69, 73, 74, 75, 163–69; motives of, 57, 58, 77, 78, 81, 83, 85–86, 107, 111, 113–14, 119, 149, 151, 152, 153, 154, 173, 179–80, 193; previous arrestees, 55, 57–58, 84, 151;

weapons carriers, 57, 60, 62, 65, 66, 67, 72, 73, 74, 76, 77, 85, 111, 113, 114, 115, 118, 150, 152; education of, 58, 59, 173; looters, 58, 60, 64, 74, 76, 77, 84, 90, 106; newcomers, 59–60, 62, 85, 118, 189; class distinctions of, 60, 70, 72, 73, 78, 84, 90, 107, 110, 153; religions of, 63, 68, 78, 80, 119; defense workers, 64–65, 66, 67, 115; misdemeanants, 68, 69, 73, 74, 76, 77, 84, 116–17; white females, 69; assault, 72, 74, 77, 80, 82, 150, 151; disturbing the peace, 73, 76, 117, 150; disorderly conduct, 73, 76, 155; race of, 73, 168; breaking and entering, 74; destruction of property, 74; entering without breaking, 75, 115, 116; black seventeen-year-olds, 76–78, 86, 168–69; white seventeen-year-olds, 76–78, 86; as victims, 89–90, 96, 110–21; handicapped, 117–19; photos of, 118; organization in, 147, 148–49; acquaintances among, 148–49; leaders in, 149–52; curfew violations, 152; outsiders among, 152; subversives among, 152–53; numbers involved, 153; nonrioters, 173; and Springfield rioters (1908) compared, 178–79; and nonrioters compared, 180–81; organizational affiliations of, 191–93; and Harlem rioters (1943) compared, 196; and New York rioters (1977) compared, 199–200; and 1960s rioters compared, 198–99; intergenerational links of, 199–207

Detroit rioters (1967): white, 12,

34; black 12, 34, 55; class distinctions of, 158, 160, 161; motives of, 160, 161–62, 165, 166, 167, 168, 172, 176; organization in, 161; acquaintances among, 161–62; leaders in, 162; origins of, 162, 171; studies of, 162, 167, 168; outsiders, 163; numbers of arrestees, 166; race of, 168; black males, 168–73; white males, 168–73; profile of, 168–73, 176; age of, 169; black females, 169–70, 171–72; white females, 169–70, 171–72; newcomers, 170; residency of, 170; Southerners, 170; previous arrests, 170; as hoodlums, 170–71; marital status of, 171–72; employment of, 172–73; education of, 173; intergenerational links of, 199–207

Detroit rioters (1943): Charles L., 5–7, 10, 30, 34, 60, 75, 79, 83, 84, 142, 143, 147, 148, 149, 150, 151, 152, 162, 202, 255; Leo T., 7, 8, 30, 34, 143, 147; John T., 8; Rudolph M., 11, 12; Roy S., 11, 12, 106; Erving M., 13, 149; Thomas H., 14; Harding D., 15, 16; Harvey G., 16–17; Mattie Mae B., 34, 75; Aaron F., 34, 78–80, 84, 141, 142, 147; Louie H., 45; Nelson B., 45, 121; Lester R., 56–57; Roy M., 56–57; James M., 57–58; John W., 58; Manley D., 59–60; Tom M., 59–60; Clifton, T., 60; Fred N., 60; Frank N., 60–61, 121; William B., 60, 85; Bedford B., 62; Walter J., 62–64, 149; Leonard O., 62, 65; Arthur O., 64; Clarence J., 64; Joseph L., 64; Richard T., 64; Henry G., 64, 65; Paul S., 64;

Donald S., 66–67; Robert B., 66–67; James A., 67; Marquis A., 67; Frances D., 70; Goldie W., 70–71, 163; Henry W., 71; Mary P., 71–72, 120; Osgood P., 71–72; Charles F., 72; Louise F., 72; Robert G., 74–75; Ralph C., 76; Rudolph R., 76; Aldo T., 80–84, 92, 132, 142, 149, 203; Anthony S., 81–83, 133, 135, 142; Armando M., 81–83, 133–35, 142, 143; Ralph T., 81–83, 133, 135, 142, 143; Robert C., 82–84, 133, 135; J. C. G., 84, 149; James G., 85; Homer E., 89, 90; William H., 89, 90; Robert D., 90; Raymond M., 96; James S., 106; Napoleon M., 111–12; Ella Mae H., 113, 114; Albert H., 114; Robert P., 114; Samuel P., 114–15; Dee G., 115–16; Isaiah J., 115–16; Howard G., 117; Lee J., 117; James G., 117–18, 121; Virgil G., 118; Edward T., 118–19; Elry T., 118–19; James N., 118–19; Duke B., 121; Edna A., 121; Ross C., 123–25, 127–28, 129–30; William P., 124–25, 127, 130, 132; Fred M., 124–28, 130, 132, 143; Albert V., 149; Leophys T., 149; Walter H., 149; George F., 150, 151, 152; Robert M., 150, 151, 152; Martin P., 150, 151, 152, 156; Mike F., 150, 151, 156; M. C. M., 152; William Lee B., 153; Willie L., 153; Thomas F., 155, 164; White, Horace A., 192. *See also* Aaron F.; Aldo T.

Detroit Street Railway, 3, 16, 28, 34, 58, 113, 118

Detroit Times, 50, 141, 192

Detroit Tribune, 20, 49, 51, 192
Deutsch, Albert, 30
D'Hondt, Frances, 141
Diggs, Charles C., 182, 185
Dies, Martin, 48
Ditzler Color Company, 98
Dixon, John, 48
Dorsey, Julius L., 164
Dorothy, P., 115
Double V campaign, 146, 191,
    195, 197
Dowling, William E., 36, 82, 157,
    247*n*91; and *The Factual Report*,
    30, 34, 35, 40, 41, 46, 53, 75, 83,
    84; and riot controversy, 30–31,
    33, 37, 42, 43–44, 48–49, 51–
    52; and Governor's Fact-Finding
    Committee, 33; opposes grand
    jury investigation, 33; back-
    ground of, 43; biases of, 43, 44,
    46–47, 49, 50, 52, 53, 103
Drob, Judah, 49
Dunlap, Vemba M., 120
Durham, North Carolina, 24

East Catholic High School, 64
East Side Merchants Association,
    102
Eastwood Park, 5, 6, 21, 77, 79,
    146, 147, 152, 155, 191, 192
Edwards, George C., 52, 192
Emergency War Conference,
    190–91

Fair Employment Practices Com-
    mittee, 183, 184
Federal Bureau of Investigation:
    and riot conspiracy, 29, 30
Fifth Columists, 10, 18, 19, 25, 26,
    27, 28, 29, 31, 120, 157
Fine, Sidney, 168, 282*n*82
Flint, Michigan, 152
Fogelson, Robert M., 167, 168

Ford Motor Company, 11, 23, 59,
    64, 65, 67, 93, 97, 115, 119, 150,
    154
Forest Club, 7, 95, 147, 148, 155
Fort Custer, Michigan, 15, 66, 68,
    147, 189
Fort Mill, South Carolina, 59
Fox, Vernon: rioter study, 39–41,
    42, 43, 44, 46–47, 62, 120;
    biases of, 46–47. *See also* Akers,
    Elmer A.
Francis Cabrini Homes (Chicago),
    196–97, 198
Frank C., 139–40
Frazer Hotel, 14, 89, 113, 148
Fred S., 139–40
Fuller, William, Sgt., 7

Gahagan, Marguerite, 141
Geschwender, James A., 167
Gillis, Joseph A., 112, 123, 125,
    127, 129, 130–33
Gilmore, John W., 129
Girardin, Ray, 164
Gomon, Josephine, 23
Gordon, Arthur E., 51
Governor's Fact-Finding Commit-
    tee: report of, 30, 33, 34, 36, 37,
    43, 53, 70, 166, 177, 187, 192;
    appointment of, 32–33, 35,
    166; composition of, 49–50;
    biases of, 50, 193, 206
Grayson, Gertrude, 125–26, 130,
    131
Great Depression, 56, 62, 145,
    183, 195
Greater Detroit Interracial Fellow-
    ship, 140
Greater Detroit Youth Assembly,
    26
Greenfield Restaurant, 21, 25, 185
Greensboro, Pennsylvania, 71
Gregory, Arkansas, 11

Grimshaw, Allen D., 177
Grover, Ira, 131
Guthner, William E., Gen., 13

Hamtramck, Michigan, 14, 15, 25, 73, 75, 93
Harper's Magazine, 50
Harriman, Tennessee, 73
Harris, Chester A., 131
Hart, Margaret, 75–77
Hastie, William H., 191
"Hate strikes," 8, 28, 49, 58, 146, 184–85, 191, 192, 197
Hawkins, Yusef, 202, 203, 205, 206
Hedegard, James, 167
Henderson, Kentucky, 70
Hicks, Robert, 134
Highland Park, Michigan, 14, 15, 73, 93, 96, 99
Hill, Charles A., 104, 182, 191, 192; on black rioters, 49; as riot victim, 90–91. *See also* Citizens Committee; Citizens Committee for Jobs in War Industries; Sojourner Truth Housing Committee
Hill, Robert, 167
Hitler, Adolph, 4, 26, 27
Hobsbawn, E. J., 175
Holyak, Ann, 93
Hoover, J. Edgar, 29

Inkster, Michigan, 191
Ionia State Reformatory, 80, 126

Jacksonville, Florida, 115
Jeffries, Edward J., Jr., 43, 138, 247 n92; and counterrioters, 13, 154, 156–57; and Harry F. Kelly, 9, 10, 13, 14, 157; and riot conferences, 9, 10; radio appeal of, 13, 14, 19, 25, 157; and

riot aftermath, 17; on riot cause, 20, 22, 29; on migrants, 22, 24, 44; on subversives, 29; and *Factual Report,* 48; and Selling study, 51, 52; on riot injuries, 87, 94; on municipal compensation, 102–03; on rioters, 119, 153; and Sojourner Truth Homes, 183; and racial tension, 183, 192, 196
Jewish Community Council, 106
Johnson, Arthur, 131–33
Juliano, Vincent, 92
Juvenile Delinquent Camp, 129
Juvenile Detention Homes, 34, 73, 128

Kelly, Edward J., 194, 195
Kelly, Harry F.: and Jeffries, 9, 10, 13; and troop request, 10, 13, 14, 15, 157; and emergency proclamation, 13; and martial law, 13, 14, 17, 157; and Ramsay study, 22, 34, 44, 47; and Governor's Fact-Finding Committee, 32, 35, 47, 84; and grand jury investigation, 33; and *Factual Report,* 44, 47, 48
Kelsey, W. K., 23, 31, 50
Kercheval incident, 158, 159
Krause, Paul E., 137–39
Ku Klux Klan, 28, 52, 145, 152; riot involvement, 27, 28, 29, 30
Kucharski, W., 25

LaGuardia, Fiorello H., 194–95, 196
Lansing, Michigan, 17
Lansing School for Boys, 129
LeBon, Gustave, 174–76, 177, 199
Leveye, James, 123
Lexington, Mississippi, 56
Lieberman, Samuel J., 102, 103, 104

Lincoln High School, 186
Locke, Hubert G., 164, 165
Long, William, Patl., 156
Lovett, William P., 23, 48. *See also*
    Detroit Citizens League
Luby, Elliot, 167

Maher, John J., 21, 100, 111
Mamie T., 102
March on Washington Committee,
    195
Marsh, Donald C., 105–10
Marshall, Thurgood, 19. *See also*
    National Association for the Ad-
    vancement of Colored People;
    White, Walter
Martin, Louis E.: and black pro-
    test, 43, 191; on Dowling, 44,
    49; on Selling study, 51, 52, 53;
    and black in-migration, 52–53.
    See also Michigan Chronicle
Marx, Karl, 175
Matthews, Anna, 125
Mayor's Committee for Human
    Resources Development, 165
Mayor's Committee on Race Rela-
    tions (Chicago), 191, 198
Mayor's Interracial Peace Commit-
    tee, 30, 33, 51, 52, 157
McCall, J. Edward, 192; on riot
    cause, 27; on rioters, 20; on
    Governor's Committee, 50; on
    Selling study, 51, 52–53. *See also
    Detroit Tribune*
McClellan, George, Insp., 35
McClendor, James J., Dr., 51, 157
McCuffie, Arthur, 200
McGill, Ralph, 22–23, 24
Mendelsohn, Robert A., 167
Merchant Marine, 66
Methodology, 209–13
Metropolitan Detroit Youth Coun-
    cil, 27, 49

Michigan Bureau of Child Wel-
    fare, 23, 35
Michigan Chronicle, 20, 21, 27, 43,
    51, 191; as riot cause, 31, 33,
    192
Michigan Civil Rights Act (1937),
    25, 185
Michigan Detective Bureau, 123,
    125
Michigan State Police, 10; and riot
    conspiracy, 26, 28, 29
Michigan State Troops: deploy-
    ment of, 10, 13, 14, 16, 18; and
    riot, 117–18, 153
Milgram, Sam, 48
Milwaukee, Wisconsin, 198
Minardo, Cosimo M., 136, 138,
    139, 140
Mitchell, Maggie, 125
Mobile, Alabama, 25
Monroe, Michigan, 73
Montgomery, Alabama, 115

National Advisory Commission on
    Civil Disorder, 159, 166–67,
    171, 172, 175, 207
National Association for the Ad-
    vancement of Colored People,
    183, 190, 195; criticism of po-
    lice, 19, 88; and riot conspiracy,
    29, 30; as riot cause, 30, 33, 191,
    192; Detroit Chapter of, 30, 33,
    106, 115, 139, 190; Emergency
    War Conference of, 190–91. *See
    also* Marshall, Thurgood; Mc-
    Clendor, James J., Dr.; White,
    Walter
National Lawyers Guild, 50, 88
National Urban League: and riot
    conspiracy, 27, 28, 29; Detroit
    Chapter of, 162, 192
National Workers League, 27, 192
Nelson, Carter B., 125–26, 130, 131

Nelson, Walter N., 136, 138, 139
New Detroit Committee, 166
New Republic, 50
New York, New York, 19, 118,
174, 176, 194–95; Central
Park wilding (1989), 201–02,
204–05; Howard Beach killing
(1986), 202; Bensonhurst killing
(1989), 202–03, 204–05, 206;
Jones Beach incident (1989),
205. *See also* LaGuardia, Fiorello
H.; Riots (United States)
New York Police Department,
194–95
Northwestern High School, 186,
188, 192
Norvell School, 186
Nowak, Stanley, 27, 157

Olander, Oscar G., 33, 50
O'Neill, Ruby, 125
Osborn, Richard W., 167

Packard Motor Company, 26, 28,
49, 92, 146, 184–85, 191, 192
Paradise Valley, 11, 14, 17, 22, 29,
41, 42, 44, 51, 52, 55, 60, 61, 63,
68, 80, 81, 85, 86, 88, 93, 98,
102, 103, 104, 107, 114, 148,
150, 152, 154, 155, 157, 197
People's Weekly, 25
Piquette Armory, 35, 149, 155
Pittsburgh Courier, 146
Pittsburgh, Pennsylvania, 193,
196, 198
PM, 30
Port Huron, Michigan, 152
Poulson, Harper, 26
Powell, Adam C., Jr., 195

Ramsey, C. F., Dr.: rioter study,
22, 35–37, 38, 39, 40, 41, 42,
44, 46, 53, 55

Randolph, A. Philip, 183
Raskin, Jack, 28, 192
Raymond T., 127–28
Receiving Hospital, 8, 20, 82, 91,
92, 93, 94, 95, 96, 97, 100, 112
Recorder's Court: and riot, 16, 39,
75, 96, 111, 112, 120; judges of,
51, 52, 75, 99, 100, 111, 112,
123, 125, 127, 128, 135, 137;
and Aaron F. case, 123, 125,
127–33; and Aldo T. case,
133–41, 143. *See also* Recorder's
Court Psychopathic Clinic; Selling, Lowell S., Dr.
Recorder's Court Psychopathic
Clinic, 22, 37, 151. *See also* Selling, Lowell S., Dr.
Reginald P., 123–25, 127–30,
132, 133
Rentie, Chester A., 29, 31
Riot theories: hoodlums, 9, 20, 21,
36, 51, 57, 70, 75, 83, 152, 166–
67, 170–71; psychopathy, 22,
38–39, 42, 43, 44, 70, 83; conspirators, 25–30; cultural deprivation, 38–39, 44, 57, 62, 70;
underclass, 39, 44, 46, 176;
riffraff, 45, 46, 168, 175, 176,
179; urban socialization, 46, 59,
75, 171, 199, 204; anomie, 59,
168; intergroup conflict, 107,
205, 206; new ghetto man, 167,
168, 175–76; relative deprivation, 168, 175; protest, 168, 175,
180, 205; blocked opportunities,
175; breakdown and contagion,
175, 176, 177; convergence,
176; newcomers, 176
Riots (Europe), 175, 176
Riots (United States), 175, 176;
Beaumont, Texas (1943), 146,
176, 193; Los Angeles, California (1943), 28, 146, 176, 193;

Mobile, Alabama (1943), 146, 176, 193; Chicago, Illinois (1919) 153, 176–77, 194; New York, New York (Harlem, 1943), 147, 177, 194–95, 196; New York, New York (Harlem, 1935), 153, 177, 201; Atlanta, Georgia (1967), 158; Cincinnati, Ohio (1967), 158; Tampa, Florida (1967), 158; Newark, New Jersey (1967), 158, 170; Los Angeles, California (Watts, 1965), 167, 170, 175; Atlanta, Georgia (1906), 176; Brownsville, Texas (1906), 176; Houston, Texas (1917), 176; New Orleans, Louisiana (1906), 176; East St. Louis, Illinois (1917), 176–77; Tulsa, Oklahoma (1921), 176–77, 179; participants in, 176–80, 200; patterns of, 176, 200–04; Columbia, Tennessee, 177; Elaine, Arkansas (1921), 177; Springfield, Illinois (1908), 178–79; Chester, Pennsylvania (1943), 198; New York, New York (1977), 199–200; Miami, Florida (1980s), 200–01, 204, 205, 206, 207; Virginia Beach, Virginia (1989), 203–04, 205, 206; future of, 205–07
Romney, George, 166
Roosevelt, Franklin D., 3, 183, 195–96, 247 n92; and deployment of federal troops, 10, 13,16
Roxy Theater, 9, 21, 88
Rudé, George, 175–76
Rushton, Herbert J., 33, 50

Sam T., 132
San Francisco, California, 85
Selling, Lowell S., Dr., 4, 23, 83, 123, 151, 152, 247 n92; rioter study, 22, 35, 37–39, 40, 42, 43, 44, 46, 51, 52, 57, 70, 75, 244 n46; biases of, 22, 44–45, 46, 47, 52, 62, 119–20; praise for, 51, 52. See also Recorder's Court; Recorder's Court Psychopathic Clinic
Shelby, Ohio, 89
Senechal, Roberta, 178
Sheffield, Horace, 191
Singer, Benjamin D., 167
Smith, Gerald L. K., 20, 28. See also America First Committee; America First Party
Sojourner Truth Homes, 4, 7, 10, 25, 27, 43, 49, 63, 79, 129, 146, 182–83, 192, 193, 197, 202
Sojourner Truth Housing Committee, 182, 191
Smullin, Isaac M., 136, 138, 139
State Prison of Southern Michigan (Jackson), 39, 123, 135, 150
Stein, Christopher E., 75, 129
St. Louis, Missouri, 91, 116
Susie F., 155
Sweet, Ossian, 7, 63, 145

Tappes, Shelton, 48, 117, 191
The Factual Report of the Governor's Committee to Investigate the Riot Occurring in Detroit on June 21, 1943: distribution of, 30, 35, 50; contents and interpretation of, 30, 48
Thomas, R. J., 26, 27, 157, 191, 192
Thompson, E. P., 175
Thurber, Donald M., 27
Tilly, Charles, 175–76
Tilly, Louise, 175–76
Tilly, Richard, 175–76
Timkin Axle Plant, 26
Toledo, Ohio, 152

Under Cover, 28
United Automobile Workers, 26, 28, 30, 157, 183, 184, 191. *See also* Sheffield, Horace; Tappes, Shelton; Thomas, R. J.
United States, 18, 92, 104
United States Army and riot, 10, 13, 15–18, 67, 68, 189; intelligence in riot, 21, 28, 152
United States Army racial incidents: Camp Livingston, Louisiana (1943), 189; Camp Robinson, Arkansas (1941), 189; Selfridge Field, Michigan (1943), 189

Vietnam War, 158
Vulcan, Michigan, 65

Whitby, Beulah T., 26
White, Horace A.: on riot cause, 19; on Dowling, 43–44; on Selling study, 51; as counter rioter, 154, 156
White, Walter F.: and police criticism, 19; on black rioters, 49; on Governor's Committee, 49; and report to Fiorello H. LaGuardia, 194. *See also* Marshall, Thurgood; National Association for the Advancement of Colored People
Williams, Claude, 28, 30
Williams, Fred Hart, 51
Williams, Nelson, Jr., 49
Winston-Salem, North Carolina, 15
Witherspoon, John H.: and riot conference, 9; defense of police, 19, 88; on rioters, 20; and Governor's Fact-Finding Committee, 33, 34; biases of, 50; on riot injuries, 94; on racial character of riot, 156. *See also* Detroit Police Department (1943)
Wood, John, 21
Woods, Anna Mae, 125
Woods, Carrie, 125
Wright, Robert, 78

YMCA (St Antoine), 17
Young, Mary Lou, 125
Young Communist League of Michigan, 27
Youngstown, Ohio, 71
YWCA (Lucy Thurman), 10

LaVergne, TN USA
13 January 2011
212365LV00005B/9/P